William Russell Smith

The History and Debates of the Convention of the People of Alabama

William Russell Smith

The History and Debates of the Convention of the People of Alabama

ISBN/EAN: 9783337796792

Printed in Europe, USA, Canada, Australia, Japan

Cover: Foto ©ninafisch / pixelio.de

More available books at **www.hansebooks.com**

THE
HISTORY AND DEBATES
OF THE
CONVENTION
OF
The People of Alabama,

Begun and held in the City of Montgomery, on the seventh Day of January, 1861:

IN WHICH IS PRESERVED THE SPEECHES OF THE SECRET SESSIONS, AND MANY VALUABLE STATE PAPERS.

By WILLIAM R. SMITH,
ONE OF THE DELEGATES FROM TUSCALOOSA.

Montgomery: WHITE, PFISTER & CO.
Tuscaloosa: D. WOODRUFF.
Atlanta: WOOD, HANLEITER, RICE & CO.
1861.

PREFACE.

I deem myself happy in having attempted to collect the materials for this book. Of the Conventions of the people that have recently been held in the seceding States on the great question of dissolving the Union, there does not seem to have been any serious effort made, in any except Alabama, to preserve the Debates. It is, therefore, my agreeable fortune, not only to be able to set an example of diligence to the sister States, but to combine, in an authentic record for future ages, both the acts of the PATRIOTS of Alabama, and the fervent words by which they were mutually animated in the discharge of their great duties.

The stirring times through which we have just passed, and the startling events which have distinguished the day, were all calculated to excite the intellectual energies to the most vigorous exertion; and whatever of eloquence or wisdom was in the possession of any citizen, may be fairly supposed to have been called into exercise. The destinies of a great Nation and the Liberties of the people were involved in the issues; and while the Past was to be measured by the statesman's Philosophy, it was as well the duty of Wisdom to lift the veil of the uncertain Future. Here was a field for the most sublime labor; and while I will not run the hazard of raising the expectation of the reader, by allowing him to look into this book for those magnificient outbursts of eloquence that dazzle, bewilder and persuade, yet I may safely promise a forensic treat, in a vast variety of speeches which breathe the genuine spirit of wisdom, animated by the liveliest touches of indignant patriotism.

The reader may rely upon the perfect authenticity of the historical parts of the book, and upon the accuracy of the speeches as to the sentiments uttered and the positions assumed by the speakers on the points arising in debate; for almost every speech in the volume, of any considerable length or importance, has been submitted to the inspection or revision of the speaker; and where this has been impracticable, and the notes confused or uncertain, the speeches have been omitted entirely, as I have been unwilling to assume the responsibility of publishing a sentiment in the name of another, on a great question, where the smallest doubt existed as to its accuracy.

In the speeches reported from my own notes, I have endeavored to adhere as nearly as possible to the language of the speaker; but to preserve the idea and sense has been my paramount design. I have attempted but little ornament either in language or metaphor; so that I have no fears that every debater will recognize his own speech as genuine, both in sentiment and language, although condensed and abridged.

Some portions of this volume will appear almost romantic. The scenes of the Eleventh of January, when the Convention was deliberating on the final passage of the Ordinance of Secession, were extremely touching. The MINORITY rose to the heights of moral sublimity as they surrendered their long cherished opinions for the sake of unity at home. The surrender was graceful and unrestrained: without humiliation on the one hand, or dominant hauteur on the other. The speeches on this occasion were uttered in husky tones, and.

in the midst of emotions that could not be suppressed, and which, indeed, there was no effort to disguise. These and other scenes which appear in the Journal and Debates, will show the impartial enquirer, that every member of the Convention was deeply impressed with his responsibility. Solemnity prevailed in every phase of the proceedings. In the debates of six weeks, on the most exciting topics, but few unkind words were uttered. Forensic invective, so characteristic of legislative assemblies, was lost in devotion to the public good, and scarcely a jar of personal bitterness disturbed the harmony of the deliberations.

While I claim nothing for myself, but due credit for the diligence and labor which I have employed in collecting and combining these materials, yet I feel proud in submitting this Book to the Public, for I am conscious of thus supplying a link in the History of Ages, and a chapter in the LIFE of LIBERTY.

EXPLANATION.

It must be noticed that this book does not pretend to give the entire debates of the Convention. This could hardly be expected in a volume of this size, since a single day's debate, if given in full, would fill fifty—perhaps an hundred pages. My object has been to preserve the *political* features of the debates; and hence I have not attempted, as a general rule, to give the discussions on the ordinary subjects of legislation. Many of the ablest speeches delivered in the Convention were upon the changes in the Constitution of the State, not touching the political necessities of the new condition of things. These speeches must be lost, however much they were worthy of preservation.

The Appendix contains the REPORTS of the Commissioners appointed by Governor Moore to the slave-holding States. These Reports are able documents, and will explain themselves. Whatever the object of the appointment of these Commissioners may have been, the documents themselves become historical, and must live in the annals of the Revolution.

INDEX.

African Slave-Trade 129, 164, 194
Alabama Secedes from the Union 118
" Flag of 119, 122

BAKER, of Barbour:
Returns thanks to the ladies for Flag.................... 120

BAKER, of Russell:
Resolution for open Sessions............................. 43
Speech on the same...................................... 47
" on Ratification of Constitution..................... 358
" on Council of State............................... 162

BARRY, Hon. Wm. S., President Mississippi Convention:
Dispatch from... 75

BEARD, Hon. A. C.:
Speech on Ordinance of Secession........................ 102
" on Dr. Fearn's resignation......................... 460

BECK, Hon. F. K.:
Speech against Coercion................................. 58
" on Council of State................................ 161

BRAGG, Hon. Jno.:
Resolutions in reference to Collector of Mobile........... 128
Report on same subject.................................. 133
Speech against excluding members of the Convention from
election to Congress.................................. 154

INDEX.

BREWER, S. D., Temporary Secretary........................... 19

BROOKS, Hon. Wm. M.:
    Elected President.. 23
    Speech against Withdrawing Troops from Florida.......... 215, 219
    Resolution of Thanks to.................................. 264
    His Farewell Speech..................................... 265

BULGER, Hon. M. J.:
    Resolutions on Federal Relations......................... 56
    Speech on Ordinance of Secession........................ 108
    Proposed to elect Deputies to Congress, by People........ 117
    Speech on Resolution against Coercion.................... 193
        " on Ratification of the Constitution................ 352

BUFORD, Hon. Jeff.:
    Speech on the Legitimate powers of the Convention....... 281

BULLOCH, Hon E. C:
    Commissioner to Florida.................................. 35
    Dispatches from.. 42
    His Report as Commissioner.............................. 115

CALHOUN, Hon. J. M.:
    Commissioner to Texas................................... 35
    His Report.. 123

CALHOUN, Hon. A. P.:
    Commissioner from South-Carolina........................ 23
    His Speech in the Convention............................ 31

CADETS of University:
    Reception and Review of................................. 188, 189

CHILTON, Hon. Wm. P :
    Elected Deputy to Congress.............................. 161

CLARKE, Hon. W. E., of Marengo:
    Speech on Confiscation.................................. 181
        " on Public Lands................................ 313, 315

CLARK, Hon. James S., of Lawrence:
    Speech on Applause in the Galleries..................... 45
        " Against Secession.............................. 81, 183
        " on Ratification of the Constitution............. 326

INDEX. III

CLOPTON, Hon. David:
 Commissioner to Delaware............................... 35
 His Report... 436

CLEMENS, Hon. Jere:
 Speech on Whatley's Resistance Resolutions............. 28
 On sending Troops to Florida........................... 50
 Minority Report on Secession........................... 77
 Speech on Secession.................................... 126
  " against excluding members of the Convention from
   being elected to Congress........................ 158
  " on sending Commissioners to Washington........... 166
  " on Withdrawing Troops from Florida............... 211-220

COLEMAN, Hon. A. A.:
 Resolution against Coercion............................ 57, 189
  " to suspend Collection of Debts................... 175

COCHRAN, Hon. John:
 Resolutions Requesting Information from Governor....... 25
 To Compliment the Governor............................. 51
 Speech on Sending Troops to Florida.................... 51
  " on the Power of Taxation......................... 300

CONVENTION:
 Resolutions calling.................................... 9
 Time of convening...................................... 19
 Proclamation for....................................... 17
 Second Session of...................................... 269
 Visit to the President in a Body....................... 461

CONFISCATION.. 174

COUNTIES:
 Size of, Proposed to be Changed........................ 169

COOPER, Hon. Wm.:
 Commissioner to Missouri............................... 35
 His Report... 405

CRUMPLER, Hon. Albert:
 Speech on the Ordinance of Secession................... 103

CROOK, Hon. Jno. M.:
 Speech on Coercion..................................... 191
 Resolution to Visit the President...................... 461

COMAN, Hon. J. P.:
    Speech on Ratification of Constitution.................... 354

CURRY, Hon. J. L. M.:
    Commissioner to Maryland............................. 35
    His Report... 400
    His Letter, with Hon. Mr. Pugh, to the Convention........ 125
    Elected Deputy to Congress.. 161

DARGAN, Hon. E. S.:
    Speech on Secession................................... 93
    Resolution to accept Flag.............................. 120
    Report of $1,000,000 Loan, and Speech on same.......... 123
        " Commissioners to Washington.................... 166
        " African Slave-Trade............................ 164
        " Power of Taxation.........................202, 299, 301
    Speech on Ratifying the Constitution.................... 325

DAVIS, Hon. Nich.:
    Resolution to submit Ordinance of Secession to the People.. 55
    Speech on Resolution against Coercion.................. 72
        " on the Ordinance of Secession.................. 110
    Elected Deputy to Congress............................ 461

DEPUTIES elected:
    To Congress.. 160
    To Convention—names of.............................. 21, 22

DOWDELL, Hon. J. F.:
    Speech against Secret Sessions........................ 47
    Resolution on the Navigation of the Mississippi River..... 174
    Speech on Coercion Resolution......................... 190
        " on Citizenship................................. 223
        " on African Slave-Trade........................ 252-253

EARNEST, Hon. Wm. S.:
    Speech on Coercion Resolution......................... 60
        " on Ratification................................ 336
    Report on Engrossing Ordinance of Secession on Parchment... 173

EDWARDS, Hon. Wm. M.:
    Speech on Secession................................... 104

INDEX.

ELMORE, Hon. John A.:
    Commissioner to South-Carolina................... 35
    His Report.. 389

FOWLER, WM. A.:
    Elected Secretary................................. 29
    His Resignation................................... 128
    Resolution Complimentary.......................... 129

FLAG of Alabama, presented by Ladies................... 119
    Sonnet to same.................................... 122

FEARN, Hon. Thos:
    Deputy to Congress—Resigns....................... 169
    Mr. Beard's Speech on his Resignation............. 16

FLORIDA:
    Troops sent to.................................... 50
    Secedes... 23

GILMER, Hon. F. M.:
    Commissioner to Virginia.......................... 35

GARRETT, Hon. J. J.:
    Commissioner to North Carolina.................... 35

GIBBONS, Hon. Lyman:
    Speeches on the Power of Taxation................. 295, 303

GREEN, Hon. Jno.:
    Speech on Secession............................... 98

GOVERNMENT:
    Report for Provisional and Permanent.............. 136
    Debate on the same................................ 137–147

HALE, Hon. S. F.:
    Commissioner to Kentucky.......................... 35
    His Report.. 373

HENDERSON, of Macon:
    Resolutions to send Commissioners to Arizona........ 124
    Ordinance for a Council of State................... 129
    Speech on Divorce................................. 308

HERNDON, Hon. T. H.:
    Motion to Amend Ordinance of Citizenship.............. 123, 127

HORN, A. G.:
    Temporary Secretary..................................... 19
    Elected Principal Secretary............................. 120
    Resolution Complimenting................................ 372

HOPKINS, Hon. A. F.:
    Commissioner to Virginia................................ 35

HUBBARD, Hon. David:
    Commissioner to Arkansas................................ 35
    His Report.. 443

HUMPHRIES, Hon. H. G.:
    Calls the Convention to Order........................... 19
    Speech on Power of Taxation............................. 305

INZER, Hon. Jno. W.:
    Speech on Secession..................................... 97

INTRODUCTION. Historical................................... 9

JEMISON, Hon. R., Jr.:
    Voted for, for President of Convention.................. 23
    Resolution to Close Doors............................... 13
    Speech on Coercion Resolution........................... 63
    Speech on Secession..................................... 93
    Motion in regard to the Formation of a Permanent Government.. 136
    Resolution to Submit same to a Convention of the People... 147
    Speech on Election of Deputies to Congress.............. 150
    On Commissioners to Washington.......................... 172
    On Withdrawing Troops from Florida...................... 218, 220
    On the Power of Taxation................................ 298
    Resolution to Refer the Permanent Constitution for Ratification to a Convention................................. 32
    Speech on Ratification of the Constitution.............. 323

JEWETT, Hon. O. S.:
    Speech on Permanent Constitution........................ 138, 144
    On Public Lands... 311, 316

JONES, Hon. H. C., of Lauderdale:
    Speech on Secret Sessions.................................... 18
    On sending Troops to Florida............................... 54
    On Resolution against Coercion............................ 65
    On Secession.. 95
    On Confiscation.. 177
    His Substitute for Ordinance on African Slave Trade...... 194
    Speech on same.. 206
    Substitute Adopted.. 264
    Elected Deputy to Southern Congress..................... 461

JOHNSON, Hon. N. D.:
    Speech on Coercion Resolution............................. 58
      " on Secession... 100
      " on African Slave-Trade.............................. 262
      " on Size of Counties.................................. 269

JUDGE, Hon. T. J.:
    Commissioner to Washington—His Report.................. 152

KIMBALL, Hon. A.:
    Speech on Sending Troops to Florida....................... 54
      " On Secession.. 99
    Resolution of Thanks to President Brooks................ 265
    Speech on Ratification... 325

LEWIS, Hon. D. P.:
    Speech on Confiscation.. 175, 182
    Elected Deputy to Congress................................. 161

MANLY, Rev. Basil: His Prayer 29

MATTHEWS, Ex-Governor:
    Commissioner from Mississippi............................. 92
    Addresses the Convention.................................... 130

M'CLANAHAN, Hon. Jno. M.:
    Speech on Reducing Size of Counties..................... 272

M'REA, Gen. Colin:
    Elected Deputy to Southern Congress...................... 161

MISSISSIPPI River: Navigation of.................................. 174

MORGAN, Hon. Jno. T.:
    Resolution Restraining Applause............................ 29

MORGAN, Hon. Jno. T.:

Speech on Secret Sessions and Applause	45
" on Coercion Resolution	61
" on excluding Members of the Convention from the Southern Congress	153
on the African Slave-Trade	195
" on Withdrawing Troops from Florida	215
" on Changing the Size of Counties	277
" on the Power of Taxation	309
" on the Ratification of the Constitution	324

MOORE, Hon. A. B., (Governor):

Letter to, by Citizens	12
His Reply	13
His Proclamation for Convention	17
Appoints Commissioners to Slave-holding States	35
Their Credentials	35
Letter to Mr. President Buchanan	41
His Message to Convention	31

PETTUS, Hon. E. W.:

Commissioner to Mississippi	35
Dispatches from	42
His Report	418

POSEY, Hon. S. C.:

Speech on Secret Sessions	44
" on Resistance Resolution	26
" on Secession	95
" on African Slave-Trade	208

POTTER, Hon. John:

Speech on Secession	100
" on African Slave Trade	210, 258
" on Size of Counties	275

PRESIDENT DAVIS:

Visit to	461
Vice-President STEPHENS' Speech at Reception	461

PUBLIC LANDS:

Debate on	311

PUGH, Hon. J. L.:

Communication to Convention	125

RALLS, Hon. John P.:

    Speech on Secession.. 105
    Size of Counties.. 274

REPORTS:

    Yancey's, on Secession.. 76
    Clemens' Minority.. 77
    Bragg's, on Money in hands of Mobile Collectors................ 133
    Committee of Conference on Relative Duties of the Convention and General Assembly....................................... 164

SANFORD, Hon. J. W. A.:

    Commissioner from Georgia... 74
    Introduced, and Addresses the Convention....................... 123

SECESSION:

    Ordinance of... 76
    Engrossed on Parchment... 76
    Mode of Signing... 135, 138

SHEFFIELD, Hon. James L.:

    Speech on Secession... 106
    Speech on Ratification of Constitution............................ 356

SMITH, Hon. Wm. R., of Tuscaloosa:

    Speech on Resistance Resolution................................... 25
    " on Sending Troops to Florida.................................. 53
    " on Coercion Resolution.. 66
    " on Secession.. 97
    " on Reception of Flag... 120
    Sonnet to Flag.. 121
    Speech on Sending Commissioners to Washington.............. 167
    " on Confiscation.. 179
    " on Navigation of the Mississippi............................ 186–187
    " on African Slave Trade.. 200
    " on Watts' Amendment—same subject...................... 259
    " on Citizenship... 227
    " on Ratification of Constitution................................ 341

SMITH, Hon. R. H.:

    Commissioner to North Carolina.................................... 35
    His Report.. 430
    Elected Deputy to Southern Congress............................. 161

SMITH, Frank L.:

    Elected Assistant Secretary... 23

SHORTER, Hon. John Gill:
 Commissioner to Georgia... 35
 His Report.. 304
 Elected Deputy to Southern Congress........................... 101

SHORTRIDGE, Hon. Geo. D.:
 Speech on Motion on Council of State........................... 55
  " on Commissioners to Washington......................... 167
  " on Confiscation.. 175
  " on Citizenship.. 221-225

STEELE, Hon. John A.:
 Speech on Secession... 103

STONE, Hon. Lewis M.:
 Speech on Resolution Against Coercion........................ 58
  " Against Excluding Members of the Convention from
   Election to Southern Congress............................ 151
  " on African Slave Trade..................................... 231
  " on Ratification of the Constitution...................... 332

TIMBERLAKE, Hon. John P.:
 Amendment to Ordinance of Secession........................ 90
 Speech on same.. 90

WYNN, R. H.:
 Elected Door-Keeper.. 23

WATTS, Hon. T. H.:
 Speech on Sending Troops to Florida........................... 52
  " on Resolution Against Coercion......................... 68
 Reads Dispatches.. 124
 Speech on Commissioners to Washington................. 166-168
 Ordinance to Confiscate Property.............................. 175
 Speech on Withdrawing Florida Troops................. 218-220
  " on Citizenship.. 226
  " on African Slave-Trade................................ 255-264
  " on Power of Taxation.................................. 298-300
  " on Public Lands... 324

WATKINS, Hon. R. S.:
 Speech on Secession.. 101

WEBB, Hon. James D.:
 Speech on Commissioners to Washington................... 168

INDEX.   XI

WEBB, Hon. James D.:
   Resolution to Review Cadets.................................... 153
   Report on same... 157
   Speech on Citizenship.. 227

WALKER, Hon. R. W.:
   Elected Deputy to Congress..................................... 161

WHATLEY, Hon. G. C.:
   Resolution of Resistance....................................... 24
   Speeches on same... 24, 30
     "   on Timberlake's Amendment.............................. 91
     "   on Permanent Government............................... 137
     "   on Commissioners to Washington........................ 160
     "   on Citizenship.. 226
     "   on Powers of Taxation................................. 300
     "   on Public Lands....................................... 315

WINSTON, Hon. Wm. O.:
   Speech on Secession.. 100

WINSTON, Hon. Jno. A.:
   Commissioner to Louisiana...................................... 35
   His Report... 113

WILLIAMSON, Hon. James:
   Speech on Resistance Resolution................................ 29
     "   on Applause in the Galleries.......................... 41
     "   on Permanent Government............................... 137
     "   on Council of State................................... 163
     "   on Withdrawing Troops from Florida.................... 215

YANCEY, Hon. Wm. L.:
   Resolution Providing for Opening the Convention by Prayer. 20
   Speech on Resistance Resolution................................ 27
   Resolution Sending Troops to Florida........................... 50
   Speech on Resolution Against Coercion.......................... 68
   Report of Ordinance of Secession............................... 76
   Speech on Timberlake's Amendment............................... 91
     "   on Secession.. 101
   Deputed by the Ladies to Present a Flag to the Convention. 120
   Report for Provisional and Permanent Government............ 130
   Speech on the same subject..................................... 133
     "   Against Excluding Members of the Convention from
           Election as Deputies to Congress.................... 157

YANCEY, Hon. Wm. L.:

    Speech on Commissioners to Washington................   176
    " on Navigation of the Mississippi River...................   184–188
    " on African Slave-Trade......................................   237

YEAS AND NAYS:

    On Resolution to submit Ordinance of Secession to the People..   55
    On Clemens' Minority Report..   80–81
    On Timberlake's Amendment.......................   92
    On the Ordinance of Secession...   118
    On Bulger's Motion to Submit to the People the Election of Representatives to Congress..................................   119
    On Jemison's Amendment to Submit the Constitution to a New Convention..   363
    On the Ratification of the Constitution.............................   364

YELVERTON, Hon. G. T.:

    Speech on Resolution Against Coercion....................   66
    Resolution to Remove Secrecy from the Vote and Proceedings on Ordinance of Secession,.......................   119
    Speech Against Excluding Members of the Convention from Congress...   158
    Speech on African Slave Trade........................   228
    " on the Legitimate Powers of the Convention.......   287

INTRODUCTION—HISTORICAL.

On the 24th day of February, 1860, the Alabama Legislature adopted the following Joint Resolutions, with great unanimity—there being but two dissenting voices:

Whereas, anti-slavery agitation persistently continued in the non-slaveholding States of this Union, for more than a third of a century, marked at every stage of its progress by contempt for the obligations of law and the sanctity of compacts, evincing a deadly hostility to the rights and institutions of the Southern people, and a settled purpose to effect their overthrow even by the subversion of the Constitution, and at the hazard of violence and bloodshed; and whereas, a sectional party calling itself Republican, committed alike by its own acts and antecedents, and the public avowals and secret machinations of its leaders to the execution of these atrocious designs, has acquired the ascendency in nearly every Northern State, and hopes by success in the approaching Presidential election to seize the Government itself; and whereas, to permit such seizure by those whose unmistakable aim is to pervert its whole machinery to the destruction of a portion of its members would be an act of suicidal folly and madness, almost without a parallel in history; and whereas, the General Assembly of Alabama, representing a people loyally devoted to the Union ot the Constitution, but scorning the Union which fanaticism would erect upon its ruins, deem it their solemn duty to provide in advance the means by which they may escape such peril and dishonor, and devise new securities for perpetuating the blessings of liberty to themselves and their posterity; therefore,

1. *Be it resolved*, That upon the happening of the contingency contemplated in the foregoing Preamble, namely, the election of

a President advocating the principles and action of the party in the Northern States calling itself the Republican Party, it shall be the duty of the Governor, and he is hereby required, forthwith to issue his Proclamation, calling upon the qualified voters of this State to assemble on Monday not more than forty days after the date of said Proclamation, at the several places of voting in their respective counties, to elect delegates to a Convention of the State, to consider, determine and do whatever in the opinion of said Convention, the rights, interests, and honor of the State of Alabama requires to be done for their protection.

2. *Be it further resolved,* That said Convention shall assemble at the State Capitol on the second Monday following said election.

3. *Be it further resolved,* That it shall be the duty of the Governor as soon as possible to issue writs of election to the Sheriffs of the several counties, commanding them to hold an election on the said Monday so designated by the Governor, as provided for in these Joint Resolutions, for the choosing of as many delegates from each county to said Convention as the several counties shall be entitled to members in the House of Representatives of the General Assembly; and said election shall be held at the usual places of voting in the respective counties, and the polls shall be opened under the rules and regulations now governing the election of members to the General Assembly of this State, and said election shall be governed in all respects by the laws then in existence, regulating the election of members to the House of Representatives of the General Assembly, and the persons elected thereat as delegates, shall be returned in like manner, and the pay, both mileage and *per diem,* of the delegates to said Convention, and the several officers thereof, shall be the same as that fixed by law for the members and officers of said House of Representatives.

5. *Be it further resolved,* That copies of the foregoing Preamble and Resolutions be forwarded by the Governor as soon as possible to our Senators and Representatives in Congress, and to each of the Governors of our sister States of the South.

The following Resolutions, adopted at the same session, will serve still further to show the spirit that animated the Legislature of Alabama:

Joint Resolutions of the General Assembly of Alabama in response to the Resolutions of South Carolina.

1st, *Be it resolved,* That the State of Alabama, fully concurring with the State of South Carolina, in affirming the right of any State to secede from the confederacy, whenever in her own judgment such a step is demanded by the honor, interests and safety of her people, is not unmindful of the fact that the assaults upon the institution of slavery, and upon the rights and equality of the Southern States, unceasingly continued with increasing violence and in new, and more alarming forms, may constrain her to a reluctant but early exercise of that invaluable right.

2d, *Be it further resolved*, That in the absence of any preparation for a systematic co-operation of the Southern States, in resisting the aggressions of their enemies, Alabama, acting for herself, has solemnly declared that under no circumstances will she submit to the foul domination of a sectional Northern party, has provided for the call of a Convention in the event of the triumph of such a faction in the approaching Presidential election, and to maintain the position thus deliberately assumed, has appropriated the sum of $200,000 for the military contingencies which such a course may involve.

3d, *Be it further resolved*, That the State of Alabama having endeavored to prepare for the exigencies of the future, has not deemed it necessary to propose a meeting of Deputies from the slave-holding States, but anxiously desiring their coöperation in a struggle which perils all they hold most dear, hereby pledges herself to a cordial participation in any and every effort, which in her judgment will protect the common safety, advance the common interest, and serve the common cause.

4th, *Be it further resolved*, That should a Convention of Deputies from the slave-holding States assemble at any time before the meeting of the next General Assembly, for the purposes and under the authority indicated by the resolutions of the State of South Carolina, the Governor of this State be, and he is hereby authorized, to appoint one deputy from each Congressional District, and two from the State at large, to represent the State of Alabama in such Convention.

Upon the election of Mr. Lincoln to the Presidency, the Governor, in pursuance of the foregoing Resolutions, called a Convention of the People of Alabama, to meet in the city of Montgomery, on the 7th day of January, 1861. The following Correspondence is worthy of preservation as a part of the history of the times:

LETTER FROM GOV. MOORE.

MONTGOMERY, Nov. 12, 1860.

To his Excellency A. B. MOORE:

Sir—At a meeting of citizens of several counties of the State, held at this place on Saturday, the 10th inst., the undersigned were appointed a Committee to confer with your Excellency, and ascertain the construction put by you on the Joint Resolutions of our last Legislature, for the call of a Convention of the people of the State. What is desired from you are, your views as to the time when you are authorized to issue your Proclamation for the call of that Convention, whether upon the election of Electors by the people of the several States, or when those Electors cast their vote for President; and also, if it be consistent with your ideas of public duty, that you would inform us when that Proclamation will be issued, and upon what day you will order the election of Delegates to that Convention.

These are questions of deep interest to the people of the State, and it is deemed of great moment that your views on those questions should be known, if you have come to a determination about them. Your answer, we hope, will be given at an early day, with permission for its publication.

Very respectfully,
J. A. ELMORE, Montgomery county.
J. D. PHELAN,   "   "
E. W. PETTUS, Dallas county.
N. H. R. DAWSON, "   "
J. B. CLARK, Greene county.
W. E. CLARKE, Marengo county.
D. W. BAINE, Lowndes county.
J. F. CLEMENTS, "   "
J. G. GILCHRIST, "   "
C. ROBINSON,   "   "
E. D. KING, Perry county.
R. FRAZIER, Jackson county.
W. L. YANCEY, Montgomery county.
J. H. CLAYTON,   "   "
G. B. DUVAL,   "   "
T. J. JUDGE,   "   "
G. GOLDTHWAITE, "   "
T. H. WATTS,   "   "
S. F. RICE,   "   "
T. LOMAX,   "   "
M. A. BALDWIN,   "   '

Executive Department, }
Montgomery, Nov. 14, 1860.

GENTLEMEN: I have received your letter of the 12th inst., asking for my construction of "the Joint Resolutions of our last Legislature, for the call of the Convention of the people of the State." You particularly desire to know when I consider myself authorized to issue my Proclamation for the call of a Convention —"whether upon the election of Electors by the people of the several States, or when said Electors cast their votes for President." You also ask me to inform you, if consistent with my ideas of public duty, "when that Proclamation will be issued, and upon what day you [I] will order the election for the delegates to the Convention."

I fully agree with you, that "these are questions of deep interest to the people of the State," and having, after mature deliberation, determined upon my course in regard to them, and not considering it inconsistent with my public duty to communicate that determination to you, with leave to publish it, I unhesitatingly do so.— The intense interest and feeling which pervade the public mind, make it not only proper, but my duty.

After stating a long list of aggressions in the preamble to the Joint Resolutions referred to, the first resolution provides "that upon the happening of the contingency contemplated in the foregoing preamble, viz: the election of a President advocating the principles and action of the party in the Northern States, calling itself the Republican party, it shall be the duty of the Governor, and he is hereby required forthwith to issue his proclamation," &c.

The Constitution of the United States points out the mode of electing a President, and directs that "each State shall appoint, in such manner as the Legislature thereof may direct, a number of electors, equal to the whole number of Senators and Representatives to which the State may be entitled in Congress." See Art. 2, §1.

Art. 12, §1, of Amendments to the Constitution, provides that the Electors shall meet in their respective States, and vote by ballot for President and Vice President." Under these provisions of the Constitution, the people of the several States vote for electors and these electors vote for President. It is clear to my mind that a candidate for the Presidency cannot constitutionally be elected until a majority of the electors have cast their votes for him.

My Proclamation will not, therefore, be issued until that vote is cast on the fifth day of December next. I regret that this delay must occur, as the circumstances which surround us make prompt and decided action necessary. There can be no doubt that a large majority of the electorial vote will be given to Mr. Lincoln, and in view of the certainty of his election, I have determined to issue my Proclamation immediately after that vote is cast. I shall appoint Monday, the 24th day of December next, for the election of delegates to the Convention. The Convention will meet on Monday, the 7th day of January next.

The day for the election of delegates has been designated in advance of the issuance of the Proclamation in order that the minds of the people may at once be directed to the subject, and that the several counties may have ample time to select candidates to represent them. Each voter of the State should immediately consider the importance of the vote he is to cast. Constitutional rights, personal security, and the honor of the State are all involved. He must decide, on the 24th December, the great and vital question of submission to an Abolition Administration, or of secession from the Union. This will be a grave and momentous issue for the decision of the people. To decide it correctly, they should understand all the facts and circumstances of the case before them. It may not be improper or unprofitable for me to recite a few of them.

Who is Mr. Lincoln, whose election is now beyond question? He is the head of a great sectional party calling itself Republican: a party whose leading object is the destruction of the institution of slavery as it exists in the slaveholding States. Their most distinguished leaders, in and out of Congress, have publicly and boldly proclaimed this to be their intention and unalterable determination. Their newspapers are filled with similar declarations. Are they in earnest? Let their past acts speak for them.

Nearly every one of the non-slaveholding States have been for years under the control of the Black Republicans. A large majority of these States have nullified the fugitive slave law, and have successfully resisted its execution. They have enacted penal statutes, punishing, by fine and imprisonment in the penitentiary, persons who may pursue and arrest fugitive slaves in said State. They have by law, under heavy penalties, prohibited any person from aiding the owner to arrest his fugitive slave, and have denied us the use of their prisons to secure our slaves until they can be removed from the State. They have robbed the South of slaves worth millions of dollars, and have rendered utterly ineffectual the only law passed by Congress to protect this species of property. They have invaded the State of Virginia, armed her slaves with deadly weapons, murdered her citizens, and seized the United States Armory at Harper's Ferry. They have sent emissaries into the State of Texas, who burned many towns, and furnished the slaves with deadly poison for the purpose of destroying their owners.

All these things have been effected, either by the unconstitutional legislation of free States, or by combinations of individuals. These facts prove that they are not only in earnest and intent upon accomplishing their wicked purposes, but have done all that local legislation and individual efforts could effect.

Knowing that their efforts could only be partially successful without the aid of the Federal Government, they for years have struggled to get control of the Legislative and Executive Departments thereof. They have now succeeded, by large majorities, in all the non-slaveholding States except New Jersey, and perhaps California and Oregon, in electing Mr. Lincoln, who is pledged to carry out the principles of the party that elected him. The course of events show clearly that this party will, in a short time, have a majority in both branches of Congress. It will then be in their power to change the complexion of the Supreme Court so as to make it harmonize with Congress and the President. When that party get possession of all the Departments of Government, with the purse and the sword, he must be blind indeed who does not see that slavery will be abolished in the District of Columbia, in the dock-yards and arsenals, and wherever the Federal Government has jurisdiction.

It will be excluded from the Territories, and other free States will in hot haste be admitted into the Union, until they have a majority to alter the Constitution. Then slavery will be abolished by law in the States, and the "irrepressible conflict" will end; for we are notified that it shall never cease, until "the foot of the slave shall cease to tread the soil of the United States." The state of society that must exist in the Southern States, with four millions of free negroes and their increase, turned loose upon them, I will not discuss—it is too horrible to contemplate.

I have only noticed such of the acts of the Republican party as I deem necessary to show that they are in earnest, and determined to carry out their publicly avowed intentions—and to show that their success has been such as should not fail to create the deepest concern for the honor and safety of the Southern States.— Now, in view of the past and our prospects for the future, what ought we to do? What do wisdom and prudence dictate?— What do honor and safety require at our hands?

I know that the answer that I shall give to these questions may subject me to severe criticism by those who do not view these matters as I do; but feeling conscious of the corrrectness of my conclusions, and the purity of my motives, I will not shrink from responsibilities in the emergency which presents itself. It would be criminal "in those entrusted with State sovereignty" not to speak out and warn the people of the encroachments that have been made, and are about to be made upon them, with the consequences that must follow.

In full view, and, I trust, a just appreciation of all my obligations and responsibilities, officially and personally, to my God, my State, and the Federal Government, I solemnly declare it to be my opinion, that the only hope of future security, for Alabama and the other slaveholding States, is secession from the Union.— I deplore the necessity for coming to such a conclusion. It has been forced upon me, and those who agree with me, by a wicked and perverse party, fatally bent upon the destruction of an institution vital to the Southern States—a party whose constitutional rights we have never disturbed, and who should be our friends; yet they hate us without a cause.

Should Alabama secede from the Union, as I think she ought, the responsibility, in the eyes of all just men, will not rest upon her, but upon those who have driven her in self-defence, to assume that position.

Has Alabama the right peacefully to withdraw from the Union, without subjecting herself to any rightful authority of the Federal Government to coerce her into the Union? Of her right to do so, I have no doubt. She is a Sovereign State, and retains every right and power not delegated to the Federal Government in the written Constitution. That Government has no powers, except such as are delegated in the Constitution, or such as are necessary to carry these powers into execution. The Federal Government was established for the protection, and not for destruction or injury of Constitutional rights. A Sovereign State has a right to judge of the wrongs or injuries that may be done her, and to determine upon the mode and measures of redress. The Black Republican party has for years continued to make aggressions upon the slaveholding States, under the forms of law, and in every manner that fanaticism could devise, and have now gained strength and position, which threaten, not only the destruction of the institution of slavery, but must degrade and ruin the slaveholding States, if not resisted. May not these States turn aside from the impending danger, without criminality? If they have not this right, then we are the slaves of our worst enemies. "The wise man foreseeth the evil and turneth aside." A wise State should not do less.

If Alabama should withdraw from the Union, she would not be guilty of treason, even if a Sovereign State could commit treason. The Constitution says: "Treason against the United States shall consist only in levying war against them, or in adhering to their enemies, giving them aid and comfort." The Federal Government has the right to use its military power "to execute the laws of the Union, surpress insurrections, and repel invasions." If a State withdraws from the Union, the Federal Government has no power, under the Constitution, to use the military force against her, for there is no law to enforce the submission of a sovereign State, nor would such a withdrawal be either an insurrection or an invasion. We should remember that Alabama must act and decide the great question of resistance or submission, for herself. No other State has the right or power to decide for her. She may, and should, consult with the other slaveholding States to secure concert of action, but still, she must decide the question for herself, and *coöperate afterwards*.

The contemplated Convention will not be the place for the *timid* or the *rash*. It should be composed of men of wisdom and experience—men who have the capacity to determine what the honor of the State and the security of her people demand; and patriotism and moral courage sufficient to carry out the dictates of their honest judgments.

What will the intelligent and patriotic people of Alabama do in the impending crisis? Judging of the future by the past, I believe they will prove themselves equal to the present, or any future emergency, and never will consent to affiliate with, or submit to be governed by a party who entertains the most deadly hostility towards them and their institution of slavery. They are loyal and true to the Union, but never will consent to remain degraded members of it.

Very respectfully, your obd't serv't,
A. B. MOORE.

The following is a copy of the Proclamation issued by the Governor:

PROCLAMATION.

Executive Department,
Montgomery, Ala., Dec. 6, 1861.

Whereas, the following Joint Resolutions were passed at the last session of the General Assembly of the State of Alabama, to-wit:

[Reciting the Resolutions on page 9.]

Now, I, A. B. Moore, Governor of the State of Alabama, by virtue of the power vested in me by the foregoing resolutions, and in obedience thereto, do hereby proclaim and make known to the people of Alabama, that the contingency contemplated in said Preamble and Resolutions has happened in the election of Abraham Lincoln to the Presidency of the United States. The qualified voters of the several counties of the State are, therefore, hereby called upon to assemble at the several places of voting in their respective counties, on Monday, the 24th December, 1860, to elect delegates to a Convention of the State of Alabama, to be held at the capitol in the city of Montgomery, on Monday, the 7th day of January next, to "consider determine and do whatever, in the opinion of said Convention, the rights, interests and honor of the State of Alabama require to be done for their protection."

In testimony whereof, I have hereunto set my hand and caused [L. S.] the Great Seal of the State to be affixed in the city of Montgomery, this 6th day of December, A. D. 1860.
By the Governor,   A. B. MOORE.
 J. H. WEAVER, Secretary of State.

HISTORY AND DEBATES OF THE CONVENTION.

FIRST DAY.

On the 7th January, 1861, the Convention assembled in the city of Montgomery, in the Hall of the House of Representatives of the State Capitol. It is a remarkable fact, that, of the one hundred Delegates of which the Convention was constituted, not one was absent. This was owing, doubtless, to the great anxiety, on the part of the Delegates, to participate in the earliest proceedings; and also, I apprehend, to the doubt that existed, previous to the organization, as to whether the straight-Secession party or the Coöperation party was in the majority. On the Sunday night before the Convention met, each party seriously claimed the ascendancy; but before the hour for organizing the Convention, it was conceded that the Secession party was the stronger.

Great precaution had been taken in advance, to secure an harmonious organization; and for this purpose it had been agreed, at first, that one member of each party, to be designated before the meeting, should approach the desk, call the Convention to order and nominate a temporary President; but the Coöperation party, convinced, by having accurately measured their strength, that they were in a minority, deemed it proper to yield the organization of the Convention to the majority; of which fact the latter were duly advised.

On motion of the Hon. H. G. Humphries, the Hon. William S. Phillips, of Dallas, was called to the Chair, as temporary President; and A. G. Horn, of Mobile, and S. D. Brewer, of Montgomery, were appointed temporary Secretaries.

Mr. YANCEY offered the following Resolutions, which were unanimously adopted:

Resolved, 1st. That the proceedings of the Convention be opened with prayer, and that the Rev. Dr. Manly be invited to perform this service to-day.

Resolved, 2d. That the President of the Convention be requested to invite some Clergyman to open the Convention with prayer each successive day of the session.

The Convention was then opened with prayer by Rev. Basil Manly, formerly President of the University of Alabama.

PRAYER.

Almighty Father, Maker of Heaven and Earth; King eternal, immortal, invisible; the only wise God! We adore Thee, for Thou art God, and besides Thee there is none else; our Fathers' God, and our God! We thank Thee that Thou hast made us *men*, endowed with reason, conscience and speech—capable of knowing, loving and serving Thee! We thank Thee for Thy Son, the Lord Jesus Christ, our only Mediator and Redeemer! We thank Thee for Thy word of truth, our guide to eternal life. We thank Thee for civil government, ruling in Thy fear; and we especially thank Thee that Thou didst reserve this fair portion of the earth so long undiscovered, unpolluted with the wars and the crimes of the old world—that Thou mightest here establish a free government and a pure religion. We thank Thee that Thou hast allotted us our heritage here, and hast brought us upon it at such a time as this. We thank Thee for all the hallowed memories connected with the establishment of the independence of the Colonies, and their sovereignty as States, and with the formation and maintenance of our government, which we had devoutly hoped might last, unperverted and incorruptible, as long as the sun and moon endure.

Oh, our Father! we have striven as an integral part of this great Republic, faithfully to keep our solemn covenants in the Constitution of our country; and our conscience doth not accuse us of having failed to sustain our part in the civil compact. Lord of all the families of the earth! *we appeal to* THEE to protect us in the land Thou hast given us, the Institutions Thou hast established, the rights Thou hast bestowed! And now, in our troubles, besetting us like great waters round about, WE, Thy dependent children, humbly entreat Thy fatherly notice and care. Grant to Thy servants now assembled, as the direct representatives of the people of this State, all needful grace and wisdom for their peculiar and great responsibilities at this momentous crisis! Give them a clear perception of their duties, as the embodiment of the people; impart to them an enlightened, mature and sanctified judgment in forming every conclusion; a steady, Heaven-directed purpose and will in attaining every right end! Save them from the disturbing influences of error, of passion, prejudice and timidity—from divided and conflicting counsels; give them one mind and one way, and let that be the mind of Christ! If Thou seest them ready to go wrong, interpose Thy heavenly guidance and restraint; if slow and reluctant to execute what duty and safety require, quicken and urge them forward! Let patient enquiry and candor pervade every discussion; let calm, comprehensive and sober wisdom shape every measure, and direct every vote; let all things be done in Thy fear, and with a just regard to their whole duty toward God and toward man! Preserve them all in health, in purity, in peace; and cause that their session may promote the maintenance of equal rights, of civil freedom and good government; may promote the welfare of man, and the glory of Thy name! We ask all through Jesus Christ, our Lord: Amen!

The Convention consisted of one hundred Delegates, each of whom being present, approached the Clerk's desk, as his county was called, and enrolled his name.

NAMES OF THE DELEGATES AS ENROLLED.

From the county of

Autauga—George Rives.
Barbour—John Cochran, Alpheus Baker, J. S. M. Daniel.
Baldwin—Jos. Silver.
Bibb—James W. Crawford.
Blount—John S. Brasher, W. M. Edwards.
Butler—Samuel J. Bolling, John McPherson.
Calhoun—Daniel T. Ryan, John M. Crook, G. C. Whatley.
Chambers—J. F. Dowdell, Wm. H. Barnes.
Cherokee—Henry C. Sanford, Wm. L. Whitlock, John Potter, John P. Ralls.
Choctaw—S. E. Catterlin, A. J. Curtis.
Clark—O. S. Jewett.
Coffee—G. T. Yelverton.
Conechu—John Green.
Coosa—George Taylor, John B. Leonard, Albert Crumpler.
Covington—Dewitt C. Davis.
Dallas—John T. Morgan, Wm. S. Phillips.
Dale—D. B. Creech, James McKinnie.
DeKalb—Wm. O. Winston, John Franklin.

Fayette—B. W. Wilson, E. P. Jones.
Franklin—John A. Steele, R. S. Watkins.
Greene—James D. Webb, Thos. H. Herndon.
Henry—Hastings E. Owens, Thomas T. Smith.
Jackson—John R. Coffey, Wm. A. Hood, John P. Timberlake.
Jefferson—Wm. S. Earnest.
Lauderdale—S. C. Posey, H. C. Jones.
Laurence—D. P. Lewis, James S. Clarke.
Limestone—J. P. Coman, Thos. J. McClellan.
Lowndes—James S. Williamson, Jas. G. Gilchrist.
Macon—Samuel Henderson, O. R. Blue, J. M. Foster.
Madison—Nich. Davis, Jere. Clemens.
Marshall—A. C. Beard, James L. Sheffield.
Marengo—W. E. Clarke.
Marion—Lang. C. Allen, W. Steadham.
Mobile—John Bragg, George A. Ketchum, E. S. Dargan, H. G. Humphries.
Monroe—Lyman Gibbons.
Montgomery—Wm. L. Yancey, Thos. H. Watts.
Morgan—Jonathan Ford.
Perry—Wm. M. Brooks, J. F. Baily.
Pickens—Lewis M. Stone, W. H. Davis.
Pike—Eli W. Starke, Jeremiah A. Henderson, A. P. Love.
Randolph—H. M. Gay, George Forrester, R. J. Wood.
Russell—R. O. Howard, B. H. Baker.
Shelby—Geo. D. Shortridge, J. M. McClanahan.
St. Clair—John W. Inzer.
Sumpter—A. A. Coleman.
Talladega—N. D. Johnson, A. R. Barclay, M. G. Slaughter.
Tallapoosa—A. Kimball, M. J. Bulger, T. J. Russell.
Tuscaloosa—R. Jemison, Jr., W. R. Smith.
Walker—Robert Guttery.
Washington—James G. Hawkins.
Wilcox—F. R. Beck.
Winston—C. C. Sheets.

As the Delegates from the county of Montgomery, Hon. Wm. L. Yancey and Hon. T. H. Watts, approached the desk to enroll their names, there were some demonstrations of applause in the gallery; whereupon Mr. Morgan offered the following Resolution:

That the members of this Convention will abstain from applause on all occasions; and that all demonstrations of applause in the galleries or lobby shall be strictly prohibited.

Mr. Morgan said:

Mr. President—I sympathise fully with the sentiment that impels the Delegates on this floor, and the people in the galleries, to indulge in demonstrations of applause, but I deprecate the effect of this excitement upon our deliberations. I have respect for the occasion, and I feel assured that the best way to evince my feeling is by a dignified and respectful course of discussion and deliberation. I have respect for the Convention and desire to see it respected by others. If every speaker on this floor is to be openly and loudly applauded or condemned, as his opinions may meet with popular favor or rebuke, we shall have much to regret before we close our labors here.

I take this early opportunity to offer a resolution on this subject, and to strike at the evil when it first begins to display itself in a compliment to our most distinguished friends, who have just enrolled their names.

The Convention then proceeded to the election of a permanent President. Mr. Beck nominated Wm. M. Brooks, of Perry ;— Mr. Davis, of Madison, nominated Robert Jemison, Jr., of Tuscaloosa.

In casting up the vote, it appeared that Mr. Brooks had received 53 votes; Mr. Jemison, 45. This was the entire vote, and was a test of the relative strength of parties—there being, including Mr. Brooks, fifty-four who favored immediate secession, and forty-six, including Mr. Jemison, who were in favor of consulting and coöperating with the other slave-holding States.

Mr. Brooks was declared duly elected; and Messrs. Bragg Winston and Humphries were appointed to wait upon him, by whom he was conducted to the Chair. He delivered an appropriate address, and assumed the duties of his office.

Wm. H. Fowler, of Tuscaloosa, was elected Secretary; Frank. L. Smith, of Montgomery, was elected assistant Secretary ; and Robert H. Wynn was elected Door-keeper.

The President laid before the Convention the credentials[*] of

---

[*] Credentials of the Commissioner from South Carolina.

THE STATE OF SOUTH CAROLINA:

Whereas, Andrew P. Calhoun has been duly elected by a vote of the Convention of the people of the State of South Carolina, to act as a Commissioner the Hon. Andrew P. Calhoun, as a Commissioner from the State of South Carolina. On motion of Mr. Yancey, it was

Resolved, That a Committee of three be appointed to wait upon the Hon. Andrew P. Calhoun, Commissioner from the State of South Carolina, and request him to address the Convention at such time as he may designate, and that he be invited to take a seat within the bar of the Convention.

Messrs. Yancey, Webb and Davis, of Madison, were appointed.

On motion by Mr. COCHRAN, it was

Resolved, That the Governor of the State be requested to communicate to this Convention any information he may have respecting the condition of the country.

RESOLUTION OF RESISTANCE.

The first debate in the Convention arose upon the following Resolutions, offered by MR. WHATLEY:

WHEREAS, the only bond of union between the several States is the Constitution of the United States; and WHEREAS, that Constitution has been *violated*, both by the Government of the United States, and by a majority of the Northern States, in their separate legislative action, *denying* to the people of the Southern States their Constitutional rights;

And WHEREAS, a sectional party, known as the Black Republican Party, has, in the recent election, elected Abraham Lincoln to the office of President, and Hannibal Hamlin to the office of Vice-President of these United States, upon the avowed *principle* that the Constitution of the United States *does not recognise prop-*

---

to the Convention of the people of the State of Alabama, and the said people of the State of South Carolina, has ordered the Governor of said State to commission the said Andrew P. Calhoun. *Now, therefore*, I do hereby commission you, the said Andrew P. Calhoun, to act as a Commissioner from the State of South Carolina, in Convention assembled, to the State of Alabama, in Convention assembled, to confer upon the subjects entrusted to your charge.

Witness, His Excellency, Francis W. Pickens, Governor and Commander-in-Chief of said State, this first day of January, in the year of our Lord, One Thousand Eight Hundred and Sixty-one, and the Eighty-fifth year of the Sovereignty and Independence of the State of South Carolina.

[Seal of State.]   JAMES A. DUFFAS,
By the Governor.   Deputy Secretary State

erty *in slaves*, and that the Government should *prevent its extension* into the common Territories of the United States, and that the power of the Government should be so exercised that *slavery, in time, should be exterminated:*

Therefore, be it Resolved, by the people of Alabama, in solemn Convention assembled, That *these acts* and *designs* constitute such a violation of the compact, between the several States, as absolves the people of Alabama from all obligation to continue to support a Government of the United States, to be administered upon such *principles*, and that the people of Alabama *will not submit* to be parties to the *inauguration and administration* of Abraham Lincoln as President, and Hannibal Hamlin as Vice President of the United States of America.

On submitting the Resolutions, MR. WHATLEY said:

Mr. President—I offer these Resolutions for the purpose, in the outset, to ascertain the sense of this body upon the question of submission or resistance to Lincoln's Administration. It is known that there are different opinions entertained by members of this Convention; many have been elected as *straight-out secessionists*, others as coöperationists, and among the coöperationists there is a diversity of opinion. Some are for coöperating with the entire South, others for a coöperation with the Cotton States, and likely *some* are willing to coöperate with a majority of the Cotton States. It is said, there are some in this body who are for absolute submission; I trust though, these suspicions are not true, and that we shall present an undivided front, in antagonism to the Black Republican administration. In the language of the Joint Resolutions, of the last session of our Legislature, let us assert that, "Alabama, acting for herself, has solemnly declared that, under no circumstances *will she submit* to the *foul domination* of a sectional Northern party." I desire, therefore, to ascertain, definitely, the sense of this body upon the question of submission or resistance. If we shall determine for resistance, as no doubt we will, then the next step will be, what kind of resistance shall we offer?

MR. SMITH, of Tuscaloosa:

Mr. President—I do not object, so much to the resolutions themselves, as to the reasons assigned by the gentleman, [Mr. Whatley,] for their introduction. It is proclaimed that this is intended as a test; the test as to *submission!* The intimation is ungenerous. It is inconsistent with the desires of harmony and con-

ciliation that have been openly expressed here by all parties. It
is an injudicious beginning of our deliberations. It is true, that it
has been ascertained by the elections which have just been had
here, that we are a minority. I am of that minority; but I do
not associate with submissionists! There is not one in our company. We scorn the prospective Black Republican rule as much
as the gentleman from Calhoun, [Mr. Whatley,] or any of his
friends.

There is, in the gentleman's speech, besides the undisguised expression of suspicion, the appearance of a desire to stir up enemies, instead of a desire to harmonize friends. If this is the
harmony you preach and practice, you will have nothing in this
Convention but the most unpleasant scenes of stubborn, sullen,
and unyielding antagonism. All good men should deprecate that.

The leading sentiments of the resolutions I endorse. I am perfectly willing to express a determination to resist a Black Republican Administration; but I may not choose to vote for this long
string of resolutions. Present a naked question of resistance to
Black Republican rule, and you will doubtless receive a unanimous vote in favor of it. But do not so interlard it with generalities and political abstractions that we shall be forced to reject
the good on account of its too close association with the evil. I
object particularly to make an intimation that I would oppose by
force the inauguration of Lincoln. I would not have anything to
do with that in any way. I deprecate the idea of intimating to
the people, even remotely, that the laws ought not to be respected.

If gentlemen are earnest in their wishes to procure here, and at
this time, an emphatic expression of resistance, I have no doubt
that the resolutions can be so amended as to meet the cordial support of all of us.

I am not willing to say, as does this resolution, that the separate action of any State has absolved Alabama from all obligation to continue to support the Government of the United States.
A State may violate the Constitution and still the General Government may not be at fault.

Let the resolutions be amended—stripped of their verbiage, so
as to present the single question of resistance, placed in its true
position, and I will support them.

Mr. Posey said:

He opposed the resolutions, because the first recital in the
preamble places resistance to Mr. Lincoln's Administration upon
the aggressions of the Federal Government, as well as those of

the Northern States. The last charge is true; the first is not true. There have been no aggressions on the part of the Federal Government; there has been an omission, it may be, in some instances, to execute the Fugitive Slave law, which we well know proceeded from the hatred of Northern Abolitionists to that law. The aggressions of which we have just cause to complain, have been made by the people in some of the Northern States, and by the Personal Liberty Bills of thirteen of these States. They have violated the Constitution of the United States, in these unconstitutional enactments.

Mr. Posey admitted the South could not submit to the principles presented in the Chicago Platform. Resistance to the issues made up in that Platform was forced upon the people of this State. They had no other alternative placed before them in the Chicago Creed, but exclusion from the Territories of the United States, with the ultimate extinction of slavery as the consequence of such exclusion and injustice, or resistance to any administration of the Government upon such principles.

These resolutions indicate, clearly, one mode of resistance only. This is not expressed, but the fair construction is, that separate State secession is the kind of resistance pledged by these resolutions; when it is well known that the coöperationists in this Convention have declared their opposition to the principles of the Black Republican party, and their determination to resist a Government administered upon their policy; but their plan of resistance is not by separate State action. We intend to resist. It is not our purpose to submit to the doctrines asserted at Chicago: but our resistance is based upon consultation, and in unity of action, with the other slave States.

If we vote for these resolutions, in their present shape, we shall have committed ourselves to separate State action, to which the coöperationists in this body stand opposed, for the reason, we greatly prefer another mode of resistance, considered by us to be safer for the country, and not less effectual in asserting and maintaining all our just rights.

Mr. YANCEY said:

Mr. President—I favor the passage of these resolutions. That they are a test—ascertaining whether there are any submissionists or not in this body, is no objection to them in my mind. It is said they are offensive because it is a test. They ought not to be offensive, in my opinion, to any Delegate who is not in favor of submitting to Lincoln's Administration. That there are such here, I am unwilling to believe, and I desire that the world shall know there are none such, if such is the fact; while at the same time, if there are any, I desire to know it, and the Convention should know it.

It has been said that this resolution will create discord amongst us—and is not conciliatory. It can only justly be so considered by those opposed to all resistance to the Black Republican power. I, for one, have no desire to conciliate persons occupying such position. I wish here, and elsewhere, to antagonise them.

The resolutions are designed, in my apprehension, to lay a basis for our future action. If we are, as I hope we shall be, united in favor of these resolutions, there can be but little difficulty in our taking some action, which will be agreeable to us all. If, however, there shall be any here opposed to these resolutions, we cannot have united action.

It will be observed, that the resolutions are carefully worded and framed. They do not designate the mode of resistance.—They offend no man's opinion upon the question of secession or revolution. They do not discriminate in favor of separate, or of coöperative State action. They simply discriminate between those who are willing to continue the Union upon the principles of the Black Republican party, and those who are willing to resist them, and to dissolve the Union rather than see the Government administered upon those principles.

With all who can vote for these resolutions, I can confer, and hope to come to a common conclusion. With those who shall vote against them, I have neither feeling or principle in common.

Mr. CLEMENS said:

Mr. President—I object to this resolution, not so much on account of its terms, as on account of the avowed motives which prompted its introduction. The gentleman from Calhoun tells us that he desires to ascertain whether there is any one here who is willing to submit to a Black Republican Administration, and he proposes this resolution *as a test*. Now, sir, the proposition to make a test on such a subject, necessarily implies suspicion, and suspicion is always more or less offensive. If, therefore, the gentleman is a correct exponent of the wishes and feelings of the majority—if that is the temper in which we of the minority are to be met, I give them warning that our session is likely to be a stormy one. We may be *persuaded* to go a long ways. We cannot be *driven* an inch in any direction, and the attempt to do it will not only result in failure, but must produce a state of things whose consequences I will not picture.

I came here, Mr. President, rightly appreciating, as I think, the difficulties before us, and prepared to do all that ought to be done to promote harmony among our own people. I see very plainly that a time is coming when our very existence as an independent people will materially depend upon a cordial union among ourselves. I am no believer in peaceable secession. I know it to be impossible. No liquid but blood has ever filled the baptismal fount of nations. The rule is without an exception, and he has read the book of human nature to little purpose who expects to see a nation born except in convulsions, or christened at any alter but that of the God of battles. So thinking, and so believing, I have felt that it was the duty of a patriot to conciliate—not to influence; to keep constantly before his eyes the one great duty of reconciling conflicting opinions, and smoothing away existing asperities. Such, I am sure, is the general feeling of my party friends. But we are men, with all the frailties of men, and the avowal of insulting suspicions—the introduction of test resolutions. and similar aggravating annoyances, will be certain to end in scenes alike discreditable to this body, and injurious to the best interests of the State.

I do not acknowledge that the gentleman from Calhoun is prepared to go any farther than I am, in resistance to Black Republican domination. There is no danger to be incurred in such a cause, so great that I will shrink from sharing it with him. There is no extremity of resistance he can propose, in which I will not join him, provided it promises to be effectual; but I do not concede his right, or the right of any man, to make a test for me.— No man shall make it; and if his purpose be to ascertain the real sense of this Convention, upon the subject-matter of his resolution. I tell him that he has adopted the wrong course, and his effort will end in failure. For one, I shall take the responsibility of voting no. My belief is, that there are forty-five others who will do the same thing, and what then becomes of his *test?* He would be very unwilling, I imagine, to let the impression go abroad that there are forty-six members of this Convention in favor of submitting to the rule of a Black Republican President, elected upon a Black Republican platform; and yet, sir, I see nothing more that he is likely to accomplish.

I shall make no proposition to amend. I shall not seek to evade a direct vote by any parliamentary expedient. I am ready to record my name upon the resolution as it stands. I shall vote no, and leave the consequences to take care of themselves.

Mr. Williamson said:

The resolutions under consideration are eliciting more discussion than I expected, since all, so far as I am informed, are agreed that Alabama cannot, and will not, submit to the Administration of Lincoln and Hamlin. The resolutions affirm nothing more. If there are any here who think otherwise, let them come out like men and say so. This would make an issue, and relieve them from the disagreeable task of resorting to parliamentary subterfuges, for the purpose of escaping discussion, and avoiding a direct vote on the main question. When I first heard the resolutions read from the Secretary's desk, I flattered myself they would be unanimously adopted without debate. I still flatter myself that the objections are to the verbiage and not to the question involved. If so, I hope gentlemen will at once point out the word or words. If opposed to the resolutions, let them state the grounds of their objections, and offer amendments indicating the desired change. I deem it important to adopt the resolutions forthwith; consequently am prepared to accommodate gentlemen by voting for any amendment not incompatible with the meaning and spirit of the resolutions, as they now stand.

Mr. WHATLEY said:

Mr. President—Gentlemen of this body have misapprehended my object in offering the resolutions at this early day of our session. The resolutions are not offered to throw a fire-brand into the deliberations of this body. I imagine, gentlemen representing the sovereign people of Alabama, are *ready, even now,* to take position upon this subject. We are misrepresented at home and abroad. We are represented North as submissionists. Even in this city, different public prints represent us in different ways, and particularly in the Northern portion of our own State are our positions misrepresented. I desire, sir, that these misrepresentations may be *speedily* corrected, and that *even during this day* the telegraphic wires may transmit the *glad intelligence abroad,* that Alabama will *never submit* to a Black Republican Administration.

This discussion was continued, with much animation, a considerable time, and the resolution was so amended as to satisfy all parties, and was passed unanimously, in the following shape:

Resolved, By the people of Alabama, in Convention assembled' That the State of Alabama cannot, and will not, submit to the Administration of Lincoln and Hamlin as President and Vice President of the United States, upon the principles referred to in the preamble.

SECOND DAY.

January 8th.—Mr. YANCEY, from the Committee to wait on the Hon. Andrew P. Calhoun, Commissioner from South Carolina, reported that the Committee had performed that duty, and that Mr. Calhoun was ready to address the Convention at such time as it should desire.

On motion by Mr. Jones, of Lauderdale, it was

Resolved, That the Hon. A. P. Calhoun, Commissioner from South Carolina to the State of Alabama, be requested to address the Convention at this time, and make such communications as he may desire.

Mr. Calhoun was then introduced, and addressed the Convention, in substance, as follows:

MR. PRESIDENT AND GENTLEMEN OF THE CONVENTION:

It is one of the most agreeable incidents of my life that the Convention of the people of South Carolina—my native State—should have elected me a Commissioner to the State of Alabama, for many years my adopted one. South Carolina could doubtless have sent an abler son to represent her, but she could not have sent one whose heart was filled with more kindness and attachment, or one who would extend the hand of fellowship with greater sincerity or regard. It was during the many years I sojourned among you, I learnt how to appreciate the intelligence and energy of your citizens, and how properly to estimate the vast and varied resources of your State: a State second to but one as a cotton producer; to none in mineral wealth, especially in coal and iron: so potent to the world, either in the mission of peace or war: a State that instructed her Governor to call a Convention in the event of the election of a Black Republican for the presumed purpose of meeting the great issue: To such a State, South Carolina would willingly have assigned the position of leadership in the great drama of events that are pressing to a rapid solution. But by a combination of accidental causes, the initiation of the contest devolved upon South Carolina. The Governor of South Carolina called an extra session of the Legislature to elect Electors to cast the Presidential vote of that State. Continuing in session for a few days, the election of a Black Republican or sectional candidate, was declared; and feeling that submission would be both degredation and annihilation, she called a Convention forthwith of the people to assemble on the 17th of December. At once the State fired up. It was an up-heaving of the people. No leader or leaders could have resisted it, or stemmed its impetuosity. The wave of public opinion swept over the lower, the middle, and leaped into the recess of the mountain districts. The result was, the Convention assembled with unprecedented unanimity. Some time was lost in consequence of a loathsome epidemic raging in Columbia, that forced the Convention to adjourn to Charleston. On the 19th a cheering voice from Alabama was heard. Your esteemed Commissioner,* who so ably represented your State, and was so acceptable to the one to which he was accredited, presented a telegram from your patriotic and popular Governor, that carried an electric thrill through every heart—"tell the Convention to listen to no proposition of compromise or delay." The next day, the 20th, came the Ordinance annulling the compact which South Carolina had entered into in 1788 with twelve other sovereign States, and resuming all delegated power, she became a free, sovereign, and independent commonwealth. At this point, the accumulated aggressions of the third of a century fell like shackles at her feet, and free, disinthralled, regenerated, she stood before her devoted people like the genius of Liberty, beckoning them on to the performance of their duty.

The argument closes here so far as Federal aggressions in South Carolina are concerned. But may we not pause in reverence and admiration before the vast monument built up by Southern genius and eloquence, in defending and warning a persecuted section of the measured approach of despotism, and that, too, in the face of the frowns and blandishments of power; and there were some who, braving the imprecations of the enemy, and the importunities of friends, persisted in performing their sacred duty to their section at all and every sacrifice.

In obedience to instructions, I now present a certified copy of "An Ordinance" to dissolve the Union between the State of South Carolina and other States, united with her under the compact entitled the "Constitution of the United Statss of America." I am also instructed to invite your coöperation with South Carolina in the formation of a Southern Confederacy, and to submit the Federal Constitution as the basis of a provisional government.— That instrument, with the Southern construction given to it, would be safe until it, or one, could be deliberately amended and perfected. The exigency requires for the present, prompt and efficient action, and for this purpose I am instructed to invite your State to meet her in Convention at the earliest practicable day.

---

* Hon. John A. Elmore, of Montgomery, Commissioner from Alabama to South Carolina.

THE CONVENTION OF ALABAMA. 33

Mr. C. proceeded to say that, before he left Charleston, the Commissioners to the several States, in a meeting, had determined to suggest the first Monday in February, the 3d. He said he had heard Montgomery suggested, but was not authorized to say anything on that point himself. Mr. C. here presented the Report and Resolutions from the Committee on "Relations with slaveholding States, providing for Commissioners to such States," and read the Resolutions appended to the report, which he then submitted to the Convention. He also submitted "The address of the people of South Carolina, assembled in Convention, to the people of the slaveholding States," and then proceeded: That no better illustration of the insidious approach and consummation of despotism can be found in history, than the progress of the Government of the United States to consolidation and the usurpation of every vestige of State sovereignty. Even the mask that covered its aggressions is now dropped, and it is making war and striking at independent States that warmed it into life. Be it so. The day of endurance is past. The government of the United States will stand out in history a mock and reproach to every friend of freedom or free institutions. We are in the midst of events, and enacting them, that will effect the condition, not only of ourselves but the world, for weal or woe. In South Carolina, we feel the justice of our cause: we will defend our State to the last extremity, be the consequences what they may. A common cause unites Alabama and South Carolina and the other cotton States. An Union at the earliest day between them will guarantee success.— We cannot be conquered; but united, we will hurl defiance at our assailants. The flag of Independence and resistance is unfurled in my State from the mountains to the sea-board. Old and young rally to its standard with the determination, if the attempt is made to coerce us, that we will "die freemen rather than live slaves."

Mr. Calhoun then laid before the Convention sundry documents, connected with his mission, which will be found in another part of this volume.

This HISTORY would not be complete if it were to conceal the great excitement that prevailed in the Convention, and the deep interest that every member felt in passing events. Telegraphic dispatches were frequently received and read, and served the purpose of keeping up the animation.

On this day Mr. Watts placed the following dispatches before the Convention:

BY TELEGRAPH FROM WASHINGTON, JANUARY 7, 1861.

"The Republicans in the House, to-day, refused to consider the border State compromise—complimented Maj. Anderson, and pledged to sustain the President."

MOORE & CLOPTON.

TELEGRAPH FROM RICHMOND TO GOV. MOORE.

"Legislature passed, by one hundred and twelve (112) to five (5). to resist any attempt to coerce a seceding State, by all the means in her power. What has your Convention done? Go out promptly and all will be right."

A. F. HOPKINS,
F. M. GILMER.

The Governor sent up the following Message, in answer to the resolution of yesterday:

EXECUTIVE DEPARTMENT, }
Montgomery, Ala., Jan. 8, 1861. }

GENTLEMEN OF THE CONVENTION:

In obedience to the resolution adopted by the Convention yesterday, requiring me to communicate any information I may have respecting the condition of the country, I herewith transmit such information as is in my possession, touching the public interests, and a brief statement of my acts in regard thereto, and the reasons therefor. All of which are respectfully submitted to the consideration of the Convention.

Very respectfully,

A. B. MOORE.

The General Assembly at its last session passed unanimously, with two exceptions, resolutions requiring the Governor, in the event of the election of a Black Republican, to order elections to be held for delegates to a Convention of the State. The contingency contemplated having occurred, making it necessary for me to call a Convention, writs of election were issued immediately after the votes of the electorial college were cast. It was my opinion that, under the peculiar phraseology of the resolutions, I was not authorized to order elections upon the casting of the popular vote. I, therefore, determined not to do so.

As the slaveholding States have a common interest in the insti-

tution of slavery, and must be common sufferers in its overthrow.
I deemed it proper, and it appeared to be the general sentiment of
the people, that Alabama should consult and advise with the other
slaveholding States, so far as practicable, as to what is best to
be done to protect their interest and honor in the impending crisis.
And seeing that the Conventions of South Carolina and Florida
would probably act before the Convention of Alabama assembled, and that the Legislatures of some of the States would meet,
and might adjourn without calling Conventions, prior to the meeting of our Convention, and thus the opportunity of conferring
with them upon the great and vital questions on which you are
called to act—I determined to appoint Commissioners to all the
slaveholding States. After appointing them to those States whose
Conventions and Legislatures were to meet in advance of the Alabama Convention, it was suggested by wise counselors, that if I
did not make similar appointments to the other Southern States,
it would seem to be making an invidious distinction, which was
not intended. Being convinced that it might be so considered, I
then determined to appoint Commissioners to all the slaveholding
States, and made the following appointments:

A. F. Hopkins and F. M. Gilmer, Commissioners to Virginia.
John A. Elmore, Commissioner to South Carolina.
I. W. Garrott and Robert H. Smith, Commissioners to North
Carolina.
J. L. M. Curry, Commissioner to Maryland.
David Clopton, Commissioner to Delaware.
S. F. Hale, Commissioner to Kentucky.
William Cooper, Commissioner to Missouri.
L. P. Walker, Commissioner to Tennessee.
David Hubbard, Commissioner to Arkansas.
John A. Winston, Commissioner to Louisiana.
J. M. Calhoun, Commissioner to Texas.
E. C. Bullock, Commissioner to Florida.
John Gill Shorter, Commissioner to Georgia.
E. W. Pettus, Commissioner to Mississippi.

All these gentlemen are well known to the people of Alabama,
and distinguished for their ability, integrity and patriotism. The
following is a copy of the commission to each of them, in substance:

EXECUTIVE DEPARTMENT, }
Montgomery, Ala., Dec., 1860. }

WHEREAS, the election of Abraham Lincoln, a Black Republican, to the Presidency of the United States, by a purely sectional vote, and by a party whose leading and publicly avowed object is the destruction of the institution of slavery as it exists in the slaveholding States, is an accomplished fact; and whereas, the success of said party, and the power which it now has, and soon will acquire, greatly endanger the peace, interests, security, and honor of the slaveholding States, and make it necessary that prompt and effective measures should be adopted to avoid the evils which must result from a Republican administration of the Federal Government; and as the interest and destiny of the slaveholding States are the same, they must naturally sympathize with each other; they, therefore, so far as may be practicable, should consult and advise together as to what is best to be done to protect their mutual interest and honor.

Now, therefore, in consideration of the premises, I, ANDREW B. MOORE, Governor of the State of Alabama, by virtue of the general powers in me vested, do hereby constitute and appoint Col. John A. Elmore, a citizen of said State, a Commissioner to the sovereign State of South Carolina, to consult and advise with his Excellency, Gov. Wm. H. Gist, and the members of the Convention to be assembled in said State on the 17th day of December, inst., as to what is best to be done to protect the rights, interests and honor of the slaveholding States, and to report the result of such consultation in time to enable me to communicate the same to the Convention of the State of Alabama, to be held on the 7th day of January next.

In testimony whereof I have hereunto signed my name, and caused the Great Seal of the State to be affixed, in the city of Montgomery, this —— day of December, A. D. 1860.

[L. S.]

A. B. MOORE.

I herewith transmit to you the reports, so far as they have been received, and will lay before the Convention any others that may be made, immediately on their receipt. I trust that my course in the appointment of these Commissioners will meet the approbation of the Convention.

Having satisfactory evidence to believe that Alabama would withdraw from the present Union, I considered it my duty to take such steps as would enable the Convention and Legislature to provide the means of putting the State in a condition to protect and defend her citizens, in the event of her secession.

Knowing that the Treasury was not provided with funds sufficient for the purpose—that bonds, at such a crisis, could not be sold out of the State, except at a great sacrifice, and believing that, at such a time, additional taxation upon the people should be avoided, if possible, I determined to take the responsibility of requesting the banks to suspend specie payments, for the purpose of retaining their specie to aid the State, provided it should become necessary. With this view, I addressed a letter to each of the banks, a copy of which will be found in the following address to the people of Alabama, published on the —— day of December, 1860. I refer the Convention to this address for a full statement of the reasons which induced my action in this matter:

Executive Department,
Montgomery, Ala., Dec. 17, 1860.

To the People of Alabama:

Strong appeals have been made to me, by many citizens from different sections of the State, to convene the Legislature for the purpose of providing the ways and means of protecting the interests and honor of the State in the impending crisis; and for the further purpose of authorising the banks to suspend specie payments, to enable them to furnish greater facilities for moving the cotton crop, and thus relieve, to some extent, the embarrassed condition of the cotton market, and the people. These appeals were made by those, whose opinions are entitled to the highest respect, and are disconnected with the banks, either as directors or stockholders. After giving to the subject the fullest consideration, and viewing it in all its bearings, I determined not to convene the Legislature, for reasons which I will now give.

I did not doubt, and do not now, that the Convention, to meet on the 7th January, will determine that Alabama shall withdraw from the present Union, at an early day.

Should this contingency occur, it will be necessary forthwith to convene the Legislature to provide for whatever the action of the Convention may render necessary, in the way of legislation.— The imposition upon the State of the expenses of the Convention, and two extra session of the Legislature at this time, when economy is a matter of the highest consideration, ought to be avoided, if it could be done consistently with the public interests. If the Leggislature could anticipate the action of the Convention, and provide for it, it would supersede the necessity of convening, after the Convention shall have acted; but this would be impossible.

It was my opinion, that if I issued a proclamation calling an extra session of the Legislature, every one would believe that the object, in part, was to authorize the banks to suspend specie payments. This would have caused an immediate run upon them, and would, in a great measure, have exhausted their specie, and thus rendered them unable to aid the State in her emergency, or relieve the people.

It appeared to me, that these difficulties could be avoided, by the banks and myself assuming responsibilities, which never should be done under any other circumstances. I considered it a matter of the utmost importance that the specie, in the vaults of the banks, should be kept there, so far as it could be done, in order to aid the State in providing the means to sustain herself in the approaching crisis. It would be inexpedient, at such a time, to tax the people, and State bonds could not now be sold, except at a great sacrifice. I considered it the duty of banks, upon whom extraordinary privileges had been conferred, to come to the aid of the State in her hour of need, and therefore determined to request them, at the same time, to suspend specie payments, and retain their specie for the benefit and security of the State, so far as might be necessary.

In this way, a run upon the banks would be avoided, and they would remain in a condition to relieve the State from immediately taxing her people, or selling bonds at a heavy discount; and render unnecessary an extra session of the Legislature, before the meeting of the Convention.

The extension of relief to the people, in selling their cotton crops would follow as an incident. In consideration of the premises, I addressed to each of the banks a letter, of which the following is a copy:

EXECUTIVE DEPARTMENT, }
Montgomery, Ala., Dec. 4, 1860. }

TO THE PRESIDENT AND DIRECTORS OF THE
CENTRAL BANK OF ALABAMA, MONTGOMERY, ALA:

GENTLEMEN:—The peculiar and extraordinary state of public affairs and the interest of the State, make it a matter of State necessity to retain in the vaults of the banks all the gold and silver in their possession.

From present prospects, there can scarcely be a doubt that Alabama will secede from the Union before the 4th day of March next. Should that contingency occur, it will be necessary for the State to raise not less than a million of dollars in specie, or its equivalent. Under the circumstances which surround us, we could not sell State bonds, either in the North or in Europe, except at a ruinous discount; and it would be inexpedient to tax the people immediately for that purpose. How, then, can the State secure the money, that may be necessary, in her emergency?

But one practicable plan now presents itself to my mind, and that is to call upon the banks of the State to come to our aid. The course of events, and the suspension of the South Carolina and Georgia banks, will create more or less uneasiness in the minds of bill-holders, and will induce many of them to draw the specie from the banks to the extent of the notes they may hold, and thus render the banks unable to aid the State, as they otherwise could do.

I am strongly urged, from various parts of the State, to convene the Legislature, for the purpose of authorizing the banks to suspend specie payments, and thus enable them to retain their specie for the purposes suggested.

I have reflected much and anxiously upon the subject. I am satisfied, were I to convene the Legislature for the purpose stated, that it would produce a run on the banks, and in a great measure exhaust their specie and defeat the object I have in view.

With the view, then, of enabling the banks to retain their specie for the purpose aforesaid, I deem it my duty, under the cir-circumstances, to advise and request them to suspend, all at the same time.

The high and patriotic motives which would induce the act, would sustain the banks and me. There can be no doubt that the Convention and Legislature, soon to meet, will sustain and legalize the act. I will sanction it, and will institute no proceedings against them; and in my message to the Legislature and Convention will urge them to sanction the act, which I am sure they will do.

If need be, after the suspension, I will write an address to the people of the State, stating the facts and circumstances under which the step was taken. I am satisfied that the banks are in a sound condition, and can maintain it through the present crisis; but it will render them unable to give the State that aid she will need.

I have written similar letters to all the banks. The contents of this communication are respectfully submitted to your consideration. Very respectfully. your obedient servant,

A. B. MOORE.

At my suggestion and request, and for the purposes stated in my letter, the Commercial Bank at Selma, the Central Bank at Montgomery, and the Eastern Bank at Eufaula, suspended this day. It is due to those banks that I should say (being advised of their condition) that they are able to sustain themselves through the crisis, and that they have taken this important step with the high and patriotic motive of sustaining the State, as shown by the response of each of them to my letter. Their letters are filed in my office, and would have been published but for the length they would give this communication.

There is no necessity for any depreciation in their notes, as there can be no question of their solvency.

The circumstances under which they have suspended, should relieve them from any censure. If censure is to fall upon any one, it should be upon me, and I rely for my justification upon the manifest propriety and necessity of the act, as well as the motives which induced it. The Bank of Mobile, and the Southern Bank of Alabama decline to suspend, but patriotically pledge themselves to raise their proportion of the amount suggested in my letter, should there be a necessity for it. These two banks being located in Mobile, can procure specie and exchange with more facility than the banks in the interior, and are not so liable to be prejudiced by the suspended banks of South Carolina and Georgia. Hence their ability to aid the State without suspending specie payments.

The Northern Bank at Huntsville, also declines to suspend, on account of peculiar circumstances which surround it.

I have now briefly stated the circumstances and facts, connected with the suspension of three of our banks, in accordance with the promise contained in my letter, and hope they will be satisfactory to the enlightened and patriotic people of Alabama, for whose benefit this great responsibility has been assumed.

A. B. MOORE.

I am authorized to say that the banks are prepared to loan the State their proportionate share of one million dollars, should her necessities require it.

The Convention is aware that I have had Fort Morgan, Fort Gaines, and Mount Vernon, occupied by the troops of Alabama.— My reasons for this important step are briefly and plainly set forth in the following letter to the President of the United States, as soon as I was officially informed that the Forts and Arsenal had been occupied:

EXECUTIVE DEPARTMENT,
Montgomery, Ala., Jan. 4, 1861.

To His Excellency JAMES BUCHANAN,
PRESIDENT OF THE UNITED STATES:

SIR:—In a spirit of frankness, I hasten to inform you by letter that, by my order, Fort Morgan and Fort Gaines and the United States Arsenal at Mount Vernon, were, on yesterday peaceably occupied, and are now held by the troops of the State of Alabama. That this act on my part may not be misunderstood by the Government of the United States, I proceed to state the motives which have induced it, and the reasons which justify it, and also the course of conduct with which I design to follow that act.

A Convention of the people of this State will, in pursuance of previously enacted law, assemble on the 7th inst. I was fully convinced, by the evidences which I had, that that Convention would, at an early day, in the exercise of an authority which, in my judgement, of right belongs to it, withdraw the State of Alabama from the Government of the United States, and place it in the attitude of a separate and independent power. Being thus convinced, I deemed it my duty to take every precautionary step to make the secession of the State peaceful, and prevent detriment to her people. While entertaining such a conviction as to my duty, I received such information as left me but little, if any, room to doubt that the Government of the United States, anticipating the secession of Alabama, and preparing to maintain its authority within this State by force, even to the shedding of blood and the sacrifice of the lives of the people, was about to reinforce those Forts, and put a guard over the Arsenal. Having that information, it was but an act of self-defence, and the plainest dictate of prudence to anticipate and guard against the contemplated movement of the authorities of the General Government. Appreciating, as I am sure you do, the courage and spirit of our people, you must be sensible that no attempt at the coercion of the State, or at the enforcement by military power of the authority of the United States within its jurisdiction, in contravention of the ordinance of secession, can be effectual unless our utmost capacity for resistance can be exhausted. It would have been an unwise policy, suicidal in its character, to have permitted the Government of the United States to have made undisturbed preparation, within this State, to enforce, by war and bloodshed, an authority which it is the fixed purpose of the people of the State to resist to the utmost of their power. A policy, so manifestly unwise, would probably have been overruled by an excited and discontented people, and popular violence might have accomplished that, which has been done by the State much more appropriately and much more consistently with the prospect of peace, and the interests of the parties concerned.

The purpose with which my order was given and has been executed, was to avoid, and not to provoke, hostilities between the State and Federal Government. There is no object, save the honor and dignity of my State, which is by me so ardently desired as the preservation of amicable relations between this State and the Government of the United States. That the secession of the State, made necessary by the conduct of others, may be peaceful, is my prayer, as well as the prayer of every patriotic man in the State.

An inventory of the property in the Forts and Arsenal has been ordered, and the strictest care will be taken to prevent the injury or destruction of it, while peaceable relations continue to exist, as I trust they will. The Forts and Arsenal will be held by my order, only for the precautionary purpose for which they were taken, and subject to the control of the Convention of the people to assemble on the 7th inst.

With distinguished consideration,
I am your obedient servant,
A. B. MOORE.

The Forts and Arsenal will be held subject to such instructions and directions as the Convention may think proper to give. Strict orders have been given the officers in command at the places mentioned, to take an inventory of the arms and ammunition, and public stores, and see that all are protected and preserved.

I am fully aware that, in all I have done in regard to the matters herein communicated, I have taken great responsibilities.— For my justification, I rely upon the propriety and necessity of the course I have taken, and upon the wisdom and patriotism of the Convention and people of Alabama. In this great and trying crisis, I have done all I could do to prepare the State for any emergencies that might occur. The great and responsible duty of protecting the rights, interests and honor of Alabama, is now imposed on the Convention; and I do not doubt that her present proud and high position will be maintained. May the God of Wisdom and Justice guide you in your counsels.

A. B. MOORE.

The President laid before the Convention the following telegraphic dispatches, from the Hon. Edmund W. Pettus, Commissioner from Alabama to Mississippi; and from the Hon. E. C. Bullock, Commissioner from Alabama to Florida:

"*Jackson, Miss., Jan.* 7.—"A resolution has been passed to raise a Committee of fifteen to draft the ordinance of secession."
E. W. PETTUS.

"The Convention met at twelve (12.) Mr. Barry is President. The State will probably secede to-morrow or next day."
E. W. PETTUS.

"*Tallahassee, Fla., Jan.* 7.—Convention, by vote of one hundred and sixty-two (162) to five (5,) adopted resolutions in favor of immediate secession. Committee appointed to prepare ordinance of secession."
E. C. BULLOCK.

PROPOSED SECRET SESSIONS.

When Mr. Calhoun addressed the Convention to-day, there was applause in the galleries and lobby, and in the Convention. It seemed difficult to restrain this disposition; and the President intimated that the galleries would have to be cleared if order was not observed. This led to a discussion, and the following propositions:

Mr. JEMISON introduced resolutions as follows:

Resolved, 1st. That all the deliberations of this Convention shall be held with closed doors, and in secret, unless otherwise directed by the Convention.

Resolved, 2d. That on a motion to open the doors of the Convention, there shall be no debate unless by consent of two-thirds of the Convention.

Resolved, 3d. That those persons invited within the bar of the Convention shall not be excluded from the secret sessions, unless so ordered by the Convention.

Resolved, 4th. That an obligation of strict secrecy, in regard to the secret deliberations of this Convention, is imposed upon all members and persons invited within the bar, and the officers of this Convention.

Resolved, 5th. That the lobby be set apart for the use of the ladies, while we are in open session.

Mr. BAKER, of Russell, moved to strike out the first resolution and insert the following:

Resolved, That whenever this Convention shall deem it necessary to hold a secret session, it may be done on motion and a majority vote of the Convention, and thereupon the Door-keeper shall clear the lobby and galleries, and that no debate shall be had on a motion to go into secret session.

MR. YANCEY said:

That he was in favor of secret sessions on certain questions. The proposition of the gentleman from Tuscaloosa [Mr. Jemison,] however, was not such as wholly met his approval. That proposition makes secret session the rule, and open session the exception. He would reverse it, and make open session the rule, and secret session the exception. Whenever any matter came up, which it would be policy to consider in secret session, it would be easy to move to close the doors.

It was a matter, however, of but little real moment, which way it was decided, and he would vote for the resolutions of the gentleman from Tuscaloosa, [Mr. Jemison,] rather than not have secret sessions.

Mr. POSEY said:

That he would prefer to confer upon the President the power to order the doors to be closed, when in his judgment it was proper to go into secret session; this would remove another objection which has been urged against closing the doors upon motion by the vote of the majority of the Convention; that is, the necessity of revealing to the house the subject-matter which required secrecy in deliberation, and thus defeat the sole object of sitting with closed doors.

The President of the Convention must know the nature of every dispatch and message from the Governor; in a word, the chair will know what is the character of all subjects demanding the deliberations of this body, and in his judgment and sound discretion the Convention may safely confide.

That there are questions of very grave importance, which prudence and the public safety alike require, should not yet be made public, Mr. P. admitted to be true; at the same time, he was unwilling to adopt the rule of secret session, and open doors the exception, for the reason that much of the business of the Convention may not be of that delicate complexion, requiring closed doors for its consideration.

The demonstrations in the galleries, Mr. P. admitted, were improper; but he thought such indiscretions would not be repeated; and he was unwilling to exclude from the galleries so many of our fellow-citizens, who, in common with the members of this Convention, were so deeply interested in its deliberations.

Mr. WILLIAMSON said:

As a general rule, applause in the lobby and galleries should not be tolerated; but regardless of rules, there are times when "out of the abundance of the heart the mouth speaketh." This, sir, is an occasion, which, in my judgment, justifies a departure from that rule. I have no doubt but that Alabama will respond in thunder tones to the noble sentiments expressed by the gallant Carolinian accredited to our State, for the purpose of notifying us officially of the secession of South Carolina from the United States. In the course of his remarks, he informed us, that she was induced to take the step, believing it to be essential to the vindication of her rights and honor, against a dominant sectional party, bent upon the destruction of the whole South. *This*, sir, many of us believe; and when told that her sons, from the mountains to the sea-shore, had determined to strike, if need be solitary and alone, in defence of Liberty, it was quite natural for those who feel deeply, and anxious, at once to unite with them in repelling insult and injury, to give expression to their feelings. I am sure, but for the deference and respect entertained for this body, the air would have been rent with a *wild shout* of approval, instead of the *almost inaudible hum* of applause from the lobby and galleries.

Mr. CLARK, of Laurence, said:

If the design of such demonstrations is to influence the deliberations of the Convention, they will prove, no doubt, utterly fruitless; and therefore, if there were no other objections, I would be in favor of permitting gentlemen to amuse themselves *ad libitum*, by hand-clapping, foot-stamping, big-smiles, or in any other manner, which their singular appetite for noise might prefer. There are other reasons, however, why this clamor from outside places should be suppressed. In the midst of the confusion it is impossible to hear; besides, it tends naturally to disturb the harmony of our counsels, and is wholly inconsistent with that calm, sober and reflecting mind which should characterize an occasion so solemn and impressive. That we are enacting a drama for history is absolutely certain; whether it is a tragedy or a farce will transpire hereafter. Therefore, unless the galleries shall be immediately cleared, the Convention should certainly adjourn to the Theatre, where the *dramatis personæ* will not only have fuller sweep to play "fantastic tricks," but applause from an enraptured auditory will be entirely proper.

Mr. MORGAN said:

Mr. President—I have before expressed my opinion that the order of this body should be preserved against all efforts to disturb it. So far, we have found it impossible to preserve proper order, and the result has been that we are unable even to comprehend much that has been said by members of the Convention. Allusion has been made by some gentleman to the fact that we represent the people, and that the people have a right to witness our deliberations. I am very fond of the people, but I have always found that the best recommendation a servant can bring to his master is, that he has done his duty, not with eye service. The impossibility of repressing applause with the feet has been referred to by some gentleman. I regret this, for while I admit that the earnest and elevated thoughts which have just been uttered by the distinguished Commissioner from South Carolina have fallen upon my heart with unusual power, I thought the occasion, the presence, and the great name which he has inherited, and lived to honor, would have moved us to a deeper and purer tone of feeling, and a more appropriate mode of expression.

I love that sort of patriotism which glows in the burning cheek and glistens in the falling tear; which brings our manhood up to the willing endurance of great suffeirng for the cause of right and justice. I approve it more than I do that zeal which rattles off rounds of applause with the feet and with canes upon the floor. The best reasons can be shown for the adoption of the resolutions of the gentleman from Tuscaloosa. It will remove from this chamber the hot impulse which moves the people to demand the immediate passage of the Ordinance of Secession. Every argument must be heard on both sides, and we must take counsel together. No man can render me a better service than to keep me in check until my judgment can fully approve a measure which every emotion of my nature urges me to adopt. I am now prepared for Secession, fully prepared, and anxious to hasten the moment of deliverance. But I must not go alone, while others, wiser than myself, may ask me to delay until they are prepared to go with me, or until their reason admonishes them that they cannot go. I speak in reference to the people of our own State. I would, at least, listen respectfully until I should be convinced that longer delay would be useless or dangerous.

We cannot debate the question properly in open Convention. Connected with the question of Secession there are many facts which, for reasons of public policy, ought not now to be stated. No Convention of the character of that now sitting here has conducted all its deliberations openly. No skillful General or prudent Diplomat would open the secrets of his counsels to the ear of his adversary or enemy. Why should we do so? Are we in a more secure position than our fathers were when the Congress, at Philadelphia, was sitting with closed doors and promulgating resolves and laws under the veil of secrecy to the people of the Colonies? Make secret sessions the rule and open sessions the exception, and the people will not be continually excited with telegrams to the effect that the Convention has gone into secret session. The people are not afraid of their representatives here. They have no fear that an American will ever attempt to establish another Star Chamber. If we trust them as implicitly as they trust us, we will need no explanation of our opinion that their interests are to be promoted by our sitting with closed doors.

Mr. DOWDELL said:

Mr. President—Two propositions are before the Convention. The one by the gentleman from Tuscaloosa [Mr. Jemison,] establishes the rule of secret sessions, open doors the exception. The substitute offered by the gentleman from Russell, [Mr. Baker,] would establish the rule of public sessions, closed doors the exception. I shall certainly support the latter proposition. There will be but little necessity and very few occasions for going into secret session. We shall have nothing to conceal from our own people; all our discussions on subjects in which they are vitally interested should be public—these will be numerous. Let them hear, and let the country know as speedily as possible, the temper and principles of this body. We speak for the people and the people should hear our voice, and fill its volume with the great chorus of accord and approbation. I am willing to admit that, in the progress of our deliberations, some subjects will arise connected with our safety and defence demanding secrecy and dispatch. We can anticipate such occasions, and on motion go into secret session. About the propriety of this no body will dispute. We are contending against a wily and an unscrupulous enemy. From him I would conceal all that we do. We despair of changing his mad policy by appeals to his reason, and we are unwilling to notify him of defensive plans which his wicked ingenuity might forestall or defeat. Open always to friends—show nothing to an enemy. Let them find out our plans in their development and execution. When secret sessions are demanded all will see the necessity, and there will be no difficulty in closing the doors at any time. But let our deliberations as far as possible be open; be public. Of our cause we are not ashamed; we speak to the world in behalf of our great cause, and we know that a response of approbation will come up from true and patriotic hearts every where. For these reasons I shall vote for the substitute, and I trust that the Convention will adopt it.

MR. BAKER, of Russell, addressed the Convention, briefly, in favor of his substitute, admitting the propriety of closing the doors on appropriate occasions, as it might become necessary to discuss certain questions, when expediency and the public good demand secrecy. But, as a general rule, he thought that the doors should remain open. The desire of the people to listen to our discussions must be great indeed, if we are to judge by the manifestations of interest which we see around us. This desire should be gratified, as far as prudence and a just regard to the public interest should allow. Not only have the people a great desire to hear and see what is going on in this body, but they have the right to hear and to see; and this right should not be abrided, except from positive necessity. And the people have not only the right to see and to hear, but they are at least to be excused, if, now and then, under a feeling of rapture, which may sometimes be uncontrollable, they should give utterance to their feelings in such demonstrations as we have witnessed to-day. He was not able at all times to control his own feelings, and he was willing to judge others by himself.

Mr. JONES, of Lauderdale, said:

I concur with the gentleman from Russell, [Mr. Baker,] in most of the remarks he has just submitted to the Convention. Like him, I believe, that on all proper occasions the people should be admitted to the galleries to witness the action of their representatives.

In times like these, when the public mind is deeply moved by passing events—when expectation is on tip-toe to catch every report in reference to the action of this body, armed as it is, with powers full and ample to tear down in an hour the Government under which we were born—it is not to be presumed that the people, interested alike with us in the great drama now being enacted, should be spectators unmoved by the sentiments expressed on this floor.

But, sir, there are bounds beyond which the exhibition of this feeling should not go.

The boisterous manifestation of applause or dissatisfaction is incompatible alike with the dignity of this body and the calm and thorough investigation of the momentous issues intrusted to us.

The gentleman from Russell says, "This applause should not be suppressed;" he says, "That when men feel deeply they *must* speak out,"—" that, it is customary in his section for persons when they go to church and get happy to shout as loud, and as much as they please, and no one dares object." To all this I agree. I will, however, suggest, that the great Methodist Church, of which I am an *outside* pillar, consider this as one of our *reserved rights*, and yet, we limit the enjoyment of this privilege to our own churches; we are always quiet when in the house of our Presbyterian or Episcopal friends. Nor is *this* the proper *house* for the manifestation of popular applause.

Mr. BAKER, of Russell, said:

He was very glad to learn that his friend from Lauderdale was a member of the church. He had known him a long time and had never suspected it before; he had recently met him at one or two places where *members* were not expected.

Mr. JONES rejoined:

As my friend from Russell is an *old member,* I should like for him to explain how *he met me there* without being *there* himself. I assure him that I am not yet a member, but when I do join, I fear I shall meet my friend from Russell but seldom, for I intend to keep out of doubtful company.

This discussion was continued, with much animation, when Mr. Baker's substitute was lost, and the Convention resolved to sit, as a general rule, with closed doors.

SECRET SESSION.

Mr. Watts presented the following dispatches received at Montgomery, Jan. 8, 1861, by telegraph from Richmond.

To Gov. A. B. MOORE:
Our friends here think the immediate secession of Alabama, not postponed to any future time, would exercise a favorable, perhaps controlling effect on the Secession of Virginia.
F. M. GILMER, JR..
A. F. HOPKINS.

Received at Montgomery, Jan. 8th, 1861, by telegraph from Pensacola.

To T. H. WATTS:
See Major Chase. Send us five hundred men immediately. Let us know.
A E. MAXWELL.
E. A. PERRY.

Received at Montgomery, Jan. 8th, 1861, by telegraph from Mobile, Ala.

To Gov. A. B. MOORE:
Shall United States armed vessels be permitted to enter harbor? If so, shall they be fired on and destroyed? Specific instructions wanted. They should not enter, else our forts have no protection.
G. B. DUVAL

Mr. YANCEY moved that a committee of one be appointed to confer with the Governor, and get any information he may have in relation to the Florida Forts. Adopted, and Mr. Ketchum appointed.

MR. KETCHUM returned and reported verbally that the Governor would make a communication as soon as it could be prepared.

TROOPS TO BE SENT TO FLORIDA.

MR. COCHRAN introduced the following resolutions:

Resolved, That the Governor of this State is requested and authorized to take such steps, and employ such measures, as in his judgment may be necessary to protect the interest of the people of Alabama; and that his action in taking temporary possession of the forts and arsenals within the borders of Alabama is approved.

Resolved, 2d, That to enable the Governor to carry out the objects of the preceding resolution, the sum of ten thousand dollars is hereby appropriated and placed at his disposal.

MR. YANCEY moved to strike out all after the word "Resolved," and insert:

That the Governor of this State be instructed to accept the services of five hundred Volunteers, to be placed under orders of the Governor of Florida, with a view to the taking possession of the forts at Pensacola, for the purpose of protecting the State of Alabama from invasion and coercion, during the deliberations of this Convention upon the question of resuming the sovereign powers of the State of Alabama; and for this purpose, ten thousand dollars be appropriated out of funds in the Treasury.

The amendment was accepted, as was also the following amendment offered by Mr. DARGAN:

Resolved, That the citizens of this State who have volunteered for the defence thereof, or who may volunteer as soldiers under the authority of our sister slaveholding States for their defence against any hostile or coercing power, shall be protected by the power of this State, against any proceeding which may be instituted against them by the Government of the United States on that account.

MR. CLEMENS said: That he doubted the power asserted in the resolution to appropriate money. But he did not regard that as important He was not satisfied that there was any real necessity for the passage of the resolution at all. If there was an emergency, he would not pause to inquire into smaller matters. But if the resolution was pressed, without further information, he should be constrained to vote against it.

Mr. COCHRAN, after earnestly urging immediate action on the resolutions, continued:

There is no necessity for delay, no wisdom in delay, but great folly. Here is an appeal from the Executive of a neighboring State, urgently requesting our aid. The Convention of the people of Florida is now in session. They must be permitted to deliberate in peace. It would be unjust in us, under the circumstances, to pause for further information. To doubt the existence of the necessity for this aid, as requested by Florida, would be an indignity to that State. If the aid is to be granted, let it be granted at once. One day's delay, and all may be lost. In emergencies, such as those which now surround us, all success depends upon the rapidity of our movements. "Secrecy in council and celerity in war," is an axiom built upon the experience of ages. We have adopted the one—let us carry out the other. Let us act now, and act promptly.

Mr. KIMBAL said:

Mr. President—I am unable to see or appreciate the necessity of the great haste of the gentleman from Barbour, [Mr. Cochran,] to send troops to Florida. I have not been apprized of any settled purpose on the part of the authorities at Washington, to wage immediate war on the South. The reverse to my mind seems conclusive. The telegraphic dispatches, on which gentlemen rely for the necessity of such precipitation, are uncertain, because of the great excitement in the public mind. In this sort of preparation, I see, as I think, motives in this matter that should not be brought into the consideration of this Convention. I fear, sir, there is too great anxiety to precipitate the country into hostilities. This thirst is replete with danger. None can see the end and dire consequences of the first blow. I entreat gentlemen to look circumspectly to these warnings. The people of Alabama are not yet freed from the burdens of taxation, heavy and long continued. It certainly would be ruinous again to be visited with another—perhaps a more onerous one. If this thing must come, let the people of Alabama know that it has not been the result of precipitancy or the recklessness of this Convention. Place not the censure at our door.

Subsequent events, I predict, Mr. President, will show the fallacy of sending 500 troops to take Pensacola, at an expense from the treasury of Alabama. This unnecessary aggression on our part, will not strengthen our cause in public estimation. We should look to that public opinion as the sheet anchor of our Southern cause. Therefore, Mr. President, we should coolly and patiently wait for the troubling of the waters. We are not now in actual war; why then exhaust our treasury, and cool the ardor of our soldiers, by quartering them in the sickly regions of Florida, when there is no necessity for it?

Mr. KIMBALL moved to refer the resolutions to the Committee of thirteen.

During the pendency of this motion, a communication was received from the Governor, which was read:

EXECUTIVE DEPARTMENT,
January 8th, 1861.

Hon. WILLIAM M. BROOKS,

President of the Convention of the State of Alabama:

In reply to a verbal communication from the body over which you preside, made by one of its members, I make the following statement. My information in regard to Pensacola is, that Governor Perry, of Florida, has informed me by dispatch, that he has ordered the Forts to be occupied by the troops of Florida, and asks aid from Alabama. The force at his command in West Florida is small, and not sufficient to take and maintain the Forts. Troops from Alabama could reach the point, before the troops of Middle and East Florida. This fact, with the importance of the position to Alabama, as well as to Florida, induces him to make the request, as I am informed. It is believed at Washington, in South Carolina and Georgia, as I am advised from high sources, that it is not only the policy of the Federal Government to coerce the seceding States, but as soon as possible to put herself in position by reinforcing all the Forts in the States where secession is expected. I need not suggest the danger to Florida and Alabama that must result from permitting a strong force to get possession of these Forts

With sentiments of high consideration and respect,

A. B. MOORE.

Mr. WATTS said:

I think there is necessity and propriety in adopting the resolutions at once. The Governor of Florida may have, and no doubt has, assumed responsibilities similar to those assumed by our own Executive. Forts and munitions of war may have passed into the possession of the State of Florida, which should be, and must be retained. Not only are the interests of Florida involved in the proposition, but also the interests of Alabama. We are here for the purpose of deliberating on the gravest questions which have ever been presented to us. Every avenue to invasion ought to be guarded.

MR. SMITH, of Tuscaloosa, said:

Mr. President—The proposition before the Convention involves many grave and important questions. The resolution contemplates an act of war; the assembling of troops to aid one of the States in some fancied or real difficulty with the Federal Government; and thus involves the more serious question of Treason against the United States. It seems to me that an hour is not sufficient time to devote to the investigation of such a proposition.

But, as there is to be no delay granted, I cannot permit the resolution to go to a final vote without expressing, in brief, my objections to it.

First, There is no emergency requiring so extraordinary a movement, so far as we are advised. If gentlemen propose to do an act, remarkable in itself, and even revolutionary in a military sense, it is incumbent on them to show the necessity. There is no necessity, and the answer to our demands for evidence of the emergency is, simply, *the Governor of Florida requests it.*

It will be observed too, that the substitute offered by the gentleman from Montgomery, changes completely the original resolution, and presents a new design; that is, that the troops are not so much for the aid of the Governor of Florida, as to protect this *Convention against* invasion during its deliberations!

Now, sir, I ask, is there the slightest apprehension in the mind of any member here, that *this* Convention will be *invaded* during its deliberations? Yet, that is now the ground upon which the resolution is urged! Is there not something specious in this?

Again, sir, I oppose the proposition because it seeks to enlarge and extend the powers of the Executive. I hold, that, until the act of secession is consummated, we have no such sovereign power as enables or authorises us to disturb, in any way, any of the various departments of the State Government, as already lodged by the Constitution in particular hands. The Constitution has defined and limited the duties and powers of the Governor of Alabama. We have not, as yet, the authority to enlarge or extend, or restrict those powers.

Again, the proposition contemplates an act of actual hostility to the General Government.

THE PRESIDENT:

The Chair would remind the gentlemen from Tuscaloosa, that the motion now pending, to refer the resolution to a Committee, does not allow a discussion upon the merits of the resolution.

Mr. WATTS asked leave to withdraw his motion to refer to a Committee of seven. Objection was made, and Mr. COCHRAN moved that Mr. Watts have leave to withdraw his motion, which was carried, and the motion was withdrawn.

MR. JONES, of Lauderdale, said:

He hoped the discussion would be closed and the vote taken on this question to-day. The minority had opposed the passage of the resolution under discussion from a deep sense of their constitutional obligations to keep the peace of the country, and to lend their aid to the passage of no hasty measures that may lead to bloodshed, and thereby close the way to a peaceful solution of the questions that divide the two great sections of this Government.

Having done this, whatever may be the result, we will stand acquitted by the record of responsibility or blame. But he was unwilling to go farther and take all responsibility from the majority by obstructing the legitimate course of legislation.

They assert, that, by the passage of this resolution, they can take peaceful possession of the Forts at Pensacola—secure the South from invasion from that quarter, and thereby prevent Alabama from becoming the "cock pit" in the coming conflict between the North and South.

This, if true, is a consummation of paramount importance to every citizen of Alabama.

The majority say, that unless this resolution is passed to-day, it will be useless—that every hour of delay tends to render it so. Why, then, postpone until all prospect of good will be destroyed, and only evil result? The majority were anxious to assume this responsibility; and if they could secure our people from invasion, and prevent our fields from being desolated by hostile armies, he was ready to sustain their action and applaud their foresight and courage. He believed that this move would end in a waste of time and money, yet, he saw no propriety in delay which would insure that result. He asked, therefore, that the vote might be taken now.

The vote was taken upon the first resolution, and it was adopted by 52 to 45, ordered to be engrossed by the Secretary and sent forthwith to the Governor.

On motion of Mr. JEMISON, the second resolution, [Mr. Dargan's amendment,] was ordered to be referred to a select committee of five to be appointed by the President.

And the Convention adjourned until to-morrow, 10 o'clock, A. M.

JANUARY NINTH—THIRD DAY—SECRET SESSION.

On motion of Mr. COCHRAN, Hon. H. L. BENNING, of Georgia, was invited to a seat within the bar of the Convention.

MR. SHORTRIDGE offered the following resolution, which was adopted:

Resolved, That the Hon. JAMES L. PUGH and Hon. J. L. M. CURRY be requested to communicate to the Convention, in writing, any facts or information which may be in their possession touching the action of Congress, and the purposes of the Black Republican party, which will, in their opinion, tend to aid this body in its deliberations.

MR. DAVIS, of Madison, offered the following resolution:

Resolved, That whatever Ordinance this Convention may adopt in its final action, contemplating or providing for a severance of the State of Alabama from the Federal Government, ought to be submitted to the people for ratification or rejection.

MR. COCHRAN moved to lay the resolution on the table, but withdrew it, at the request of Mr. BAKER, of Russell, for explanation; and Mr. Baker renewed the motion.

The ayes and noes were called for, and resulted, ayes 53 noes 46.

Those who voted in the affirmative are—Messrs. President, Baily, Baker, of Russell, Baker, of Barbour, Barnes, Beck, Blue, Bolling, Bragg, Catterling, Clark of Marengo, Cochran, Coleman, Crawford, Creech, Crook, Curtis, Daniel, Dargan, Davis, of Covington, Davis, of Pickens, Dowdell, Foster, Gibbons, Gilchrist, Hawkins, Henderson, of Macon, Henderson, of Pike, Herndon, Howard, Humphries, Jewett, Ketchum, Love, McClanahan, McPherson,

McKinnie, Morgan, Owens, Phillips, Rives, Ryan, Shortridge, Silver, Smith, of Henry, Starke, Stone, Watts, Webb, Whatley, Williamson, Yancey, Yelverton—53.

Those who voted in the negative are—Messrs. Allen, Barclay, Beard, Brasher, Bulger, Clarke, of Lawrence, Coffey, Coman, Crumpler, Davis, of Madison, Earnest, Edwards, Ford, Forrester, Franklin, Gay, Green, Guttery, Hood, Inzer, Jemison, Jones, of Fayette, Jones, of Lauderdale, Johnson, Kimball, Leonard, Lewis, McClellan, Posey, Potter, Russell, Ralls, Sanford, Sheets, Sheffield, Smith, of Tuscaloosa, Slaughter, Stedham, Steele, Taylor, Timberlake, Watkins, Whitlock, Wilson, Winston and Wood—46.

MR. Clemens absent and not voting.

MR. EARNEST moved to take from the table the reports from Commissioners to the slaveholding States, as communicated by the Governor. Carried.

MR. BAKER, of Russell, moved to go into open session.

MR. DOWDELL moved an amendment, that when this Convention is in open session, the flag of Alabama shall be raised from the Capitol. The amendment was accepted, the motion adopted, and the doors of the Convention opened.

OPEN SESSION.

MR. BULGER introduced the following preamble and resolutions, which, on his motion, were referred to the Committee of Thirteen :

WHEREAS, Anti-Slavery agitation, persistently continued in the non-slaveholding States of this Union for a long series of years, and in the late election was triumphant in the election of a President who sympathises with the enemies of Domestic, or African slavery, thereby rendering our property and our institutions insecure ; and

WHEREAS, we have been summoned together in Convention to "consider, determine and to do whatever, in the opinion of the said Convention, the rights, interest and honor of the State of Alabama require to be done for their protection ;"

And, WHEREAS, This Convention, taking into consideration the actual situation of the country, as well as reflecting on the alarming circumstances by which we are surrounded, can no longer doubt that the crisis is arrived, at which the conservative men of the United States are to decide the solemn question, whether they will, by wise and magnanimous efforts, secure and perpetuate the blessings of a *Union* consecrated by the common blood of our fathers; or whether, by giving way to unmanly jealousies and prejudices, or to partial and transitory interests, they will renounce the auspicious blessings, prepared for them by their Revolutionary fathers, and furnish to the enemies of free government an eventual triumph;

And, WHEREAS, The same noble and extended policy, and the same paternal and affectionate sentiments which originally determined the citizens of the independent colonies to form a confederation, and the people of the States, afterwards, to form a more perfect Union, cannot but be felt with equal force now, as motives to lay aside every inferior consideration, and to concur in such further provisions as may be found necessary to secure every section of our vast country in all their just rights, and throw around the weaker portion (the Southern States,) such guarantees as will make them to rest securely in the Union, and restore peace and quiet to the country;

Therefore, be it Resolved, That separate State secession, in the present emergency, is unwise and impolitic; and Alabama will not secede without first making an effort to secure the coöperation of the Southern States.

Resolved, 2d, That the Convention invite each of the Southern (Slaveholding) States to meet the State of Alabama in a Convention of Delegates, equal in number to the several Representatives in the Congress of the United States, at   on the   day of   for the purpose of consideration and agreement as to the wrongs that we suffer in the Union, and the dangers that we are threatened with; and to determine what relief we will demand for the present, and security for the future; and what remedy we will apply if our just demands are not complied with.

Resolved, 3d, That the President of this Convention be requested to forward forthwith, by the most speedy conveyance, a copy of this preamble and resolutions to the Governors of the several Southern States, with a request that they give them such direction as will be most likely to secure the object desired, to wit: The coöperation of all the Southern States, in securing their rights in the Union, or establishing their independence out of it.

AID TO THE SECEDING STATES AGAINST COERCION

Mr. COLEMAN introduced the following resolution:

Resolved by the people of the State of Alabama in Convention assembled, That they pledge the power of this State, to aid in resisting any attempt upon the part of the United States of America to coerce any of the seceding States.

Mr. DAVIS, of Madison. moved to refer the resolution to the Committee of Thirteen.

MR. BECK said:

He saw no necessity for a reference; he thought the resolution ought to be passed, and passed promptly. The cause of South Carolina was the cause of Alabama; indeed, of the whole South; but particularly were the States that contemplated secession, interested in sustaining each other. Alabama cannot stand by and see force used against a seceding State. It would, continued Mr. Beck, be the policy of the Federal Government to conquer the States in detail. They must, therefore, sustain each other. This matter was well understood in Virginia, who, though she had taken no step towards secession, had already, through her Legislature, resolved almost unanimously, that she would resist, by force, any attempt to coerce a seceding State. We owed it to ourselves and to the position we now occupy, not to be behind Virginia in giving prompt expression to our determination to stand by and uphold the seceding States in their efforts to resist Black Republican rule.

MR. JOHNSON said:

Mr. President—The last sessions of this body having been held in secret, forbids an allusion in detail to its action, and hence, cogent reasons which might otherwise be offered in favor of a reference of this motion, are precluded.

Without expressing any opinion as to the policy embodied in the resolution, I think it would be, under the circumstances, discourteous to the minority to press it upon them at this time; and particularly, as it would have the effect of placing them in a false position before the country. I hope, therefore, the resolution will be referred to the Committee of Thirteen.

MR. STONE said:

Mr. President—I fully concur with the gentleman from Montgomery, [Mr. Yancey,] in the propriety of immediately passing the resolution now under consideration. All the powers of the State of Alabama should be pledged to aid in resisting any attempt to coerce a seceding State back into the Union. Sir, the Southern States recognize the *right* of secession. It constitutes the very essence of State sovereignty, and is inseparable from it. A State is the best and sole judge of her own grievances, and as a party to the Federal compact must, *herself*, decide in the last resort "as well of the infraction as of the mode and measure of redress." If, in her sovereign capacity, she determines to resume her independence, can we, who have a common interest in the protection of this right, look calmly on and see her invaded by Federal soldiers? Sir, the Convention which framed our Constitution expressly refused to grant to the General Government the power to employ force against a State. The States came into the Union " free, sovereign and independent." They have never parted with their freedom or sovereignty. They established a Government to act as their agent; and now, to permit that agent to employ force against the States would be to sanction the grossest usurpation. It would be converting the Government into a despotism. Sir, the Union was never intended to be preserved by force. The fact that the power to employ force against a State was refused in the Convention which framed the Constitution, proves that those who constructed our Government knew that it could not be maintained by force. Of what value would the Union be, if the States composing it had to be reduced to obedience by the strong arm of military power? The permanence and security of our Government depend alone upon the principle of common affection and common interest. Force is the last argument of kings, and cannot keep these States together. If then, we recognize the right of secession, and intend to maintain that right against any power that may resist its exercise, why not so declare by passing this resolution? This course will give encouragement to our Southern sisters It will give strength to the Southern cause. It may secure peace. If the Government at Washington is informed that the coercive policy with which South Carolina is now threatened will be resisted, and that the first Federal gun fired against Charleston will summon to the field every Southern man who can bear arms, it may produce a peaceful solution of the pending difficulties. If it should not, then the responsibility will rest alone upon our assailants. All we can now do is to warn them against the madness of attempting coercion. We wish peace—we do not intend to provoke war—we shall act on the defensive. But if war is forced upon us, our enemies should know, that the Southern States, whose rights, whose honor, and whose independence are alike at stake, intend to stand side by side in the contest, prepared to make common cause and to meet one common fate.

Mr. EARNEST said:

Mr. President—I have examined the resolution of the Hon. gentleman from Sumter, and anxiously listened to the arguments of the friends of the measure with the object, if I could, to vote for the resolution.

I am not prepared to condemn the action of our Governor, or of the patriotic gentlemen for whose benefits the resolution is introduced. In fact, from the force of circumstances with which they were surrounded, I must say that I commend their actions, for if they have erred, it has been on the side of their country. I fully recognize the doctrine, that a sovereign State, acting in her sovereign capacity, can withdraw or secede from the Union; and that, after that, any acts she or her citizens may do, to protect her rights or to defend her independence, even to bloody war, is not and cannot be treason. But the State must act in her sovereign capacity; no other act, by any body or individuals, can withdraw her from the Union or relieve her citizens from the laws of treason, if overt acts are committed by the citizen or the State against the General Government. Entertaining these views of Constitutional rights and individual rights, I am estopped from voting for the resolution. The Hon. gentleman from Montgomery, [Mr. Yancey,] has made an ingenious argument, an appeal to members on this floor, predicated on the resolution of the Virginia Legislature. I reply to the Hon. gentleman, by saying, that resolutions are harmless things when not connected by overt acts. Such was the case of the Virginia resolution. But very far from that is our situation. This resolution is introduced to cover acts of hostility—acts that amount, unexplained, not to a declaration of war only, but to war itself. Hence, to vote for the resolution is only to subject us to the penalties of treason, without aiding those for whose benefit those resolutions are introduced. I confess, Mr. President, that since we met here, my mind, as to expediency, has undergone a great change. And while I cannot vote for the ordinance of secession, I believe that there is a majority of this Convention that will pass the ordinance, and thereby sever our allegiance from the *General Government.*— That being done, my allegiance is due alone to the State of Alabama, and in me she shall find no laggard or luke-warm friend.— As my allegiance is now due to the United States, I can do no act inconsistent with that relation. No one regrets more than I do, the Constitutional barrier that prevents me from voting for the resolution. I have already intimated that the course of our Governor, and the patriotism of our volunteers find no condemnation in me, but as peace measures I approve them as eminently wise and prudential.

THE CONVENTION OF ALABAMA. 61

Mr. Morgan said:

Mr. President—The resolutions adopted on the first day of this session, by the unanimous voteof the Convention, leaves us no alternative but resistance to the attempt to place the United States under the Government of the Black Republican party. I entertain no doubt that this resistance will be accomplished by the withdrawal of this State from the Union. But the question is still open as to the mode of resistance. It does not follow, from the adoption of the Resolution of the gentleman from Sumter, that we are confined to any special mode of resistance, or resistance at a particular time. But this does follow: that no seceding State should be coerced or conquered, whether we remain in the Union and fight abolitionists and abolitionism, or whether we withdraw.

The question is not debateable, whether blood should be shed in a Southern State, with impunity, by a people whom we consider as oppressors. The people of Alabama have asserted, in their written Constitution, under which they were admitted into the Union as a State, that "all political power is inherent in the people, and all free governments are founded on their authority, and instituted for their benefit, and, therefore, they have at all times an inalienable and indefeasible right to alter, reform or abolish their form of government in such manner as they may think expedient."

If we had thought of confining this declaration alone to the people of Alabama, or had intended to deny its application to every other State of the Union, we should have entered that Union not as the equals, but as the superiors of the other States in political rights. We have not been guilty of such arrogance. Upon our own doctrines, then, the people of South Carolina are fully justified in "altering or abolishing their form of government." But I am persuaded that I need not go into an argument to establish the right of South Carolina to secede, as a predicate for the clear duty of Alabama to aid her in her defence against hostile fleets or armies. We are one people, and can never be dissevered. Every interest and sympathy that can unite two peoples are wrought into the golden chain by which we are bound together. The secession of South Carolina will naturally, and, in time, inevitably, lead to the secession of Alabama. But if our secession is for the time retarded or prevented by an unmatured course on our part, still our hearts, our interests, our duty, will force us to declare that all the power and resources of men and means within the control of Alabama, are pledged to the defence of every seceding State against coercion by the United States Government.

If we are unable to withdraw from the Union, we will be able to assist the cause of justice and free government. In the Union or out of it, a war upon South Carolina is a war upon Alabama. We will so accept the issue when it is needed, and let us now prepare for it. We may force a war upon South Carolina by refusing to align ourselves with her. We may refuse to shelter her until her enemy will cease to fear her power of resistance. We may invite war by our hesitancy, at the moment when decisive action would secure peace; but we cannot see the blood of her sons shed in a conflict for right, and against oppression, and refuse to open our veins in her cause.

The effect of the resolution is, that South Carolina may recruit her armies in Alabama, and that our treasury shall stand open to her demands so long as she shall need the means of defence and protection. Sir, you cannot shut the treasury against her. You may close the door, but the treasure will flow with accelerated freedom from the pockets of the people. No army could be placed along our borders to prevent our soldiery from swarming to the standard of the Palmetto. The mothers of our country would be the recruiting sergeants for South Carolina, and the fathers would curse those children who should hesitate to spring to their guns in her defence. There can be no valid reason why we should not at once assume this attitude, and announce our Resolution. The argument of precipitancy is constantly employed to check every movement in this direction. Some persons may be inclined to summary and decided steps, but this is not precipitancy. It is a sound calculation, deliberately made, that there is more to be lost than there is to be gained by delay. This position is true beyond question. The Northern States are hastily pledging themselves to contribute men and money to aid them in coercing the seceding States. Perhaps their haste in making the pledge will stand in singular contrast with their haste not to fulfil the promises. But whether they would badger us, or whether they are in solemn earnest, we should attribute to them at least a respectable inclination to do as they promise. This is a matter that will not admit of delay. If we remain in the Union we will act upon the principles of the resolution under discussion. If we withdraw, we should lose the happy moment to give our evidence of our magnanimity. unless we pass the resolution now.— After we are out of the Union, we might have many reasons for adopting such a *resolve*, in which we would not be wholly disinterted.

It has fallen from the lips of a friend of secession, in the course of this debate, that he would rather secede to-day with a majority of one, than to wait until next Saturday and secede with a large majority. I fully appreciate and applaud the zeal which prompted this declaration, but I take occasion to dissent entirely from the position assumed. I would prefer to delay the secession of Alabama one month, or until some new danger should appear to follow from delay, and go out with twenty majority, than to go out to-day with one majority. I cannot distrust the position of the delegates opposed to me in opinion, as to the time and manner of secession, until I am forced to do so. They have all declared for resistance. There is no submissioni-' amongst them, if their votes are any evidence of their opinions. Moreover, this State is divided in policy by a geographical line: no line divides us on the point of duty and honor. I wish to erase that line; and we will see no more of it after we have withdrawn from the Union, unless we grave it upon the map with our own hands.— The people of the mountains have been represented as being very decided in their opinion on the questions of the time and manner of secession. I do not doubt it. It was my fortune to be raised amongst the people of the mountains, and I can bear witness that they are an earnest and brave people. But love of country is with them a religious sentiment. The State has many perils to encounter yet, and you will find that, in her greatest agony, she will repose faithfully upon the hearts of these people. They will never deceive the State. These men will pour like torrents into the army—the best and bravest of men. I wish to hold free counsel with these delegates on this floor, and am determined, if this is not the case, the fault shall not be mine. If they want time to consider, to debate, to hear from their people, they must have time. If they want time to betray me into submission, they shall not be deceived in me, but I shall be grossly deceived in my estimate of them. But, sir, there is no evil spirit of deception here, and I allude to it only to repel the idea.

Let us pass the resolution, and our enemies will, at least, form correct opinions of our condition and sentiments.

Mr. Jemison said:

Mr. President—I see no necessity for immediate action upon the resolution. We have no reliable information on which to act. [Hon. Mr. Dowdell read a dispatch, saying hostilities had commenced, &c.] Yes, we have various telegrams, the authenticity and reliability of which seem to be confided in, and are fully satisfactory to gentlemen of the majority. But as for myself, being no wire-worker, and having nothing to do with the working of wires in these days of telegraphic information, I am disposed to question the authenticity of much of what we hear. The aims are made to tell whatever is most appropriate for effect. They keep the public mind in a continued state of excitement; and, for whatever matter under consideration here, we have a telegram suited to the occasion. Whatever is wanting in argument is supplied by telegraph. If we will not be reasoned into a measure, we must be frightened into it. We are kept by these ready and continued rumors in a state of excitement and alarm, that in a good degree prevents considerate and wise counsels. I was brought up, Mr. President, on the Indian frontiers where we were subject to frequent inroads and attacks from hostile parties. By common consent and general understanding, my father's house was the place of rendezvous in cases of alarm. We had no telegraphs in those days, yet we were not without news-mongers, who delighted in getting up a sensation. Hence we had very many alarms. I am reminded, by the excitements frequently caused amongst us by telegrams, of a scene that occurred during these border alarms, when I was quite a boy. At a dead hour of a beautiful moonlight night, the slumbers of the family were broken by a general ingathering of the neighbors. They came in all manner of style: some dressed, some half-dressed, and some scarcely dressed at all. Everything was excitement and confusion. This person was killed—that family massacred; not one left to tell the details of the horrid and heart rending tragedy. At length, two of the party, somewhat incredulous, determined to visit the scenes of reported slaughter. The first place visited was where a negro woman was reported as killed, who was found so *dead asleep* that she was not aware she had been left alone on the place. The next, was where the husband had abandoned an invalid and bed-ridden wife, whom he reported as killed. They found her also, but suffering all the anticipated horrors of the tomahawk and scalping knife. The next and last place visited was where the whole family was reported as butchered; there all was quiet and safe, the family had heard nothing of their danger, and were rejoiced they had escaped the indiscriminate massacre allotted to them by Madam Rumor. [Here the gentleman from Chambers remarked, that the dispatch he had read stated, the firing of guns had been heard.] Yes, Mr. President, so was firing of guns heard in the case I have related. With others of my father's hands, I had that day been engaged in firing dead hickory trees, in a second year's new ground, to burn them down and burn them out of the way. When the alarm was started these trees had just got into a fair way of falling! The excited and alarmed people supposed they heard the firing by platoons.

I would not be understood to say there is no danger of hostilities between State and Federal troops; but I do intend to say, I believe that the prospect of immediate collision is magnified; that the aid of the wires has been evoked to operate on our prejudices and our fears. I am therefore in favor of the reference. I am not disposed to be hurried—see no reason for hasty action. A reference is more likely to result in harmonious as well as prudent action.

Mr. JONES, of Lauderdale, said:

He was sorry the gentleman from Sumter had introduced these resolutions; they could lead to no practical good, and would only consume the time of the Convention in useless discussion. He was placed in a position of great delicacy, and hoped the resolutions would be referred to the proper committee and not be pressed to a vote now.

There was no necessity for the hot haste manifested by the gentlemen of the majority. There is no hostile army battering at the gates of Charleston—no invading foe desecrates her soil. There is no voice from that quarter demanding our aid—there is no money wanted, no munitions of war needed, no soldiers asked. The resolutions are at best, but an empty profession—a meaningless tender of what is not expected to be performed. Why, then, cannot gentlemen wait? Wait at least, until to-morrow, when it is morally certain that the Ordinance of Secession will be passed, and the members of this Convention absolved by the sovereign authority of Alabama from their allegianc to the Federal Government. Until the State so absolved him, he could not and would not vote for resolutions proposing to declare war on the Government of the United States. He had in both ends of this Capitol, and at sundry other places, solemnly sworn to support the Constitution of the United States. He knew that others thought differently on this subject, he only spoke for himself. Each one must act according to his own conscience. But whilst this State continued a member of the Union he would not vote for resolutions which propose directly or indirectly to bring about a collision between this State and the Federal authorities. The gentleman from Montgomery had said that "when we shall have seceded, a resolution tendering aid to other seceding States will be considered as asking, rather than offering, aid." He could not see that offering aid to-day and seceding to-morrow, before notice of the offer could reach the ears of our sister States, will afford any very over-powering proof of our disinterestedness. He would say, in conclusion, that he felt assured that when the soil of South Carolina, or any Southern State, is invaded to subvert her institutions or subjugate her people, the men of the South will move to arms as by one common impulse to repel the invader. And when this dire necessity shall arise, he hoped to be behind no gentleman on this floor in vindicating the honor and defending the soil of the section to which he belonged.

Mr. YELVERTON said:

Mr. President—While I advocate the reference in a spirit of conciliation, I surrender nothing. I need not appeal to the members on this floor with whom I have been associated to bear evidence of my devotion to the principles enunciated in the excellent resolution under consideration. Sir, I take it for granted that I am as well understood and as *strongly defined* on all the questions connected with immediate separate State action—prompt secession—as any other gentleman of this Convention.

This resolution has the approval of my heart; it commends itself to the calm and manly consideration of every member, with a force of truth and reason, which seems to me to be irresistible.

The assurances we have from honorable gentlemen of the minority, that the reference is sought only with the great patriotic view of understanding the resolution, and understanding each other, and thus to enable them to vote with us, *for the resolution*, is an appeal all powerful to me.

I hold, Mr. President, that it would be exceedingly disgraceful to our gallant State, to have a single vote cast against this resolution; and if I did not go for this reference with the assurances I have, I should feel myself to that extent responsible for that disgrace. Then, I appeal to gentlemen who are already prepared to vote for the resolution, and, as the delay will be but temporary and the result not doubtful, to vote for the reference, that our friends of the minority may have no cause of complaint, and that the resolution may be adopted unanimously.

I have the honor to be a member of the Committee of Thirteen. I know the material of which it is composed. I think I hazard nothing in saying that an unanimous report in favor of the resolution would follow such a reference.

Mr. SMITH, of Tuscaloosa, said:

Mr. President—I am ready to vote upon the resolution now, so far as I am concerned. It contains but the expression of a sentiment that I heartily endorse. I know of no feeling more agreeable 'than that which prompts a generous heart to offer assistance to a friend in danger. There is no feeling more pleasant—except, perhaps, it be the gratitude that accepts such assurance. But in order that this pleasure should be perfect, it is necessary that this assurance should be made with the whole heart; there must be no deception. Now, sir, some of the gentlemen who are known here to be in the minority, and with whom I have the honor to act, request a day's delay—or the reference of the resolution to a Committee, in order that they may have an opportunity to examine it, expressing at the same time a desire to vote for it. This request you are about to refuse!

Sir, what will be the inevitable result of your disposition to press the minority to immediate and final action upon such resolutions, without giving them the usual legislative delay for reflection? The attempt to force your measure upon us must result in this: that you will pass this resolution and others of no less importance, by a meagre majority of six or eight votes; (for that is the majority by which you elected your President.) Do you wish to do this? Would you not prefer that *this* resolution particularly should receive all the votes here? I am satisfied that if this resolution is referred to a Committee, as proposed by the gentleman from Madison, [Mr. Davis,] and as acquiesced in by the mover of it, [Mr. Coleman,] so that a day's delay may be had upon it for reflection and examination, it will be adopted by this Convention without a dissenting voice.

An assurance, by a bare majority of this Convention, of aid to be given by the State of Alabama, would be considered by South Carolina almost as an insult. She might be delighted at first to hear and receive such an assurance; but when she learned the fact that the resolution had been adopted by a bare majority, she would be inspired with disgust; and she would swell with indignation, if it should appear, (as it may, upon a calm and thorough examination, and a comparison of the facts and figures) that the minority here were really the representatives of a majority of the sovereigns of this State. [Here there was some conversation—in questions by Mr. Morgan and Mr. Yancey—as to Mr. Smith's source of information upon the popular vote of the State.] I receive my information from tables in the public prints; I do not assert them to be true; but I believe that a popular majority of the State is represented here by the minority.

But that is not now material. If you press this resolution now, you will pass it by a meagre majority; and so soon as South Carolina is advised of this disagreeable fact, she will consider your promises as unreal; she will exclaim: Poor Alabama! she sent us an apple with gold on its outside, but with ashes on its core—

> "Dead sea fruits that tempt the eye
> But turn to ashes on the lip."

I have the greatest respect for South Carolina; her sons are gallant, her statesmen are wise, her clime is genial, her history is great, her aspirations are sublime. She is to be revered for one thing, if for nothing else: she has given to this age a Demosthenes; that is her immortality—may it not be her last and her greatest glory. And because I respect her, I would deal with her in a way not to deceive—not to disappoint her. I would gratify her, and at the same time satisfy myself.

Sir, we of the minority ask of the majority but the ordinary civilities of parliamentary decorum; time to deliberate and examine. We claim that our errors are errors of the head, and we concede to others what we claim for ourselves. If there be here a sincere desire to cultivate kindly relations, and to harmonize on the great questions upon which we are now called to act, this disposition on the part of the majority to press upon us measures to final action upon an hour's notice, must be abandoned. You may have the power to do as you please; but indiscreet haste will neither promote the popularity of your measures, nor convince the public that you are right.

I can but admire the wise and deliberative tone in which the gentleman from Coffee, [Mr. Yelverton,] has just expressed himself on this subject. Yielding nothing of the ardency of his opinions, he yet sees no harm in a day's delay. "A week's delay," in the patriotic language of the gentleman from Montgomery, [Mr. Watts,] "would be cheerfully yielded by him, for the sake of a unanimous vote in favor of the resolution."

For my part, I wish the resolution adopted; and I am satisfied, sir, that on to-morrow it would be passed unanimously, and I sincerely hope that it will be referred.

MR. YANCEY said:

Mr. President—The gentleman from Tuscaloosa has sneeringly said, that it will be but poor consolation to South Carolina, when we tender the promise to aid her against coercion by the General Government, by a meagre majority of one. I think, sir, I understand the allusion. It is useless to disguise the fact, that in some portions of the State there is disapprobation towards our action; and, I venture to tell the gentleman from Tuscaloosa, that when that Ordinance shall be passed, even if it be by the meagre majority of one, it will represent the fullness, and the power, and the majesty of the sovereign people of Alabama. When it shall be the supreme organic law of the people of Alabama, the State upon that question will know no majority or minority among her people, but will expect and demand, and secure unlimited and unquestioned obedience to that Ordinance. If gentlemen imagine, or indulge the hope, that there will be opposition to that expressed will of the people, I tell them that it will not be from any portion of *the people* of Alabama, but from the enemies of the people of Alabama. The State is a unit in its sovereignty; the people of the State constitutes a unit in allegiance to its high decrees. If there shall be found any who shall dare oppose it, they will not be of the people; they will not be of a minority or majority of the people, as some choose to call them. They must throw off the character of citizenship in this State, and assume a new character in accordance with their new position. It is useless, Mr. President, to disguise the true character of things with soft words. Men, who shall, after the passage of this Ordinance, dissolving the union of Alabama with the other States of this Confederacy, dare array themselves against the State, will then become the enemies of the State. There is a law of Treason, defining treason against the State; and, those who shall dare oppose the action of Alabama, when she assumes her independence of the Union, will become traitors—rebels against its authority, and will be dealt with as such. Sir, in such an event, the nomenclature of the Revolution of 1776 will have to be revived. The friends of the country were then called Whigs, and the enemies of the colonies were called Tories. And I have no doubt that, however they may be aided by abolition forces, the God of Battles and Liberty will give us the victory over the unnatural alliance, as was done, under similar circumstances, in the Revolution.

In this great contest there are but two sides—a Northern and a Southern; and when our Ordinance of Secession shall be passed, the citizens of the State will ally themselves with the South. The misguided, deluded, wicked men in our midst, if any such there be, who shall oppose it, will be in alignment with the abolition power of the Federal Government, and as our safety demands, must be looked upon and dealt with as public enemies.

The above is a very brief report of Mr. YANCEY'S speech on this occasion. It is here inserted from the "*Montgomery Mail,*" and is supposed to have been drawn up, so far, by Mr. Yancey himself. The speech as delivered, occupied nearly half an hour; was uttered with great vehemence, and embraced many topics not here reported. It threw the Convention into the highest excitement.

MR. WATTS said, [in substance:]

Mr. President—I regret exceedingly the tone of the speech just made by my colleague [Mr. Yancey.] This is no time for the exhibition of feeling or for the utterance of denunciations. The minority have simply asked a parliamentary courtesy, which ought not to be denied; especially, as there is no emergency calling for immediate action on the resolution. It is extremely desirable that this resolution should be passed unanimously; and I earnestly hope that the motion to refer it may prevail; and, I believe, that on to-morrow, it can, and will be passed by a majority of One Hundred—all the votes of this Convention.

[MR. WATTS retained the floor some considerable time, seeming to have been actuated by a desire to mollify the feeling, and quiet the excitement that prevailed in the Convention.]

MR. JEMISON said:

Mr. President—I had not intended to say more upon the resolution under consideration; but I cannot permit to pass in silence, the extraordinary and unprovoked remarks of the gentleman from Montgomery, [Mr. Yancey.] I say unprovoked, for they were wholly uncalled for by any thing that fell from either my colleague or myself. The gentleman charges me with having spoken of his native State, South Carolina, with levity—slightingly. I have done no such thing. I have never spoken of that gallant State slightingly. I have differed with her leading politicians, but I have not spoken disrespectfully of them, or their State. I can differ with men upon measures of policy, and yet believe them honest and patriotic. But, sir, nothing was said by me as to the State of South Carolina, her politicians, or her policy. I spoke only of the dispatches, or telegrams, that have been poured in upon us in such profusion, upon every subject and every occasion. Some of them, it is true, were from the gentleman's native State; some from other States—they came from all quarters. They came so thick and fast, they seemed like snow-flakes, to fall from the clouds. Of these telegrams, but without singling out those from any particular State or locality, I did speak with levity and incredulity. I spoke as I thought, as I felt, and as I believe, but without disrespect to any State, individual or class.

The gentleman from Montgomery has made the remarks of myself and colleague, the text or rather the pretext of reading for the benefit of ourselves and the minority of this Convention, a long, and very racy and pointed commentary upon the law of *Treason.* He tells us the political nomenclature of "76" will be revived; that parties will be known and distinguished as of yore, by the names of Whig and Tory; that in times past the friends of the country were known as Whigs, and its enemies as Tories. He tells us further, that there is such an offence as Treason, and reminds us that though the Ordinance of Secession may pass by a majority of a single vote, that those who shall not submit to it are guilty of the crime of treason, and must, and will be punished as traitors.

For whom and by what authority does the gentleman speak? He speaks in the plural. In all frankness, said he, "*we* speak thus, *we* tell our opponents," &c. Are we to understand him as speaking for himself alone, or does he speak as the organ of the majority party in this Convention, of whom he is the acknowledged leader? I cannot believe that he has spoken the sentiments of the majority, or any member of it but himself. I cannot think such sentiments are entertained by any other member of this Convention. I had not expected to hear such sentiments from any quarter. They are unmerited—they are uncalled for and unprovoked by any thing that has been uttered by my colleague or myself, or by any other member of the minority; they are unjust; they are unbecoming any gentleman on this floor. [Hon. Mr. Yancey rose, and the President called Mr. J. to order, whereupon he took his seat. There was much confusion at this moment, and Mr. Yancey, also, was called to order by the President.] After order was restored, Mr. J. proceeded. Mr. President, when I took upon myself the duties of a delegate to this Convention, it was with a full knowledge and proper appreciation of all its difficulties and responsibilities. I took my seat here with a fixed and firm resolution, not only to preserve the courtesies of debate, but to cultivate friendly intercourse and relations with each and every one, but to encourage calm and friendly discussion; to keep down every crimination or recrimination by pouring oil upon the troubled waters. My most earnest desire has been to see good feeling and harmony preside over our deliberations; that whenever we should take final action, that all should cordially and cheerfully unite in support of that action. This has been my most ardent desire—this my most settled determination. From this determination and from this purpose, I cannot be driven by any ill-timed or unmerited remarks, come from what source they may. But, sir, when the great leader of the majority shall call the minority party *tories*, shall denounce us as *traitors* and pronounce against us a *traitor's doom*, were I to pass it in silence, the world would properly consider me worthy of the denunciation and the doom.

[Here Mr. YANCEY rose to explain. He said his remarks were not applicable to, or intended for, the minority of this Convention; they were intended for those in certain portions of the State, where it was said the Ordinance of Secession, if passed, would be resisted.]

Mr. JEMISON continued:

I am glad, Mr. President, to hear the gentleman disclaim any imputation of disloyalty to the minority in this Convention. But has he bettered it by transferring it to the great popular masses in certain sections of the State where there is strong opposition to the Ordinance of Secession, and where it is said it will be resisted? Will the gentleman go into those sections of the State and hang all who are opposed to Secession? Will he hang them by families, by neighborhoods, by towns, by counties, by Congressional Districts? Who, sir, will give the bloody order? Who will be your executioner? Is this the spirit of Southern chivalry? Are these the sentiments of the boasted champions of Southern Rights? Are these to be the first fruits of a Southern Republic? Ah! is this the bloody charity of a party who seeks to deliver our own beloved sunny South from the galling yoke of a fanatical and puritanical abolition majority? What a commentary on the charity of party majorities! The history of the reign of Terror furnishes not a parallel to the bloody picture shadowed forth in the remarks of the gentleman. I envy him not its contemplation. For the interest of our common country, I would drop the curtain over the scene; and palsied be the hand that ever attempts to lift it.

After the explanation and disclaimer of the gentleman [Mr. Yancey,] it is due to him, and to myself, that I should say—which I do with great pleasure—that the particular remark of mine to which he excepts, was intended to illustrate my notions of parliamentary decorum, and not to apply to him individually.

Mr. DAVIS, of Madison, said:

Mr. President—I cannot allow this occasion to pass without saying a word in reply to what has fallen from the gentleman from Montgomery, [Mr. Yancey.] Under other circumstances, his remarks might pass unnoticed; but I feel that I owe it to those I represent, at least, correctly to state the position which they hold, upon the question so unexpectedly brought before this body. I claim, sir, to know their views, and I say to this Convention that they have not intended to resist its action, when in conformity to the wishes of the people of the State. The question with them, sir, is: does the Convention represent the popular will of the State? If it does, they will stand by it, no matter what its decision may be. Now, sir, I need scarcely say that the act of this Convention will not be conclusive in this matter. And why? Because, as every one knows, the popular vote of this State may be one way; the Convention another, and this resulting from the *manner* in which it was called, by those who are guilty of an usurpation of power. In short, Mr. President, the sovereignty of this body is denied, and its action will be sustained or resisted, as the popular will may be reflected through it.

The gentleman from Montgomery, [Mr. Yancey,] asserts upon the authority of a newspaper statement, the vote to be one way: the gentleman from Tuscaloosa, [Mr. Smith,] upon like authority, claims it to be another. I submit, sir, that in deciding a question of such moment, the proof on either side, is unsatisfactory. The people of the State will so regard it. We have the means in our hands of ascertaining their will, by submitting our action for their ratification or rejection; and should a course so manifestly just, be refused, a Committee of this Body, with the evidence at the door, can arrive at a satisfactory conclusion. In either event, I pledge those I represent to stand by the expressed will of the people. I repeat, that I know this to be the position of my constituents, and such, so far as my knowledge extends, is the position of the people in North Alabama.

Mr. YANCEY:

I said nothing about the people in North Alabama.

Mr. DAVIS:

No sir, you did not, but it is very well understood by every member on this floor to whom your remarks were applicable. If it should turn out that the popular vote is against the Act of Secession, should it pass, I tell you, sir, that I believe it will and ought to be resisted. The minority of the people of this State ought not to control the majority. But we are told that this is a representative Government—not a pure Democracy, and in this form minorities may rule. If our State Government be representative in this sense, who made it so? The people who, in Convention, framed its Constitution and organic law. They set it on foot, and whilst it moves in the orbit which they prescribed, grant that it is representative, and has the feature which is claimed. Secession, however, destroys that Constitution, and the people are muzzled in this Convention by a Legislature, which derived its existence from the instrument to be destroyed. But I do not propose to discuss this matter. Judging from the speech of the gentleman from Montgomery, [Mr. Yancey,] that is not the mode in which it will be decided. We are told, sir, by him, that resistance to the action of this Convention is treason, and those who undertake it, traitors and rebels. The nomenclature of the resolution will then be revised, and the epithet of tory, in future, may ornament the names of Alabamians. I cannot accept this as applicable to my constituents; nor neither do I perceive the fitness or force of the intended illustration. The Whigs of the Revolution were the friends of this Government—the Tories its enemies. If names shall hold the same relation to the Government now as then, I shall have no objections to the historical reminiscence. And not less odious, in my estimation, than the name of tory, is the doctrine which is claimed of the right to coerce an unwilling people. We must be dealt with as public enemies. But yesterday, sir, this Convention condemned this doctrine. With one voice, you declared against it, and expressed your determination to meet such an invasion of your rights as it ought to be met, with arms in your hands. It will be asserted as readily against a tyrant at home as abroad; as readily by the people of my section against usurpation and outrage here, as elsewhere. And when compelled to take this course, they will cheerfully, no doubt, assume all the responsibility that follows the act. I seek no quarrel with the gentleman from Montgomery, or his friends. Towards him personally, I entertain none other than the kindest feeling. But I tell him that should he engage in that enterprise, he will not be allowed to boast the character of an invader. Coming at the head of any force which he can muster, aided and asisted by the Executive of this State, we will meet him at the foot of our mountains, and there with his own selected weapons, hand to hand, and face to face, settle the question of the sovereignty of the people.

The Convention adjourned without having taken any further action on the resolution.

FOURTH DAY—SECRET SESSION—JANUARY 10.

Gen. J. W. A. SANFORD, Commissioner from the State of Georgia to the State of Alabama, was invited to a seat within the bar of the Convention.

THE CONVENTION OF ALABAMA.   75

The President laid before the Convention an official dispatch from the State of Mississippi.

Received at Montgomery January 9th, 1861, by telegraph from Jackson:

To Hon. WM. M. BROOKS:

I am instructed by the Mississippi State Convention to inform you that the State of Mississippi, by a vote of her Convention, approaching unanimity, has seceded unconditionally, from the Union, and desires, on the basis of the old Constitution, a new Union with the seceded States.   WILLIAM S. BARRY,
President of the Convention.

And also dispatches from Charleston, as follows:

Received at Montgomery January 9th, 1861, by telegraph from Charleston:

To John A. ELMORE:

The Steamer with reinforcements, was fired into by the Forts, disabled, retreated and lying at anchor. This is certain. The reports of her hauling down her colors I do not vouch for.
WM. E. MARTIN.

Received at Montgomery January 9th, 1861, by telegraph from Charleston:

To J. A. ELMORE, or the President of the Convention:

Anderson, it is said and believed, intends firing upon our shipping, and cutting off communication with the fort.
WM. E. MARTIN.

Received at Montgomery January 9th, 1861, by telegraph from Charleston:

To JOHN A. ELMORE, or President of Convention:

Anderson writes to the Governor he will fire into all ships. Governor replies, and justifies what we did. Now Anderson replies, his mind is changed, and refers the question to Washington.
WM. E. MARTIN.

ORDINANCE OF SECESSION

MR. YANCEY, from the Committee of Thirteen, reported as follows:

The Committee to whom it was committed to consider upon, and report, what action was necessary to be taken by this Convention, in order to protect and preserve the rights and independence of the people of the State of Alabama, beg leave to report, that they have calmly and thoughtfully considered the great matter committed to them; and they have instructed me to report the accompanying Ordinance and Resolutions.
W. L. YANCEY,
Chairman.

An Ordinance to dissolve the Union between the State of Alabama and other States united under the compact styled " The Constitution of the United States of America."

WHEREAS, the election of Abraham Lincoln and Hannibal Hamlin to the offices of President and Vice President of the United States of America, by a sectional party, avowedly hostile to the domestic institutions and to the peace and security of the people of the State of Alabama, preceded by many and dangerous infractions of the Constitution of the United States by many of the States and people of the Northern section, is a political wrong of so insulting and menacing a character as to justify the people of the State of Alabama in the adoption of prompt and decided measures for their future peace and security ; therefore,

Be it declared and ordained by the people of the State of Alabama, in Convention assembled, That the State of Alabama now withdraws, and is hereby withdrawn, from the Union known as " the United States of America," and henceforth ceases to be one of said United States, and is, and of right ought to be, a Sovereign and Independent State.

SEC. 2. *Be it further declared and ordained by the people of the State of Alabama in Convention assembled,* That all the powers over the Territory of said State, and over the people thereof, heretofore delegated to the Government of the United States of America, be and they are hereby withdrawn from said Government, and are hereby resumed and vested in the people of the State of Alabama.

Be it resolved by the people of Alabama in Convention assembled, That the people of the States of Delaware, Maryland, Virginia, North Carolina, South Carolina, Florida, Georgia, Mississippi,

Louisiana, Texas, Arkansas, Tennessee, Kentucky and Missouri, be and are hereby invited to meet the people of the State of Alabama, by their Delegates, in Convention, on the 4th day of February, A. D., 1861, at the city of Montgomery, in the State of Alabama, for the purpose of consulting with each other as to the most effectual mode of securing concerted and harmonious action in whatever measures may be deemed most desirable for our common peace and security.

And be it further resolved, That the President of this Convention be, and is hereby instructed to transmit forthwith, a copy of the foregoing Preamble, Ordinance, and Resolutions to the Governors of the several States named in said resolutions.

Done by the people of the State of Alabama, in Convention assembled, at Montgomery, on this, the eleventh day of January, A. D., 1861.

MINORITY REPORT.

Mr. CLEMENS, from the minority of the same Committee, made a report with resolutions as follows:

The undersigned, a minority of the Committee of Thirteen, to whom was referred all matters touching the proper mode of resistance to be adopted by the State of Alabama, in the present emergency, beg leave to present the following

REPORT:

Looking to harmony of action among our own people as desirable above all other things, we have been earnestly desirous of concurring with the majority in the line of policy marked out by them, but, after the most careful consideration, we have been unable to see in Separate State Secession the most effectual mode of guarding our honor and securing our rights. Without entering into any argument upon the nature and amount of our grievances, or any speculations as to the probability of our obtaining redress and security in the Union, but looking alone to the most effectual mode of resistance, it seems to us that this great object is best to be attained by the concurrent and concerted action of all the States interested, and that it becomes us to make the effort to obtain that concurrence, before deciding finally and conclusively upon our own policy.

We are further of opinion that, in a matter of this importance, vitally affecting the property, the lives and the liberties of the whole people, sound policy dictates that an ordinance of secession should be submitted for their ratification and approval. To that and, the resolutions which accompany this report have been prepared and are now submitted to the Convention.

The undersigned purposely refrain from a detailed statement of the reasons which have brought them to the conclusions at which they have arrived. The action proposed by the majority of the Committee is, in its nature, final and conclusive—there is no chance for rehearing or revision; and we feel no disposition to submit an argument, whose only effect will be to create discontent, and throw difficulties in the way of a policy, the adoption of which we are powerless to prevent. In submitting our own plan, and using all fair and honorable means to secure its acceptance, our duty is fully discharged; to insist upon objections when they can have no effect but to excite dissatisfaction among the people, is alike foreign to our feelings, and our conceptions of patriotic duty.

The resolutions hereinbefore referred to, are prayed to be taken as part of this Report, and the whole is herewith respectfully submitted.
JERE. CLEMENS,
DAVID P. LEWIS,
WM. O. WINTSON.
A. KIMBAL,
R. S. WATKINS,
R. JEMISON, Jr.

WHEREAS, repeated infractions of the Constitution of the United States by the people and States of the Northern section of the Confederacy have been followed by the election of sectional candidates, by a strictly sectional vote, to the Presidency and Vice Presidency of the United States, upon a platform of principles insulting and menacing to the Southern States; and WHEREAS, it becomes a free people to watch with jealous vigilance, and resist with manly firmness every attempt to subvert the free and equal principles upon which our Government was originally founded, and ought alone to be maintained; therefore,

Be it resolved by the people of Alabama in Convention assembled, That the States of Delaware, Maryland, Virginia, North Carolina, South Carolina, Georgia, Florida, Mississippi, Louisiana, Texas, Arkansas, Tennessee, Kentucky and Missouri, be and they are hereby requested to meet us in general Convention in the city of Nashville, in the State of Tennessee, on the 22d day of February, 1861, for the purpose of taking into consideration the wrongs of which we have cause to complain; the appropriate remedy therefor, and the time and manner of its application.

Be it further resolved, That the State of Alabama shall be represented in said Convention by nine delegates, one to be selected from each Congressional district, and two from the State at large, in such manner as shall hereafter be directed and provided for by this Convention.

"*Be it further resolved.* That our delegates selected shall be instructed to submit to the general Convention the following basis of a settlement of the existing difficulties between the Northern and the Southern States, to wit:

1. A faithful execution of the Fugitive Slave Law, and a repeal of all State laws calculated to impair its efficacy.

2. A more stringent and explicit provision for the surrender of criminals charged with offences against the laws of one State and escaping into another.

3. A guarantee that slavery shall not be abolished in the District of Columbia, or in any other place over which Congress has exclusive jurisdiction.

4. A guarantee that the inter-State slave trade shall not be interferred with.

5. A protection to slavery in the Territories, while they are Territories, and a guarantee that when they ask for admission as States they shall be admitted into the Union with or without slavery as their Constitutions may prescribe.

6. The right of transit through free States with slave property.

7. The foregoing clauses to be irrepealable by amendments to the Constitution.

Be it further resolved, That the basis of settlement prescribed in the foregoing resolution shall not be regarded by our delegates as absolute and unalterable, but as an indication of the opinion of this Convention, to which they are expected to conform as nearly as may be, holding themselves, however, at liberty to accept any better plan of adjustment which may be insisted upon by a majority of the slaveholding States.

Be it further resolved. That if the foregoing proposition for a conference is refused, or rejected, by any or all of the States to which it is addressed, Alabama, in that event, will hold herself at liberty, alone, or in conjunction with such States, as may agree to unite with her, to adopt such plan of resistance, and mature such measures, as in her judgment may seem best calculated to maintain the honor and secure the rights of her citizens; and in the meantime we will resist, by all means at our command, any attempt on the part of the General Government to coerce a seceding State.

Be it further resolved, That the President of this Convention be instructed to transmit copies of the foregoing preamble and resolutions to the Governors of each of the States therein named.

And also the following resolution from the same :

Be it resolved by the people of Alabama in Convention assembled, That an ordinance of secession from the United States is an act of such great importance, involving consequences so vitally affecting the lives, liberty and property of the citizens of the seceding State, as well as of the States by which it is surrounded, and with which it has heretofore been united, that in our opinion it should never be attempted until after the most thorough investigation, and discussion, and then only after a full and free ratification at the polls by a direct vote of the people, at an election held under the forms and safeguards of the law in which that single issue, untrammelled and undisguised in any manner whatever, should alone be submitted.

Mr. CLEMENS moved that the preamble and first series of resolutions be taken up and substituted for the ordinance.

The ayes and noes was demanded.

The ayes and nays were then called on the motion of 'Mr. Clemens, and it was lost. Ayes, 45, nays, 54.

Those who voted in the affirmative are Messrs. Allen, Barclay, Beard, Bulger, Clarke, of Lawrence, Clemens, Coffee, Coman, Crumpler, Davis, of Madison, Earnest, Edwards, Ford, Forrester, Franklin, Gay, Green, Guttery, Hood, Inzer, Jemison, Jones, of Fayette, Jones, of Lauderdale, Johnson, Kimball, Leonard, Lewis, McClellan, Posey, Potter, Russell, Sanford, Sheets, Sheffield, Slaughter, Smith, of Tuscaloosa, Steadham, Steele, Taylor, Timberlake, Watkins, Whitlock, Wilson, Winston, Wood—45.

Those who voted in the negative are Messrs. President, Bailey, Baker, of Barbour, Baker, of Russell, Barnes, Beck, Blue, Bolling, Bragg, Catterling, Clarke, of Marengo, Cochran, Coleman, Crawford, Creech, Crook, Curtis, Daniel, Dargan, Davis, of Covington, Davis, of Pickens, Dowdell, Foster, Gibbons, Gilchrist, Hawkins, Henderson, of Pike, Henderson, of Macon, Herndon, Howard, Humphries, Jewett, Ketchum, Love, McClanahan, McPherson, McKinnie, Morgan, Owens, Phillips, Ralls, Rives, Ryan, Shortridge, Silver, Smith, of Henry, Starke, Stone, Watts, Webb, Whatley, Williamson, Yancey, Yelverton—54.

Mr. CLEMENS offered the following amendment:

Provided, however, that this ordinance shall not go into effect until the 4th day of March, 1861, and not then unless the same shall have been ratified and confirmed by a direct vote of the people.

The ayes and noes were taken on the amendment, and were: ayes, 45, nays, 54, and the amendment was lost.

Those who voted in the affirmative are, Messrs. Allen, Barclay, Beard, Bulger, Clarke, of Lawrence, Clemens, Coffee, Coman, Crumpler, Davis, of Madison, Earnest, Edwards, Ford, Forrester, Franklin, Gay, Green, Guttery, Hood, Inzer, Jemison, Jones, of Fayette, Jones, of Lauderdale, Johnson, Kimball, Leonard, Lewis, McLellan, Posey, Potter, Russell, Sanford, Sheets, Sheffield, Slaughter, Smith, of Tuscaloosa, Steadham, Steele, Taylor, Timberlake, Watkins, Whitlock, Wilson, Winston, Wood —45.

Those who voted in the negative are Messrs. President, Bailey, Baker, of Barbour, Baker, of Russell, Barnes, Beck, Blue, Bolling, Bragg, Catterling, Clarke, of Marengo, Cochran, Coleman, Crawford, Creech, Crook, Curtis, Daniel, Dargan, Davis, of Covington, Davis, of Pickens, Dowdell, Foster, Gibbons, Gilchrist, Hawkins, Henderson, of Pike, Henderson, of Macon, Herndon, Howard, Humphries, Jewett, Ketchum, Love, McClanahan, McPherson, McKinnie, Morgan, Owens, Phillips, Ralls, Rives, Ryan, Shortridge, Silver, Smith, of Henry, Starke, Stone, Watts, Webb, Whatley, Williamson, Yancey, Yelverton—54.

Mr. YANCEY moved to take up the Ordinance of Secession, and that it be adopted.

Pending this motion Mr. CLARK, of Laurence, said:

Mr. President—As separate secession is not a right, so it is not a remedy. - As a question of policy, merely, a more appalling picture can scarcely be presented to the eye of the patriot and philanthropist, than that of separate State secession. There is something repulsive in the very exclusiveness of its name.

It is no remedy, because it would remove no evil. The slavery question, the "Iliad of all our woes," would not be decided in our favor, or even settled in any way. It would still continue a vital and ever-present issue. If we succeed in quieting or removing this cause of disturbance, we have accomplished all—if we fail, nothing. How shall separate secession effect this result? It would be a revolution of the Government, it is true, but it would not revolutionize the Northern mind. It would neither hush the pulpit, calm the forum, nor purify the quarters of Black Republicanism.

This mode of action certainly can afford no relief for the past. It is equally clear, it can provide no security for the future. Destitute of the ordinary means of self-defence—in no condition to demand an alliance, and without the power to invite one—the General Government provoked into hostility by our disobedience —other governments refusing to acknowledge our independence— the surrounding States forced to become enemies by our dictation; shut out from the Pacific on the West, the Atlantic on the East; with Federal fleets cautiously watching our manœuvres from the Gulf of Mexico—our border exposed on every side—abolitionism always ready to foray upon us—with no fugitive slave law to protect our property—without a treasury, an army or a navy—we should be, indeed, the Niobe of nations. Intimidated by our own weakness, distressed by our exposed condition, and exhausted by destructive efforts at self-preservation—all history teaches that but one fate would await us. The proud spirit of our people bruised, broken, and at last overcome by these combined agencies, would demand protection, as the dernier resort, from some stronger power—and Alabama ultimately become a dependency of Great Britain, or of France, or perhaps be forced to return "in secret, in silence and tears" to the American Confederacy ! The minor States of ancient Greece, alternately paying tribute to Sparta or Athens, great as the power of one or the other was paramount, afford a mournful and instructive lesson upon this melancholy subject. The small feudatories of the eleventh and twelfth centuries, in England, also offer sad examples of the well established historical truth, that a weak State can only maintain a nominal independence—a sort of political wardship when environed by more powerful neighbors. Separate secession, therefore, so far from enabling us the more effectually to secure the interests of slavery, would only invite the descent and make us the easy prey of Northern marauders. Nations are not improvised. They are the slow and steady growth of centuries. "A thousand years scarce seem to make a State."

The sense of insecurity, which our forlorn condition would beget, most certainly, would drive capital away; just at the time, too, when we should need it most. The cost of administering a government is in inverse proportion to its size. Federal officers with Shylock avidity, would seize the public revenue in every collection district, and direct taxation would be the only resource for funds with which to support the machinery of government. Our people, oppressed to the earth by a system of taxation more intolerable than that of despotic Austria, and impelled likewise, by the instinct of self-preservation, would strike their tents and emigrate to the West. Thus deserted by population, our lands would pass out of demand, and depreciate; and our negroes, too, cease to be valuable for want of a market. This emigration would go on chiefly from the white population, and the dismal proportion of negroes which we have already, would then become absolutely alarming. Our lovely State, with its few Caucasian inhabitants, would be converted into a kind of American Congo.

Should Alabama and South Carolina withdraw their representation in Congress, the democratic majority there, which makes the present of slavery secure, according to the infamous Phillips, would be destroyed; and Virginia, Kentucky, Missouri and Tennessee, the great central slave and border States being left—ungenerously abandoned to the implacable vengeance of their relentless foe, would seek safety for their slaves in emigration, and fair equivolency in Southern markets; and, besides crowding the Gulf States with a ruinous surplus of the black race, would themselves, by gradually yielding up their lands to the exclusive culture of incoming whitemen from the North, become free States. Thus the institution of slavery, gradually receding before the Northern avalanche of abolitionism, pressing down upon it like a glacier in the gorges of the eternal Alps, and coming southward from State to State, would finally perish. We should then believe, but all too late, the recent declaration of Senator Wade, "separate State secession is the decree for universal emancipation." This evil could not be remedied by laws prohibiting the immigration of negroes to the State. In thus attempting to avoid Charybdis, we should be wrecked upon Scylla. To obstruct the inter-slave-trade, is, at once, to "clip the golden hair from the head of Nisus." The Black Republicans desire nothing more. It is the policy, therefore, of Alabama to remain, if not in the Union, at least in the South with Virginia, Tennessee and Kentucky, interposed between her and the region of danger, if for no other purpose than to give protection to her own property. But she owes this much, at least, to those States themselves. Her patriotism, chivalry and magnanimity could never be excused for ingloriously deserting them in this hour of awful peril. The hostile tread of abolition invaders will only desecrate the virgin soil of Alabama, when the courage of the Old Dominion becomes a myth and the Kentucky rifle a fable.

Surely, Alabama ought to exhibit no indecent haste in cutting the companionship of Virginia. She is a powerful auxiliary—a tried friend. If the State of Virginia, losing annually a hundred times as much property as our own, and submitting to a thousand indignities to which our people are strangers, can remain in the Union, at least long enough, to select with some deliberation the best mode of retiring from it, certainly Alabama's honor will not be compromised by the determined abandonment of a friend, so dear and invaluable. It is said that if Virginia and Kentucky do not wish to be deserted, let them follow Alabama. But is it not eminently discourteous, selfish and unkind, for any one State to arrogate the Supreme Dictatorship of fourteen equals?

Southern sentiment is opposed to separate State secession; and if not a majority, at least a large minority of our own people are violently hostile to it This circumstance, alone, should be conclusive against the policy. A large part of the produce of North Alabama finds a market in Tennessee, or passes through that State on its way to it. North Alabama has no idea of permitting her citizens and cotton to run the gauntlet of passports, custom houses, and the other machinery of a foreign government as they go to market. Already many of her best and truest citizens are speaking of secession from Alabama and annexation to Tennessee: thus illustrating at once the utter absurdity of the doctrine of secession, as well as foreshadowing the storm that is impending over our own State. Shall we ever live to behold the day when Alabama, having assumed the untried responsibilities of separate secession, shall find herself torn, convulsed and rent in twain by the dissensions of her own people? Shall the martial roll of the warlike drum ever be heard reverbrating through the deep ravines of the Sand Mountains, calling the clansmen of the hills against our brothers of the South? Shall grim-visaged war lift his horrid front" above the Arcadian valley of the Tennessee, and bestain and overspread with slaughter's pencil those beautiful and picturesque landscapes, brighter than any scene which ever flashed admiration upon the shepherd's soul among those flowering peaks, where "smooth Peneus glassy flood reflects purpureal Tempe's pleasant scene?" Shall the very Eden of peace, become the home of strife, of carnage and of destruction? The bare probability of such a thing "fills me, and thrills me with terrors no mortal ever felt before." Great God forbid it!

In her name, and by her authority, I implore you to yield something, for once, to the demand of North Alabama—to your brothers who have the same common cause, danger and destiny, the same fathers and mothers to watch over and pray for you; who love and cherish you, and whose brave hearts and strong arms will bleed and strike for you in peril's darkest hour. Although cautious in council, North Alabama, when the conflict comes, if come it must, will lead your army to victory and to glory.

What abolition aggression do you resist by going out of the Union alone? Will it repeal the personal liberty bills of the North? Will it return a single fugitive slave? Can it prevent the abolition of slavery in the District of Columbia? or the suppression of the inter-State-slave trade? Alabama by seceding, voluntarily relinquishes whatever of interest she has in the golden fruitage of the territories—the Hesperides of America. Has the cotton bloom no interest in the Indian territory worth Alabama's attention? Can you witness without a pang the federal assetts go to enrich the coffers of your enemies? Will you shed not a tear when you bid farewell to that army and navy, around which so many glorious recollections cluster, and in which Southern valor has won such unperishable laurels? But above all, to say nothing of the grave of Washington and the home of Clay, are you ready tamely to surrender the Temple of the Constitution—the Jerusalem of our hopes—to the Saracens who beleager it? Southern patriots! can you repose in quiet upon your pillows while the Constitution of your fathers—the grandest effort of human workmanship—writhes in the harpy hands of Black Republicanism? Can you prevent this deplorable consummation by separate State action? Delude not yourselves with the vain hope, that if this Government is picked to pieces by fragments, it, or any considerable portion of it, can, upon some self-adjusting principle, ever reünite in sufficient strength to demand and assert our claim to any of the Federal property which we shall abandon. Has history been written in vain? Shall we not profit by the experience of the past? If our fathers, surrounded by all of the terrors of the Revolution, could scarcely form a Union, how can their sons expect, in times of peace, to restore the unity of a disintegrated South? If a few weak and nerveless colonies—without money and without men—doubted long, and finally agreed with great reluctance, do you suppose that fifteen Sovereign States, as you so love to call them, would mingle again gracefully into one? Said Mr. Madison, in 1829, "In the event of a dissolution of the Union, an impossibility of ever renewing it is brought home to every mind by the difficulties encountered in establishing it. But you ask me, where then would be a unity of interest, a unity of climate and a unity of soil—what would prevent a union in politics? The same causes which came so near defeating the hopes of liberty under the Articles of Confederation, and which rendered the present Constitution a necessity. The same causes which have operated in all ages and in all instances wherever the federative system has been attempted. History abounds with examples. The bad passions of men, and the passions of bad men. The ambitious schemes of selfish, political leaders, and the honestly entertained views of others—petty rivalry and jealousies—various views of government, questions of boundary, perhaps, and conflicting commercial regulations."

But suppose you could succeed, after striking Alabama from the constellation of States, in provoking a war with the General Government, if it was not imposed upon you, and by thus desolating her fair borders and slaughtering her peaceful citizens, draggoon the other Southern States unto your assistance and a union with you, would you do it? Every instinct of philanthropy, and common humanity answers for you a thousand times, no. My chief objection, therefore, to separate secession, is, that it would be a disunion of the South: a thought so gloomy and awful that it needs only to be mentioned.

These are a few of the numerous objections to peaceable separate State secession. But could this policy be carried out peaceably? I think not. It must be followed sooner or later, by an appeal to the high arbitrament of arms—where the eloquence of artillery would debate, and the bayonet's bloody point decide. The annals of all time furnish but few, if any, instances of a people changing their allegiance by a bloodless revolution. If the General Government were to attempt to coerce the State, that would determine the question at once. If the incoming administration, however, should adopt the constitutional constructions of its predecessor, the unpleasant alternative will be presented of engaging in a civil war, or of submitting to the collection of the Federal revenue. A brave people, ground down by taxation, will not be long in deciding that question. I shall not argue to it. A settled gloom comes over the mind and deadly sickness steals upon the heart at its mere contemplation. One paragraph from that magnificent burst of oratory, uttered by Mr. Webster in the great strife of 1850, which gathers new splendor from the impending crisis, is worth more than all of my argument: "Who is so foolish—I beg everybody's pardon—as to expect to see any such thing? Sir, he who sees these States now revolving in harmony around a common centre, and expects to see them quit their places and fly off without convulsion, may look the next hour to see the heavenly bodies rush from their spheres and jostle against each other in the realms of space, without causing the wreck of the universe. There can be no such thing as peaceable secession. Peaceable secession is an utter impossibility. Is the great Constitution under which we live—covering this whole country—is it to be thawed and melted away by secession as the snows on the mountains melt in under the influence of a vernal sun, disappear almost unobserved and run off? No, sir! No, sir! I will not state what might produce disruption of the Union: but sir, I see as plainly as I see the sun in heaven what that disruption itself must produce. I see it must produce war, and such a war I will not describe in its twofold character."

The only hope for a peaceable secession is in a United South; and that alone can afford certain security to the future of slavery. Now is the time, too, if ever, that it can be effected. Southern sentiment, although opposed to separate secession, is ripe for a Union of the South. That moral revolution which must always precede political changes, has been already wrought. Lincoln's election—a standing menace to slavery—by a party organized upon a basis of hostility to that species of property, in which all of the Southern States are so largely interested, will force the South into unity of idea.

A united South! What music to the patriot's ear! In it would be realized the brightest dreams of Southern statesmanship—the life-long ambition of the great Calhoun consummated—and the institution of slavery protected forever against the propagandism of the Northern mania. A united South implies all that is profitable in practice, beautiful in theory, and stupendous in conception. A salubrious climate, fertile soil, and nearly nine hundred thousand square miles of slave territory; fifty navigable rivers, unlocked by the rigors of winter; a sea coast by ocean and gulf almost immeasurable; a population in the year 1850 of nearly ten millions; her property worth, exclusive of slaves, in round numbers, three billions; and fifty-five millions of acres of improved land, groaning beneath the richest of harvests. The cash value of her farms, two billions of dollars; her farming implements alone worth sixty millions of dollars; her agricultural products, estimated at six hundred and thirty-two millions of dollars; each agriculturist earning in the sweat of honest industry, an average of one hundred and seventy-one dollars per annum: a capital of ninety-six millions of dollars employed in manufactures, and working up in raw material a value of eighty-seven millions of dollars. [Here Mr. Clark enlarged upon the resources of the South, and continued:] Besides, the South is the nursery of the Arts and Sciences, the land of the philosopher; the home of the orator and statesman, the poet, the historian and the divine. Its chivalry unvanquished by flood or by field, and its beauty blooming like "wild roses by the abbey towers" in every hamlet and village. While these statistical facts, taken indiscriminately from the census of 1850, augmented by a decade's increase, demonstrate that the South, under the present Government, has attained a distinction almost unrivalled in material progress, they admonish us to exercise great patience before we destroy the Constitution which has supplied us with so much nourishment, growth and wealth. They also show that the South, united, possesses within herself, all of the elements of greatness, prosperity and independence. Our independence would then be acknowledged, and our power, influence and vast resources would invite alliances. Coercion would then become a thing impossible, and even fanaticism itself would not attempt it. The united freemen of the South, standing above the soil of their nativity, and battling around the urns and sepulchres of their fathers, can never be conquered. We should then possess, in short, all of the requisites of a great nation; the evils incident to separate secession above alluded to, would be prevented; and in this way, if at all, the long train of deplorable disasters consequent upon civil war, avoided.

The North know that we are injured and that the grounds of our complaint are just. They know that if there is any wrong in the fugitive slave law, we are indebted to them for it. Almost before their tracks were dry on the decks of the May-flower, in 1643, only twenty-three years after,

> "A band of exiles moor'd the bark
> On the wild New England shore."

Commissioners from Connecticut, New Hampshire, Massachusetts, Rhode Island and other places enacted a Fugitive Slave Law.

Let the South in her united majesty once more come forth "with her cohorts gleaming in purple and gold," and, lifting her mighty voice, like the sound of many waters, above the granite hills of New England, utter again to Abolitionism, the edict of heaven: "thou shalt not steal." We owe it to the interests of liberty—to republican institutions, and to the great rights of man throughout the civilized world. We owe it to that long line of posterity which shall rise up and bless us—to the present with all of its untold grandeur—and to the illustrious past.

An act, involving such momentous consequences as the tearing down or building up a government implies, should not be done in passion, pique or precipitation. We should at least determine the successor before we dethrone the incumbent—agree upon the form of a new government before we destroy the old. Our ancestors were nearly a century and a half in erecting the present government of the United States; and in the Convention which assembled in Albany in 1754, its ruling spirit, Dr. Franklin, and his associate commissioners, unlike our separate secession advocates, spurned the idea of separate Confederacies. Indeed, colonial history fully proves that the great statesmen who were acting under a high and patriotic sense of their responsibilities to mankind, and whose deliberations resulted in the formation of a government, which up to the present moment has been regarded with wonder and admiration by the civilized world, were controlled by two principles, which obtain but little favor with the government makers of the present day: the greatest caution and a strong desire for united action. They were acting, too, under circumstances ten times more alarming than those which surround us, and with precisely the same object in view—self-protection against external danger. Even after hostilities had commenced in the province of Massachusetts, they published resolutions renouncing trade with Great Britain, Canada and the Colonies; they preferred petitions to the King; and it was only after argument, persuasion, remonstrance, entreaty, non-intercourse and every other conciliatory measure had been exhausted, that they struck the final blow which made America free.

What a change has come over the spirit of South Carolina's dream! Then she was prudent, cautious, full of delay; even up to the first day of July, 1776, although her arms had flashed forth at Fort Moultrie in a blaze of glory, she had not given in her adherence to the Declaration of Independence; and the reason, still more singular, was that one of her deputies wanted time to *unite others in the project.*

For these reasons, with many others, it is the policy of Alabama, clearly indicated, to invite a Conference of the Southern States for consultation and endorsement. What should be the policy of that Convention, it is not for me to anticipate. But, that great good would result from it we may safely hope. If some plan of reconciliation were derived by it which should satisfy the demands of the Southern States, as I confidently believe would be done, certainly every good patriot would hail it with delight. But if, after we have made this last appeal to the justice of the North— after we have exhausted, like our revolutionary fathers, argument, persuasion and entreaty, injustice and wrong shall continue to rule their counsels—thus manifesting the determination to wage the " irrepressible conflict" until the foot of the slave shall no longer tread the soil of the South—then no constitutional scruples abou. State sovereignty or Federal coercion will be mooted; the South in grand, unbroken and consolidated unity, would appeal to that right which is higher than all constitutions—which tears down and sets up governments—which topples dynasties and crushes empires—which dethrones kings and decapitates tyrants—the implacable right which the Great God of the Universe has granted to man in the eternal charter of the skies—the right of every community to freedom and happiness, and of every people, when the government established over them becomes incompetent to fulfill its purposes, or destructive of the essential ends for which it was instituted, founded upon the law of nations and the reason of mankind, and supported by the best authority and most illustrious precedents, to throw off such government and provide new guards for their future security. If the wisdom, the patriotism and the experience of the land, assembled in solemn council, after calmly surveying the facts and maturely, considering the consequences of their act, shall be of the opinion that the dearest interests of our people require the destruction of the government, let them quietly ascertain and define our grievances; and then having adopted the example of the immortal fathers of the first revolution, in vindication of the second, "let facts be submitted to a candid world." But if this Convention should neither restore peace nor declare independence, our condition would be no worse than it is now. Once more, therefore, in the names of Liberty, of Peace, of happy hours—of the aged, of the poor, of our mothers, of our sisters—of helpless humanity throughout the borders of our State, I implore you to concede something to the counties of North Alabama.

MR. TIMBERLAKE offered the following amendment:

Amend by inserting the following after the second section of the Ordinance, viz:

And it being the desire of the State of Alabama to form a Provisional Government, and a Southern Confederacy, upon the basis of the Constitution of the United States of America, with such of the slaveholding States as will join in forming the same; and the present resumption of its powers are declared to be for that purpose.

MR. TIMBERLAKE said:

In proposing this amendment, he hoped to so explain an ordinance by the adoption of which, Alabama proposes to resume the powers heretofore delegated to the Federal Government, as to confine the future action of the State, in the exercise of those powers, to the formation of a Confederacy of Southern States. He was unwilling to clothe Alabama with those powers for any other purpose; he could but regard the experiment of States, (formerly belonging to the United States,) setting up for themselves separate independent Governments, as being dangerous and unwise in policy, and as it had been a question upon which the parties in this Convention differed in the late canvass, both agreeing that the object and purpose of secession was the formation of a new Confederacy with Southern States. The Ordinance thus explained, will be complete for that purpose. He was willing that Alabama should resume the delegated powers for that purpose and for no other.

This Convention has power to adopt all measures for the defence of the interest and honor of Alabama, as well before as after the act of separation.

Mr. WHATLEY said:

The amendment of the gentleman from Jackson, is already incorporated in the Ordinance proposed by the Committee. The only spirit and object of the Ordinance is to accomplish what the gentleman proposes. It seems that no explanation or solicitations by the Chairman of the Committee, and other members, can suit the taste of the gentleman from Jackson; I therefore move to lay his amendment on the table.

Mr. YANCEY said:

He was willing to vote for a proposition that it was the desire and intention of the people of Alabama in seceding, to join other seceding States in erecting a Southern Confederacy of States upon the principles of the Constitution of the United States of America. But he could not vote for the proposition of the gentleman from Jackson, [Mr. Timberlake,] because it announced such design as the sole motive in seceding from the Union. He asked the attention of the gentleman from Jackson to this distinction. If he really desired an announcement, upon the part of delegates, that they intended to use all proper efforts to frame a Confederacy of Southern States upon Republican principles, let him alter his amendment so as to express that idea, and he will receive a hearty support from the friends of secession in this Convention. For us to vote for this amendment as now worded, is to ask us to declare a motive for secession which was never entertained by its friends.

The advocates of secession placed their action upon far higher grounds. They believed that the rights and liberties of the people of Alabama were assailed, and endangered by the Northern majorities, who control a majority of the States, and who are about to control the legislation of the Union.

Believing this, secession, or withdrawal of the State from under the power of that hostile majority, was advocated purely for the purpose—for the purpose alone—of protecting and preserving the endangered rights of the people of this sovereign State— even though not another State should follow our example. Though this was the sole purpose of secession, yet we all believed that other States would secede, and in that event it was our hope that they would join us in forming a new Confederacy upon old-fashioned Republican principles.

After a short discussion, Mr. WHATLEY renewed his motion to lay the amendment on the table.

The ayes and noes were called, and resulted: ayes 62—noes 37.

Those who voted in the affirmative were Messrs. Brooks, Allen, Bailey, Baker of Barbour, Barnes, Beck, Blue, Bolling, Bragg, Catterling, Clarke of Marengo, Clarke of Lawrence, Cochran, Coleman, Crawford, Creech, Crook, Curtis, Daniel, Dargan, Davis of Covington, Davis of Madison, Davis of Pickens, Dowdell, Foster, Gibbons, Gilchrist, Green, Hawkins, Henderson of Macon, Henderson of Pike, Herndon, Howard, Humphries, Jewett, Jones of Lauderdale, Ketchum, Lewis, Love, McClanahan, McClellan, McPherson, McKinne, Morgan, Owens, Phillips, Ralls, Rives, Ryan, Sheets, Shortridge, Silver, Smith of Henry, Starke, Stone, Watts, Webb, Whatley, Williamson, Wood, Yancey, Yelverton —62.

Those who voted in the negative were Messrs. Baker of Russell, Barclay, Beard, Brasher, Bulger, Clemens, Coffey, Coman, Crumpler, Earnest, Edwards, Ford, Forrester, Franklin, Gay, Guttery, Hood, Inzer, Jemison, Jones of Fayette, Johnson, Kimball, Leonard, Posey, Potter, Russell, Sanford, Sheffield, Slaughter, Smith of Tuscaloosa, Stedham, Steele, Taylor, Watkins, Whitlock, Wilson, Winston—37.

MR. YANCEY moved the following amendment, to be inserted immediately after the Ordinance, and before the resolutions:

"And as it is the desire and purpose of the people of Alabama to meet the slaveholding States of the South, who may approve such purpose, in order to frame a provisional as well as permanent Government, upon the principles of the Constitution of the United States."

The amendment of Mr. Yancey was adopted.

MR. WATTS announced the presence of Ex-Governor J. W. Matthews, Commissioner from Mississippi, who was, on motion, invited to a seat within the bar of the Convention.

On motion of Mr. JEMISON, the Convention then adjourned until to-morrow (Friday), at 11 o'clock, A. M.

FIFTH DAY—JANUARY ELEVENTH.

The President laid before the Convention the following official dispatches from the State of Florida:

TALLAHASSEE, Jan. 10.—Florida has seceded unconditionally, by a vote of sixty-two to seven.   M. S. PERRY.

The other was from Hon. E. C. Bullock, Commissioner from Alabama to Florida, precisely similar to the one from Gov. Perry.

The President announced that the special order before the Convention for this day, was the report of the majority from the Committee of Thirteen, and the Ordinance of Secession.

MR. JEMISON, who was entitled to the floor, said:

That he had thought of submitting to the Convention, this morning, some extended remarks touching this most important question; but, upon reflection, he would decline to do so. His own mind had long been made up to acquiesce in whatever the majority of the Convention might do. He was pledged, unconditionally, to his constituents to this course; and he would cheerfully carry out his pledge; and, he trusted, to their satisfaction. He would not only acquiesce himself in the passage of the Ordinance of Secession, but, upon his return to his constituents, he would use all honorable exertions, if need be, to satisfy the people with the action of this body. This he deemed to be his duty, as suggested by every consideration of patriotism. The public welfare demanded unity of action; and, so far as he was concerned, the best energies of his mind would be devoted to that end.

MR. DARGAN said:

I wish, Mr. President, to express the feelings with which I vote for the secession of Alabama from the Government of the United States; and to state, in a few words, the reasons that impel me to this act.

I feel impelled, Mr. President, to vote for this Ordinance by an overruling necessity. Years ago I was convinced that the Southern States would be compelled either to separate from the North, by dissolving the Federal Government, or they would be compelled to abolish the institution of African Slavery. This, in my judgment, was the only alternative; and I foresaw that the South would be compelled, at some day, to make her selection. The day is now come, and Alabama must make her selection, either to secede from the Union, and assume the position of a sovereign, independent State, or she must submit to a system of policy on the part of the Federal Government that, in a short time, will compel her to abolish African Slavery.

Mr. President, if pecuniary loss alone were involved in the abolition of slavery, I should hesitate long before I would give the vote I now intend to give. If the destruction of slavery entailed on us poverty alone, I could bear it, for I have seen poverty and felt its sting. But poverty, Mr. President, would be one of the least of the evils that would befall us from the abolition of African slavery. There are now in the slaveholding States over four millions of slaves; dissolve the relation of master and slave, and what, I ask, would become of that race? To remove them from amongst us is impossible. History gives us no account of the exodus of such a number of persons. We neither have a place to which to remove them, nor the means of such removal. They therefore must remain with us; and if the relation of master and slave be dissolved, and our slaves turned loose amongst us without restraint, they would either be destroyed by our own hands—the hands to which they look, and look with confidence, for protection—or we ourselves would become demoralized and degraded. The former result would take place, and we ourselves would become the executioners of our own slaves. To this extent would the policy of our Northern enemies drive us; and thus would we not only be reduced to poverty, but what is still worse, we should be driven to crime, to the commission of sin; and we must, therefore, this day elect between the Government formed by our fathers (the whole spirit of which has been perverted,) and POVERTY AND CRIME! This being the alternative, I cannot hesitate for a moment what my duty is. I must separate from the Government of the United States, and abandon the Government of my fathers, one under which I have lived, and under which I wished to die. But I must do my duty to my country and my fellow-beings; and humanity, in my judgment, demands that Alabama should separate herself from the Government of the United States.

If I am wrong in this responsible act, I hope my God may forgive me; for I am not actuated, as I think, from any motive save that of justice and philanthropy!

Mr. Posey said:

Mr. President—Before the vote is taken, I desire to offer some reflections, not arguments, upon this solemn occasion. I admit the time for argument is passed. The test votes taken upon the question clearly indicate the determination of a majority on this floor, to withdraw Alabama from the Government left us by our fathers, and which all here once valued as our richest inheritance.

"I come to bury Cæsar, not to praise him." Mr. President, I know you are a man, having the feelings of a man, and can appreciate the sensations of the minority. Reflect how you would have felt before you had been prepared, head and heart, to dissolve our relations with the Federal Government. We of the minority have not advanced so far; we would make one more effort to preserve the Federal Government, and by united action with the other Southern States, demand and sustain all our just rights; and should such united demands be refused by the States of the North, then to withdraw together from the Union.

The minority believe the Ordinance of Secession ought to be submitted to the people; our constituents believe the same, and would submit more willingly to the vote of the people themselves. This Ordinance will be more distasteful to them, because they have not been allowed to ratify or reject it. I hope they will acquiesce in the action of a majority of this Convention. Division at home would be worse than Secession; this is the opinion of the minority on this floor, upon mature reflection. The first impression of some of us, was, if the Convention refused to submit the question to the people, to bolt the Convention and return home. This intention we have abandoned; the conciliatory course of the majority on this floor, was wise and prudent, and has induced us to remain; and as we conceive, without being responsible for the Act of Secession, we can stay here and aid in providing for the emergencies of the future.

Mr. Jones, of Lauderdale, said:

That he had not wasted the time of the Convention by factious opposition to the action of the majority; he did not desire to do so now, yet he thought the act about to be performed would justify him in occupying the time of the Convention for a few moments.

This had been the most solemn hour of his life—he expected to feel no more solemn when he should stand in the presence of the King of Terrors.

We are to sever the ties that have hitherto bound us to the Federal Union, and enter upon an unknown sea of experiment. He would not argue the propriety of that act. The whole history of this Convention proves that the decision is already made—that each member has determined the course he will pursuse, and is prepared to meet the responsibility of his acts both now and hereafter.

Knowing this, he would not have said one word, but for the fact that it was reported and believed by many, that the constituency he represented were submissionists: this is a great mistake.

The people of Lauderdale are as jealous of their rights, and as ready to resent an infraction of those rights, as any people represented on this floor—they have solemnly and unanimously declared, time and again, that they would not submit to Black Republican rule on the principles enunciated by that party—they hold doctrines announced in your resolutions of Monday last to be their principles, and stand pledged to maintain them.

'Tis true, they differ with you about the time and mode of redress; they think that hasty secession is not the proper remedy: they think it unwise, impolitic and wanting in proper courtesy to our brethren of the border States. Thus you see, we do not differ about the *fact*, but the manner of redress—the remedy. But whether your mode or ours be wisest, he would not argue; that must be left for future history to decide.

He had been much moved by the remarks offered by the gentleman from Green, [Mr. Webb.] Seventeen years ago he had met that gentleman in the House of Representatives, when they were mere boys; since then, they had met in both ends of the Capitol, and he had ever found him ready to accord full and ample justice to my section. North Alabama had never drawn a draft on him, he did not honor. Then, sir, if the danger which he describes shall befall his section of the State, he will find us ready and willing to share every toil and divide every danger. Though differing totally from the majority on this subject, yet he was a son of Alabama, born and reared upon her soil, he had not, nor expected to live beyond her limits. To her he owed his first allegiance, and through her a second to the Federal Union. When Alabama shall sever this last allegiance and bid him stand in her defence, he had but one course of duty left. When her banner was unfurled he should stand beneath it—her friends should be his friends and her enemies his.

These opinions were widely known to his constituents, and they sent him here because they endorsed them. He would only add that he had a boy 15 years old now training in your ranks, and his mother says that when he is called his father must go with him; and he could not shrink from the responsibility.

Mr. INZER said:

Mr. President—This is the most solemn period of my life. Although a young man, I have been looking forward for years to a dissolution of the States composing this Confederacy. The Great Compact has already been broken. South Carolina, Florida and Mississippi have seceded, and before the going down of the sun the State of Alabama will have declared her independence, and no longer be one of the United States of America. I am pledged to oppose the Ordinance. I told the people of the county which I have the honor to represent, that if elected, I would most assuredly vote against immediate separate secession; and to-day I stand here ready to redeem my pledge, and will vote against the Ordinance. But when it becomes the organic law of my State, I will support it, as I believe it to be my duty to do so. I believe the people of my county will stand by the action of the State in her sovereign capacity; and I am in hopes that Alabama will go on with her great work to independence and prosperity. I told the people of St. Clair, [Mr. Inzer's county,] while canvassing the county, that I was in favor of coöperation; but said, if Alabama should secede separate and alone, I would go with her and stand by her in every peril, even to the cannon's mouth; and I now repeat it, I am for Alabama under any and all circumstances.

Mr. SMITH, of Tuscaloosa, said:

Mr. President—I will not at this time express any argument of opposition I may entertain towards the Ordinance of Secession. I have many reasons for this course.

I meet here a positive, enlightened and unflinching majority. I have respect for them, and I despair of being able to move them.

In times like these, when neighboring States are withdrawing one by one from the Union, I cannot get my consent to utter a phrase which might be calculated, in the slightest degree, to widen the breaches at home. My opposition to the Ordinance of Secession will be sufficiently indicated by my vote; that vote will be recorded in the book; that book will take up its march for posterity; and the day is not yet come that is to decide on which part of the page of that book will be written the glory or the shame of this day.

It is important to the State that you of the majority should be right, and that I should be wrong. However much personal gratification I might feel hereafter in finding that I was right on this great question, and that you were wrong, that gratification would indeed be to me a poor consolation in the midst of a ruined and desolated country. Therefore, as the passage of the Ordinance of Secession is the act by which the destiny of Alabama is to be controlled, I trust that you are right, and that I am wrong. I trust that God has inspired you with His wisdom, and that, under the influence of this Ordinance, the State of Alabama may rise to the highest pinnacle of national grandeur.

To show, sir, that the declarations I now make are not forced by the exigencies of this hour, I read one of the resolutions from the platform upon which I was elected to this Convention:

"*Resolved*, That we hold it to be our duty, *first*, to use all honorable exertions to *secure* our rights in the Union, and if we should fail in this, we *will maintain* our rights *out of the Union* —for, as citizens of Alabama, we owe our allegiance first to the State; and we will support her in whatever course she may adopt."

Thus, Mr. President, you will observe that the course I now take is the result of the greatest deliberation, having been matured before I was a candidate for a seat in this Convention; and there is a perfect understanding on this subject between me and my constituents.

It but remains for me to add, that when your Ordinance passes through the solemn forms of legislative deliberation, and receives the sanction of this body, I shall recognize it as the supreme law of the land; my scruples will fall to the ground; and that devotion, which I have heretofore, through the whole course of my public life, given to the Union of the States, shall be concentrated in my allegiance to the State of Alabama.

Mr. GREEN said:

He would vote against the Ordinance, but would sustain the action of the Convention. His people would ratify and fully endorse it. Mr. G. spoke feelingly, and said he hoped the people of Alabama would be a unit.

He had been elected as a coöperationist; and would now greatly prefer a consultation with the slaveholding States before he severed the bonds of the Union. But, he would not withhold his acquiescence from the will of a majority here, however much he might be convinced, in his own mind, of the propriety of coöperation. In this great day of interest, it becomes all good men to be united in the same ranks to promote the general welfare of the people, and to oppose our enemies in a solid and determined body.

MR. KIMBALL said:

Mr. President—The passage of the Ordinance is now a settled fact; and I do not rise, sir, to make factious opposition to its passage. It is due to myself, it is a duty I owe the people whom I represent on this floor, that I should express to this body, the power delegated to me by my people. Now, sir, I represent in part, thirty-three hundred votes, as good and true people to the South as lives on Alabama soil. It is true they were opposed to separate secession; that opposition, nevertheless, made them none the less opposed to Black Republicanism; but in my opinion, the more effectual. In all my intercourse with my fellow-citizens, I found none who did not cordially desire a united South, not a dissenting voice. In the "Advertizer" of this morning, I find a dispatch expressing the opinion of Gen. Scott, who is said to be the great War Spirit, who unhesitatingly says, that with a certain unanimity of the Southern States, it would be impolitic and improper to attempt coercion. This is the effect we expected to consummate by the action of coöperation. We believed it would be effectual with less loss of blood and treasure. Now, sir, to show our sincerity in effectual resistance, I read from the platform, published to the people, on which we went before them for the position we occupy on this floor. One of the resolutions in said platform, says:

"That in order to secure the coöperation of the South as a unit, and justify ourselves in the eyes of the world, we consider it wise and politic that a general Convention of all the Southern States should be called to adopt an ultimatum to the Northern Republicans, and that unless such ultimatum so presented be adopted, that then our safety, and the preservation of our rights, demand that those rights should be maintained, even if it result in the secession of the State of Alabama and the rupture of the Union."

Now, sir, this shows a laudable effort on the part of the people of Tallapoosa, to avoid the horrors of war by securing a united action of the South on an ultimatum. The rejection of which, would certainly greatly tend to our unanimity—a most desirable object.

Another objection I have to the passage of the Ordinance, under existing circumstances, is the evident disposition and settled purpose of this Convention not to submit this Ordinance to the people for their rejection or ratification. It is right and proper, this should be done. The sovereign people of the State of Alabama, on a great question of this sort, should be consulted; they are the parties whose interest is to be affected. In this opinion all parties were agreed, and I now read the resolution to which none (of the candidates,) in Tallapoosa objected:

"That the Sovereignty of Alabama remains with the people thereof, and that the result of the Convention called by the Governor, let it be what it may, should be referred back to the people for their rejection or ratification."

As one of the Committee of Thirteen, I desired this should be done; but as this Convention has decreed otherwise, as a loyal citizen of Alabama, I must yield; and I am satisfied my constituents will concur, and will stand by Alabama in weal and woe.

Mr. Johnson said:

Mr. President—Similar reasons to those assigned by gentlemen as having influenced them in arriving at the conclusion to sustain the Ordinance when passed, has operated upon and influenced me in forming a similar conclusion. This question differs very materially from all ordinary political questions. To have opposed the policy of separate State secession, before any action taken or expression given by this Convention, was certainly legitimate, and, I think, wise; but having ascertained that there is a well-defined majority of this body in favor of that policy, further resistance should cease.

It is either factious or revolutionary, or both; and hence, in my opinion, should not be persisted in.

The minority of this body, with which I have acted, have voluntarily and patriotically pledged themselves, unanimously, to resist abolition aggression.

We have had an opportunity of expressing our preference as to the mode and measure of resistance which we would offer to present and anticipated aggressions.

We preferred the calling of a Convention of all, or as many of the slaveholding States, as would meet us in such Convention, in order that we might avail ourselves of their counsel, their grievances, and their simultaneous action. This Convention decided that to be impracticable.

Then, sir, acting upon the principle that the people are sovereign, and should be permitted to exercise their inalienable right to supervise the action of their agents, in a matter involving their dearest rights and destiny, we proposed to refer the action of this Convention to the people, for their ratification or rejection.

This was decided to be impolitic or unnecessary. Having thus failed, sir, to induce the Convention to adopt our policy or mode of resistance, the alternative is presented: Will we adopt Secession as a mode of resistance? or will we say to the world that we prefer Submission to this mode of resisting abolition aggression?

I prefer secession to submission, and will not only sustain your Ordinance when passed, but will go farther, and say that, if responsibility attaches to its passage, I will share that responsibility.

I will vote for the ordinance, believing that Talladega county is unwilling to shun a responsibility which other counties of the State are willing to assume. The entire delegation from Talladega, as well as those from Coosa, will vote for the Ordinance.

We are not influenced, in casting this vote, by a desire to conciliate the majority here, or to obtain popularity elsewhere, for the records of this body will show our preference, and views as to the mode of resistance which should be adopted. We desire that our common enemy should know and appreciate, that so far as relates to a determination to resist their aggression, there is but one feeling in Alabama: and although we may and do differ as to the means by which we will protect our rights and our institutions, yet I wish them to see and feel that, although our line of policy is rejected by a majority of a Convention of that people, yet we will accept another means and another policy.

I have no hesitancy in saying, sir, that I believe the entire people of Alabama will sustain this Ordinance when passed, and I humbly hope we may go on in our course of greatness and prosperity, and that this action may redound to the honor and interest of the entire people.

Mr. WATKINS said:

Mr. President—The Ordinance before us, proposing the severance of this State from a Government so deeply rooted in the affections of the people, is a matter of such grave concern, and involves so many great and vital considerations, as to make it necessary that I, in common with others who have preceded me, should say something touching the vote I am about to give.

A native of one of the Southern States, who, for more than twenty years of continued residence in this State, has enjoyed her beneficence and protection, because wedded to her soil, identified with her institutions, and, withal, jealous of her honor and watchful in guarding against any infraction of the rights of her people, I feel it to be a duty, no less of affection than gratitude, on this great occasion, to declare the most devoted fealty to her, and to pledge all I have and am in her behalf, whatever may be her fate.

The constituency I represent—with whose sentiments I fully

coincide—are deeply and strongly attached to the Union of the American States; and, although they acknowledge and feel that grievous evils exist, which call for prompt and efficient resistance, they believe that a more satisfactory, safe, and effective remedy can be had, by a coöperative effort on the part of all the Southern States, than by the more desperate and hazardous expedient of separate State secession, proposed in the Ordinance before this Convention. I shall vote against the Ordinance, in obedience to the will of the people I represent, and will cheerfully await the verdict of the future as to the wisdom which actuates it.

MR. BEARD said:

Mr. President—I came to this Convention a warm friend to the policy of consulting and coöperating with all the slaveholding States, or with as many of them as would agree to meet us for the purpose of consultation. I have labored faithfully to carry out my desires—as much so as any member here; and I still believe that that would be the best, safest and wisest course for Alabama to adopt in this trying emergency. But my opinions in this regard will not lead me to stubborness in my opposition to what this Convention, in its wisdom, may decide to do. That I am, and have been, in favor of resistance to the rule of Black Republicanism, has already been shown by my vote on the resolution which was adopted by this Convention on the first day of our meeting. If this Convention shall decide on immediate secession, as the surest and wisest mode of resistance; and if, in the wisdom of the counsel that prevails here, it shall be decided that this is the remedy for the surest redress of our grievances, while I may not agree to endorse this with my vote, I am the last man in the State of Alabama who would lift a voice of opposition to your decree. I will acquiesce in your action, and I will support, heartily, the State of Alabama, in all the difficulties that may beset her now or hereafter, so long as I am able to raise my voice in her councils or my arm in her defense. And I can safely say as much for the people of my county—who, though by a large majority, have been in favor of coöperation and consultation with the slaveholding States, yet they will earnestly support the State of Alabama in all her troubles, even though the necessities of the times should call them to take up arms, and to muster in the ranks of the army in military array. I, as well as they, will be prepared, under whatever emergencies may arise, to shoulder my musket and to do as good service for our country as any man on this floor. We will be found to be in the rear of none in our readiness to *act* when the moment of danger comes.

I shall vote against the Ordinance of Secession, but to that extent alone will my opposition be carried.

Mr. STEELE said:

That he would stand with the bravest and truest of Alabama's sons in support of the action of the Convention, and in defence of the honor and independence of Alabama. Though opposed to the Ordinance, and in favor rather of the policy of consulting with the other slaveholding States, yet he would not carry his opinion so far as to embarrass, in any manner, the will of the majority of the delegates in this Convention. In the hour of danger he would know no country but Alabama; and he would be ready, he hoped, to show his allegiance, in some practical way, whenever the State should need his services.

Mr. CRUMPLER said, in substance:

[Speaking for himself and colleagues,] that he and his colleagues were elected on the coöperation ticket, and had acted and voted with the coöperation party on every measure before the Convention. He now felt it to be his duty, with the facts before him, to vote for the Ordinance of Secession and the resolutions. His colleagues, Col. Taylor and Maj. Leonard, would cheerfully vote with him. We pledge ourselves to do all in our power to induce our constituents to sustain and fully sanction the action of the Convention, believing now that Secession is the only proper and effectual mode of resistance. Our first plan being defeated, we feel bound to vote for prompt and immediate secession—that being the only effectual plan now left us by which to preserve our rights, our honor, our equality and our liberties. Let all patriotic citizens now UNITE AND RALLY, AS ONE PEOPLE, around the standard of free and independent Alabama, and all will be well.

Mr. CLARK, of Laurence, said:

After having manifested by my remarks of yesterday, a more decided opposition to the passage of the Ordinance of Secession than any other member of this Convention, the observations I am about to make, I trust, may not be deemed wholly inopportune. Sir, I have loved, honored and revered the Union of our fathers. I have cherished it for the good it has accomplished—the liberty it has secured, and the public and private prosperity it has dispensed. The treasure expended in its defence, the privations patriotically endured, and the many heroic lives voluntarily sacrificed to purchase the blessings it affords, I have never forgotten, and can never forget.

Where now are Columbia's classics? What becomes of her legends and her traditions? Where are her anniversaries—her Bunker Hills, her Lexingtons, her Yorktowns? Where, her national airs—her hymns of freedom? Entombed in the storied urns and sepulchres of the Past.

These recollections will be treasured up in the hearts of our countrymen as the sacred mementoes of a dead friend. They are Liberty's bright gems, sprinkled upon the page of oblivion, which patriotism, in after years, will delight to gather and string around the neck of memory. I have opposed the Secession movement from its incipiency to its completion. Coöperative action I have thought was the better policy, and my opinion is, now, unchanged. I shall vote against the Ordinance. But when the Ordinance shall become the LAW of the State, the same reasons which have been urged with so much force against Secession, apply with equal cogency in favor of acquiescence. Resistance to this Ordinance could only result in strife and dissension among our people. If any one believes that I would be guilty of inciting hostile divisions between different sections of the State, and thus enkindle the flames of civil war throughout the borders of Alabama, he has very much mistaken his man.

MR. EDWARDS said:

Mr. President—I have opposed the passage of the Ordinance of Secession in every honorable way that I possibly could. I am opposed to separate State action, but to carry this opposition further, is wholly unnecessary now in this Convention. I have opposed it, sir, because I believed such a course unwise on the part of Alabama. Again, I oppose its passage because in all cases where the fundamental principles of Government are to be changed, such changes should be submitted to the people for their approval or disapproval. It is contended by the friends of the Ordinance, that the majority of the people have spoken out in regard to this matter; but, sir, this is doubtful. Then, sir, as there are some doubts in regard to which way the majority stands in this particular case, I do contend, that the action of the Convention ought to be submitted to the people for their adoption or rejection at the ballot-box. Mr. President, the people whom I have the honor to represent upon this floor, did not presume to think that this Convention would pass an Ordinance of Secession without its reference to them; but, sir, they, together with many others in Northern Alabama, will be greatly disappointed in that respect. My constituents made it obligatory upon me, to use my best exertions to have the action of the Convention referred to them. This I have done to the best of my ability. But I, together with the party with whom I have acted, have signally failed. Inasmuch, therefore, as the action of the Convention is final, I am not prepared at this time to say, whether the people of my county will acquiesce in it or not. I know, sir, they are excited to a considerable extent, and when the news reaches my county that Alabama has seceded from the Union, I anticipate the excitement will run much higher.

Sir, when I return home, I am in duty bound, to state to my fellow-citizens the action of this Convention, and in doing so, I will here state, that I will use no effort on my part to excite them to rebellion.

Mr. RALLS said:

Mr. President—I rise not for the purpose of making a speech, but simply a remark or two. My position as a delegate, is in some respects peculiar. I am not a coöperation secessionist.

The people who have sent me here have no demands to make of the North. One of the resolutions adopted at the meeting nominating me, was that secession was the only remedy.

Straight-out, was the phrase used in the canvass, instead of separate State action; although it was explained to the people that every State must act for itself, as one State could not for another. One word as to the term *straight-out*. At the time I was nominated, the Union was unbroken, and the subsequent action of South Carolina furnished an example of straight-out secession, as understood by my people; that is to say, secession without an assurance that any other State would assume the same attitude; and against this I was pledged.

Now, what are the circumstances by which we are surrounded? South Carolina is out; so also is Florida; so also is Mississippi; and there can be no doubt that Georgia, my native State, will take the same proud position next week, and that Louisiana and Texas will follow in rapid succession. Yea, Mr. President, may I not go a step further and say, that there is good ground to hope that the border slaveholding States will wheel into line and unite their destiny with the extreme Southern or cotton States?

I find then around me the coöperation that my constituents desire—that is, coöperation in seceding.

That these seceding States, impelled by a common danger, and attracted by common interests and sympathies, will unite again in the establishment of a republican form of government, thus securing the liberty and peace of the people, is in my mind, a question that admits of no doubt. This opinion has been long entertained, publicly expressed, and the developments of every day confirm me in it.

The way is clear. I shall vote for the Ordinance.

MR. SHEFFIELD said:

Mr. President—I rise with great diffidence, on this occasion, knowing my inability to do justice to the subject before the Convention. I merely wish to state my position before the vote is taken on the Ordinance. I have known, for days, that the Ordinance would pass.. I have used every exertion to prevent it, but without a hope of success. I have written home to my constituents, that such would be the case, and asking them whether, in that event, they desired me to sign it. As an individual, I will sustain the action of my State, honestly and zealously; and if war should come, I will not only counsel my people to submit to the decision of the Convention, but to maintain it with arms in the field. I have opposed secession as long as opposition was of any avail. Now that the Ordinance will pass, as a patriot, I feel bound to take the side of my native State in any contest which might grow out of it. I will vote against the Ordinance.

MR. POTTER said:

Mr. President—Sir, as every member of this body must necessarily take position, either for or against this measure, by the vote which will very soon be cast, I feel in duty bound to offer some reasons why my vote shall be cast against the passage of this Ordinance at the present time.

Sir, the decision which we make to-day upon this, in all human probability, the most momentous question that shall ever be settled by the people of Alabama, may, for weal or woe, tell more potently upon all ages to come, than any which will ever claim our consideration or demand our action.

Now, sir, I desire to say to the members of this honorable body, that when I first entered this Hall I came with decided convictions as to the true policy of our State, in the present emergency; and I am now prepared to state that nothing which has occurred here, nor any developments which have been made elsewhere, have at all changed my previous opinion.

I maintain now, as I have maintained before, that separate State secession, if a remedy at all for our political grievances, is not the only remedy—nay, is not the best remedy. And laboring as I do under this conviction, I cannot advocate the adoption of this measure, until I become convinced of my error.

Sir, there are a few plain, simple propositions which should claim the serious consideration of every member of this Convention.

First—Our grievances should be redressed. This is what we all desire, and only differ in regard to the proper method to be adopted. For one, I have not been able to see that secession is the best mode, and therefore I cannot adopt it.

Second—All our rights should be secured and maintained. It cannot be denied that our rights and interests have been disregarded and set at nought by many of our sister States. But can we come up to the full measure of duty, and secure all to which we are entitled by the act of secession? I think not; and therefore I cannot adopt it as our true policy.

Third—It is very desirable to have security at home. Will secession give us this? It may, or it may not. And it really appears to me, sir, that in this respect we are about to make a very doubtful experiment, which may lead to a most disastrous result. And as there does not appear, to me, to be any positive necessity for taking this course now, in justice to myself, and to those whom I represent, I feel called upon to oppose it.

Fourth—Our honor should be vindicated. Now, sir, if secession can be shown to be the best means of its vindication, then will be presented at least one powerful argument in favor of this measure. But I must confess, sir, that to my mind, the truth of this proposition has not yet been shown. There is among men a morbid sense of honor which often leads them to extremes, and involves them in disgrace while they vainly seek to maintain their false views of true honor. Against these false views and fatal extremes, it is the part of wisdom for us to be carefully guarded. Entertaining these views of propriety and prudence, I cannot do otherwise, under present circumstances, than withhold my support from a measure whose wisdom and policy are so doubtful.

Fifth—We ought to do ourselves justice. Now, it is apparent to me, sir, that the act of secession will cost us such a sacrifice of interest in the public property of the United States, as will do the people of Alabama great injustice. If, sir, this were the only line of policy possible to be pursued, then we should adopt it at once, let it cost what it might; but until we are fully satisfied that no better line of policy can be pursued, we should hesitate to adopt a measure so hazardous in itself, and involving so great a sacrifice.

Sixth—We wish to perpetuate Southern institutions. This, sir, is an imperative duty which we owe to ourselves and to posterity. And the great question for us to solve, is this: Will secession secure the perpetuity of these institutions? Sir, I am so well satisfied that there is a better way, a more certain method of securing this object, so desirable, nay, so necessary, that I cannot give my consent to the adoption of this extreme measure.

Seventh—We want harmony among ourselves. This, sir, is of so much importance to our success, that, so far as possible, it ought to be secured. In view of the conflicting opinions now so prevalent, I am unable to see how it is possible to do justice to public sentiment if we now pass this Ordinance, and refuse to refer the action of this Convention to the people of the State for their ratification or rejection. And this, sir, will evidently be the result, if this measure shall be sustained by a majority of this body. For these, and other reasons not mentioned, I am constrained, sir, to act upon the principle that what my judgment condemns my hand shall not indorse. I therefore vote in the negative.

Mr. Bulger said:

Mr. President—Being as I am among the oldest, as well as the humblest of the members of this Convention, it is perhaps proper that I should be one of the last to speak on this, the most important question that has ever been debated in the State of Alabama. Sir, believing as I do, that separate State secession is unwise and impolitic, and not a remedy for any wrong of which we complain in the Union, I deem it unnecessary for me at this time to attempt an array of reasons that bring me to this conclusion. This I did before the people that sent me here. When we had an exciting contest, I told my friends that secession was a vital issue, that they should consider coolly; that if it was decided against them, it would become their duty to acquiesce; that we were all on board of a common bark—if it foundered and went down, we must all go down together; that we could not, if we would, separate our destiny from those with whom we differed. And now, sir, finding as I do, that secession, immediate and separate, without reference to the people for their ratification or rejection, is a foregone conclusion, and having voted against every proposition leading to that conclusion, except one, on which I was prevented voting by severe indisposition, I will now content myself with recording my vote against the final act of secession. Having done so, I will have discharged my whole duty to those whom I represent on this floor. The act of secession having been consummated by the majority of this Convention, whether rightfully or wrongfully, it becomes the action of Alabama; I feel it to be my duty to cease all opposition to that act, and coöperate with the majority, to the best of my ability, in reconstructing a Government adapted to the new state of affairs by which we are surrounded. That done, my first and paramount allegiance is due to the State of Alabama; and if an attempt be made to coerce or invade her, although I am advanced beyond the ordinary age of a soldier, I will seek some humble position in an army of defense, where I can render some service in support of the rights, the interests and the honor of my country.

Mr. WINSTON said, in substance:

That he would say a few words, now that the important measure for which the Convention was called, was about to be disposed of; that he was opposed to the hasty step about to be taken, and should record his vote against it; that the die was cast—it was the determination of the majority of the Convention to pass the Ordinance of Immediate Secession. That being the will of this Convention, the sovereignty of Alabama, sink or swim, live or die, survive or perish, the same destiny awaited all. He represented a constituency opposed to this hasty dissolution of the best Government the world ever knew; they were a brave and patriotic people, and notwithstanding their veneration for the Union of their Fathers, they, he had no doubt, would acquiesce in and sustain their State in this its final determination; and will rally to the standard of Alabama whenever their services shall be needed to repel Black Republican force, should the same ever be employed to subjugate them. He had contended, and so declared by his vote, that this Ordinance about to be passed, should be referred to the people for their approval or rejection, and that an effort should be made, in the Union, to adjust our existing difficulties with the North, by calling a Convention of all the slaveholding States, and proposing as an ultimatum certain concessions to be made by the Northern people, which, if not granted, then to separate. But these had been voted down by the majority of the Convention, and now the Ordinance of Immediate Secession was about to be passed by that same majority, severing the link which binds Alabama to the Federal Union, and no alternative is now left the minority but to acquiesce in that determined act of the majority. This done, Alabama stands forth as an independent sovereignty—in anticipation of which event, he had written to his son, then a cadet at the military academy at West Point, to resign his position there and return home, that he might unite his destiny with that of his native State—that for nearly two years in that excellent school, the knowledge he had acquired of military tactics might be of some service in the approaching stormy times. He assured gentlemen that whatever glory might attach to this act of precipitation, would belong to the leaders of that movement—to all of which they were most clearly entitled.

In conclusion, he was then ready to record his vote against it.

Mr. DAVIS of Madison, said:

Mr. President—I, too, have a word to say upon this occasion. I cannot remain unmoved amid such solemn occurrences. I shall speak briefly and I hope frankly. It cannot be denied that circumstances have greatly changed since this Convention met on last Monday. We have seen State after State, in the exercise of its sovereign powers, withdrawing from the Union in the few past days. Florida has seceded; Mississippi has seceded—each by overwhelming majorities. It is now no longer a serious apprehension that Alabama will stand alone in this movement of secession. It is confidently asserted that Georgia and Louisiana and Texas will follow. Under this aspect of the case, it is not remarkable that a great change has also come over the Convention—a change clearly indicated by the speeches that have been this day delivered in this hall.

I shall vote against the Ordinance. But if Alabama shall need the strong arm of her valorous sons to sustain her in any emergency which, on account of this Ordinance of Secession, may arise within her borders, by which her honor or the rights of her citizens are likely to be endangered, I say for myself and for my constituents—and I dare say for all North Alabama—that I and they will be cheerfully ready to take our part in the conflict. We may not indorse the wisdom of your resolves, but we will stand by the State of Alabama under all circumstances.

Mr. YANCEY said:

Mr. President—If no other gentleman desires to address the Convention, I will exercise the usual parliamentary privilege accorded to the Chairman of the Committee reporting a measure—that of closing the debate by assigning a few reasons why the measure before you should be adopted. In common with all others here, I feel that this is a solemn hour, and I congratulate the Convention that the spirit that prevails is both fraternal and patriotic—that whatever of irritation or suspicion had prevailed in the earlier hours of our session, has been, in a great degree, dissipated, and has given way to a juster appreciation of the motives and the conduct of each other. In the Committee, the majority yielded to the minority all the time that they desired for deliberation; and since the report has been made, the majority in the Convention has also yielded to the wishes of the minority in this respect, and every delegate, who desired to do so, has addressed the Convention in explanation of his vote, and has taken as much time as, in his judgment, was necessary to his purpose. If, in the earlier stages of our proceedings, it has been thought, as it has been said by some gentlemen, that an undue celerity of movement was pressed by the majority, I beg those gentlemen to believe that this conduct on our part was dictated solely by our convictions of duty, and not from any—the least desire to precipitate others into a vote, before they were prepared to give it understandingly. Time was deemed, by the friends of independent State action, to be either success or defeat in the inauguration of this great movement—success, if there was a prompt and unequivocal withdrawal from this Union—or defeat, if time was used to delay and to dishearten. You who were opposed to such action, from a sense of duty, would necessarily be for all such delays as would aid in accomplishing its defeat; we who were for it, from a like sense of duty, were necessarily in favor of a prompt decision of the question. Each has acted, doubtless, upon well-founded ideas of duty. All that was necessary to a better understanding of each other, was a belief in that fact, a belief in the good faith of each other; and I rejoice that to-day has furnished ample evidence that we now mutually entertain that belief; and, on the part of the majority, I return sincere thanks to the venerable delegate from Lauderdale, [Mr. POSEY,] who, though compelled to vote against this Ordinance, yet has characterized the conduct of the majority in this matter, as giving evidence of "wisdom, discretion, and a spirit of conciliation."

As to the measure itself, [the Ordinance and Resolutions,] whatever of merit it possesses, is the result of consultation between the majority and minority of the Committee. I am sure that the members of that Committee will indulge me in alluding to what passed in its sessions. The majority decidedly preferred to adopt a simple Ordinance of Secession. But determined, for the sake of harmony, to do all in their power to disarm prejudice, and to bring about a fraternal feeling, they did not hesitate to yield their own cherished desire in this particular, when my friend from Madison [Mr. Clemens] proposed to amend our proposed Ordinance by adding thereto the preamble and resolutions, which form a part of his report. It is well known that some of the people have been led to believe that the friends of secession desired to erect Alabama either into a monarchy, or into an independent State, repudiating an alliance with other States. As for myself, I can truly declare that I have never met with any friend of secession, entertaining such views. The proposition submitted by my friend from Madison, [Mr. Clemens,] being in perfect accordance with the wishes and desires of the majority, and amply refuting these misconceptions, the one which we would have preferred to have voted upon separately, was at once agreed to, and the result is, the measure now before us for consideration.

On the first day of our session a resolution was unanimously adopted, declaring that the people of this State would resist the administration of Lincoln for the causes and upon the principles there enunciated. On the question of resistance, then, there is no difference in this Body—all are for resistance. But there is a difference between members as to the mode, the manner of resistance. Some believe that when the rights of our people are denied or assailed by the parties to the Federal compact, or by the Federal Government, that secession from this compact is the rightful remedy. Others believe that secession is wrong, and that the remedy is revolution. A careful reading of the Ordinance on your table will show, that the resistance therein provided may be called revolution, disunion, or secession, as each member may desire. The caption styles it "an Ordinance to dissolve the Union," &c. In the body of the Ordinance, the people of the State are "withdrawn from the compact," &c. It is true, that the mode of resistance is organic; it is an organic coöperation, not of States, but of the people of this State in resistance to wrong. In this respect it harmonizes differences. Another difference, both in the popular mind and in that of delegates, is, that resistance should be by coöperation of States, and not by independent State action. That difference has been harmonized by the conjunction of the Ordinance and Resolutions, as reported by the Committee. Coöperation and separate State action, as far as they can be effected, under our obligation to the Federal compact and in harmony with the principles of State sovereignty, have been joined in this measure. It is true, there are a class of coöperationists, whose views are not met by this measure—those who have advocated coöperation to secure submission—to defeat resistance. But there are none of that character here. While the friends of independent

State action in this Ordinance do obtain a declaration as to the rights of the people of Alabama; and as to our determination to sustain them, the friends of coöperation, for the purpose of effectual resistance, also obtain a declaration of our desire and purpose to unite with all of the slaveholding States who entertain a like purpose, in confederated or coöperative resistance, and in a confederated government upon the principles of the Federal Constitution.

As far as it was possible, then, to do so, without yielding principles, the friends of resistance have used every reasonable effort to meet on a common ground. And I rejoice in the belief that the effort has been successful, and that there will be a far greater unanimity manifested when the vote shall be taken on this measure, than was even hoped for, when we first met in this Hall — From the remarks of gentlemen to-day, many will be compelled to vote against this measure by reason of instructions of their people, who otherwise would vote for it. I sincerely respect these motives, and think that those occupying such positions act correctly in their premises.

Mr. President, we are fortunate in having the example of our Revolutionaay fathers sustaining the plan of action here proposed —separate State action and then coöperation in confederating together. South Carolina, after several months deliberation, with a view to resisting British aggression, formed a State government early in the year 1776. Virginia did so in June, 1776, declaring her separate and independent secession from the Government of Great Britain. Afterwards, on the 4th of July, 1776, the Congress of the United States agreed upon and adopted a joint Declaration of Independence. It was after the colonies had acted separately and independently, that both the Declaration of Independence and the Articles of Confederation and the Constitution of the United States were severally adopted.

The friends of independent State action have also cause to congratulate themselves, that as far as the people of the Southern States have spoken, they have unanimously expressed themselves in favor of independent State action.

South Carolina, Mississippi, and Florida, have each already acted independently. In this Convention a majority are known to be in favor of that kind of action. We have already received information that a majority of delegates in favor of such action has been elected, both in Georgia and Louisiana. I commend this significant fact to all who feel disposed to condemn an independent State movement.

Some have been disposed to think that this is a movement of

politicians, and not of the people. This is a great error. Who, on a calm review of the past, and reflection upon what is daily occurring, can reasonably suppose that the people of South Carolina, Georgia, Florida, Alabama, Mississippi and Louisiana who have already elected conventions favorable to dissolution, and the people of Arkansas, Tennessee, North Carolina and Virginia were contemplating an assembling in their several conventions, have been mere puppets in the hands of politicians? Who can for a moment thus deliberately determine that all these people, in these various States, who are so attached to their government, have so little intelligence that they can be thus blindly driven into revolution, without cause, by designing and evil minded men, against the remonstrances of conservative men? No, sir! This is a great popular movement, based upon a wide-spread, deep-seated conviction that the forms of government have fallen into the hands of a sectional majority, determined to use them for the destruction of the rights of the people of the South. This mighty flood-tide has been flowing from the popular heart for years. You, gentlemen of the minority, have not been able to repress it. We of the majority have not been able to add a particle to its momentum. We are each and all driven forward upon this irresistible tide. The rod that has smitten the rock from which this flood flows, has not been in Southern hands. The rod has been Northern and sectional aggression and wrong, and that flood-tide has grown stronger and stronger as days and years have passed away, in proportion as the people have lost all hope of a constitutional and satisfactory solution of these vexed questions. In this connection, I would say a few words upon the proposition to submit the Ordinance of Dissolution to a popular vote. This proposition is based upon the idea that there is a difference between the people and the delegate. It seems to me that this is an error. There is a difference between the representatives of the people in the law-making body and the people themselves, because there are powers reserved to the people by the Convention of Alabama, and which the General Assembly cannot exercise. But in this body is all power—no powers are reserved from it. The people are here in the persons of their deputies. Life, Liberty and Property are in our hands. Look to the Ordinance adopting the Constitution of Alabama. It states " we the people of Alabama," &c., &c. All our acts are supreme, without ratification, because they are the acts of the people acting in their sovereign capacity. As a policy, submission of this Ordinance to a popular vote is wrong.

In the first place, we have gone too far to recede with dignity and self-respect. Such a submission involves delay dangerous to our safety. It could not well be effected before the 4th of March.

The policy is at war with our system of government. Ours is not a pure Democracy—that is a government by the people—though it is a government of the people. Ours is a representative government, and whatever is done by the representative in accordance with the Constitution is law; and whatever is done by the deputy in organizing government is the people's will.

The policy, too, is one of recent suggestion; if I am not mistaken, it was never proposed and acted upon previous to 1837. Certainly the Fathers did not approve it. The Constitutions of the original Thirteen States were adopted by Conventions, and were never referred to the people.

The Constitution of the United States was adopted by the several State Conventions, and in no instance was it submitted to the people for ratification. Coming down to a later day, and coming home to the action of our State sires, we find another example against such submission. The Constitution of the State of Alabama was never submitted for popular ratification.

One other and most important consideration is, that looking to the condition of the popular mind of the minority of the people on this question, such a course will but tend to keep up strife and contention among ourselves. Such a submission, it is clear to my mind, will but result in a triumph of the friends of secession—and an additional amount of irritation and prejudice be thus engaged in the minds of the defeated party. Some gentlemen seem to think that in dissolving the Union, we hazard the "rich inheritance" bequeathed to us. For one I make a distinction between our liberties and the powers which have been delegated to secure them. Those liberties have never been alienated—are inalienable. The State Governments were formed to secure and protect them. The Federal Government was made the common agent of the States, for the purpose of securing them in our intercourse with each other, and the foreign powers. The course we are about to adopt makes no war on our liberties—nor indeed upon our institutions—nor upon the Federal Constitution. It is but a dismissal of the agent that first abuses our institutions with a view to destroy our rights, and then turns the very powers we delegated to him for our protection against us for our injury. These powers were originally possessed by the people of the sovereign States, and when the common agent abuses them, it seems to me but the dictate of common sense, as well as an act of self-preservation, that the States should withdraw and resume them.

The Ordinance withdraws those once delegated by Alabama—and the resolutions accompanying it, propose to meet our sister

States in Convention, and to confederate with them on the basis of the very Constitution, which was the bond of compact and union between Alabama, and the other States of the Union. We propose to do as the Israelites did of old, under Divine direction —to withdraw our people from under the power that oppresses them, and, in doing so, like them, to take with us the Ark of the Covenant of our liberties.

There is but one more point upon which I desire to say a few words. My venerable friend from Lauderdale, asked us to forbear pressing the minority to sign the Ordinance. In my opinion it is not a necessity that it be signed by members. Its signature does not necessarily express approval of the act. Signing it is but an act of attestation, in one sense, as when the President of the Senate signs an act of the General Assembly, which he has voted against. I am willing to vote for all reasonable delay, to enable members to consult their constituents. But I beseech gentlemen to bear in mind that when the Ordinance shall be signed, the absence of the signatures of any members will be a notice to our enemies that we are divided as a people—and that there are those in our midst who will not support the State in its hour of peril. The signature of the Ordinance, while waiving no vote given against it—while giving up no opinion, is an evidence of the highest character that the signer will support his country.

It will give dignity, strength, unity to the State in which we live, and by which each of its citizens should be prepared to die, if its exigencies demand it. I now ask that the vote may be taken.

Mr. CLEMENS said:

Mr. President—In many of the sentiments just expressed by the gentleman from Montgomery, [Mr. Yancey,] I concur; in many of them I do not concur; and I think it would have been much better if many of them had not been expressed.

I have a word or two, sir, which I wish to say, before the final vote is taken upon the Ordinance, giving my reasons for my vote—but I would prefer to state those reasons when my name is called.

When Mr. CLEMENS' name was called, he said:

Mr. President—Each member of this Convention, however unpretending may have been the obscurity of his past life, this day writes a name in history which will endure long after we ourselves shall have passed from the stage of action. In honor or reproach; in glory or in shame, there it is stamped, and stamped forever. Under such circumstances, I feel that a word of explanation as to my course, will not be out of place.

I shall vote for this Ordinance; but frankness and fairness requires me to say that I would not vote for it, if its passage depended upon that vote. If it was left to me to decide whether this plan of resistance, or another, should be adopted, I have already indicated a strong preference for that other which you have voted down.

As matters now stand, my vote will not affect the decision of the question here in one way or the other. I am looking beyond this hall, and beyond this hour. The act you are about to commit, is, to my apprehension, treason, and subjects you, if unsuccessful, to all the pains and penalties pronounced against that highest political crime, or noblest political virtue, according to the motives which govern its commission. Whatever may be my opinion of the wisdom and justice of the course pursued by the majority, I do not choose that any man shall put himself in danger of a halter in defence of the honor and rights of my native State, without sharing that danger with him.

I give this vote, therefore, partly as an assurance that I intend in good faith to redeem the pledge which I have made again and again, in public or in private, in speeches, and through the press, that whenever the summons came to me to defend the soil of Alabama, whether it was at midnight, or at mid-day—whether I believe her right or wrong, it should be freely, promptly answered.

Sir, I never had a *doubt* as to the course it became me to take in such an emergency as this. I believe your Ordinance to be wrong—if I could defeat it, I would; but I know I cannot. It will pass, and when passed it becomes the act of the State of Alabama. As such, I will maintain and defend it against all and every enemy, as long as I have a hand to raise in its defence. As an earnest that I mean what I say, I am about to place myself in a position from which there can be no retreat.

I have other reasons, Mr. President, which I do not mention here, because to do so would in some measure counteract them. They are known to my friends, and there I shall leave them, until time and the course of events shall render their publication proper. For the present, it is enough to say that I am a son of Alabama; her destiny is mine; her people are mine; her enemies are mine. I see plainly enough, that clouds and storms are gathering above us; but when the thunder rolls and lightning flashes, I trust that I shall neither shrink nor cower—neither murmur nor complain. Acting upon the convictions of a life-time, calmly and deliberately I walk with you into revolution. Be its perils—be its privations—be its sufferings what they may, I share them with you, although as a member of this Convention I opposed your Ordinance. Side by side with yours, Mr. President, my name shall stand upon the original roll, and side by side with you I brave the consequences. I vote in the affirmative.

Mr. YANCEY, by leave of the Convention, corrected a clerical error in the resolution of the Ordinance, by changing "third" to "fourth" day of February.

The question being upon the adoption of the Preamble, Ordinance of Secession and Resolutions as amended, the vote was taken by ayes and noes, and they were adopted—ayes 61, noes 39.

Those who voted in the affirmative are: Messrs. Brooks, Baily, Baker, of Barbour, Baker, of Russell, Barnes, *Barclay*, Beck, Blue, Bolling, Bragg, Catterling, Clarke, of Marengo, Cochran, Coleman, *Clemens*, Crawford, Creech, Crook, *Crumpler*, Curtis, Daniel, Dargan, Davis, of Covington, Davis, of Pickens, Dowdell, Foster, Gibbons, Gilchrist, Hawkins, Henderson, of Macon, Henderson, of Pike, Herndon, Howard, Humphries, *Johnson*, Jewett, Ketchum, *Leonard*, Love, McClanahan, McPherson, McKinne, Morgan, Owens, Phillips, Ralls, Rives, Ryan, Shortridge, Silver, *Slaughter*, Smith, of Henry, Starke, Stone, *Taylor*, Watts, Webb, Whatley, Williamson, Yancey, Yelverton—61.

Those who voted in the negative are: Messrs. Allen, Beard, Brasher, Bulger, Coffey, Coman, Clarke, of Lawrence, Davis, of Madison, Earnest, Edwards, Ford, Forrester, Franklin, Gay, Greene, Guttery, Hood, Inzer, Jemison, Jones, of Lauderdale, Jons, of Fayette, Kimball, Lewis, McClellan, Posey, Potter, Russell, Sanford, Sheets, Sheffield, Smith, of Tuscaloosa, Stedham, Steele, Timberlake, Watkins, Whitlock, Wilson, Winston, Wood—39.

Those in *italics*, who voted for the passage of the Ordinance of Secession, were elected as coöperationists.

Mr. President BROOKS announced the result of the vote, and that the Ordinance of Secession was adopted, and that Alabama was a free, sovereign and independent State.

Mr. YELVERTON introduced the following resolution:

Resolved, That the secrecy be removed from the proceedings of this day, and that the President of the Convention be requested to telegraph the information of the passage of the ORDINANCE OF SECESSION to our members of Congress, and to the Governors of the slaveholding States.

Mr. YELVERTON'S Resolution was adopted, and by motion of Mr. Yancey, the doors were thrown open.

It would be difficult to describe with accuracy the scenes that presented themselves in and around the Capitol during this day. A vast crowd had assembled in the rotundo, eager to hear the announcement of the passage of the Ordinance. In the Senate Chamber, within the hearing of the Convention, the citizens and visitors had called a meeting; and the company was there addressed by several distinguished orators, on the great topic which was then engrossing the attention of the Convention. The wild shouts and the rounds of rapturous applause that greeted the speakers in this impromptu assembly, often broke in upon the ear of the Convention, and startled the grave solemnity that presided over its deliberations.

Guns had been made ready to herald the news, and flags had been prepared, in various parts of the city, to be hoisted upon a signal.

When the doors were thrown open, the lobby and galleries were filled to suffocation in a moment. The ladies were there in crowds, with visible eagerness to participate in the exciting scenes. With them, the love songs of yesterday had swelled into the political hosannas of to-day.

PRESENTATION OF THE FLAG.

Simultaneously with the entrance of the multitude, a magnificent Flag was unfurled in the centre of the Hall, so large as to reach nearly across the ample chamber! Gentlemen mounted upon tables and desks, held up the floating end, the better thus to be able to display its figures. The cheering was now deafening for some moments. It seemed really that there would be no end to the raptures that had taken possession of the company.

Mr. YANCEY addressed the Convention, in behalf of the ladies of Montgomery, who had deputed him to present to the Convention this Flag—the work of the ladies of Alabama. In the course of his speech he described the mottoes and devices of the flag, and paid a handsome tribute to the ardor of female patriotism.

The writer has to regret that he has been unable to obtain a copy of Mr. Yancey's speech, and that he has no notes from which he can make a satisfactory report of it.

Mr. DARGAN offered the following resolutions:

Resolved, That the flag presented by the ladies of Montgomery be received, and that the President of the Convention be requested to return to them the thanks of the Convention.

Resolved, That the flag shall hereafter be raised upon the Capitol, as indicative whenever the Convention shall be in open session.

Mr. SMITH, of Tuscaloosa, said:

Mr. President—I was not prepared for this surprise. I knew nothing of this intended presentation. The suddenness with which this gorgeous scene has been displayed before us, overwhelms me with emotions that impel me to give utterance to the sentiments that inspire me.

In looking upon this flag, a thousand memories throng my mind. The battle fields of my country are spread out before me—and amid the smoke and clamor of contending armies, I see floating above a gallant and triumphant soldiery, The Star-Spangled Banner:—a flag sacred to memory, embalmed in Southern song—baptised in the best blood of the greatest nations of the earth, and consecrated in history and in poetry as the herald of Liberty's grandest victories on the land and on the sea.

Under the *Star-Spangled Banner* still float a thousand ships, whose appearance is cheered in every port. Under the Star-Spangled Banner, battles have been won, whose victories, as they adorn the annals of an age, proclaim to posterity the untameable valor of an infant people. Under the Star-Spangled Banner, as the lurid eyes of the British Lion have grown dim, British swords have been surrendered:—and, in later days, in the ancient home of kings, on the dismantled towers of dismembered nations, the Star-Spangled Banner in triumph has been displayed.

In parting, shall we not salute it? Have we no gratitude for the past? No recollection of the glories that have been achieved under the glittering folds of the Star-Spangled Banner? No thanks for the fame that it has brought to the country? In the memory of the gallant soldiers that lie on the field of death, enshrouded in its folds; in the name of Perry and Decatur, of Lawrence and Jackson, and a long line of illustrious heroes—" Let him who has tears to shed, prepare to shed them now"—*now*, as we lower this glorious ensign of our once vaunted victories.

We accept *this Flag*. It is presented by the ladies of Alabama. I see upon it, a beautiful female face.

"Oh! woman! in our hours of ease,
Uncertain, coy, and hard to please,
And variable as the shade
By the light quivering aspen made;
When pain and sorrow wring the brow,
A ministering angel thou."

Presented by the daughters of Alabama! The history of the world teaches, that in times of trouble and danger to her country, woman is always in the van. Her heroism is reserved for revolutions. She has been known to tear the jewels from her ears, the diamonds from her neck, and the rings from her fingers, and sell them to buy bread for the starving soldier. Nay, in order to aid a struggling army, we see her cutting away the glorious locks that adorn her beauty, and consent even for them to become the "dowry of a second head." What wonder, then, that now, in these stirring times, when "grim visaged war" wrinkles the brow of Peace—what wonder that the daughters of Alabama should thus endeavor to impart to our veins the burning currents of their own enthusiasm! What wonder that they should strive, by these graceful devices of female ingenuity, to lift us up to the height of their own hallowed inspiration!

We accept this flag; and, though it glows with but a single star, may that star increase in magnitude and brilliancy, until it out-rivals the historic glories of the Star-Spangled Banner!

Mr. Dargan's resolutions were adopted, and the President deputed Mr. Baker, of Barbour, to return the thanks of the Convention to the ladies.

Mr. Baker ascended the President's stand, and in a very beautiful and appropriate speech returned to the ladies the thanks of the Convention for their patriotic present. This speech was eminently worthy of preservation. The writer of these pages has made several earnest but unsuccessful efforts to obtain a copy of it for publication.

Amid the wild enthusiasm that had taken as well possession of the hall as of the streets and the city, the Convention adjourned.

The roar of cannon was heard at intervals during the remainder of this eventful day. The new flag * of Alabama displayed its virgin features from the windows and towers of the surrounding houses; and the finest orators of the State, in harangues of congratulation, commanded until a late hour in the night the attention of shouting multitudes. Every species of enthusiasm prevailed. Political parties, which had so lately been standing in sullen antagonism, seemed for the time to have forgotten their differences of opinion; and one universal glow of fervent patriotism kindled the enraptured community.

---

* The writer will be pardoned for appropriating a corner on this page to the preservation of the Sonnet below. He knows of no better location for it. And perhaps only the fervor of such enthusiasm as prevailed at this time, could tolerate the extravagant hyperbole.

THE LOST PLEIAD FOUND.

Long years ago, at night, a female star
  Fled from amid the Spheres, and through the space
Of Ether, onward, in a flaming car,
  Held, furious, headlong, her impetuous race:
She burnt her way through skies; the azure haze
Of Heaven assumed new colors in her blaze:
Sparklets, emitted from her golden hair,
Diffused rich tones through the resounding air;
The neighboring stars stood mute, and wondered when
The erring Sister would return again:
Through Ages still they wondered in dismay;
But now, behold, careering on her way,
The long-lost PLEIAD! lo! she takes her place
On ALABAMA'S FLAG, and lifts her RADIANT FACE!

SIXTH DAY—JANUARY TWELFTH—OPEN SESSION.

Mr. Cochran, from the Committee to wait on the Commissioners from Georgia and Mississippi to this State, introduced to the Convention Gen. J. W. A. Sanford, Commissioner from the State of Georgia, who addressed the Convention upon the subject of his mission.

The Reporter regrets that he has been unable to procure a copy of Gen. Sanford's speech on this occasion. It was listened to by the Convention with profound attention. At the close of the address, there was an interesting colloquy between the Commissioner and Judge Posey, touching the coast defenses of Georgia.

Mr. Dargan read an Ordinance authorizing the Governor to raise one million of dollars for State purposes, by the issuance of State bonds, to run not less than five nor more than twenty years; and the bonds not to be sold at a discount.

Mr. Dargan said:

That there was a necessity to raise money. The people would see that such necessity existed, and their patriotism would be equal to the occasion. If Alabama lives, the bonds would be good; if Alabama dies, of course our property, which will be pledged for the bonds, will also die. He wished the people of Alabama to take the bonds, but people of other States should also have the privilege. In South Alabama he knew there was a great deal of money that was lying idle in the hands of trustees and others, which here would find a source of sound investment. He asked the reference of the Ordinance to the Committee of Finance, which was done.

The following dispatch was laid before the Convention, by the President:

CHARLESTON, January 12, 1861.

Large steamship off the bar, steaming up; supposed to be the Brooklyn. Expect a battle. R. B. RHETT, JR.

Mr. Watts placed before the Convention the following dispatch:

HUNTSVILLE, January 12, 1861.
To Gov. A. B. MOORE:
I leave for Montgomery to-day. It is absolutely certain that Tennessee will go with the South. L. P. WALKER.

Mr. Henderson, of Macon, offered the following Resolution, which was referred to the Committee on Foreign Relations:

Resolved, That the Committee on Foreign relations be instructed to inquire into the expediency of sending a special Commissioner, or Commissioners, to the Territories of New Mexico and Arizonia, for the purpose of securing, if possible, the annexation of those Territories to a Southern Confederacy, as new States, at the earliest practicable period.

A communication from the Governor was received and read, with reference to affairs at Pensacola, as follows:

EXECUTIVE DEPARTMENT, January 12, 1861.
To Hon. WM M. BROOKS, President State Convention:

Sir: The following resolution, passed by the Convention, has just been handed me by the Secretary of that body:

"*Resolved*, That the Governor be requested to communicate to the Convention any information he may have as to the condition of military operations near Pensacola."

I regret that it becomes my duty to inform the Convention that the Federal troops have deserted the Navy Yard and Fort Barancas, and now occupy Fort Pickens, with about eighty men. The guns are spiked at Barancas and the Navy Yard, and the Public Stores removed to Fort Pickens. This fort commands Fort Barancas and the Navy Yard, and can only be taken by an effective force, and by bold and skillful movements.

Fort Pickens was garrisoned on Wednesday night. Col. Lomax left Montgomery on Wednesday night, at 7 o'clock, with two hundred and twenty-five men, and arrived at Pensacola last night at 10. The three hundred troops ordered from Mobile to the same point, under the resolution of the Convention, were telegraphed, when about to sail for Pensacola, by Major Chase, in command at Pensacola, to remain in Mobile until the receipt of further orders.

The Governor of Mississippi has ordered troops, at my suggestion, to Pensacola. They will halt at Mobile, I presume, until ordered to sail for Pensacola.

This is all the information I can give at this time. I expect a messenger to-night with full information. Very respectfully,
A. B. MOORE

SEVENTH DAY—JANUARY FOURTEENTH.

The Convention met in the Senate Chamber to-day, for the convenience of the members of the House of Representatives— the Legislature having assembled in obedience to the call of the Governor. The Senate accommodated itself in the Supreme Court room, and the Judges of that Court held their sittings in the Library.

Mr. BRAGG, by leave, read dispatches from Mobile, as follows :

MOBILE, January 13, 1861.
To JOHN BRAGG—Have you passed the Ordinance for collection of duties, clearance of vessels, and disposing of United States property? I have resigned, and I hold treasure for the State, waiting its instructions. Please answer.
THADDEUS SANFORD.

Mr. BRAGG, by leave, offered the following Resolution, which was adopted:

Resolved, That the Chairman of the Committee on Imports and Duties be authorized to transmit to Thaddeus Sanford, the Collector of the Port of Mobile, a telegraphic dispatch informing him of the passage of the above Ordinance, and requesting him to repair to this city immediately, to confer with the Committees on Commerce and Finance, and Imports and Duties, in reference to matters appertaining to his office, and the interests of the State.

Mr. BAKER, of Barbour, by leave, read a dispatch from Gov. Perry of Florida, as follows :

TALLAHASSEE, FLA., January 14, 1861.
To Gov. A. B. MOORE, Executive Department.
Telegraph received. Can you send (500) five hundred stand of arms to Col. Chase?   M. S. PERRY.

The communication from Messrs. Pugh and Curry, former members of Congress from this State, was read as follows :

MONTGOMERY, ALA.
January 10, 1861.

HON. WM. M. BROOKS,
  President of the Convention :
SIR—In response to the Resolution, adopted by the Conven-

tion, requesting us to communicate, in writing, any facts or information which may be in our possession, touching the action of Congress and the purpose of the Black Republican party, which would aid the body in its deliberations; we state, with a due appreciation of the high compliment contained in such a request, that the facility and frequency of communication between this city and Washington, are so great as to render accessible to every reader of the public prints, nearly every source of information which is open to a member of Congress.

It gives us pleasure to comply, so far as we can, in presenting the object of your assembling.

Early, in the session, a Committee of Thirty-three was appointed by the House of Representatives to consider the perilous condition of public affairs and report thereon to the House. The *materiel* of that Committee represented the conservatism of the Union men, South, and the Republicans, North. After frequent attempts to agree on some adjustment of political difficulties, several Southern members withdrew from its deliberations, and the Committee at last utterly failed to adopt or agree upon any terms satifactory to the most moderate and yielding.

At a later day, a Committee of Thirteen, for a similar purpose, was appointed by the Senate. It was composed of the representative men of both sections and all parties, and after several fruitless and earnest efforts, reported inability to agree upon any plan of settlement.

The belief prevails with no well informed man of either section in Congress, excepting those who are willing to submit without terms to the election of Lincoln and Hamlin, that any settlement can be had in the Union.

The determination is universal with the Republicans of all degrees of hostility to slavery, to abate nothing from their principles and policy, as defined in the Chicago platform. It is the fixed purpose of the Republican party to engraft its principles and policy upon the Federal Government. Prominent Republicans have represented to us, that if they were faithless enough to retract from the platform on which they obtained power, their constituents would crush them.

We have been assured by many resistance men in the Border Slaveholding States, that they have no hope of a settlement of existing difficulties in the Union, and are anxious for the Cotton States to secede promptly. Some favor, or have favored, a consultation of all the Southern States to negotiate for new guaranties, with but little or no expectation of obtaining them, but for the purpose, in the event of failure, of securing the ultimate contemporaneous secession of such States. Our settled conviction is, that a large majority of our friends in the Border States, disposed to resist Republican ascendancy, desire the immediate secession of the Cotton and Gulf States; in which event, the only question left for such States will be to select between the seceding and friendly States and a hostile government; and on the determination of that issue, there will be but an inconsiderable opposition.

It is the concurrent opinion of many of our friends in the Border and Northern States, that the secession of the Cotton States is an indispensable basis for a reconstruction of the Union. Possibly the most important fact we can communicate is, that the opinion generally obtained in Washington, that the secession of five or more States would prevent or put an end to coercion, and the New York *Tribune*, the most influential of Republican journals, concedes that the secession of so many States would make coercion impracticable.

We have the honor to be, most respectfully,
Your obedient servants,
J. L. PUGH,
J. L. M. CURRY.

After the reading, the document was laid on the table.

Mr. Dowdell offered the following resolution, which was adopted:

Resolved, by the people of the State of Alabama, in Convention Assembled, That the Commissioners heretofore appointed by the Governor of this State, to the several Slaveholding States, be and they are hereby directed to present to the Conventions of said States the Preamble, Ordinance and Resolutions adopted by the people of the State of Alabama, in Convention, on the 11th day of January, 1861, and to request their consideration of, and concurrence in, the first resolution.

EIGHTH DAY—JANUARY FIFTEENTH.

Mr. Cochran, from the Committee on the Constitution, reported the following Ordinance, which was adopted:

An Ordinance to change the oath of office in this State.

Be it declared and ordained, and it is hereby declared and ordained by the people of the State of Alabama, in Convention assembled.

That the first Section and sixth Article of the Constitution of the State of Alabama be amended by striking out of the fifth line of said Section the words "Constitution of the United States and the," after the word "the" and before the word "Constitution" where they occur.

And be it further ordained as aforesaid, That all officers in this State are hereby absolved from the oath to support the Constitution of the United States heretofore taken by them.

RESIGNATION OF MR. FOWLER.

The President read the following communication from the Secretary:

MONTGOMERY, January 15, 1861.

Hon. WM. M. BROOKS, President Convention—

Sir:—I have received a notification that my company the "Warrior Guards," Tuscaloosa county, starts to-day for Fort Morgan by order of the Governor, and it is my duty as well as my inclination to join it forthwith.

I therefore resign my place as Secretary to your honorable body. Respectfully,
W. H. FOWLER.

Mr. HENDERSON, of Macon, offered the following resolution, which, on motion of Mr. Clemens, was laid on the table:

Resolved, That in accepting the resignation of the Principal Secretary, Mr. W. H. Fowler, who has tendered the same for the purpose of obeying the call of our State to defend her from invasion, and while we entertain a high appreciation of his services as an officer of this body, we yield to the exigency which deprives us of his able services; and our best wishes accompany him to the post of danger to which he is called.

The President afterwards read the following letter from Mr. Fowler:

MONTGOMERY, ALA., January 15, 1861.

Hon. WM. H. BROOKS—

Sir:—Learning through yourself that my resignation as Secretary, for the purpose named, was not accepted by the Convention, I beg to say that, fully appreciating the kindness of those who desire me to remain in this position, yet, I feel in honor bound to join my company, and with due respect to the Convention I must do so. Very respectfully,
W. H. FOWLER.

On motion, the resolution offered by Mr. Henderson, of Macon, was taken up and adopted.

Mr. WHATLEY moved to go into the election of a Secretary, which was adopted, and the name of Mr. A. G. HORN, of Mobile, being put in nomination, he was elected by acclamation, there being no opposition.

Mr. YANCEY made a report from the Committee of Thirteen upon the formation of a Provisional and Permanent Government between the seceding States—and on his motion the Report and Ordinance were laid on the table, and 200 copies ordered to be printed for the use of the Convention.

Mr. POSEY, by leave, introduced "An Ordinance to prohibit the African Slave Trade," and asked to have it made the special order of the day for Monday next.

On motion of Mr. WHATLEY, it was referred to the Committee on Foreign Relations.

Mr. HENDERSON, of Macon, introduced "An Ordinance providing for a Council of State," which, on his motion, was referred to the Committee on Military Affairs.

NINTH DAY---JANUARY SIXTEENTH.

The Convention having assembled in the Hall of the House of Representatives, [for the accommodation of the Legislature and the large audience,] on motion, a Committee of three, consisting of Cochran, Herndon and Bailey, were appointed to wait upon Ex-Gov. Matthews, the Commisssioner from Mississippi to Alabama, and inform him that the Convention was ready to hear him.

On motion, the members of the General Assembly were invited to seats within the Bar of the Convention, on this occasion, and the President of the Senate and Speaker of the House of Representatives, were invited to seats on the stand by the President of the Convention.

The Committee having returned, with Ex-Gov. Matthews, he was introduced by the President, and addressed the Convention in an elaborate and eloquent speech in relation to the object of his mission.

[The Reporter has not been able to obtain a copy of Ex-Gov. Matthews' speech.]

When Gov. Matthews had spoken about an hour, upon motion by Mr. Whatley, the Convention repaired, in a body, to their own Hall, and resumed a secret session; when the Commissioner continued his address, upon subjects which it was thought advisable should not be made public.

A message from the Governor communicated resolutions adopted by certain Southern Senators, and a letter from Senator Clay, which were read, and, on motion of Mr. Morgan, they were referred to the Committee on Foreign Relations.

On motion, by Mr. Yancey, the special order of the day, being the Report of the Committee of Thirteen, "upon the formation of a Provisional and Permanent Government between the Seceding States," was taken up.

The following is the Report:

REPORT AND RESOLUTIONS.

From the Committee of Thirteen, upon the formation of a Provisional and Permanent Government between the Seceding States.

The Committee of Thirteen, beg leave to report that they have had under consideration the "Report and Resolutions from the Committee on Relations with the Slave Holding States," providing for the formation of a Provisional and Permanent Government by the Seceding States, adopted by the people of the State of South Carolina, in Convention, on the 31st December, 1860, and submitted to this body by the Hon. A. P. Calhoun, Commissioner from South Carolina, which report and resolutions were referred to this Committee.

They have also had under consideration the resolutions upon the same subject, referred to them, which were submitted by the delegates from Barbour and from Tallapoosa. All of these resolutions contemplate the purpose of forming confederate relations with such of our sister States of the South as may desire to do so. The only disagreement between them is, as to the details in effecting that object. The Committee unanimously concur in the purpose and plan proposed by the Convention of the people of South Carolina. In the opinion of the Committee, there has never been any hostility felt by any portion of the people of Alabama against the Constitution of the United States of America. The wide-spread dissatisfaction of the people of this State, which has finally induced them to dissolve the Union styled the United States of America, has been with the conduct of the people and Legislatures of the Northern States, setting at naught one of the plainest provisions of the Federal Compact, and with other dangerous misinterpretations of that instrument, leading them to believe that the Northern people design, by their numerical majority, acting through the forms of government, ultimately to destroy many of our most valuable rights.

With the people of South Carolina, we believe that the Federal Constitution "presents a complete scheme of confederation, capable of being speedily put into operation;" that its provisions and true import are familiar to the people of the South, "many of whom are believed to cherish a degree of veneration for it;" and that all "would feel safe under it, when in their own hands for interpretation and administration; especially as the portions that have been, by perversion, made potent for mischief and oppression in the hands of adverse and inimical interests, have received a settled construction by the South; that a speedy confederation by the South is desirable in the highest degree, which it is supposed must be temporary, at first, (if accomplished as soon as it should be,) and no better basis than the Constitution of the United States is likely to be suggested or adopted." This Convention, in the resolutions accompanying the Ordinance dissolving the Union, has already responded to the invitation of the people of South Carolina, to meet them in Convention for the purposes indicated in their resolutions, and have named Montgomery, in this State, and the 4th day of February, as the appropriate place and time, at which to meet. In fixing the time and place, this Convention but concurred in the suggestions of the honorable gentleman representing the people of South Carolina before this body. We are aware that several of our sister States, which have indicated a disposition to secede from the Union, and have called Conventions of their people, may not be able to meet us, at so early a day; but the great importance to the States, which have already seceded, and which are likely to secede by that date, of having a common government to manage their federal and foreign affairs in the emergency now pressing upon them, outweighed, in the opinion of the Committee, the consideration which suggested delay. The Committee more readily came this conclusion, as the Convention which will meet on the 4th of February, will at first be engaged in the formation of a Provisional Government—leaving the more important question of a Permanent Government to be considered of at a later day; by which time it is hoped and believed that all the Southern States will be in a condition to send deputies to the Convention, and participate in its councils. It was thought, also, that the proposition to form the Provisional Government upon the basis of the Federal Constitution, so much revered by all the Southern States, would meet with the approval of all those which may secede. The Committee are also of opinion that the election of the deputies to meet the people of our sister States in Convention, should be made by the Convention. To submit the election to the people would involve a dangerous delay, and it would be impracticable to secure an election by the people before the 4th of February next.

The Committee, therefore, recommend to the Convention the adoption of the following resolutions, [here printed as amended,] viz:

Resolved, That this Convention cordially approve of the suggestions of the Convention of the people of South Carolina, to meet them in Convention at Montgomery, in the State of Alabama, on the fourth day of Februrary, 1861, to frame a Provisional Government, upon the principles of the Constitution of the United States, and also to prepare and consider upon a plan for the erection and establishment of a permanent Government for the seceding States, upon the same principles, which shall be submitted to Conventions of such seceding States for adoption or rejection.

Resolved, That we approve of the suggestion that each State shall send to said Convention as many deputies as it now has, or has lately had, Senators and Representatives in the Congress of the United States; and that each State shall have one vote upon all questions upon which a vote may be taken in said Convention.

Resolved, therefore, That this Convention will proceed to elect, by ballot, one deputy from each Congressional District in this State, and two deputies from the State at large, at twelve o'clock, meridian, on Friday, the 18th of January, instant, who shall be authorized to meet in Convention such deputies as may be appointed by the other slaveholding States, who may secede from the Federal Union, for the purpose of carrying into effect the foregoing, and the resolutions attached to the Ordinance dissolving the Union; and that deputies shall be elected separately, and each deputy shall receive a majority of the members voting.

Mr. JEMISON moved to change the word "for" to "from," where it occurred in the first line of third resolution. Withdrawn.

Mr. SMITH, of Tuscaloosa, renewed the motion, and it was adopted.

Mr. BRAGG, moved to amend the third resolution of the report by inserting in first line, after the word "elect," the words "by ballot, without nomination."

Pending the consideration of Mr. BRAGG's proposition to amend.

Mr. YANCEY said:

That he desired to make a proposition to the members of the Convention, after it had adjourned, which he thought would obviate the objection of the mover of the last amendment.

On motion, the Convention then adjourned.

TENTH DAY—JANUARY SEVENTEETH.

The Convention met pursuant to adjournment, and was called to order by the President, at 10 A. M.

Mr. BRAGG, from the Committee on Imports and Duties, to whom was referred the communication of His Excellency the Governor, transmitting to the Convention a telegraphic dispatch from Thaddeus Sanford, the Collector of the Port at Mobile, to the effect, that a draft dated January 7, 1861, for the sum of twenty-six thousand dollars, had been drawn on his office by the Treasury Department of the Government of the United States; and asking to be instructed whether he should pay the same; have had the same under consideration, and ask leave to report:

That it appears from the dispatch that the draft was drawn on the 7th of January, inst.; a date anterior to the passage of the Ordinance withdrawing Alabama from the Federal Union. The draft is in favor of the U. S. Navy Agent at Pensacola, and the object of it is stated to be, to pay certain merchants and mechanics in Pensacola, for goods furnished and labor performed for the United States; and certain other merchants in the city of Mobile for supplies furnished by them to the same Government.

In annulling the office of Collector at the Port of Mobile, as a United States office, and reclaiming that Port as embraced within the jurisdiction of, and appertaining to, the State of Alabama in her sovereign capacity, the Convention, in its Ordinance passed to effect that object, imposed upon the Collector, thereby appointed as an officer of the State, the duty of retaining in his hands, until the further order of the Convention, all such money as might be in his possession at the date of the passing of said Ordinance.

Under the circumstances by which the Convention was surrounded, it was deemed advisable to pursue such a course, not with a view of laying violent hands upon the funds of the United States in the possession of an officer of the United States, but simply as a measure of self-protection, and with the purpose of facilitating a fair settlement of the various complicated questions that must necessarily arise in the future between the Government from which she has withdrawn and the State of Alabama.

From the date of this draft, it will be seen that it was drawn before the passage of the Ordinance requiring the Collector to retain such funds in his hands, as well as before the Ordinance of Secession. It will also be seen that it was drawn for certain purposes involving the interests of third parties, who seem to be interposed in such a manner as to take from the case the simple features of a question between the Government of the United States and the State of Alabama. Those parties performed services, and, furnished goods and supplies for the Government of the United States previous to the withdrawal of Alabama from the Union. There was an obligation imposed on the Government, of which Alabama was a constituent part, to pay for this labor and these supplies; and it seems to your Committee that every principle of good faith, and an honest desire to preserve inviolate the sanctity of contract, require that these parties should be paid their just dues. The best way to secure justice to ourselves is, to do justice to others. But, it may be said, why not continue to retain this money, and remit these parties to the Government of the United States, to be paid out of other funds in the Treasury of the Government? The answer is, this is the fund out of which such obligations as arise at the points indicated, (Pensacola and Mobile,) are accustomed to be paid ; and to which, no doubt, the parties looked when the supplies were furnished and the labor performed. To send these parties back now to the Government of the United States for payment, when the monetary affairs of the country are in such a condition, that men of the amplest means and largest credit are scarcely able to sustain themselves; to require them to rely on the crippled treasury of a mere fragmentary Government for payment; when the obligation was incurred when that Government was a whole, and when such a course would amount to an indefinite postponement of payment, seems to your committee to involve the grossest injustice to those parties, as well as a departure from the manifest policy that should govern the action of the Committee in its relations with the Government of the United States as well as our own people.

The Committee have accordingly instructed me to report the following resolution to the Convention, and ask its adoption :

Resolved, That in response to the dispatch received from T. Sanford, Collector of the Port of Mobile, in reference to a U. S. Treasury draft, bearing date the 7th January, 1861, drawn on his office for the sum of twenty-six thousand dollars, the Governor be authorized to inform him that it is the sense of this Convention that he pay the same. JOHN BRAGG, Chairman.

Mr. JEMISON offered the following resolution:

Resolved, That the future deliberations and action of this Convention shall be restricted and confined to such changes and modifications of the organic or fundamental law, as have become necessary by the present political status of our State.

Mr. CLEMENS moved to postpone the resolution until Monday next, which was carried.

Mr. KETCHUM offered the following resolution:

Resolved, That the Ordinance of Secession adopted on the 11th instant, be ordered to be engrossed on parchment—sealed with the Great Seal of the State—and at 12 M., on Saturday next, the 19th day of January, instant, in the hall of the House of Representatives, publicly, and in the presence of all the public authorities of Alabama, be signed by the members of the Convention who may desire to do so at that time.

Mr. PHILIPS moved to amend by adding the words "and that afterwards it lie on the table to be signed by such others as may choose to do so," which was accepted.

Mr. MORGAN moved to amend, by striking out all after the word "resolved,". and inserting in lieu thereof the following as a substitute:

That the Ordinance of Secession adopted on the 11th of January, 1861, be engrossed on parchment and laid upon the table to be signed by such members of the Convention as may desire to do so, during or before the final adjournment of this Body.

This substitute was adopted.

PROVISIONAL AND PERMANENT GOVERNMENT.

At the suggestion of Mr. YANCEY, the President now announced as the special order, The Report of the Committee of Thirteen, on the formation of a Provisional and Permanent Government be tween seceding States.

The question was on Mr. BRAGG's motion pending, to insert after the word "elect" in the first line of third resolution, as per printed report, the following words: "by ballot, and without nomination."

Mr. CLARK, of Marengo, called for a division of the question upon the proposed amendment, so that the sense of the Convention might be taken separately on the two clauses, "by ballot" and "without nomination;" and the words "by ballot" were adopted as an amendment.

Mr. BRAGG withdrew the latter clause, "and without nomination."

Mr. BRAGG moved to amend, by inserting in the second line of the first resolution, after the word "Convention" the words, "on the fourth day of February, at the city of Montgomery."— Amendment adopted.

Mr. JEMISON moved to strike out all after the words "United

States," where it occurs in the third line of the first resolution; "and also to prepare and consider upon a plan of Permanent Government for the seceding States."

Mr. WHATLEY said:

Mr. President—I am utterly opposed to the proposition of the gentleman from Tuscaloosa, [Mr. JEMISON.] I am unwilling that it shall be said by posterity, that we had the power to tear down, but were unwilling to reconstruct a new Government upon the ruins of the old. This was the very argument used by our enemies in the late canvass. They said we intended to destroy this Government, and that chaos and confusion would rule in the place of order and good Government. I am for establishing *speedily* another Government upon the basis of the old Federal Constitution, and to avoid, if possible, the abuse of it by a fanatical majority. Our people love their Government—they are a loyal and patriotic people—I am ready to give my energies, and my feeble ability, to lay the foundations of a more permanent Government, and that *at no distant day.*

It is said that the Border States are not ready to participate in the establishment of a new Government at this time. That may be true, but that is not our fault: we will have the Cotton States by the 4th of February, and with them, we can establish a Government great in resources, and boundless in territory. Gentlemen say our speedy action will tend to drive the border States from us. Not so, sir—our speedy action will be an invitation to them to join us in this great movement. By the formation of a new Government, we offer to the Border States, who join us, a guaranty of protection against Northern coercion and Northern tyranny.

MR. WILLIAMSON said:

Mr. President—I should very much regret to see the amendment proposed by the gentleman from Tuskaloosa [MR. JEMISON], adopted. It would, in effect, be declaring to the world, that we are not yet prepared to approach the altar with our sister Southern States, and unite with them in pledging our lives, our fortunes, and our sacred honor, in defence of the course we, but a few days since, deemed it our duty to pursue. If we fail to provide for establishing a Permanent Government at the earliest day practicable, we shall have acted in bad faith to the people, and will subject ourselves to the scorn and contempt of every true friend of our cause. During the war of '76, if the colonists had united and presented an unbroken front, the British Lion would have been much sooner expelled—millions saved to the Treasury, and our fathers spared the shedding of much blood—the result of a protracted war, not only with foreign enemies, but traitors in their midst.

There is no use in disguising the fact: We are in the midst or a revolution; thus far bloodless, it is true, yet its effects are present and palpable. Look, sir, to the deplorable condition of our financial and commercial affairs. Confidence lost, gloom and despair depicted in every countenance. Every intelligent man knows that our great staple ought to have advanced. Yet millions have already been and will continue to be lost to the South by its depreciation, if we do not demonstrate to the World that we are in earnest, and intend, regardless of cost, at every hazard, and to the last extremity, to present an unbroken front in defence of our nationality and rights. This can only be done by establishing a Permanent Government. To-day the people are with us, and expect us to act. If disappointed and left for an indefinite time, surrounded by difficulties more intolerable to an intelligent and brave people than war itself, no one can predict the consequences. Our present position is untenable. We cannot recede. There is no half-way house. Consequently, we must press forward, and my life upon it, that in less than two months, the skies will brighten, and if we are not at peace, we shall find ourselves amply able and fully prepared to conquer a peace.

MR. JEWETT said:

Mr. President—I shall support the motion of the gentleman from Tuscaloosa. His amendment affects only the appointment of delegates to a Convention to form a Permanent Government, and leaves those we propose to select, in the resolution before us, full power to organize and put into operation a Provisional Government.

It is of pressing necessity that we shall have a Provisional Government organized at the earliest practicable period; and that it shall be in the full exercise of its functions before the 4th of March next, when Mr. Lincoln is expected to take control of the Federal Administration of those States which still adhere to the old organization. If our delegates meet in the early part of February next, as proposed in the resolution reported by the Committee, they will have ample time to adopt a plan for the temporary government of those States, which shall, by that time, have dissolved their connection with the present United States Government; and to select and place in power able and patriotic men, charged with its administration; and by the time Mr. Lincoln assumes the control of those States united under the old Government, we shall have a new Government for our Gulf Confederacy in operation—with a treasury and an army, capable of protecting us against foreign invasion, and of securing domestic tranquility.

This same Convention, it is true, might proceed further, and adopt the plan of a Permanent Government, to be submitted to such States as might hereafter withdraw from the old Federal Union, and ask admission into the new one. But when we consider that, at this time, there are only four States in a position to enter this proposed Convention, I think a proper respect to the other slave States demands of us the postponement of our action in the formation of a Permanent Government. I do not wish to defer action to a remote day—but to a day sufficiently far off to enable Georgia, Louisiana and Texas—States whose sympathy with us has already been indicated by their recent elections—to come into our Convention, and take part in the discussions of those questions which must arise in the formation of any system of Government; and which, of necessity, each member of the new Confederacy must feel a vital interest in. But, besides the States just named, we ought not to ignore the claims of Virginia, North Carolina, Tennessee and Arkansas, which are moving in the same direction as the Gulf States; and although they have not called Conventions, up to this time, I am not hazarding too much to say, they will, in a short time, do so.

There are within the limits of those States, men as true and reliable as any we have within our borders!—men who have taken the front rank in the advocacy of immediate secession, and whose influence, we may confidently expect, will be all powerful in placing their States, in good time, along side of ours.

The States have a right, I say, to be heard in the formation of the new Government—they must pursue a similar policy—they have a kindred blood—and above all, upon the great question of the day—that involving the perpetuity of our domestic institution of slavery—they are bound to us by every tie of feeling and interest; shall we not extend an invitation to them to join us in laying the formation of a Gulf Confederacy that shall embrace every slave State?

Mr YANCEY said:

Mr. President—The people of South Carolina have invited the people of Alabama to meet them in Convention to frame Provisional and Permanent Governments for the seceding States. In the resolutions accompanying the Ordinance dissolving the Union—the Ordinance of Secession—this Convention accepted that invitation; and adopting the suggestion of the Commissioner from South Carolina, we invited those, as well as the other Southern States, to meet us in Convention in this city, on the 4th of February, 1861, for the purpose of framing Provisional and Permanent Governments, for our common future peace and security.

The object of the report and resolutions now under consideration, is simply to carry into effect the design then and thus announced; and therefore, no delegate who voted for the Ordinance and Resolutions attached can consistently vote against the report.

Several objections have been urged against the report, which I propose briefly to consider. One is, that by the report deputies to that Southern Convention are to be elected by this body, and not by the people; and also that no provision is made for the election of another Convention to consider the plan for the Permanent Government to be submitted for ratification. The points are correctly stated, but constitute no objection with me. The people have had this question of secession before them for a long time, and have maturely considered it in two late elections, namely: those for Electors of President, and for delegates to this body. The issue was as distinctly made in one as in the other, and in both they decided the issue in favor of secession.

They have intrusted their delegates with unlimited power—power to "consider, determine, and do whatever, in the opinion of this Convention, the rights, interests and honor of the State of Alabama require to be done for their protection." The laws that authorized the election contained that enumeration of ample authority, and the people endorsed it. We have been selected for our supposed wisdom, experience in public affairs, integrity and courage to take all proper responsibility in the premises. In my opinion, the seven States that will be out of the Union by the 4th of February, will need a common Government in order to meet a common enemy, as soon as one can be organized.—It is plain that, with divided councils, and divided resources, and divided action, these States cannot contend against the united power of the Northern States, as well as if they met their enemy with the strength and wisdom of union, in council and action Hostilities already exist between the seceding States and the Federal Union. Coercion is the policy at Washington. To postpone the meeting of the Southern Convention until we could submit the election of deputies to the people, would postpone its meeting till the 4th of March; and that, in my opinion, would be hazardous to the last degree. Such an act would be suicidal—one to be looked for, perhaps, from a friend of reconstruction of the Union, but not from a friend of a Southern Confederacy.

But, it is said, why not call another Convention to ratify the Permanent Government to be adopted? I answer, because it is unnecessary. A Permanent Government for a Southern Confederacy was looked for by the friends of secession—was spoken of and entered into all the discussions in the late canvass. It was a part of the plan of secession, and when the people decided for secession, they decided for a Southern Confederacy. Therefore, on that point we already know the views of the people, and no new expression of opinion is needed. Neither is such expression needed as to the character of the Permanent Government. That character the people have indicated, and it is expressed in the report—it must be a government as nearly similar as possible to the Federal Constitution. We need no discussion before the people, nor other expression of their views on that point. Besides these views, in themselves conclusive to any mind, no statesman would willingly throw such grave issues before the people after once receiving their decision, until the irritations and prejudices and passions of the previous contest had cooled. It is eminently wise, before throwing off upon the people the responsibilities which attach to us, to consider the condition of the public mind. Gentlemen here have told us of an excited and unhealthy state of public feeling in some sections of the State, and asked time for reflection, in order to its correction. Who is not aware that it was a great misfortune that the election for delegates to this body came off so soon after the heated Presidential contest? Who is not aware that in one section of the State the angry passions and prejudices of that contest entered very largely and almost exclusively in that section into the election for delegates? And is it wise, is it not eminently unwise, to throw this whole question again before such a people, to blow off the ashes and revive once again the glowing embers of that bitter strife?

There is another reason why I oppose the election of another Convention. Such a proposition has a tendency to reöpen the question of secession, by bringing up the issue of a reconstruction of the Federal Government. It allows such an issue to be made—it invites it, in fact. And under what circumstances? From the signs of the times, it would seem that coercive measures were to be adopted. If so, about the time of such an election, the people will be bearing the burthens of such a contest. Commercial and agricultural interests will be suffering. Debts will be hard to pay.

Provisions will be scarce. Perhaps death at the hands of the enemy will have come to the doors of many families. Men's minds, thus surrounded and affected by strong personal and selfish considerations, will not be in that calm and well balanced condition, which is favorable to a correct and patriotic judgment of the question. The very state of things will perhaps exist, which our Black Republican enemies predict will exist, and which they sneeringly rely upon to force our people to ask for rëadmission into the Union. Shall we, the selected friends and deputies of the people, aid these wily and malignant enemies of our State by laying this whole question, as it culminates in its progress, on the very eve of final triumph, back to the consideration of a people thus surrounded and influenced by most unpropitious circumstances? To do so might well accord with the purposes of a friend of the Federal Government, but in my opinion is a policy which every true friend of the people should condemn.

Mr. President, I avow myself as utterly, unalterably opposed to any and all plans of rëconstructing a union with the Black Republican States of the North. No new guaranties—no amendments of the Constitution—no peaceful resolution—no repeal of offensive laws can afford any, the least, inducement to consider even a proposition to rëconstruct our relations with the non-slaveholding States. This opinion is not founded on any objection to a confederation with States, North of Mason & Dixon's line, on principles mutually agreeable to them; but it is founded on the conviction that the disease, which preys on the vitals of the Federal Union, does not emanate from any defect in the Federal Constitution—but from a deeper source—the hearts, heads and consciences of the Northern people. They are educated to believe slavery to be a religious as well as a political wrong, and consequently, to hate the slaveholder. Mr. Seward was right, when he declared that there was "an irrepressible conflict," which would not cease until slavery was exterminated. But, sir, the elements of that conflict are not to be found in the Constitution, but between the Northern and Southern people. No guaranties—no amendments of the Constitution—no compromises patched up to secure to the North the benefits of Union yet a little longer, can rëeducate that people on the slavery issue, so as to induce them, having the majority, to withhold the exercise of its power in aid of that "irrepressible conflict." To accept of such rëconstruction would, in my opinion, be but salving over the irritated surface of the deep-rooted cancer, which has been eating into the vitals of the Union, affecting perhaps an apparent, a deceitful cure, while still the loathsome and incurable disease keeps on its fatal progress, and daily weakens the body politic, until finally it breaks forth again with renewed, becaused temporarily repressed, vigor and the victim sinks in death.

One other objection has been raised by my friend from Clarke, [Mr. Jewett,] which would seem to be fundamental in its nature; and that is, that by the fourth of February, but five States will meet on that day, and he cannot consent that five States should make a government for fifteen; for, in his opinion, all the Southern States will secede by the fourth of March; and when they do so, if this report is adopted, ten of them will find a Provisional and perhaps Permanent Government in operation, which they had no voice in making. If the Seceding States had the command of events; if time was to them, at this juncture, a matter of but little moment; if circumstances did not demand extraordinary promptitude and action, in order to give unity, strength and effect to the movements of defence on the part of the Seceding States, I concede that the proposition of my friend from Clarke, would at once command universal assent. But such is not the case. War is already commenced on South Carolina. The same hostile movements have been made upon Florida. We daily hear of preparations for military coercion. The Federal Government seems to be under control of a military chieftain. Prompt action in establishing some common Government is imperiously demanded.

The resolutions, as they are now presented, it seems to me, obviate the chief force of the objection of my friend from Clarke, in this; that the resolutions indicate the character of both the Provisional and Permanent Government to be formed. They are both to be formed on the principles of the Federal Constitution. This Constitution is well known to all the Southern people. It is revered by them. There has been no desire to oppose or to alter it. On the contrary, such a policy has always met with public disfavor. The interpretation of that instrument has been generally uniform at the South, ever since the passage of the celebrated Virginia Resolutions of 1798. That Constitution has been uniformly held up by the South, as its great shield and buckler against Northern aggression. The South is content with it now —will be content with it hereafter.

If all the Southern States were in convention, who doubts that they would unanimously frame the government for a Southern Confederacy upon the principles of the Federal Constitution? None of us doubt it; and if the five or seven States that may assemble in Convention on 4th of February next, do proceed at once to frame a Provisional Government upon the basis of that

Constitution, and afterwards frame a Permanent Government upon the like principles, who doubts that every seceding State, as it retires from the Federal Union, will at once ask admission into the Southern Confederacy? For one, I do not doubt. One great and prime obstacle to the earlier movements of the border States in favor of secession has been a wide spread belief that the Gulf States designed in seceding, to establish a Government, differing essentially from the Federal Constitution; and especially that the African Slave Trade would be reopened. I have received many letters from distinguished gentlemen in various parts of Kentucky, Virginia, North Carolina and Tennessee, upon that very point, informing me that, were it not for the fear of the new Confederacy reopening the African Slave Trade, there would be a much stronger and more general movement in those States in favor of dissolution.

Those resolutions quiet such fears. The action upon them by the Southern Congress, instead of being an obstacle in the way of other States joining the Southern Confederacy, will be hailed by them with delight—will be considered by them as wise—and will command their respect and admiration, as much as the present Union commanded that of Texas, when she asked admission into the Union, although having had no voice in framing the Constitution. A Southern Confederacy, with the Federal Constitution slightly altered to suit an entire slaveholding community, will be an invitation to Southen States, yet in the Union, to leave it and seek for peace and security and liberty within a Union, having no enemies—no irrepressible conflicts—and being a confederacy of slaveholding States, under the Constitution of our slaveholding sires.

I now ask that the vote may be taken upon the resolutions.

MR. JEWETT said:

Mr. President—I do not wish to be misrepresented, and I do not intend to be misunderstood in my position upon the question under debate. The gentleman from Montgomery intimates that I have receded from my position as an advocate of immediate secession, and that my course to-day, is not consistent with my vote upon the Ordinance of Secession. I deny it. I stand to-day where I stood on the 11th January, and where I have ever stood, at home, in my own county, in the recent canvass. I maintained our right and our duty to secede from the Union, even if we had to take that step alone. In my vote on the Ordinance of Secession, I carried out my opinions by action, and gave to the world the only assurance in my power, that I was not disposed to tolerate hesitation or delay upon the great question of withdrawing Alabama from a Federal Union with non-slaveholding States.

The gentleman says the time at which we were to form this Provisional Government was indicated in the Ordinance of Secession; and that those who voted for that Ordinance are estopped from saying that any other day is suitable or proper for the meeting of that Convention of seceding States.

It is true that a resolution was reported by the Committee of Thirteen, and attached to the Ordinance of Secession, designating a day upon which we were will'ng to meet the other seceding States in Convention. But what States did we design to meet in Convention, and for what purpose did we desire to meet them?

The resolution adopted by us was in response to the invitation extended by South Carolina. Now, what was that invitation? It was in the following words:

"*Resolved, Third,* That the said Commissioners be authorized to invite the seceding States to meet in Convention, at such time and place as may be agreed upon, for the purpose of forming and putting in motion such Provisional Government, and so that the said Provisional Government shall be organized and go into effect at the earliest period previous to the 4th day of March, 1861, and that the same Convention of seceding States shall proceed forthwith to consider and propose a Constitution and plan for a Permanent Government for such States; which proposed plan shall be referred back to the several State Conventions for their adoption or rejection."

In our acceptance of this invitation, we designate such States as we propose to meet in Convention, and embrace therein every one of the fifteen slaveholding States.

With what show of consistency can we ask fifteen States to meet us in Convention, when it is perfectly apparent that we have fixed a day for their assemblage, so early, that not more than four or five of them can be represented in it?

I am satisfied that the spirit and meaning of our resolution are fully met when we accept their invitation to join in the formation of a Provisional Government, on the 4th day of February next. And upon examination of the report "from the Committee on Relations with the Slaveholding States, providing for Commissioners to such States," presented to our Convention by the Commissioner from South Carolina, I am confirmed in my opinion. In that respect, the Committee say (referring to certain modifications proposed in the plan suggested for a Provisional Government,) "yet these modifications may be safely left to a period when the articles of a Permanent Government may be settled, and that, meantime, the Constitution referred to will serve the purpose of a temporary Confederation, which the Committee unite in believing ought to be sought, through all proper measures, most earnestly."

That I did not desire or insist on any unnecessary delay, in the formation of the plan of a Permanent Government, will be shown by a resolution I proposed to offer, at the proper time, in case the Convention sustained the motion to amend, offered by the gentleman from Tuscaloosa. That resolution I now have, and I propose to read it, to show what I contemplated doing upon this subject. It reads as follows:

"*Resolved*, That this Convention hereby extends, to such slaveholding States as have already withdrawn from the Union, and also to such other slaveholding States as, by the 25th day of February, 1861, shall have withdrawn therefrom, its invitation to meet Alabama in Convention, on the 4th day of March, 1861, at Montgomery, Alabama, to propose a plan for a Permanent Government of such seceding States; which plan of Government, when so formed, shall be submitted to each State respectively, for its ratification or rejection."

I am not desirous now of postponing the meeting of that Convention beyond a day when we can meet the representatives of such States as have already called Conventions, or which, before the 4th of March next, may call them, in a Federal Congress of Slaveholding States; and I will even go so far as to say, that I do not desire to make choice of new delegates, but am willing that the same delegates whom we elect to frame our Provisional Government, may proceed, after performing that labor, to the consideration of a plan for the Permanent Government. But I desire them to extend invitations to all States which may have seceded, within a reasonable time, to be specified even by them, to whose discretion I am willing to leave the matter, and that they shall adjourn over to a subsequent day, to meet all such representatives as shall then present themselves from seceding slaveholding States, for the purpose of forming a permanent and lasting Government. I have no doubt representatives will be found there from Virginia, and from the other border States, and that we shall have a united South, ready to join in every measure calculated to advance the interests and promote the happiness and glory of the slaveholding States.

Mr. POTTER offered the following as the substitute for the amendment of Mr. Jemison, and to take the place of the first resolution reported:

Resolved, That the Convention cordially approves of the suggestion of the Convention of the people of South Carolina, to meet them in Convention to frame a Provisional Government, upon the principles of the Constitution of the United States; and also, to prepare a plan for the creation and establishment of a Permanent Government for the seceding States, upon the same principles; which plan shall be submitted to the Conventions of such States, for adoption or rejection.

Mr. JEMISON arose to a point of order; that the substitute was not in order. Overruled.

Mr. POTTER asked leave to withdraw his substitute. Not granted.

The question being on substituting the amendment of Mr. Potter, for the amendment of Mr. Jemison, to take the place of the first resolution, it was carried without a dissenting voice.

Mr. YANCEY moved to amend, by inserting, in the substitute, after the word "Convention," in the third line, the words "on the 4th day of February, 1861, in the city of Montgomery." Adopted.

Mr. JEMISON offered the following amendment to the substitute

"*Be it further Resolved*, That the plan for a Permanent Government proposed by the Conventions of the seceding States, shall be submitted for ratification or rejection to the Legislatures of the several States, or to Conventions hereafter to be elected by the people of the several States, as may be proposed by the Convention of seceding States." This was, by leave, withdrawn.

Mr. DARGAN moved the following amendment to be added to the substitute, which now stands for the first resolution:

"And no Provisional Government that may be formed shall be inconsistent with the Constitution of the State of Alabama." Lost.

Mr. BULGER offered the following, to be added to the last resolution, by way of amendment:

"The members of which shall be elected by the people."

On a motion to lay it on the table, the ayes and noes were called.

Those who voted in the affirmative were Messrs. President, Bailey, Baker of Barbour, Barnes, Beck, Blue, Bolling, Catterling, Clarke of Marengo, Cochran, Coleman, Creech, Crook, Curtis, Daniels, Dargan, Davis of Covington, Dowdell, Foster, Gibbons, Gilchrist, Hawkins, Henderson of Macon, Henderson of Pike, Howard, Humphries, Jewett, Ketchum, Love, McClannahan, McPherson, McKinne, Morgan, Owens, Rives, Ryan, Shortridge, Silver, Smith of Henry, Starke, Stone, Watts, Webb, Whatley, Williamson, Winston, Yancey, Yelverton.—49.

Those who voted in the negative were Messrs. Allen, Barclay, Brasher, Bulger, Clarke of Lawrence, Coman, Crawford, Crumpler, Davis of Madison, Edwards, Ford, Franklin, Guttery, Hood, Inzer, Jemison, Jones of Fayette, Jones of Lauderdale, Johnson, Kimball, Leonard, Lewis, McClellan, Posey, Potter, Russell, Sandford, Sheets, Sheffield, Slaughter, Smith of Tuscaloosa, Stedham, Steele, Taylor, Timberlake, Watkins, Whitlock, Wilson, Wood. —39.

The question being upon the adoption of the report and amendment,

Mr. WATTS offered the following amendment, to be added to the last resolution :

" And that the delegates shall be elected separately, and each delegate shall receive a majority of the members voting."

And the report and resolutions were adopted. And the Convention adjourned.

ELEVENTH DAY—JANUARY EIGHTEENTH.

A Message was received from the Governor, by his private Secretary, Mr. Phelan, communicating certain resolutions adopted by the New-York Legislature, which the Governor of said State had sent to him, entitled " Concurrent Resolutions, tendering aid to the President of the United States in support of the Constitution and the Union." [See Appendix.]

Objection was made to the reading of the Resolutions, and

Mr. YANCEY raised the question of reception, and moved to lay that on the table, which was done.

A communication was also received from the Governor, transmitting the report of Hon. E. C. Bullock, Commissioner to the State of Florida, which was temporarily laid on the table. [See Appendix for all reports of Commissioners.]

At 12 o'clock, M., the President announced that the hour to go into the election of Deputies to the Convention of Seceding States, to assemble at Montgomery, Alabama, on the fourth day of February, 1861, had arrived.

Mr. JEMISON moved to postpone the election until to-morrow at 12 o'clock, M., which the Chairman (Mr. Smith, of Tuscaloosa, in the Chair,) decided to be out of order.

Mr. JEMISON appealed from the decision of the Chair, and the Chair was sustained.

Mr. EARNEST asked leave to offer a resolution as a distinct proposition, as follows:

Resolved, That no member of this Convention, or of the present Legislature, shall be eligible to election on a seat in the Southern Congress provided for by the Ordinance adopted by this Convention.

The question of order was raised.

The CHAIR (Mr. Smith, of Tuscaloosa, presiding) decided that the Resolution was in order.

Mr. YANCEY appealed from the decision of the Chair.

The CHAIR stated, that the Resolution would not be in order under Parliamentary usage; but that there had been an agreement in the Convention last night, when the vote was about to be taken on the Resolutions providing for this election, that this Resolution should be considered, if the gentleman from Jefferson desired to press it. On this account, the Chair rules that the Resolution is in order.

Upon a vote taken on Mr. Yancey's appeal, the Chair was sustained.

Mr. PHILLIPS moved to lay the Resolution on the table, which was lost—ayes 44, noes 55.

Mr. BROOKS, the President, (Mr. Smith, of Tuscaloosa, in the Chair,) moved to amend by striking out "eligible to election on," and insert "shall be elected by this Convention to," which was accepted by Mr. Earnest.

Mr. JEMISON said:

That it had been a rule with him, through the whole course of his political and legislative life—a period of near thirty years—never, under any circumstances, to vote for a member of the Legislature for any office created by that Legislature. He had adhered to this rule rigidly, and often at the great sacrifice of personal feeling; for, on many occasions, he had reluctantly been compelled to vote against his best friends.

There is a law on our Statute Book which positively forbids the election of a member of the Legislature to any office created by the body during the time for which he may have been elected. It is true, that that law does not apply to this case, as a law; but yet, it is a principle, and he must adhere to it.

If there was any occasion that would authorize a departure from this rule of action, it would be this; for there were many gentlemen here whom I would be glad to see elected to this position—nay, sir, to other and more prominent positions. He might be permitted to refer to one who is at the head of the Military Committee, whose name has been mentioned in connection with a high military appointment. There were many others in our midst who stand no less deservedly high in the public estimation for their abilities and patriotism. Hence, continued Mr. J., though I shall adhere to my rule, I confess that this is an occasion, if any, which might authorize a departure from that rule.

MR. CLEMENS said:

Mr. President—I do not consider the adoption of this resolution a matter of the slightest importance in reference to offices which are to be filled by the Convention itself, since it is plain that the same majority who have power to adopt the resolution, have the power to defeat any candidate who may be placed in nomination. I should not, therefore, have participated at all in the debate, if direct allusion had not been made to me by the gentleman from Tuscaloosa [Mr. Jemison.] The terms of the allusion were complimentary, it is true, and for that I thank him; but still, it was so made as to demand some reply.

I do not agree that there is any propriety in excluding ourselves from offices which are to be filled outside of the Convention, and by a power over which we have no control. There may be some reason for excluding ourselves from offices to which we retain the power of election; but when we have surrendered that power to other hands, the reason is removed, and the disfranchisement becomes an act of simple and unadulterated tyranny. The military appointments referred to by the gentleman from Tuscaloosa, are vested in the Governor. The Military Committee have voluntarily deprived themselves of all voice in their selection, and I think I have a right to say for that Committee, that they have not been swayed one hair's breadth in their action by any consideration but the public good. I do not believe that a single member of it has had any consultation with the Governor, as to the individuals who should be appointed: no one has made a suggestion to, or received an intimation from, him on the subject. Looking alone to the efficiency of our military organization, we vested the appointment of the officers in him, hoping that the discretion thus given him would be exercised wisely, and intending that it should not be obstructed by importunities on our part.

As to the appointment for Major-General, I must be allowed to say that no man is fit for the office who stoops to seek it. It is one of grave responsibility, surrounded by innumerable difficulties; and it will be a fatal mistake to confer it upon any man from personal or partisan motives. No one should be selected whose qualifications, apart from the recommendation of friends, do not point him out unmistakably as the man for the place and for the times.

The gentleman from Tuscaloosa has alluded to me in connection with this office. Sir, I have intimated to no one any desire to fill it. I know too much of its responsibilities and its difficulties, and though I have been accustomed to take the one and encounter the other, these are of a nature which I could only be induced to shoulder by controlling considerations of public duty. In the trying times which are before us, I know that my place will be in the field; and I know, too, that there I shall have a position commensurate with any military abilities I may possess, no matter what ordinances you may pass. I have no fears of being overlooked—no apprehensions that my services will be dispensed with; but the passage of this resolution may cripple us in other respects, and, therefore, I shall vote against it.

Mr. STONE said:

Mr. President—I cannot permit the vote to be taken upon the Resolution of the gentleman from Jefferson, without rising to protest against its adoption. Sir, that Resolution, if adopted, will deprive the State of the services of some of her most talented and eminent sons, and at a time, too, when she peculiarly needs in her councils the services of her wise and patriotic men. In the organization of a Southern Confederacy, the State will need her best talent—her men of intellect, her statesmen; and to such alone should be confided the great trust of organizing the new government. It makes no difference where these men are to be found, whether in the Legislature, in this Convention, or elsewhere in the State—if they are the *right men*, we should call them to the public service, without regard to their being members of this or of any other body. We should have our whole State from which to make our selection of delegates to this Congress, and should not, by the adoption of this Resolution, so restrict ourselves as to be forced to exclude and ostracise some of our most faithful and eminent statesmen. Sir, is the fact that such men have been endorsed by the people, and have come to this body, entrusted with their dearest rights, a reason why *we* should pronounce them disqualified for the position of Deputy? Not at all. It is rather a recommendation. But we owe it not only to our own State, but to our sister States, whom we are to meet in Convention, and with whom we are to counsel with regard to the rights of all, that we should send our most eminent men to aid in the deliberations of that important body. Sir, as the whole responsibility of this new government will rest upon the secession party, I call upon *them* to see to it, that the organization of the Southern Confederacy is entrusted to its friends and not to its enemies; to men who have been true to the cause of the South through evil report as well as through good report; to men who are thoroughly identified with it; whose fidelity is above suspicion, and who, in good faith, will use their best efforts to secure the organization of a government that will prove satisfactory to the people. Any inefficiency or failure of this new government—any inconvenience or hardship that may result from its establishment, will be charged upon the Secessionists; and it therefore behooves us to place this work of constructing the Southern Confederacy in the hands of its tried and its best friends. In such hands we should feel that the work was safe and secure. In this way we may obtain a full guarantee that the rights of those whom we represent will be amply protected. Sir, I trust the Resolution will not be adopted. It is unjust to our State, that now, in her perilous condition, she should be deprived of the services of some of her ablest citizens. It is ungrateful to those noble and gallant spirits who, in the face of every sacrifice and of the most bitter denunciations, have accomplished so much for the rights of our people and the honor of our State; that now, at the very moment of the triumph of the Southern cause, to which they have ever been so faithful, we should repudiate and discard them as unworthy of the public confidence. Sir, I cannot thus discriminate against our friends.

MR. MORGAN said:

He had desired that the Convention would not place any restraint in its action in the selection of deputies to the Congress to meet on the 4th February, by a formal resolution ; but he was equally anxious that the selections should be made from persons outside of the Convention and of the Legislature ; and had hoped that a tacit agreement on this point would relieve us from all embarrassment. As the resolution had been presented, he would vote for it, if it was kept in its original form, so as to exclude members of the Convention and of the Legislature. If the propositions were presented separately, he should vote against both.

Our State adopted the principle in its original organization that the Legislature should not fill an office created by itself, from its own membership, existing at the time the office was created. I see no occasion here to depart from this principle of government. I would include the Legislature for many reasons. The most important reason is, that this election ought to go to the people. The people ought to select their deputies. But we have not time to refer the election to the people, and we ought to make the nearest approach we can to them, and select the deputies from their midst. They have selected their delegates to this Convention, and their members to the Legislature, because they wanted certain men in certain positions. They had other men to represent them in Congress. We have abrogated these offices, and created others of a similar character under a different Government. As it was under the Old Government, so it should be under the New Government. These representatives should be selected by the people or from the people.

It is no reflection on the Legislature or the Convention if we go outside of those bodies for our deputies. It is rather a compliment to the State that she has many citizens capable of such high duties. A position in this body ought to gratify any ambition. An honor conferred by this body on one or more of its members would be of great value, I confess; but it would be subject to a decided drawback if we should come under the unjust censure of attempting to elevate our members to posts of distinction, merely because they are members of this body, and we have the power. There are gentleman on this floor whom I would gladly place in any high and responsible position, but their constituents have higher claims

on them than we have, and they have signified their preference.
Let us abide by it.

MR. BRAGG said:

That, in rising to submit a few remarks to the Convention upon
the proposition under consideration, he begged to be permitted to
say that no feeling in reference to himself personally, had the
slightest influence on his action here. If he had ever had any
appetite for political preferment or high official position, it had
long since been appeased. Neither his temperament nor his tastes
led him to seek such things : that he was here, a member of this
Convention, was owing to no action of his own, but simply because
those, whose principles he had been called on to vindicate as corresponding with his own, had invaded his peaceful retirement and
demanded such a sacrifice at his hands. In opposing, then, the
proposition of the gentleman from Jefferson, [Mr. Earnest,] to exclude members of this Convention and of the State Legislature
from eligibility to the office of Deputy to the Southern Convention, he was governed solely by considerations affecting great public interests, and the honor and dignity of the State.

The same reasons seemed to Mr. B. to justify his opposition to
the plan of confining the election of Deputies to the respective
Congressional Districts, presented themselves with additional force
when applied to the still further restriction now proposed. He
had deprecated the first step taken in this direction, because he
thought the Convention should allow itself the broadest range of
selection; and repudiating mere ideal lines of demarkation, should
appropriate the best material, without regard to locality, where-
ever it could be found in the State. We are engaged here in no
every-day work, no ordinary adventure ; but States and Nations
waited on our action. While the present called aloud on us for the
exercise of the best faculties with which God had endowed us, the
future no less demanded that we should look well to the instruments we propose to employ to reconstruct the fabric intended to
shelter and protect posterity. He was afraid that gentlemen were
taking too narrow a view of the great duty before them. He knew
the difficulty of breaking up old habits of thought, and going out
of channels along which we have been accustomed to glide smooth-
ly; but new circumstances ought to inspire new ideas. These were
no times for resorting to mere routine, to continue to do now what
we had always done, simply because there were some who might
expect it, and who perhaps had already trimmed their little sails
to catch any popular breeze that might be passing by. For his

part, said Mr. B., he desired the largest liberty on this subject. He was not particular about lines of latitude; if he could not find the right man in South Alabama he would go to North Alabama; if he failed there he would go elsewhere. He protested against all restriction; he wished the whole field to be open for exploration; he wished to seek candidates for this important position, and did not wish to be sought by them—in no other way could this Convention vindicate its own dignity, and at the same time do its duty to the people and the State. Mr. B. said, he was persuaded there was a great error prevailing in the public mind in reference to this matter of confining this action to particular Congressional Districts. Although it had been the uniform custom under the Constitution of the United States, and the laws of the States, to elect members of Congress from the districts in which they resided, yet such limitation was now strictly legitimate; and it would have been allowable had the people desired, and any great emergency required it, for them to have gone beyond the boundaries of any particular district and selected for their suffrages any distinguished citizen in any part of the State whose services they might have deemed it proper to demand. He [Mr. B.] remembered one memorable occasion at least, on which this was done; when the distinguished Wm. B. Giles, of Virginia, was taken up by the people and elected a member of Congress in a district far removed from that in which he resided; and yet we are told we shall be removing ourselves too far from the people in this election unless we give them a member from each Congressional District. Mr. President, said Mr. B., my experience has taught me that the people, when let alone, are often more capable of taking elevated views of public affairs than their agents. It was so in the case of the election of Mr. Giles, and if they could speak to us to-day it would be so now.

But much, said Mr. B., as he was opposed to being tied down to these Congressional Districts, he was still more opposed to the additional restriction proposed to be placed upon the Convention by the gentleman from Jefferson. And here he was sorry to differ so radically with his friend from Tuskaloosa, [Mr. Jemison,] for whose fine practical talents he entertained the highest respect and with whose views he had very often concurred during the sittings of this Convention. That gentleman had said it was a principle with him, (and no man was more pertinacious in adhering to a principle,) that no deliberative or legislative body should reserve to itself to fill offices, which the body itself had created.— Now, sir, said Mr. B., as a general rule this may be a good one, but who would insist in its universal application? This post of Deputy is not an office of profit; it is not one that can be ranked under the head of governmental patronage; it is not one that it will be necessary to fill at stated regular periods—leading to that suit of bargaining and huckstering that we sometimes see in public bodies; but it is one that grows out of a great and extraordinary occasion, not likely soon to recur, and presenting no analogy in any of its features to what we ordinarily denominate public office. Why, then, seek to apply a rigid principle to an exceptional case?

It would be remembered that before the accession of Gen. Jackson to the Presidency, he enunciated the doctrine, that in dispensing the patronage of the Government, it should be done to the exclusion of members of Congress from all the offices of the country. The theory seemed to be unexceptionable, looking as it did, like a sort of check to that tendency to management and corruption that marked the times. But no sooner had Gen. Jackson reached the chair of State than he was the first to violate his own principle. Looking at the mere abstraction it was well enough, but when he came to work the machine of government, like a man of sense, he looked around for the best instruments, and he selected these from amongst those who by education and experience were best qualified to suit the purpose in view, whether they were found in or out of Congress. That is precisely what we ought to do here. Let us put off these unwise trammels, and take for our Deputies our best and ablest men wherever we can find them.

Mr. B. said that one idea advanced by gentlemen had greatly surprised him. We had been told that unless we disfranchised the Convention and the Legislature in this election, and went out of them to select these deputies from among the people, we should excite the jealousy of the people, and be wanting in a proper respect for them by showing a disposition to absorb the power which belonged to themselves. Mr. B. took a very different view of that matter; the members of these bodies were the chosen recipients of the people's favor and confidence; they had been selected on account of their wisdom and experience to represent the greatest public interests, many of them for a long series of years. If the object, then, was to vindicate the sagacity and intelligence of the people, how could it be better done than by making this election out of the material they themselves had furnished? It would be a singular way of evincing our respect for the people by rejecting as worthless and counterfeit, that very coin whose face had been stamped by the people's approbation.

Mr. B. besought gentlemen, then, to lift themselves up to a comprehensive view of the field of action before them. These were no times when we should hearken to the small counsels of small politicians, and give ourselves over to the mandates of cross-road caucuses, and little local arrangements looking to the gratification of mere personal ambition, and heedless of the great interests committed to our charge. Was the poverty of intellect so great in this body that we could find no one here to represent us in this Congress? Was there so little wealth of mind and worth in the Legislature that that body too must be excluded? Mr B. did not know how others felt on this subject, but for himself, when he looked around and saw South Carolina selecting her best men for the approaching Congress—when he reflected that Georgia, whose pride it was to be first among the foremost in the great movements of the day, would unquestionably send to that body her wisest and truest statesmen—when other States all around us might be expected to pursue a similar course—he should feel mortified and humiliated at the spectacle, if our own State, with abundant material out of which to make a most creditable selection, should content herself by sending inferior men to this important body; and dwarf herself down to mere mediocrity, when she ought to present herself as a peer of the greatest and best of her sister States. The State of Alabama is rich in intellectual treasures; let us group them all together; let us take from the mass the purest and brightest jewels, and combining these, let us throw into the approaching Congress all the light we can command. By doing this, we should vindicate the dignity of this Convention, exult the character of the State, and best consult the honor as well as the interests of the people.

Mr. YANCEY said:

Mr. President—I am opposed to the proposition of the gentleman from Jefferson upon principle. In its practical operation I have not the least interest. I may say, I hope without being considered as egotistic, that many members of the Convention have expressed a desire to have me elected as one of the deputies to the Southern Convention, and that for reasons satisfactory to myself if not to them, I have positively declined to have my name considered in that connection. I have thought it proper to allude to this, in order that my opposition to this proposition of the gentleman from Jefferson may be considered as upon principle, and not as upon selfish considerations.

The Southern Congress will be composed of deputies representing the people of Alabama, elected by this body. The people have a right to a selection from their entire number. This proposition adopted will confine that selection to a portion only of the people; to a large portion, it is true, but still it will be a restriction to a particular class of the people. Besides, that objection, there is another: it will be a disfranchisement of a portion of the people; a small portion it is true, but still a part of the people; certainly not inferior to any other part of the same number, whether intelligence, skill in public affairs, or patriotism is considered. That this part of the people that will be disfranchised—thus forbidden to aspire to this high trust, loses none of its importance, in that connection, when it is considered that the people have heretofore selected them as worthy of their confidence and trust. They number two hundred and thirty-three, and have each and all received the stamps of public approval, on the very issues which will yet agitate the public mind.

The great fundamental principle, lying at the foundation of all our institutions, is equality of citizens in our State, and its antagonistic principles. The recognition of privileged classes, has ever met with universal condemnation. That equality of citizenship would be grossly violated by the adoption of this amendment. No matter what course delegates may individually take in making their selection, let us not mar our records by placing upon them such a declaration.

Mr. YELVERTON said:

Mr. President—It is perhaps proper that I should mention that I did at first favor this resolution, believing that deliberative bodies should not create offices for themselves; and without looking at the question in any other light I so expressed myself to some of the members of this body. But an examination of this question has satisfied me that the object sought to be accomplished by this resolution is not consistent with this view of the subject. I am still free to maintain my own position and approve, with all my heart, the general principle of this resolution. But I am now satisfied that this proposition is full of mischief, *leveled at certain gentlemen, or perhaps at a certain gentleman;* and not intended to secure fair competion to all. Again, sir, the elections to be made by the Convention, and the places to be filled are of such vast magnitude, that they are placed beyond the reach of ordinary rules, and ordinary considerations; and the men should not be selected from mere favoritism.

I was for separate State action first, and for the formation of a great Southern Confederacy next; and for everything necessary to accomplish these great purposes. The people, I have the honor to represent, were openly and boldly for these things. As their standard-bearer, by unanimous choice of their own, with these purposes plainly inscribed upon their banner I took it and bore.

it aloft over a field warmly contested. I paid my devotion to it, in open and free discussion, taking issue with Union, coöperation and submission, in all its forms and places. I was sent here to honor, not to dishonor it; the first I will do by being true to its principles, and to *its true men*; the last I will never do.

I proudly join my voice and action with those of the gallant and eloquent gentlemen from Pickens, [Hon. L. M. Stone,] and Barbour, [Hon. Alpheus Baker,] and call upon, and appeal to, the gallant and true Secession members of this body to vote this measure down. I ask to make this appeal the more impressive, because of the decided manifestation for its adoption. I make it in good faith, and under the impression that others as well as myself have mistaken the object of the resolution. I shall exempt the gentleman who introduced this resolution from the imputation of mischief-making, and I do this because I know him, and believe him to have been influenced by a different motive; but those gentlemen, who are pressing it so earnestly in an easy, cautious way; I may indulge the belief as to them, that they are not, to say the least of it, prompted by a very great desire to advance the claims of gentlemen, who have been the most prominent in the Secession movement. I could perhaps charge that some men, who were not themselves qualified for seats in the Southern Congress, would aid to crush others, who had the qualification. I might use stronger language, and say, that a very distinguished gentleman was most eminently qualified, and that the object was to *victimize him.*

I am opposed, Mr. President, to lend myself directly or indirectly to such a warfare; and if my suspicions be well-founded, the act would be in utter violation of my own sense of propriety. I would be the last to desert *the man* who has labored most to make Secession prominent. Sir, I not only believe it to be right, but I believe it to be the only remedy—the only passport from vassalage to freedom. The resolution, viewed in any aspect, is proscriptive, and unjust on that account. The State has a perfect right to call into active service the ablest and truest men; and we should keep an eye to the service, and the effect of the service; and in no event proscribe gentlemen because they have been honored with the confidence of the people. We may yet be told that in such men the people had the greater confidence. The resolution is softened by the amendment proposed by the honorable gentleman from Perry, (the President of the Convention,) but sir, I am for an open field, free competition, free choice, and the greatest amount of ability and experience, along with the *truest men* to the service and the principle. If secessionists believe that this resolution is to prevent them from sustaining one or more of the great and gallant men in this body, and the Legislature, who have labored gloriously and successively for the cause, they would certainly do themselves great injustice, do violence to their constituency, and deal oppressively towards their own favorites by voting with their enemies against their friends. Sir, so great is the demand for the most eminent ability in this State, now to be employed in this arduous and exalted service, that if there is even a doubt as to the propriety of the Resolution we should reject it. We ought to move with abundant caution and circumspection. I think it equally clear, that we should not give preference to gentlemen, simply because they are members of the Convention or the Legislative body.

Mr. President, I warn the Convention to be on its guard. I am in favor of acting out openly and boldly, and for taking my share of all responsibilities in a direct way. No harm can result from rejecting the Resolution. We are now covered up in secrecy. To this I have been, and am opposed, for the reason that I believe that the people, whose rights, interests, and sovereignty are in our hands, have a perfect right to see, hear, and know all that we do for them, and in their name. They may say that they would have protested against such action if they could have had access to us. Vote for, and adopt this Resolution; proscribe your friends, including leaders and the acknowledged champions of your cause; and then when the light breaks in upon your proceedings, well may outsiders exclaim: " the Convention preferred darkness rather than light, because of its deeds were evil." Sir, before I would place myself in that predicament, this right arm should fall from my body. I will not vote for the Resolution as a rule or an expression of opinion. It would work general injustice and special ingratitude.

There were some other speeches made upon this Resolution, and a great variety of amendments proposed, when Mr. Webb moved the *previous question*, which was sustained; and upon a vote taken, the Resolution was lost—yeas 46, noes 50.

The Convention then proceeded to the election of Deputies. The election was commenced on the afternoon of Friday, and completed on Saturday, and resulted in the following selections:

DEPUTIES FOR THE STATE AT LARGE.

Hon. Richard W. Walker, of Lauderdale.
Hon. Robert H. Smith, of Mobile.

DEPUTIES FOR THE DISTRICTS.

1st. District—Gen. Colin J. McRae, of Mobile.
2nd.   "   Hon. John Gill Shorter, of Barbour.
3rd.   "   " W. P. Chilton, of Montgomery.
4th.   "   " S. F. Hale, of Greene.
5th.   "   " David P. Lewis, of Lawrence.
6th.   "   Dr. Thos. Fearn, of Madison.
7th.   "   Hon. J. L. M. Curry, of Talladega.

THIRTEENTH DAY—JANUARY TWENTY-FIRST.

After the adoption of a resolution offered by Mr. Dowdell, to remove the injunction of secrecy as to all previous business of the Convention, the gallery was thrown open.

PROPOSED COUNCIL OF STATE.

Mr. COCHRAN called up the Ordinance reported by the Committee on the Constitution, to appoint a Council of State.

Mr. SHORTRIDGE offered the following amendment:

"Whose duty it shall be, when required by the Governor, to advise with him on all matters which may be submitted to their consideration; and that a record of such consultation shall be kept: Provided, nevertheless, that the Governor shall, in all cases, decide upon his own action."

MR. BECK said:

He was opposed to the amendment offered by the gentleman from Shelby. He saw no good to result from its adoption. The object of the Committee that reported the Ordinance was two-fold: first, to afford the Governor that assistance which he required in the altered state of our affairs, by giving him a Council with whom he could advise and consult, in cases of doubt and difficulty, and at the same time would relieve him of much of the actual labor now incident to his office. Secondly, it was intended, that while the labors of his office were lessened, the Governor should be held to the full measure of all his responsibilities. He is to select his counsellors, and be accountable for his and their conduct. The amendment proposed by the gentleman looks to a division of responsibilities between the Governor and his counsellors, the result of which would be unfortunate.

Mr. SHORTRIDGE replied:

The proposition, Mr. President, which emanated from me, is a copy from the Ordinance adopted by South Carolina, on a subject identical with the Ordinance now under consideration. So far from complicating the matter, as argued by the gentleman from Wilcox [Mr. Beck], its tendency is to make it plain and explicit. It provides that the Council shall advise the Governor, when he demands their advice; that a record shall be kept of their consultations; and, finally, the Governor shall decide on his own action. It occurs to me that it is wise and prudent that a record of the proceedings of the Council should be kept; and it is not less so that the Governor should at last decide upon his own action, and be responsible to the country for that action.

I can assure the gentleman from Wilcox, that the proposed amendment is not, as he intimates, intended to embarrass the passage of the Ordinance. My course is dictated by no unfriendly spirit. On the contrary, it is to meet and to remove objections which I know to exist in some quarters. For my own part, I am prepared to vote for the Ordinance, with or without the amendment. Public good demands the establishment of a Council; and the sooner the want is met the better. At the same time, however, I prefer to adopt the safeguards which have been thrown around it by the Convention of South Carolina. It is a good example, and those who follow will not greatly err in a crisis like this.

Mr. BAKER, of Russell, said:

We will probably have no use for this Council. The Governor will soon be surrounded by advisers. He is now surrounded by the wisdom of Alabama; the Convention is here; the Legislature is here; the Supreme Court is here; the Attorney General is here. Certainly, in the civil department, the best judgment in the State is now at the service of the Governor; and there will be no difficulty whatever, in the way of consultations, for every man will feel a pride and pleasure in being called on for his advice touching the interests of the State in this important day.

But it is said that the Governor, not being a military man, must have military advisers. The answer to that is: we are organizing, with all haste, a Military Board. The military department will soon be in existence, and in active operation. It will be a part of the Government; and the Governor and his Council, if he had one, would be compelled to yield, at last, to the edicts of the leaders of the military department.

If I thought that Alabama would remain separate from the other States, in her independent capacity, I might favor this measure. But it is to be hoped that we will soon be under a National Union. There will then be greater advisers over us; for then the wisdom of the Confederate or Federal Union will dispense its guardian influences to us. Thus, sir, we will have no need whatever for this "COUNCIL OF STATE." The Governor will have the very best advice, without the creation of this new institution.

Then, if there is no necessity for this, why erect a new and novel department of State, which will necessarily greatly increase our expenses? Sir, the State will suffer no injury by the refusal of this body to adopt this new plan. The people have abundant confidence in the Governor, and he can get along just as well without this Council as with it. Let the wisdom of the past give us confidence for the future.

We have as yet suffered no terrible convulsions. We have seceded from the Union; that is true, but the sun still rises and sets with its accustomed regularity, and shines with its usual splendor. As long as the elements are not convulsed, there is no necessity of creating a fictitious state of affairs, whose apparent solemnity will be calculated to alarm the people.

MR. WILLIAMSON said:

That he could not agree with the gentleman from Russell [Mr. Baker]. The Governor asks our assistance. Doubtless he is of opinion that he needs it, and thinks that it is important for the State that the best and wisest of her sons should be called into Council. This request reflects great credit on the modesty as well as the wisdom of the Governor. The Council should be established.

It is not contemplated that this institution should be permanent, but only for the time being. The Governor will use them only so long as it may be important for the State.

This debate was continued for some time by Messrs. Cochran, Webb, Yancey, and others. When, upon a vote being taken, the Ordinance was defeated. Ayes 40—noes 52.

FOURTEENTH DAY—JANUARY TWENTY-SECOND—OPEN SESSION.

Mr. DARGAN, from the Committee on Foreign Relations, made the following report on an Ordinance referred to the Committee for the prohibition of the African Slave Trade :

Mr. President—Your Committee to whom was referred an Ordinance to prohibit the introduction into the State of Alabama, of slaves, not born or held to service in any one of the slave States of North America, have had the same under consideration, and have instructed me to report that the power to regulate or prohibit the Foreign Slave Trade will more properly belong to the Confederacy of the Southern Slaveholding States, when formed, than to any single State, and they believe this power will be assumed and exercised by said Government.

But it is the opinion of your Committee that such trade ought to be prohibited, and by way of expressing such opinion, and to provide, in the mean time, against the opening of such trade, the Committee have instructed me to report an Ordinance upon the subject, and to ask that the same be adopted.

Mr. DOWDELL moved to print 200 copies, and make it the special order for Thursday next, at 11 o'clock, A. M., which was carried.

Mr. JEMISON made the following report :

The Joint Committee on the part of the two Houses of the General Assembly and this Convention, to confer with each other, to ascertain and fix the respective duties of this Convention, and the General Assembly, having discharged that duty, instruct me to report, that it is understood and agreed between the said Committee representing the General Assembly, and the committee representing this Convention, that the action of the latter body, shall henceforth be confined to such changes in the organic law of the State, as may be demanded by the present exigencies, and that, with this exception and such Ordinancies as have already been adopted by this Convention, the whole business of Legislation will be left to the General Assembly.

R. JEMISON, Jr., Chairman,
on the part of the Convention.
E. C. BULLOCK,
on part of the Senate.
S. F. RICE,
on part of the House of Representatives.

INSTRUCTIONS TO SENATORS AND REPRESENTATIVES.

Mr. Dargan, from the Committee on Foreign Relations, reported as follows:

Your Committe to whom were referred certain resolutions, adopted by many of the Southern Senators and members of the House of Representatives of the Congress of the United States, have had the same under consideration. They believe that the Ordinance of Secession adopted by the people of the State of Alabama, severs completely all the connexion between the State of Alabama, and the Government of the United States. That the State of Alabama is no longer entitled to, and ought not to be represented in the Congress of the United States. Therefore, they have instructed me to report the following Resolution:

Resolved, That our Senators and Members of Congress of the Government of the United States, at Washington City, be informed that the State of Alabama is not entitled to and ought not to be represented in the Congress of the United States, as one of said United States.

The report of the Committee was concurred in and the resolution adopted. [For Senator Clay's speech upon withdrawing from the Senate, see Appendix.]

COMMISSION TO WASHINGTON.

Mr. Dargan, Chairman of the Committee on Foreign Relations reported resolutions to authorize the Governor to appoint two Commissioners to proceed to Washington City.

Mr. Shortridge enquired:

Does this resolution emanate from the Committee, or is it an independent proposition of the gentleman from Mobile?—[Mr. Dargan.]

Mr. Dargan replied:

The subject was discussed in Committee, and I drew up this as what I supposed to be the sense of the Committee, but I did not read it to the Committee, nor take a vote on it.

Mr. JEMISON said:

Then, Mr. President, it is out of order, for it is not in the legitimate line of a Committee's duty to originate business.

Mr. WATTS said:

I differ with the gentleman from Tuscaloosa, [Mr. Jemison.] What is the use of Committees if they may not originate business? It is true, that usage has adopted a certain degree of formality by which business is brought to the attention of Committees. But these formalities are not esssential; they have not matured into absolute rules. They are often inconvenient, and if followed strictly, produce great delays and vexations. Instead of facilitating they retard business, and cramp the action, not only of the Committees, but of any deliberate body who adheres to them as absolutely binding.

The Resolution embraces a subject of the greatest importance, and it ought to have been adopted long ago.

Mr. CLEMENS said:

I do not favor this resolution. There is no necessity for it. Shall we reenact the farce which has made the State of South Carolina rediculous? Shall we send a Commissioner to Washington simply that he may be sent back to us? Shall we seek an insult that we ought to know is waiting for us? No, Sir. Let the Government at Washington send Commissioners to us. I do not see what our Commissioners have to negotiate for. The example of South Carolina is quoted. She was differently situated. We have our forts in our own possession, she had not.

Mr. DARGAN said:

The views of the gentleman from Madison, [Mr. Clemens] have not escaped my reflection. I have worded the Resolution very cautiously. The Governor is not bound to appoint Commissioners immediately. It may or may not be necessary to send Commissioners. But I am not prepared to admit that even the South Carolina Commissioner, Mr. Hayne, did no good by his visit to Washington. Mr. Hayne's Commission was not without its good effects, as will be seen from the correspondence which I read, [here Mr. D. read the correspondence touching Mr. Hayne's interview with President Buchanan.]

Mr. SMITH, of Tuscaloosa, moved to strike out "two" and insert "one."

Mr. Smith said:

Mr. President—I prefer that there should be but one Commissioner. This official will occupy, to some extent, the position of a Minister. He ought to be clothed with sufficient dignity to command attention, and the respect especially of the Government to which he is sent. It will not do to divide responsibilities or honors. Two Commissioners would not command as much respect as one; because the more you concentrate honor, the brighter it is; the more you concentrate authority, the more potent it is. Besides, men do not like to divide their laurels; men do not care to toil for honors unless they have a fair prospect of wearing them. The best way to get good work out of an ambitious man is to crowd him with all the responsibilities, and give him a chance for all the honors.

Again, sir, there is some trouble in getting audiences with great men. The President can be more easily approached by one man than by two. Conferences are more solemn when the numbers are few; therefore more confidential and more decisive.

One minister cannot disagree with himself, therefore his councils will not be divided. He has no body to pull him back, therefore he goes forward. He has nobody to lean upon, therefore he depends upon himself. He has nobody to share his defeat, therefore he wars against discomfiture; nobody to divide his honors, therefore he the more eagerly seeks them.

There is something too in the expense. In excitements, such as those with which we are now surrounded, we are too apt to feel and speak contemptuously of money matters; but true economy is a jewel wherever found. Extravagance of Government is the crying evil of our day. It has been the fatal curse of the Government which we have just broken. Let us avoid this in our beginning. It is no harm to have an eye to the expense. One Minister the less to Washington will give us another for a more important place.

Mr. Shortridge said:

That he did not wish to be misunderstood. When he inquired whether or not the proposition was one directly from the Committee, he did not intend to be understood as being opposed to it. He merely wished the Committee to be put right on the subject. He might, and probably would support the resolution.

Mr. Blue,

Concurring with the gentleman from Madison, [Mr. Clemens] and believing that there is no serious necessity for the official proposed thus to be created, moved to lay the resolution on the table.

Mr. Watts:

Requested the gentleman from Macon [Mr. Blue] to withdraw his motion a moment. He did not agree with the gentleman from Madison, [Mr. Clemens.] Alabama had heretofore been a member of the United States. Having assumed an independant position, it becomes her duty to let the former Government know her reasons for this, and her policy if need be for the future. Commissioners should be sent to inform the Government at Washington officially, that we have seceded; to propose terms of negotiation, offer plans of adjustment upon different questions; proclaim our Freedom, and demand the recognition of our Independence.

Such was the course of the fathers of the Revolution. They did not wait for Great Britain to send Commissioners to us. The best men in the new Republic were sent as Ministers to England to seek a restoration of amicable relations; to secure a recognition of Independence, and to establish international Commercial intercourse.

The State of Alabama having assumed new powers, ought to seek to act up to the dignity of those powers—and to arrest them to the fullest extent—not by words merely but by acts.

There are many grave and delicate points to be settled between the new and the old Governments. The object asserted in the Resolution is one of the greatest importance, and ought to be attended to at once.

It is nothing to us whether the Government at Washington refused to receive the Commissioners from South Carolina or not; that refusal is no insult to us, and we should not so regard it. We are not advised that South Carolina has construed the conduct of the Government at Washington towards her Commissioner as an insult. South Carolina is amply able to protect her own honor.

Sir, let us adopt this resolution. It is our policy not only to seek a peaceable adjustment of our difficulties with the Government at Washington, but we should court alliances of peace with all the world.

Mr. Webb said:

Are we prepared to recognise the United States as a Gov

ernment? Certainly. The effect of the Ordinance of Secession is not to abrogate the United States Government. The withdrawal of a State does not necessarily destroy the Government of the United States. Alabama stands precisely toward the Government at Washington as she does toward the Government of France. Alabama is a nationality; so is the United States. The United States has not yet ceased to exist as an independent power.

Then, why not send Commissioners to Washington? It is admitted that there are grave questions to be settled. They must be settled, either by the pen, the voice, or by the sword. Let us seek a peaceable solution of our troubles.

It is said that the South Carolina Commissioners have been treated with contempt. Whether this be so, or not, it is of no importance to us. Let us put the Government at Washington in the wrong, if she chooses to take the wrong; but do not let us presume, in advance, that she will take the wrong.

To send these Commissioners will take nothing from the dignity of Alabama, as a new and independent State. On the contrary, it will show to the world our amicable intentions.

I have heard nothing yet in the nature of a substantial objection, and I shall therefore vote for the resolution.

Mr. WHATLEY said:

Mr. President—It is contended by gentlemen that we should not send a Commissioner to Washington, for the reason that the Government at Washington has refused to receive the South Carolina Commissioners, and therefore we are absolved from all obligations to treat with them But, sir, is it true, in fact, that the old Government has rejected the Commissioners of South Carolina? Although the first Commissioners were not received, only as *distintinguished citizens*, yet, sir, even at *this time*, the State of South Carolina has her Commissioner there. I read from the "Montgomery Mail," of this morning, that Mr. Hayne is there, making his propositions, and that matters are *more pacific*.

But, sir, if we admit, for the sake of the argument, that the South Carolina Commissioner is not received, does that justify us in breaking off negotiations? *Not at all.* I desire, sir, that if there is a collision of arms, between the old and the new Governments, that we shall not be responsible for *so dire a calamity*. It is our duty to hold out the olive branch of peace—to offer to negotiate and arrange all matters of difference between us; and if war and bloodshed come upon the country, we can go before the civilized world exculpated from all guilt, and released from all blame, and place the responsibility where it properly belongs.

True, sir, we have taken the forts and arsenals within the State of Alabama; but we have not taken them as a robber or a trespasser. We have seized the guns lest they should be turned against us, and become the instruments of our own destruction. We had a right to take them; we are a retiring partner from the common partnership, and we have a right to hold the assets in our possession until the final settlement, particularly when we have not obtained our full share.

Mr. President, we are ready to account, and we should send on our Commissioner, clothed with full power, to make the settlement, and bring about an amicable adjustment. But should the Government at Washington refuse to treat, we impose upon them the *fearful responsibility* of rejecting our Commissioner.

MR. WILLIAMSON said:

I think the amendment offered by the gentleman from Tuscaloosa [Mr. Smith], should be accepted, and the Ordinance adopted. One Commissioner can accomplish everything that can be accomplished by two or more. As to the expense, I admit we should keep one eye, at least, on the treasury; husband our resources and prepare for the worst. But, sir, under the provisions of the Ordinance the expense of sending one Commissioner to Washington is a mere trifle. It has been urged, as an objection, by several gentlemen, that if we should send a Commissioner, he will not be received in his official capacity. Suppose he should not, we, at least, will have done our duty by having shown that we are ready to come to a fair settlement—thereby placing it out of the power of our enemies to slander us by saying we were seizing everything we could lay our hands on, and refusing to account for anything. Thus far the honor of Alabama is untarnished. Her motto, "Good Faith and Fair Dealing," should be strictly adhered to by this Convention; as it will be vindicated, protected, and defended by her sons, if need be, on the tented field.

MR. YANCEY said:

That he concurred with his colleague as to the propriety of entering into negotiations, and having these questions equitably and peaceably settled. He also concurred with him in the opinion that the Government at Washington was a Government *de facto*, with which we could negotiate. I believe, however, that it is not a Government *de jure*. I cannot vote for the resolution, however, for several reasons, the chief of which is that, on the 4th of February, a Convention of the seceding States will assemble; and that Convention will have jurisdiction over the whole question, and will be the proper authority to make negotiations with the Government at Washington, as to all the public property in all the seceding States.

The example of South Carolina is not one in point. There had been an understanding between the Government at Washington and that of South Carolina, that the military status of the forts in the harbor of Charleston should be preserved unchanged. This understanding was violated, and the whole military power of the United States, in that harbor, was concentrated in Fort Sumter, commanding the whole harbor. Though South Carolina, at once, possessed herself of all the other forts, yet Fort Sumter overlooked and commanded them all. South Carolina then sent Commissioners to Washington to negotiate upon that change in the military status of the United States troops in the harbor. The President refused to receive them, save as citizens of South Carolina, and referred their communications to Congress. The second Commissioner sent to Washington by that State, according to the best information we have, was to obtain the withdrawal of the United States troops from Fort Sumter. The President has refused to receive him, as a Commissioner, and the telegraph informs us that Col. Hayne has returned to Charleston.

Now, Mr. President, Alabama occupies an entirely different position. There is no such military exigency now pressing on Alabama, and therefore the example of South Carolina is not exactly in point.

There is, however, another view, Mr. President. Alabama is not alone interested in this property. Our sister seceding States have equities in all the property in this State, lately held by the United States. Alabama does not represent all the rights in this property, and therefore she cannot settle those rights by negotiation. But in less than two weeks there is every possibility that the Convention will assemble here that will represent all the interests of the seceding States in this property, and in like property in all of those States.

That Convention then will embody the representation of all interests in the property outside of the Federal Union, and will take jurisdiction of the question, and doubtless negotiate with the Government at Washington upon the subject.

In the event that this resolution passes, your Commissioner might be found to have progressed in his negotiation, and agreed upon the basis of negotiation, and have nearly completed his labors: and at that point should a Commissioner from the Southern

Confederacy arrive in Washington to negotiate on the subject, it would be found, perhaps, that the Alabama Commissioner had proceeded upon the basis that his State was alone interested, and had otherwise so complicated the whole matter, as to render a satisfactory solution difficult, if not impossible.

I am for peace, Mr. President, and the only peaceful solution of this question is to recognise not only the equitable rights of the seceding States, but of every State of the late Federal Union. The forts are built on land, the title to which Alabama never held. The public lands were ceded to all the States by Georgia, and Military Stores and Custom Houses were made or purchased at the common expense of all the States. It is true, in withdrawing our State from the Union, all this property can be claimed by us; and if the sword is drawn, may be retained by the sword. But if we Confederate with other States, we must recognise the equity that each held in this property when members of the same Union. And if we are determined to negotiate with the United States, we must also recognise the equitable rights of every member of the late Confederacy.

The most expedient mode of doing this, is to carry on the negotiation through the Federal authority of the Southern Confederacy.

Mr. JEMISON said:

Gentlemen speak contemptuously of *expenses*. We may so think and so speak here, but the people will think of expenses. There is an old saying that "*many mickles make a muckle.*" I tell this Convention that we are now running up a formidable bill for the tax-payers. We have already incurred expenses rashly, and without necessity. We have a large number of troops in Florida; they might as well be in the Moon, at present, for all practicable purposes. The expense of a measure is, of course, a secondary consideration, when that measure is an absolute necessity, or even when good sense and wisdom seem to favor it. But in this case there seems to me to be not the slightest necessity. It will amount not only to a waste of money, but of time.

The gentleman from Montgomery [Mr. Yancey] is right on this subject. Diplomatists move slowly and with great deliberation. The two or three weeks which remain between this time and the time when our Provisional Government will, in all probability, be in full operation, would hardly suffice to procure our Commissioners an introduction into the presence Chamber of the President.

It seems to me there is no more propriety or necessity in our sending a Commissioner to Washington now, than in sending off Ministers to all the other Courts in Christendom.

The amendment of the gentleman from Tuscaloosa [Mr. Smith] was adopted, and the Resolutions passed. [For Mr. Judge's Mission and its results, see Appendix.]

ENROLLMENT OF THE ORDINANCE OF SECESSION ON PARCHMENT.

Mr. EARNEST, from the Committee on Enrollments, made the following report:

The Committee on Enrollments, to whom was referred the Engrossed Ordinance, withdrawing the State of Alabama from the Union of the United States, and who reported the Ordinance as correctly enrolled on parchment, in pursuance of a Resolution, have instructed me to make this supplemental Report—

That a copy of said Ordinance, written with indelible ink by Mr. Joseph B. Goode, of Montgomery, has been furnished the Committee, which being a neat and correct copy of said Ordinance, they recommend that this copy be adopted as the original, and filed in the office of the Secretary of State, and that the former copy of said Ordinance assigned, be deposited in the Historic Society of the State of Alabama, at the University of said State, at Tuscaloosa. W. S. EARNEST, CHAIRMAN.

Resolved, That this Convention deeply appreciates the spirit of zeal, patriotism and disinterestedness that induced Mr. Joseph B. Goode, of Montgomery, to voluntarily Engross upon parchment the Ordinance of Secession, as adopted on the 11th January, 1861.

Resolved, That this Convention hereby tenders its most hearty thanks to Mr. Goode for the elegant and creditable manner in which he has Engrossed the Ordinance—it being (as near as circumstances would admit) a perfect specimen of Penmanship.

Upon motion, the report was concurred in, and the Resolutions adopted.

And, on motion, the Convention adjourned till 10, A. M., tomorrow.

FIFTEENTH DAY---JANUARY TWENTY-THIRD.

Mr. DOWDELL asked a suspension of the Rules, to offer the following Resolution:

Resolved, That it is the opinion of this Convention that the Navigation of the Mississippi should remain free to the people of the States and Territories lying upon it and its tributaries, and no obstruction to the enjoyment of this privilege should be offered, except for protection against a belligerent and unfriendly people.
Not granted.

Mr. GILCHRIST, Chairman of the Committee on Foreign Relations, made the following report:

The Committee on Foreign Relations, to whom was referred a Resolution instructing them to enquire into the expediency of sending Commissioners to New Mexico and Arizona, for the purpose of securing the annexation of those Territories to the Southern Confederacy as new States, have had the same under consideration, and instructed me to Report, that they deem it inexpedient for the Convention to take any action thereon, as the same more appropriately belongs to the Southern Congress.

Mr. WATTS, Chairman of the Committee on the Judiciary and Internal Affairs, to which was referred "An Ordinance in relation to the Collection of Debts, &c., reported that the Committee had had the same under consideration, and had instructed him to report the accompanying Ordinance, and recommend its adoption as a substitute for the one referred:

CONFISCATION OF PROPERTY.

Be it Ordained by the people of Alabama in Convention assembled, That full power to confiscate Property belonging to enemies at war with the State of Alabama is hereby invested in the General Assembly of this State. And the power to suspend the collection of Debts, and all obligations to pay money due or owing persons, artificial or natural, in the non-slaveholding States of the United States of America, may be likewise exercised by the General Assembly of this State, in any manner they may see proper; any provisions in the Constitution of the State to the contrary notwithstanding.

Mr. SHORTRIDGE moved to refer the Report and Ordinance to the Committee on Printing, and make it the special order for Friday at 12, M.

Mr. LEWIS offered the following Resolution:

Resolved, That the Ordinance and amendments now before the Convention be referred to the Committee on the Judiciary, with instructions to report an Ordinance giving the Legislature the war-making power until the formation of a Southern Confederacy.

Mr. COCHRAN moved to lay the whole matter on the table, but withdrew his motion to enable

Mr. COLEMAN to offer the following:

Be it ordained by the people of Alabama in Convention assembled, That the collection by law of any and all Debts due, to citizens of non-slaveholding States which have passed "Personal Liberty Bills," or tendered aid to the General Government to coerce a seceding State, be suspended for nine months.

Mr. WATTS said:

The original Ordinance which was referred to the Committee, undertakes now to confiscate the property within the borders of Alabama, belonging to the citizens of any of the Liberty-Bill States. The Substitute Ordinance of the Committee proposes to give to the Legislature the power to do this whenever it may become necessary. He preferred greatly this course. Let the Legislature act upon this subject at the proper time.

Mr. SHORTRIDGE said:

Mr. President—It occurs to me the Ordinance reported by the Chairman of the Judiciary does not meet the question boldly and fully. The Legislature of New-York, as we are officially informed, has actually tendered to the Government at Washington ten millions of money, to aid in the attempt to subjugate the seceding States. It is understood that Massachusetts, Maine and Ohio, and perhaps other Northern States, have adopted similar coercive measures. This action on the part of those States amounts to a declaration of war on Alabama. It, therefore, becomes this Convention, if it would preserve its own dignity and the honor of the State, to meet this hostile legislation in the most emphatic and decided manner. This is done, it seems to me, in the first section of the Ordinance I had the honor to introduce. It provides that the doors of our Courts shall be closed against the collection of such debts as may be due from our citizens to citizens of such States as have assumed this warlike attitude, or have passed the so-called Liberty Bills, or have judicially denied the right of transit, to persons owning slaves, with their property. The amount of indebtedness due from the South to the North amounts to several hundred millions of dollars. The people of Alabama owe probably as much as eleven millions in the city of New-York alone. Whilst I do not propose to violate the law of nations, I insist that, under the circumstances which surround us, we should hold in abeyance this immense debt. To pay it now would be to drain us, and to bestow upon our enemies the means and the sinews of war. In view, too, of the pressure existing in monetary affairs, as a measure of relief, it is entitled to serious consideration. If the merchant is indulged by his creditor, he can indulge those indebted to him.

The substitute offered by the Committee proposes to leave the question to the Legislature on the happening of an actual war. I wish the Convention to act on things already developed, and to act promptly. I wish to let the States of the North know that we are willing to meet the issue which they have presented. I wish them to know that so long as the obnoxious laws remain unrepealed, and the hostile judicial decisions remain in force, to which I have alluded, that neither the comity of nations, nor a regard for peace and tranquility, can make us quail, when our honor is involved.

In the second section of the original Ordinance, it is proposed to release the citizens of Alabama from their indebtedness to Northern creditors only when those creditors endeavor to evade, by a transfer or assignment of their evidences of debt, the provisions of the first section. This was deemed necessary to give vigor and effect to those provisions, and reaches, and was only intended to reach such creditors as attempt fraudulently to creep into our Courts.

I do not pretend, Mr. President, that the original Ordinance is perfect. It was drawn hastily, and in the midst of multiplied labors. It was intended to be more suggestive than otherwise, in the hope that wiser and abler heads than mine, after examination and reflection, would aid in bringing it as near perfection as may be.

It will also be perceived that it is contemplated to leave the subject, by my Ordinance, ultimately in the hands of the Legislature. But now is the time for this Convention to make the proper reply to New-York, and this is the body on whom this duty devolves. Let us not temporize, nor fear to look dangers and difficulties like these full in the face.

With regard to those sections which contemplate confiscation in the event of actual war, I see no great difference in principle between the original Ordinance and that reported by the Committee. I am, therefore, indifferent whether they are adopted *now* by the Convention or not. It may be time enough when hostilities have commenced, to proceed to the extreme of confiscation.

Mr. JONES, of Lauderdale, said:

Mr. President—The substitute of the gentleman from Montgomery, (Mr. Watts,) proposes to confiscate all debts due by the citizens of Alabama to citizens of the Northern States at war with this State. I must confess, sir, that I did not like the proposition when it was first read at your Clerk's table, nor was my dislike at all removed by the remarks of the mover of the substitute under consideration. I am opposed, sir, to every description of robbery. But when it is proposed to inaugurate a new Republic by perpetrating a flagrant outrage upon our just creditors, I must signify my dissent, and ask to stand acquitted by the record from any participation in the deed.

Who, let me ask the gentleman from Montgomery, are the enemies of Alabama? If I do not greatly misunderstand the law, whenever a government declares war upon Alabama, every citizen of that Government, whatever may be his private opinions, becomes *eo instanti* an enemy to our State, and must be treated as such under the rules of war.

If this be true, and the President of the United States should attempt to "*enforce the law*" (which is only a honeyed phrase for invasion and subjugation,) then the merchant of New York City becomes, by the legal construction of this amendment, the enemy of Alabama, notwithstanding he has recognised our Constitutional rights, braved the whole abolition pack of his State, and wasted time and money, and lost political caste at home in defense of our property. This amendment, then, proposes to do what I believe a great wrong. It is not only wrong in morals, but it is clearly contrary to sound policy.

I think I may safely say that nineteen-twentieths of the debt of Alabama, due to the North is due to our political friends.

Indeed, it is no great compliment to Southern merchants to suppose that they have traded to any extent with the enemies of Southern Institutions; and if they have not, then, it is clear, that nearly the entire debt is due to those true men of the North, who are now the sheet-anchor of our hope to over-awe the Abolition army, that would invade, to coerce us, and thus involve us in an unnatural fratracidal war.

These Northern men have a deep merit in preserving peace. They are men of Commerce; and Commerce never fails to elevate the mental horizon, and expand the range of vision; it is, and ever has been the sworn foe of bigotry and fanaticism. These merchants have comprehended our constitutional rights, and acknowledged and defended our equality. They clearly see the priceless value of our productions, and stand aghast at the reckless folly of that pestilent set, that would strike down the production of the great staple upon which the industry, the prosperity, the very civilization of the age depends.

Then, sir, for years these merchants have carried on an extensive and lucrative trade with the Southern people. They have found our people honest, liberal, and punctual; they have trusted our merchants up to the very hour of Secession, relying on our spotless, uncorrupted integrity. Then, let our honor be sustained —let these debts be paid to the last farthing. But if this substitute must pass, let us change its caption to " An Ordinance to concentrate the entire North against the State of Alabama." This will be a much more fitting caption, and better adapted to the practical results of this measure. It is also unnecessary and precipitate. By the Ordinance of Secession, you have destroyed the Federal Courts, and the foreign creditor will be driven to seek his remedy in the State Courts. It is now certain (and I deeply regret it,) that the present Legislature will pass some sort of Stay Law, by which the collection of all debts will be delayed. Thus, time will be given to learn the policy and temper of the Northern people on the subject of coercion. In the mean time the $11,000,000, due from our people to the North will be held as a hostage for peace. This is certainly a wiser course than hasty absolute confiscation as proposed by the amendment. But honest, prompt payment is better than either.

I hope the Convention will place the seal of its disapprobation both on the Ordinance and amendment, that, standing, as perhaps we do, on the verge of a great revolution, in the progress of which the old land-marks of truth and justice may be lost sight of, will not at the outset demoralize our people by the perpetration of an act, which public necessity does not demand, and sound morality cannot justify.

Mr. Smith, of Tuscaloosa, said:

Mr. President—The subject of confiscation, as presented in this Ordinance, is one of the most interesting, as it is one of the most important questions that will come before this Convention.

The deliberate act of confiscation, by the war-making power of a State, is regarded, amongst civilized nations, as equivalent to a declaration of war.

It is not the custom of nations to confiscate the property of any, except their actual enemies—enemies in war; not of a political enemy merely, nor of one that may hereafter become an enemy.

Some States, of a tyrannical power, exercise the right of confiscating the property of their own citizens, for treasons and other offences; but the question raised here has reference only to the confiscation of the property of the State's enemies.

Sir, I maintain, that, in a belligerent sense, we have no enemies. And I understand it to be the desire of this Convention that we should not so govern our movements here as to create enemies. As I deprecate hostilities, so I deprecate any action whatever, upon this question, at this time, as premature. There is no necessity for this action yet. Do you wish to provoke retaliations? Set the example here, and your own citizens who own property at the North will be the first to suffer; for in matters of money and property, the people of the North are amply able to protect themselves; and they are proverbially as keen and sagacious in their apprehensions as they are quick in the exercise of their resources.

Mr. Watts:

If the gentleman from Tuscaloosa, [Mr. Smith,] will read the Ordinance, he will see that he does not interpret it properly.

Mr. Smith:

The language of the Ordinance is not as distinct as is stated by the gentleman from Montgomery, [Mr. Watts.] There will be left in it, an open question for the Legislature. The Ordinance ought not to carry on its face a doubtful meaning. An ingenious constructionist could strain a power which it might not be our intention to give. At the proper time, in order to restrict the power proposed to be conferred, I will offer a *proviso*, "That the powers hereby conferred on the General Assembly shall not be exercised except in case of actual war, or until hostilities shall have been commenced.

The gentleman from Lauderdale, [Mr. Jones] has the true conception of this subject. He has told you that this confiscation would reach our friends first. How true is this; let us pursue this idea: In the city of New York, in the late election for President, *our friends* carried the polls by nearly forty thousand votes! In the State of New York, in the same election, we were defeated by less than forty thousand majority. We have in the State of New York, 313,000 voting friends—nearly half the State—nearly enough *voting friends* to make four States as populous as Alabama! And it should not be forgotten that, in the city of New York, where our friends are forty thousand majority, is due the bulk of the Southern debt, and due to our friends. This debt might be confiscated, under the power you propose to confer upon the Legislature, by this Ordinance.

In connection with the idea of the number of our friends in New York, I will refer to another subject: A few days ago, we received a communication from the Governor of Alabama, transmitting to us the New York Resolutions, in which the Legislature of that State had offered aid to the General Government with an appropriation of 10,000,000 of dollars, for the unholy purpose of coercing the seceding States. I was not surprised at the feeling of indignation that seized the Convention, when the subject of the Resolutions was disclosed. I was not surprised that the reading of the execrable document was brought suddenly to a close, and that it was consigned to the oblivion of silent contempt. No man could read it or hear it read, without feeling his blood burning his veins. But notwithstanding the hostile character of the document; in our more quiet and reflecting moments, we cannot forget that those Resolutions expressed but the opinions of a dominant majority; an accidental power, which in a single turn of the wheel of political fortune, might be hurled from its position. The triumph of party is transient. There is no stability in parties. There is no tenure so uncertain as political power. Especially is this true in New York. Ten years of its history will show as many political revolutions. Yesterday there may have been one hundred thousand marjority one way, to-day there may be two hundred thousand majority the other way. And I verily believe that in the next election, the revolution which is now working its rapid wheels in that State, will hurl this Black Republican party from power; and the same voice that uttered that threatening proclamation, will assume towards the South the gentler tones of friendship, of sympathy, and, if need be, of assistance. The question arises, then, shall we destroy our friends? Shall we cast off those whose past conduct and present inclinations evince a sincere regard for our rights? In this moment of indignant excitement, let us not depart from the true policy pointed out by enlightened deliberation.

Sir, in every act, here we ought to look towards the preservation of peace. This seems to be the inclination of many. It is my intention thus to act. I am not one of those who have lost all hope of a restoration of our relations with the General Government. I have not despaired of the Republic. I trust that, in the progress of a peaceful Revolution, a sense of duty on the part of our political enemies, will bring them to the footstool of justice; and that they will there yield to our reasonable demands. I have faith in this Revolution. For the first time, during the existence of the Government, the NORTH is reading the sad lesson by which she is taught practically, how much she depends upon our friendship, and how much she loses by the withdrawal of our trade. Trade rules the World. The prince merchant and the moulder of candles alike depend upon trade. New elections which are to be had during this year, will present a great change on the face of Northern affairs. I cannot say that I believe all will be made right; but I do look forward with the fondest hopes, that the day is not far when upon a basis perfectly satisfactory to the South, there *may* be a *Reconstruction* of the Government. I pray for the day that may bring with it a redress of our grievances; indemnity for the past; complete and unequivocal guarantees for the future.

Sir, we are in no condition to drive away our friends. We should do nothing here leading to hostilities. We shall not need to invade any territory We will defend our own. In times of "peace, we may prepare for war." I am ready to do this—this is the duty of every people who wish to preserve their liberties. I am ready to vote supplies to any extent. But I would hold the Olive Branch above the Sword, until honor and safety should advise the sad alternative of war.

Mr. CLARKE, of Marengo, said:

From the reading of the Ordinance, it appears that we but confer a power on the Legislature to be exercised hereafter, only in time of war. I can see nothing objectionable in this. The sort of confiscation provided for in the Ordinance is authorized by the laws of nations, and generally carried out in times of war. The arguments of the gentlemen do not reach the Report and Ordinance, but only suggest objections to the exercise of the power now, or to its exercise before hostilities are commenced. The Legislature could do nothing, under this Ordinance, except against persons whose Government might be at war with us at the time of the exercise of this power.

I do not adopt the suggestions of gentlemen as to the friendly feelings of the people of the North. Gen. Sanford has already tendered his services, and the services of Regiments of men, to the Federal Government. The New York Legislature has appropriated ten millions of dollars for the military use of the General Government! God save us from such friends.

That the Southern debt is large, need not be denied. There is no wish nor intention to avoid the payment of this debt. Every creditor who would pay without this law would pay with it. In actual war the debt would necessarily be suspended and the creditor delayed.

But there is another view of this subject. Gentlemen wish to preserve peace. I regard this as a peace measure. If the Northern people are so attached to money as they are said to be, may not the very idea of the confiscation of this debt, as a necessary consequence of hostilities, keep down war? There are more ways than one to keep peace. Harsh measures are sometimes necessary to keep peace. Peace must be sometimes conquered. It often requires armies moving with threatening banners, and assuming hostile attitudes, to keep peace. Prospective dangers promote peace.

This Ordinance, if adopted, will injure no man; but the North will be reminded by it of one of the dire consequences of war, and this may have its effect towards the preservation of peace.

Mr. LEWIS said:

The chief objection to this Ordinance, in my mind, is that it gives to the Legislature a power and authority which ought not to be held by any but the war-making power. The power to confiscate property is an incident of war. The Legislature of the State has not the war-making power. I am disposed to give it such power temporarily. This power at present, so far as Alabama is concerned, can reside no where except in this Convention. The States have surrendered it to the General Government. That Government lodged it and restrained it in the Congress. We have resumed it—but we have not yet prescribed the mode by which it is to be exercised.

This war-making power, if the expectations of the people should be realized, will be lodged in its appropriate place—in the Congress of the Confederacy, for whose speedy construction we have made provision.

Mr. MORGAN said:

This matter had better be referred. The Ordinance would necessarily be provisional and of short duration—and it ought not to be allowed to interfe with the more important business, the amendments to the Constitution of the State.

The question being on Mr. Lewis' motion to re-commit, it was carried.

SIXTEENTH DAY—JANUARY TWENTY-FOURTH.

RECEPTION OF THE CADETS OF THE UNIVERSITY OF ALABAMA.

Mr. Webb, by leave, offered the following preamble and resolutions:

WHEREAS, The Corps of Cadets, composed of the students of the University of Alabama, under the command of Col. Hues, have, by authority of the Governor, presented themselves at the Capital of the State, in order that the Representatives of the people may have some practical knowledge of the operations and effect of the Law of the last session of the General Assembly of the State, establishing a Military department of the University, and judge of the future usefulness and efficiency of the corps, in the event their services should be needed by the State;

Resolved, first, That a Committee of Three be appointed to act in concert with a Joint Committee of the General Assembly, to make such arrangements for the reception of the Officers and Corps, and for ascertaining, in such mode as they deem best, their progress in military knowledge.

Resolved, second, That a copy of these resolutions be presented by the Secretary of the Convention, to the President of the Senate and Speaker of the House of Representatives.

The resolutions were adopted; and the President appointed, on the Committee, on the part of the Convention, Messrs. Webb, Clemens and Shortridge.

Message from the House of Representatives, delivered by S. B. Brewer, Assistant Clerk of the House of Representatives.

HOUSE OF REPRESENTATIVES,
January 24, 1861.

Mr. President—The House of Representatives, having adopted a similar resolution to that which was contained in the communication from your body to the House, relative to the Corps of Cadets from the University of Alabama, now present at the Capital of the State, request me to communicate to your body, that they have appointed Messrs. Hale, Tait of Wilcox, and Irby, as the Committee, on the part of the House of Representatives, to make such arrangements for the reception of the Corps as they may think proper. S. B. BREWER,
Assist. Clerk House Rep.

The Senate, through Mr. Taul, its Secretary, reported, in a Message to the Convention, that that body had appointed a Committee to act with the Committees from the House of Representatives and of the Convention, for the purpose of making arrangements for the reception of the Corps of State Cadets under the command of Col. Hues. Messrs. Toulmin, McIntyre, and Jackson, are the Committee on the part of the Senate.

THE NAVIGATION OF THE MISSISSIPPI RIVER.

Mr. Yancey offered a resolution in reference to the navigation of the Mississippi river, and moved its adoption.

Mr. YANCEY said:

That the resolution offered by him was designed to meet a state of public opinion in the North-Western States, which, based as it was upon a misrepresentation as to Southern views, is to be regretted, and to be removed if possible.

We have a few intelligent friends in the North-West, who are embarrassed in their efforts to set our cause in a proper light before that community, by this very question.

I have not the least doubt that it has never been intended by any of the seceding States to shut out the commerce of the States lying on the Mississippi and its branches, from egress through the mouth of that great stream. And I would have that intention expressed by the seceding States.

Some restrictions should be laid upon the commerce of the States of the Federal Union passing over the mouth of the Mississipi. As all who pass over it have the benefit of lights and buoys, necessary to its safe navigation; all such should, of course, pay some charge necessary to an equal distribution of these burthens.

Our peculiar domestic institutions, too, may require some laws to be observed by foreign citizens navigating said stream, through the seceding States; and the resolution provides for that policy.

I believe, Mr. President, that the policy of the South, of the cotton-growing States, should be to leave Commerce as unrestricted as possible, having reference to our State and Federative necessities. "Free Trade" should be our motto; and as, in my opinion, these natural and commercial affinities between the South and the great North-West, however unnaturally disturbed by the prevalence of certain fanatical ideas there prominent, I believe that it would be wise for the South to combat the fanaticism of the North-West with the more enlarged, and enlightened and friendly commercial policy indicated in my resolution.

Offered in a spirit of comity, I have no doubt that the people of Louisiana and Mississippi will look upon the resolution as one in which all their seceding sisters are interested.

Mr. Dowdell offered the following, as a substitute for Mr. Yancey's resolution:

Resolved, That it is the opinion of this Convention that the navigation of the Mississippi river should remain free to the States and Territories lying upon it and its tributaries; and no further obstruction to the enjoyment of this privilege should be offered except for purposes of protection against a belligerent and an unfriendly people; laying such tonnage duties as may be necessary, to keep open and make safe the navigation of the mouth of said river.

Mr. Smith, of Tuscaloosa, moved to lay both the resolutions on the table, and print them, and that they be made the special order for Saturday, 26th January. Lost.

Mr. SMITH, of Tuscaloosa, said:

The resolutions present many interesting and important questions. I am not unfriendly to an expression of opinion on this subject. On the contrary, I think it eminently proper that there should be some action had upon it. But it will be observed, in looking around the Hall, that there is hardly a quorum of the members present; and it is now within fifteen minutes of the time of our regular adjournment. This is doubtless the reason why so many members are absent. I suggest the propriety, and I appeal to the gentleman from Montgomery [Mr. Yancey], that a vote upon the Resolutions be delayed until tomorrow; and if it be agreeable, I move to make this proposition the special order of the day for to-morrow, at 12 o'clock.

[Objections were made].

MR. SMITH—I am determined, in justice to the absent members, that the vote shall not be taken now. Gentlemen know very well that, by parliamentary strategy, a vote may be easily prevented. This course would be perfectly legitimate now. Still I would rather not resort to it, and I again request that the question be delayed by consent; or I shall feel it my duty to move a call of the Convention, in order that the absent members (nearly half of this body), may have an opportunity of recording their votes, and of expressing their views on the Resolutions. The gentleman [Mr. Yancey,] has urged, in his argument, the vast importance of the subject, and has even referred to the war aspect of the question. A desire to cultivate peaceful relations with the North-West, is most laudable; and the main difference between my views and those of the mover of the Resolutions, I apprehend, will be, that I am in favor, at this time, of going much farther, and of declaring that no obstruction whatever should be thrown in the way of the free navigation of the Mississippi river, so far as the States are concerned.

But I will not now make an argument; and as the gentleman seems determined on having an immediate vote, in order to prevent that, I move that the Convention adjourn, and call the ayes and noes.

The motion to adjourn was lost.

The question being on the adoption of the substitute, the ayes and noes were demanded; and pending the call, the hour of 4 o'clock arrived, and under the rule the Convention stood adjourned until 10 o'clock A. M., to-morrow.

SEVENTEENTH DAY---JANUARY TWENTY-FIFTH.

RECEPTION OF THE CORPS OF CADETS OF THE UNIVERSITY.

Mr. WEBB, by leave, made a Report from the Joint Committee of the Convention and General Assembly, of the programme of reception of the corps of Cadets.

The Joint Committee of the Convention and General Assembly, beg leave to report that they have waited upon the Officers and Corps of Cadets of the University of Alabama, now on a visit to the Capitol, and report the following arrangements for their reception:

The Convention, General Assembly, Governor and other Officers of State, will receive the Alabama Corps of Cadets in front of the Capitol to-day at 12 M., when an address will be delivered by the Speaker of the House of Representatives, and replies by the Officers of the Corps. After which the Corps will be Reviewed by the Governor, and the presiding officers of the Convention and General Assembly; and a Company or Battalion Drill will be had.

J. D. WEBB,
Chairman of Committee.

NAVIGATION OF THE MISSISSIPPI RIVER.

The Convention proceeded with the business under consideration when it adjourned yesterday, which was Mr. Yancey's resolution, with pending amendment, upon the subject of the Navigation of the Mississippi.

MR. SMITH, of Tuscaloosa, offered the following substitute, coupled with a motion to postpone:

Resolved, That in the opinion of this Convention the *Navigation of all the Rivers within the limits of the United States, as the Union lately existed*, ought to be, and remain open and free to the citizens of *all* the States which composed the Union.

Resolved, That in the opinion of this Convention, the system of Free Trade, as it existed between the said States before the dissolution of the Union, be and remain as it was before the dissolution.

MR. YANCEY said:

That he could not vote for the motion, though desirous of yielding all proper courtesy to the gentleman from Tuscaloosa, [Mr. Smith,] for the reason, that it in some measure undermined the Ordinance of Secession. That Ordinance separates us, root and branch, from the late Federal Union. The resolution of the gentleman from Tuscaloosa, [Mr. Smith,] reconstructs the most material elements of the late Union into a Commercial Union. We all know that the Articles of Confederation were set aside, simply because each State could obstruct as it pleased commercial relations with its sister States. The Union had its birth in that difficulty, and was based very largely upon its adjustment. The resolution, then, of the gentleman from Tuscaloosa, calls upon this body to recede, and adopt the fundamental policy upon which the late Union was based, and give to the Commerce of Maine and Massachusetts the same privilege upon our navigating rivers, as the citizens of the seceding States possess.

The policy is broad, comprehensive, profound, and its effects would be a discrimination in favor of New England Commerce against European Commerce. It would effect extensive privileges in favor of the citizens of States now using every effort to subdue us, against a Commerce that seeks our shares upon liberal and pacific principles.

I move to lay the substitute on the table. This motion prevailed.

The President announced the next question to be, on Mr. Dowdell's amendment, and Mr. Yancey accepted it.

MR. YANCEY'S original resolution as amended, reads thus:

WHEREAS, The Navigation of the Mississippi River is a question in which several Northern States and Southern States, yet in the Federal Union, are deeply interested;

And whereas, the people of the State of Louisiana are about to consider of the propriety of seceding from said Union; And whereas, the Mouth of said River is within the boundaries of said State;

And whereas, this is a subject which will properly come under the consideration of the Convention of seceding States to meet on the 4th day of February;

Be it Resolved, That it is the deliberate sense of this Convention, that the Navigation of the Mississippi River, to the people of the States and Territories of the Federal Union, residing upon it and its tributaries, should remain free, and no restriction upon the privilege should be made,. further than the tonnage duties, to keep open and make safe the navigation of the mouth of said River, and for purposes of protection against a beligerent and unfriendly people.

The question being now upon the adoption of the resolution as amended, it was adopted.

REVIEW OF CADETS.

MR. IRBY, from the House of Representatives, announced to the Convention that the House was ready to attend to the reception of the Cadets.

The Convention thereupon took a recess, and repaired to the front steps of the Capitol, and assisted in the demonstration according to the programme announced by the Joint Committee.

This Corps of Cadets of Alabama, a fine body of young men, numbering about 125, under command of COL. HUES, the accomplished Military Commandant, and DR. L. C. GARLAND, the President and Superintendent, were thus complimented with a public reception by the two Houses of the Legislature of Alabama, and the Convention. After going through an admirable drill on the Capitol grounds, the Corps was Reviewed by Gov. MOORE, and an address was made to them in behalf of the two public bodies by Hon. A. B. MEEK, Speaker of the House of Representatives. To this, responses were made by Col. HUES and Dr. GARLAND. The scene, altogether, was a highly interesting one, and indicative of the spirit of the times.

This Reception was followed by a COMPLIMENTARY BALL to the Cadets, given by the citizens of Montgomery.

The friends of the State and of the University had great cause to congratulate themselves on the handsome appearance and the admirable demeanor of the young gentlemen composing this Corps, during their stay at the Capitol.

AID TO THE SECEDING STATES AGAINST COERCION.

MR. COLEMAN called up his resolution offered heretofore on the 12th January, 1861, as follows:

"*Resolved*, By the people of Alabama in Convention assembled, that they pledge the power of this State, to aid in resisting any attempt upon the part of the Government of the United States of America, to invade or coerce any of the seceding States."

MR. BAKER, of Barbour, offered to amend by inserting after the word "seceding" and before the word "States," the word slaveholding, which was accepted.

MR. COMAN offered to amend by adding the following: Provided such seceding State, or States, are not averse to entering into a Southern Confederacy, based upon the principles of the Federal Constitution.

MR. DOWDELL moved to strike out Mr. Baker's amendment, to-wit: the word "slaveholding."

MR. DOWDELL said:

I have made the motion to strike out the words indicated not without consideration. The resolutions as originally introduced meet my approbation. As the great right of a sovereign State to resume her delegated powers for reasons satisfactory to herself and for purposes of safety and liberty, has been asserted, I see no reason why should withhold her sympathy or her power, if necessary, to aid in the vindication of that right, any other sister State. To much said by my eloquent friend from Barbour, [Mr. Baker,] I give my hearty concurrence. And yet I think his opposition to the motion which I have made, limits the very principle for which I am contending, and defeats the policy which he himself designs to promote. He is willing to pledge the power and resources of Alabama to aid any slaveholding State taking a similar position of independence. I go with him in that. And I go one step further. It is not possible that any hostile State bent on coercion, through the agency of the Federal Government, will secede from the Federal Union. But it is possible. I hope probable that some of the western and north-western States will oppose coercion. They are united to the South by strong natural ties—a link stronger than hooks of steel binds them together. The great Mississippi River insures friendly feeling between those who occupy its mouth and those reside upon its head waters and its tributaries. Suppose now the populous North should make war upon us for purposes of conquest or subjugation—we are few in number—we have aggressed upon nobody—we have not wronged them—we ask simply to be let alone—we have dealt justly by them—we propose nothing but what is just and right—we fight on the defensive, to preserve intact our altars and firesides. Are we not in a condition to challenge the admiration of mankind, and to claim and receive the sympathies of the good and pure all over the world? In this state of affairs, when Alabama shall be struggling manfully, patriotically, for the dear bought inheritance of their fathers, some one of the great States of the north-west, following the example of a patriotic Senator of that section, [Mr. Pugh,] who stood up manfully for State Rights and Southern Rights against the prejudices of the North, throws herself in the breach—stems the tide of tyranny and arrests the march of fanaticism—shall we withhold the power of Alabama from her assistance when the enemy shall have turned upon such an ally? Shall we not rather pledge all that we have and are to her support? Would not our sympathies gather around her—her success become our success—her defeat our defeat? And would not our gallant sons rush to the rescue of her sons thus struggling in our own behalf against a common enemy? Who doubts it? Then if we say anything about pledging our assistance, let us say all that our hearts approve, and our actions will vindicate when the time comes. Let us not limit the principle, but assert it fully, as we doubtless mean its application. In this great controversy of State independence against Federal tyranny, the friends of States rights are our friends, and we are and shall be their friends. Relying confidently upon the strength of our cause, and the ability of our own sons to maintain our own independence, we shall not and ought not to withhold our aid from an ally in the same cause, and reject coöperation come from quarter it may. For these reasons I have made the motion to strike the words indicated from the resolutions, so as to leave them as first introduced, susceptible of the largest application of the principle set forth.

Mr. CROOK said:

Mr. President—It does appear to me, that the debate on the Resolution offered by the gentleman from Sumter, when we take into consideration their plain, positive and unmistakable character, has assumed a very wide range, and one not likely to bring about such an expression of opinion with that promptness and dispatch which is desirable to me, and which the protracted session of this Convention, in my opinion, justly demands. Why, sir, this Body has been near three weeks in session, and has had under consideration the most important subjects ever entertained by a deliberative assembly; subjects vitally affecting the rights and liberties of the Republic. How important, then, that these useless debates should cease, and that we should engage in the discharge of our legitimate duties. So far as the amendment of the gentleman from Barbour is concerned, it is not needed to give expression to the views entertained by the people of the State of Alabama; for, if I understand the object of the Resolution, it is to give an expression of our views on the great principle of State sovereignty, by a pledge of our sympathy and material support to all such States as now have assumed, or may assume to act for themselves, as the Republic of Alabama has done. The principle is the same whether the act be the act of a Slaveholding or a non-Slaveholding State. True, a similarity of interests and institutions might justify a more determined support to the action of the one than of the other; yet the great principle of human rights would be involved alike in both; hence I look upon the amendment as uncalled for at this time, and believe, under all the attendant circumstances, it would have been better to have adopted the Resolution in its original form. My opinion, then, is that the amendment is objectionable alone, on the ground that it was, and is unnecessary to a just expression of the views of this Body on the subject matter under consideration. But, sir, to the amendment of the gentleman from Limestone, I have insuperable objections. What does he propose? If my understanding is correct, he proposes to sacrifice Principle upon the altar of Interest. He proposes aid and comfort, not to all of those States occupying the position now occupied by our own beloved Alabama—relying upon the God of battles, and the brave hearts, and strong arms of her fondly cherished sons, for support in this her time of trial—but inserts a provision requiring a sovereign power to perform certain acts, amongst which is that of joining a Southern Confederacy, before we will give them that aid which a kindred act entitles them to expect from all those engaged in the same holy cause. If a State has the right to secede, which is no longer a question in Alabama, she then has a right to set up for herself, independent of all the powers of the world. And whether her decision be to remain a separate power, or unite her destinies with other States in a Southern Confederacy, is a matter proper for the decision of her own people without regard to what may, or may not, be the views and opinions of others. I contend, sir, that there is a great principle involved in the decision of this question. So well am I satisfied that the great question of independent State action is involved in this decision, that I shall most assuredly record my vote against the Resolutions, though fully approved by me in its original shape, if this amendment shall be engrafted on it. With due respect for the opinions of the gentleman from Limestone [Mr. Coman], which induced him to offer the amendment, I would ask him to withdraw it. It can do no possible good; and, with a little reflection, I feel satisfied that he must come to the conclusion that it conflicts with both the views and acts of a majority of this Body. Now, sir, in order to put a stop to this protracted debate, so that the Convention may proceed with business now requiring action, I move to lay the amendments on the table.

MR. BULGER said:

Mr. President—I appeal to the gentleman from Calhoun, [Mr. Crook,] to withdraw his motion to lay the amendment on the table for one moment, to allow me to explain the course that I feel it my duty to pursue, on the subject now under consideration. [The motion to lay on the table being withdrawn, MR. BULGER continued:] *Mr. President*—The position that I occupy in this Convention, renders it necessary for me to explain the reasons that induce me to give the vote that I will give on the subject now pending. Sir, I regret that the Resolutions were introduced, because they are but a reïteration of declarations already made by the Convention, by which every member upon this floor, and every loyal citizen of the State of Alabama, is bound, and for the maintainance of which all that we have, and all that we are, is pledged. But as they are here, they must be disposed of. I am not entirely satisfied with the Resolution as introduced, hence I will vote for the amendment offered by the gentleman from Barbour [Mr. Baker], which proposes to strike out Southern States, because I am unwilling to withhold our friendly greetings from any of the border Free States that may desire to secede and join us in an independent Confederation. But this amendment adopted, and it is thought the Resolutions are too broad, and the gentleman from Limestone, [Mr. Coman,] offers a *proviso*, which restricts our encouragement to States seceding with the intention of joining with us in a Government. This amendment the gentleman from Mobile, [Mr. Dargan,] opposes, he says, because if New Hampshire and Maine were to secede, they would be entitled to our sympathy and our respect. In this I disagree with the gentleman. Suppose, sir, Vermont and Massachusetts were to secede from the Union because the General Government concedes to the Southern Slaveholding States their just and constitutional rights; then would the gentleman say those States, seceding for this cause, would be entitled to our support in resisting coercion or invasion? I suppose not.

Then let us say what we mean—let us adopt both the amendment of the gentleman from Barbour, and the *proviso* offered by the gentleman from Limestone, and then adopt the Resolution. Then we pledge all the resources of the State to the support of such States as have, or may hereafter secede, with an intention of joining with us in a common Government, whether it be South Carolina, Texas, Indiana, Ohio or Pennsylvania, and withhold all encouragement from States that may secede for other and different purposes, whether they be Slave or Free. For these reasons, sir, I will vote first for the amendment offered by the gentleman from Barbour, and if that be adopted, I will then vote for the *proviso* offered by the gentleman from Limestone, and if that is adopted, I will vote most Cheerfully for the Resolution thus amended; but otherwise, I will vote against it.

After some further discussion, the Resolution was passed over without a final vote.

DEBATE ON THE RE-OPENING OF THE AFRICAN SLAVE TRADE.

Special order under consideration again.

The question was upon concurring in the Substitue of the Committee proposing it for the original of Mr. Posey, which had been referred to them.

MR. POSEY offered an amendment:

Amend the second Resolution by adding to the same the words, " not below the grade of felony."

MR. JONES, of Lauderdale, offered the following as an amendment:

Resolved, That it is the will of the people of Alabama, that the Deputies elected by this Convention to the Southern Convention, to meet in the city of Montgomery, on the fourth day of February next, to form a Southern Republic, be, and they are hereby instructed to insist upon the enactment, by said Convention, of uch restrictions as will effectually prohibit the importation of slaves into such Republic, from any other place or country, other than the slaveholding States of the late United States of America.

Mr. Yancey raised a point of order, and stated it thus:

The amendment is incongruous, because the subject matter reported by the Committee is an Ordinance to be the supreme law of the land. The amendment is a Resolution of instructions.

The point of order was sustained.

Mr. Jones, of Lauderdale, offered his Resolutions as a substitute for the Ordinance reported.

Mr. Morgan offered the following Preamble as a preface to Mr. Jones' substitute:

"Whereas, the people of Alabama are opposed, on the ground of public policy, to the reopening of the African Slave Trade"— which was accepted.

The question was on the adoption of the substitute proposed by Mr. Jones, of Lauderdale.

Mr. Morgan said:

Mr. President—Before giving expression to my opinion on the Report of the Committee, and the Ordinance proposed for our adoption, I desire to state distinctly that I am opposed, on grounds of public policy, to the opening of the African Slave Trade. I confine my opposition to this traffic to the only tenable ground upon which it can be placed by any statesman, who has a respect for the wise economy displayed in the different aptitudes of the several races of mankind, for the different labors assigned to the human family. I confine my opposition to this traffic to grounds of public policy; because, if I were to feel at liberty to carry out my convictions of what a pure Christian philanthrophy requires at the hands of this generation—if I could consent to commit the State to the active work of Christian evangelization—I should pledge all its powers to go to Africa and to bring over ship loads of poor, savage slaves to a country where they could be raised to the condition of Christian slaves, which is the highest point that the negro race can reach, consistently with Divine Law, and with their mental and physical organization. It is impossible that I can give a vote on this question which will hereafter be the subject of doubt with those who choose to know the grounds of my action. We have long been assailed throughout those nations who claim that they are enlightened and Christianized, as guilty parties to a barbarous code of slave laws, and to an inhuman traffic in human flesh.

It may be accounted a singular circumstance that the seven millions of the South, and some millions of the North, are so blinded to the great sin charged upon us, that we are all unable to perceive the wrong, or unwilling to cease to do evil. So many people have rarely been so undivided in a course which is even the subject of serious dispute. But I will not stop to make a defence here of a right and a duty which has just led us to record the most solemn and portentous decree ever adopted by the State. The Ordinance of Secession rests, in a great measure, upon our assertion of a right to enslave the African race, or, what amounts to the same thing, to hold them in slavery. The most fatal and scandalous declaration ever made by the late Federal Government against the people of the South, as it has affected our standing amongst the nations of the earth, especially those who are strangers to our social organization, is contained in those acts of Congress which denounce the African Slave Trade as piracy—a declaration at once degrading to every slaveholder, and a living rebuke to the Federal Constitution, which expressly prohibited the suppression of the trade prior to the year 1808. From this source, many arguments have been adduced against the inter-State Slave Trade, in the late Union, by the people on this continent and abroad, and this not without a strong show of plausibility. The traductions embodied in the terrible word "piracy," have been wrought into every shape, and pointed with every sting with which to torture and malign the South. The laws of Congress, sustained by the South for reasons of public policy, but repudiated and despised for the calumny couched in the word piracy, have been a constant shelter to all those who have assailed us, whether upon religious or political grounds. We are now free from those laws, and the question is, whether, in attempting to free the country from a dangerous and exciting topic, we shall still continue liable to the imputation of being pirates, or to any possible inference that one course of action is predicated on any distrust of the morality of slavery. In the present state of opinion amongst the people of the North, and other countries, we ought not to remain silent as to the reasons which may impel us to take any action looking to the repression of the Slave Trade. We cannot, under such circumstances, prevent misapprehension nor repel misrepresentation. Before the report of the Committee was amended to meet this view of the case, and to place the proposed Ordinance on the ground that public policy alone required such action at our hands, I could not have voted to concur in the report. Even now it is not so clear and decided in its negation of other grounds for our action, as to make the report a complete expression of my opinions. The importance of this matter cannot well be over-estimated. If any slave trade in negroes is objectionable on grounds of morality or Christian duty, I would much more readily conclude that it was wrong to bring a Christianized and enlightened negro from Virginia to Alabama, than it was wrong to bring a heathen and savage slave from Africa to Alabama. If I have to forge chains for men at the expense of the opinions of people professing Christianity, I prefer that those chains shall lead the slave without the reach of the genial rays of that Christianity. But if, as I believe, these bonds are Christian bonds, I shall not hesitate to keep them where they were placed by the ALL-WISE, and where they have proven to be the only powers which could bring the negro within the reach of a proper moral and political government. We cannot defend the inter-State Slave Trade on the great truth of its coincidence with the revealed will of God, and, at the same time, condemn the African Slave Trade on moral grounds. I oppose the Ordinance reported by the Committee, because of its silence on these points. I have thought that it ought to be express and more emphatic in its statements of the grounds of our action. The Ordinance will go out disconnected from the report, and will be liable to become injected with such reasons, and arguments, and inferences, prejudicial to us, as abolition malignity and cunning may choose to invent. Our justification will not go with the act, and we will be placed under the shadow of self-reprobation.

Other reasons of the most important nature operate against the incorporation of the Ordinance into our organic law. It is, at most, a question of policy, and must always continue such, so long as negroes are held as slaves in this State. It was a question of policy when the Federal Constitution was formed. The policy then was to keep the trade open and unrestricted, except by a light tax, until a period should arrive in which a full supply of slave labor could be obtained from Africa. There was no prohibition of the Slave Trade placed in the organic law of the Union. There was, indeed, strong opposition to the Slave Trade, but it was not then so strong as to be able to carry this feature into the Constitution; on the contrary, the anti-Slave Trade party did not succeed in prohibiting interference with the Slave Trade for a time. The restriction was in favor of the Slave Trade, and not against it. Why should we, who are the friends of negro slavery, go so far as to incorporate the prohibition of the Slave Trade into our State Constitution, while those who are its enemies have been content to rely for its prohibition upon acts of Congress, which, in this case, are but the expression of popular will? I can see no occasion for such a radical step. It does not consist with present policy; it is not demanded by any well-founded distrust of the liability of the people to become mercenary to the destruction of their peace or their general prosperity. It would be unjust to posterity, because it would settle in the most solemn form, as a principle of Government, a matter which is only a question of policy, and not a principle of Government. It has been urged that Virginia, and Maryland, and North Carolina, require a solemn act of condemnation, on our part, of the African Slave Trade; and that they will hesitate to unite with us if we hesitate to adopt this Ordinance. Perhaps it might be as truthfully said that Texas and Louisiana would demur to a settlement of this question by the sovereign States to whose counsels they have no access; and these States might hesitate to meet with States that preclude all discussion of this question. It is much to be desired that Virginia should unite with us, and that every slave State should join readily in this movement. But I would neither bribe nor threaten Virginia, nor any other slave State. Let them act on their own convictions of duty. Some recent indications in the Virginia Legislature are not much to be applauded. It is rather a deplorable and humiliating spectacle to see a great State—the largest slaveholding State—in a serious debate on the question whether her destiny is with the North or with the South. In the event the decision should be in favor of the Northern alliance, I would not hesitate to say that, if she looks to the North for alliance and sympathy, she must look elsewhere than Alabama for a slave market. It seems to be doubtful whether our true policy is not to be found in stronger measures than in petitions, concessions and adulations. We have planned our action without reference to the opinions of any other people, and our cause will at least stand on its merits, or fall for the want of merit. The justification of our action is placed on our right to determine our own destiny; and it is to be neither stronger nor weaker because another State may approve or disapprove our course. It has not been taken without the most careful efforts to procure the harmonious action of the slave States. We have been deferential to our sister States of the South. Able Commissioners have been sent to all the States of the South, but none have come to us with any message of fraternity, except from South Carolina,

Georgia and Mississippi. This is no ground of complaint, perhaps, but it is a noticeable fact, when we enquire how far Alabama is to be compromitted in her policy by a feeling of mere deference to other States. If we leave the African Slave Trade to rest under a distinct condemnation as a measure of policy, and on grounds of policy, Virginia ought to be satisfied, and will be satisfied that we do not propose to cut off or check the Virginia Slave Trade. She can join us in the discussion of that question, and if it is her opinion that this trade should be condemned in the Federal Constitution, or in the State Constitutions, she can vote in the one case and set the example in the other. In reference to its influence upon our State, I oppose the Ordinance and prefer the Resolutions of the gentleman from Lauderdale, [Mr. Jones.] His resolutions declare a policy, and display the grounds of that policy. He has made the argument that if the suppression of the African Slave Trade is left to the action of the States alone, it will only prove to be the best means of throwing the whole country open to the traffic. Any State may open it, and no one State could prevent it. No number of States could prevent it without war, if one State should have the right to open the Slave Trade with Africa. That argument has not been answered. It appears to be conclusive on the point that this matter should not be left alone to the States. Such is the effect of the Ordinance, or else its effect is to cease when a Provisional Government is formed, and in that view it would be useless now.

The Ordinance is not framed provisionally. It is to become a settled principle of organic law in the State. I will not go into the condemnation of the African Slave Trade because, at this time, we have a stock from which enough slaves will spring to supply the demand of agriculture for perhaps twenty years in the South. If we then need more slaves, we can so order it by a change of measures to suit the altered conditon of the country. I am opposed to placing fetters on the hands of posterity. Every generation of freemen should be allowed to use the blessings of Government to their own advantage. We can trust our posterity with the destiny of their successors, just as far as we can trust ourselves with their destiny. The young State, now taking her first steps in the great march of events, ought to be left free to choose her own course; her feet ought not now to be fitted to iron shoes. The Chinese system cramps the foot of the infant, and brings a decrepitude upon youth which is never overcome. It is better to leave everything free to those who are to follow us, except the principles which we esteem to be the vital elements of good government. These we must solemnly ordain for our own security and welfare, and if our successors choose to abolish them, we will leave to them this privilege, but will not sanction the course by our own example. We are ready now to declare that public policy forbids the reopening of the African Slave Trade, but we will leave it to the generations that may occupy the Gulf of Mexico, and rule over the Islands of the adjacent seas, to determine for themselves how much of this property they need; and they ought not to be compelled to uproot the foundation of the Government before they can reach the subject.

Mr. SMITH, of Tuscaloosa, said:

Mr. President—I hope the Ordinance will be adopted as reported. It is complete in itself and needs no amendment. Whatever we say on this subject ought to be positive in its terms; it ought to be more than the mere expression of an opinion; it ought to be the fundamental law of the land.

Some of our friends here are too prone to defer action on many important questions to the Southern Congress. Let us act for ourselves. To us the responsibility belongs; let us not shift it upon others.

The gentleman from Dallas, [Mr. Morgan,] thinks that a resolution expressive of our opinion merely, would be preferable to an Ordinance, because an Ordinance would tend to cramp and trammel our Deputies in the Southern Congress. This objection does not strike me with great force. The organic law of the State, as by us framed, will necessarily have to be accommodated to the Federal Constitution, if there should be one; so that the Ordinances we may adopt here will be, at last, but expressions of our opinions. So far, then, our Ordinances would operate on our Deputies as indications only of our wishes. But even if this Ordinance should be considered as deliberate instructions to guide and control the Deputies in this case, it is no harm that it should be so. There ought not to be two opinions here on this question. The Convention should be unanimous in its opposition to reopening the African Slave Trade.

The gentleman from Dallas, [Mr. Morgan,] is unwilling to admit by his vote that the reopening of the African Slave Trade would be in itself immoral. I have deference to his opinions and respect for his scruples; but I do not think that there is any admission in the Ordinance, as reported, that the reopening of the African Slave Trade would be immoral. It is true, that the Ordinance contemplates a *penalty* for the *violation* of the law; but a prohibitory statute could not be enforced, if no penalty attach to its violation. It would be an absurdity to declare, "*you shall not do this*"—without prescribing a penalty for disobedience. Penal statutes may rest upon policy alone.

But this question of morality does not necessarily arise here. As a matter of opinion, I do not believe that the African Slave Trade would be immoral in itself now—or that it ever has been immoral. I hold, that the African, taken from his native wilds and placed in the ranks that march onward from savage to civilized life, is greatly benefitted. He is humanised and christianised. He rises from the condition of a brute into the position of a christian man. The present condition of the Alabama negro, illustrates this. Place a native African side by side with an Alabama negro—how vast is the difference in stature as well as in intellect. The one has the graceful and sinewy limbs of a Hercules —the other is a mere mongrel. In nine cases out of ten, in positive contentment, the Alabama slave is happier than his master. His cottage is built for him, his food provided, his meals prepared; his hearth to spread with substantial comforts, and his long nights are for those blissful dreams that are undisturbed by the knowledge of coming necessities. He has no cankering cares, no buffetting with fortune, no aspiration for expanding acres, no cares for rain or sunshine. He has neither cloth nor meat to buy; he is free from debt, he is above all civil law—and he looks forward to Christmas, not as the maturity time for his bills, but for his holidays. Sir, there can be nothing immoral in placing a savage in such a condition as this.

The gentleman from Dallas, [Mr. MORGAN,] supposes that hereafter—in the possibility of things, it might become his duty, from motives of *public policy*, to favor the reopening of the African Slave trade; and he does not wish to be cramped by a vote given now, denouncing or seeming to denounce its morality. Such a contingency is impossible. The arguments against the reopening of this African Slave Trade are overwhelming. Policy will never demand it. Take a single argument: We double our population as a general rule every twenty years, and the negroes multiply more rapidly than the whites. We have now over four millions of slaves in the Southern States. In twenty years, we will have eight millions; in forty years, sixteen millions; in sixty years, thirty-two millions; in eighty years, sixty-four millions; in a hundred years, one hundred and twenty-eight millions of slaves!

Shall we legislate for this day alone? Is that the duty of statesmen? Shall our foresight not reach the outlines of a single century? When Solon gave laws to Athens he looked afar into the deep future. When Lycurgus gave laws to Sparta, he planned for a thousand years in advance. When Numa framed the Roman Code in the solitary cell of Egeria, he beheld, through the vista of long centuries, Rome towering in her grandeur, as in her palmiest days up-borne on the colossal shoulders of Cicero and Cæsar. Shall it be reserved for us, who boast of wise fathers, and of free and enlightened institutions, to limit our sagacity to a single age! to labor alone for the generation that lives? We are here for higher duties. He is indeed poorly entitled to the name of patriot or statesman, who legislates for the present and not the future.

But admit that on this subject the vision of our sagacity is bounded by the shadowy walls of one hundred years; what do you behold? You see huddled together 120,000,000 of negroes, circumscribed within the limits of a dozen States; and this immense slave population will be accumulated from the natural increase of *native* slaves without any importation from Africa. Will you crowd this population still more by fresh importations? Will there be any room left for the white man? What is to become of the hardy pioneer who first cleared away the wilderness, and erected his cabin on some distant knoll, proud and happy in the possession of his little kingdom—his forty acres of land? Is he to be driven away from his happy dominions by the ominous advance of this ebony giant? This must not be. This shall not be. Surely no man here wishes this to be.

> "Ill fares the land, to hastening ills a prey,
> Where wealth accumulates and men decay;
> Princes and lords may flourish or may fade;
> A breath can make them, as a breath has made;
> But a bold peasantry, their country's pride,
> When once destroyed can never be supplied."

This question of the increase of our native slave population assumes new importance now from our present position. Heretofore we have looked abroad into the Territories for *extension*. Our recent troubles have grown out of this desire of ours for extension for our slaves into the Territories. Extension for slavery was a necessity, as the protection of slavery as property in the Territories was a demand. The one made the other indispensable. Twenty days ago, we could look abroad for extension. We had a share in boundless Territories. But what is our condition to-day? We have seceded from the Union, declared our independence, and assumed before the world the attitude of a nation. We are circumscribed now within the limits of Alabama.

We carry with us nothing except what is within our geographical limits; no rights of property outside of the State; nothing but our liberties and our *eminent domain*. Whatever else we may claim must remain to be settled hereafter by some of the modes of adjusting international disputes.

A new confederation cannot be expected to embrace more than fourteen States—and this immense negro population must be confined to the limits of the new Confederacy. Where can we go? Through Texas to Mexico? That is the only outlet. Do we desire this? For what did we fight and conquer Mexico? In order to get homes upon the soil? Surely not. How many of all the American Soldiers remained or desired to remain in Mexico? Do you wish to send your slaves away and not go with them? Not so. Even the slave would degenerate in Mexico. The slave would lose his subordination, and the institution itself would lose its vitality. American slavery, in half a century, would there be transformed into Mexican peonage. Upon Mexican soil, teeming as it is with all the enervating influences of languor; fertile only in excuses for sloth and idleness, the negro, who now in Alabama makes ten bags of cotton a year for his master would become like Shakspeare's Caliban—a " mere moon calf"—a " hedge-hog"—a " fish—legged like a man"—a "most ridiculous monster"—fit only "to dig pignuts" and to " show jay's nests."

Upon Mexican soil your negro would return to Africanism; his christianity would go back to superstition; and his frame would lose those noble and graceful proportions which physical labor so completely developes. His brawny shoulders relaxed, his vigor gone, his spirit rebellious, his disposition satanic, his head full of the rampant spirit of revolution which is become an ever-prevailing epidemic in Mexico; he would indeed be a terror instead of a servant. His petty larcenies would swell into highway robberies; and he would aspire to admission into the ranks of the brown bandits of Mexico. That would be the end of him.

But if the negro would degenerate in Mexico, would not the white man—his master? Send Alabamans to Mexico for room! Sir, that enervating climate would reach the loftiest nature and drag him from his grandest heights. The change upon a single generation would be magical. Sober American gravity would grow fantastical: American gravity would sink into Mexican frivolity; and dignity itself would be content with the grown of the harlequin. Ambition would be satisfied with the weight of a spur, or the massive adornment of a bridle; and the spirit that, in this clime, would have aspired to rival the glory of a Jackson, would there be proud to approach the immaculate excellence of Santa Anna! Virginians, Kentuckians, Carolinians, Georgians, Tennesseeans, Alabamans, Mississippians, noble in intellect, brave by nature, chivalrous by instinct, accomplished by culture; symmetrical in shape and feature; high-spirited, splendid specimens of the Anglo-American, yearning after fame and proud of their sires and their climes; God forbid that the race of such men should be degenerated under a Mexican sun!

The gentleman from Dallas [Mr. Morgan,] thinks that the passing of this Ordinance would arm our Northern enemies with legitimate bludgeons to beat us; that it would amount to a stigma upon the institution of slavery—solemnly uttered and sanctioned by us. I do not think so. The passing of this Ordinance, in my opinion, would have a contrary effect. It would disarm our Northern foes. They have branded us in advance. that one of the leading causes of our desire to break up the Union, is to escape the law which denounces and punishes the African Slave Trade. They charge us that we wish and that we intend to re-open the African Slave Trade. Sir, the passage of this Ordinance by a solemn vote of this Convention, instead of arming, would disarm our Northern foes, and prove that on this question they were either deceived in their judgments, or that they were deliberate slanderers.

There has been, in the acts of this Convention, extreme haste on many momentous questions. I am not an advocate for haste in radical changes or in important innovations; but on this great question I am anxious to make haste to adopt this Ordinance, that the world may be relieved; that our designs may be known, and, above all, that our Northern foes may be forced to seal their lips, and to cease proclaiming, to the great injury of our cause, the deliberate and unmitigated slander, that Southern slaveholders wish to break up the Union for the paramount purpose of reopening the African Slave Trade.

Take another view of this question. Shall we increase our troubles? Having assumed our independence and resumed delegated powers—having sundered the ties that bound us to the Union of the States, it is wise in us, in our first acts, to bid defiance to the whole civilized world? Have we grown so great in the brief period of a single week, that we shall court the frowns of all Christendom, and bring down upon our earliest deliberations the anathemas of all Europe? The war-ships of the most respectable governments of Europe continually cruise the high seas in search of African slavers—the United States ships setting the example of diligence, vigilance and determination to check the African Slave Trade. We have recognized it a crime for half a century, and have acquiesced without murmur in the enforcement of the penalties. Shall we increase our troubles? Shall we multiply the causes and thereby the probabilities of war? Should an English ship intercept an American vessel engaged in the African Slave Trade, it would not now be cause of war, simply because this trade is prohibited by the laws of the United States. But suppose we declare the trade legitimate, and recognize it as part of our policy; suppose, even, we refuse to pass laws to prohibit it, then the foreign intercepting of a vessel belonging to us, though engaged in the direct importation of African slaves, would be an act hostile to our commerce and equivalent to a declaration of war. Are we to suppose that an English or an American ship, crusing for the very purpose of intercepting and seizing slavers, would relax their vigilance so as to let Alabama, alone of all the nations of the earth, carry on this trade? Certainly not. If one of our slavers should be taken on the high seas, the act of intercepting it would be an indignity; and the consequence of such an event would be war, or a disgraceful surrender of our national dignity and honor.

Sir, in every act of mine, in this Convention, I shall look towards peace. I would not wantonly provoke any nation, nor would I favor a law which would not be likely to receive the approbation of the wisdom of the age.

There is no wisdom in war. It is the most brutal occupation of mankind. It should never be courted. The glory of American history is found in the fact that all her wars have been thrust upon her. We have conquered on almost every battle-field; we have vindicated our courage and our prowess before the eyes of the world; and have sent forth the historic heralds of our fame to proclaim to posterity, the achievements of our arms. We have a right now to rest—and to court the more inviting shades of peace, without being suspected of cowardice, or charged with an inglorious disposition to avoid danger. Peace, then, is our policy; for in peace alone can agriculture flourish. If COTTON IS KING, his THRONE is peace, for WAR, that turns the ploughshare into the sword, will deprive him of the implements of his power and strip away the habiliments of his Royalty.

Sir, the blessings that are to come upon the State from this revolution, must be the blessings of Peace. You can do nothing without commerce—there can be no commerce without peace. You have achieved a revolution, but you have yet a great work to accomplish—you have a country to build up. You are not merely working out a dazzling reputation. You are not to be satisfied with having pulled down a government. You have not created a political storm for the unholy purpose of filling the history of the times with stirring events and disastrous accidents. You are not merely opening the womb of emergencies, that great warriors, great orators, great statesmen, and great poets may spring out of it. You are not only creating an era, an age— that may be an age of bronze—an age of iron—an age of gold— or an age of blood. You are here for the loftiest of all purposes —*to build up a country*—for the lasting happiness, and the permanent prosperity of the millions that inhabit the land. Look, then, to Peace—that stately and commanding Queen—

"Beneath whose calm inspiring influence
Science his views enlarges, Art refines,
And swelling Commerce opens all her ports."

MR. JONES, of Lauderdale, said:

Mr. President—Situated as we are, this is one of the most important questions for our consideration. It has been charged that the object of the Cotton States in seceding from the Union, is, to reöpen the African Slave Trade. This opinion seems to have taken possession of the minds of the people of the Border Slave States, and will not fail, if not promptly repudiated by each seceding State, to engender distrust as to our future policy on the vital question. He would not now enter upon a discussion of the policy or morality of this trade. The gentleman from Barbour, [Mr. Cochran] will see that this resolution does not conflict with the views he has just submitted to the Convention, for the amendment offered by the gentleman from Dallas, [Mr. Morgan,] places the action proposed by the resolution, solely, on the ground of public policy. In every action the question of policy should yield to that of morality. The maxim that "what is immoral is always impolitic," is as true in regard to nations as individuals. But when, as in the present instance, all agree that a measure is impolitic, and some say that it is immoral, it is a useless waste of time to inquire who has the better reason for the vote he is about to give? The only pertinent question is that stated by the gentleman from Mobile, [Mr. Bragg.] Will the Ordinance submitted by the Committee on Federal Relations or the substitute offered by me better accomplish the end proposed? The Ordinance simply proposes to declare by *Organic Law* that the African Slave Trade shall be prohibited in Alabama. To his mind this did not meet the necessities of the case, and consequently he offered as a substitute the resolution now pending. This resolution instructs the Deputies elected by us to the Southern Convention, to assemble at Montgomery, Alabama, on the 4th day of February next, to insist on the adoption of such restrictions as will effectually prohibit the African Slave Trade. The Ordinance of the Committee, if adopted, provides no penalty for its violation, and without some legislation will be wholly powerless to accomplish the end proposed. The Legislature can do, under the present Constitution of the State, precisely what this Ordinance proposes. Indeed, section 2058 of the Code covers the whole case and renders any further legislation by this State unnecessary.

Mr. Bragg:

Will the gentleman read the section named?

Mr. Jones:

Certainly—the section reads thus: "If any slaves or persons of color, have been or are hereafter brought into this State in violation of the laws of the United States prohibiting the Slave Trade, the Governor," &c.

Mr. Bragg:

The act of Secession repealed all the laws of the United States, and hence this section is not now in force.

Mr. Jones said:

He thought not. The section recited, only refers to certain laws of the United States; these laws are *descriptive* of a certain class of offences. Now, sir, in enforcing this law of Alabama the act of Congress is looked to for a description of the offence—the Statute 2058 declares, that the act so described is, when committed within the limits of Alabama, an offence, and prescribes the penalty—precisely as you would look to the Common Law of England for the description of an offence, the laws of Alabama pro poses to denounce and punish.

He held, that so far as Alabama is concerned, this traffic is not only fully but wisely and amply provided for. It commits us to no pseudo philanthropy to pay thousands, to recommit men redeemed from barbarism back to hopeless bondage unmitigated by a ray of christianity or civilization.

Another objection to the proposed Ordinance is, that it will have no *extra territorial* effect, and will leave us at the mercy of neighboring States. I care not how stringent the laws of Alabama may be on this subject, if the State of Florida should allow or connive at the traffic, this race will be imported, domiciled, and then smuggled over on our borders, or brought in droves under the general laws of commerce between the United States.

But, sir, it is conceded that Alabama does not design to remain as a separate State—that she will be a member of a Confederated Republic in a few weeks, is as certain as that the Sun will rise to-morrow. The Slave Trade will then belong appropriately to the Republic, as it has ever done to the General Government of the United States. We have clearly proclaimed that the New Government is to conform to the *model* made by our ancestors; why then attempt to depart from the good old way so soon and on a subject of such deep interest to our people and to civilized man every where? A prohibition by the new Republic will suppress the Slave Trade alike in all the States entering into the New Government, and will encourage others to enter and give strength, stability and respectability to the New Government. That Government will have a Navy to capture Slavers, and thus suppress the trade. It will have foreign alliances to aid in this great work of humanity.

But suppose this State shall determine to take this subject under her own jurisdiction—the State having claimed in every case jurisdiction—your delegates cannot surrender it to the New Government. Other States will follow the policy marked out by us, and thus there will be no *general law* but an interminable conflict ending in a total failure to enforce the laws.

The separate States will be utterly powerless to prevent a traffic which the greed and avarice of the worst and boldest men of the age attempt to carry on. All the power of the General Government, aided by the most powerful maratime nations of Europe, have been unable to fully suppress this trade. Then, if left to the action of the separate States, there will not be a decent show of opposition. Some may even permit it, and thus another horde of barbarians will be poured upon us.

Gentlemen may hold their own opinions, they may sanction the traffic if they chose, but for myself and my constituents, I solemnly protest now and forever against any course that will permit another African to land upon the soil of Alabama.

Mr. POSEY said:

I am for the substitute reported by the Committee, in preference to the amendment offered by my colleague [Mr. Jones].

The Committee have not prohibited the Slave Trade by making it a felony. The Ordinance, introduced by me, did. This is the principal difference. The amendment proposed by my colleague to the Committee's Ordinance, is a mere declaration of opinion against the Slave Trade, and instruction to our delegates in the Convention of the seceding States, to vote for a prohibition in the Constitution against the traffic.

The effect of the amendment under consideration would be to leave our ports open to the trade, until the Southern Congress prohibited the traffic. I would have the prohibition inserted in the Constitution of Alabama. Public sentiment, in this State, is against the Slave Trade. Why should not this opinion of the people of Alabama be incorporated in their Organic Law? Is it probable that there will be any change in public sentiment upon this subject? I think not. I see nothing in the new relation in which secession places us to other States and Governments, likely to bring about such change. Did we need more territory before secession, for the expansion of our peculiar institution? We yet have the same need for more territory. The rapid increase of our slaves, points to the necessity of acquiring more territory before we import slaves from Africa. The same rules which apply to the prosperity of individuals, are applicable to the welfare of nations. He who employs more slaves, or buys more than he has land for their profitable employment, does not act as wisely as does the man who keeps an eye to the due proportion of each. When we look at the extent of our territory, the number and the increase of the slaves upon our soil, which do we need most, more slaves, or more land for those we now have? Mr. President, the fierce strife we have had with the Northern States, which has led to the disruption of the Government, is a trumpet-tongued answer to this question. They have declared, by the election of Lincoln, "There shall be no more slave territory—no more slave States." To this the Cotton States have responded by acts of secession and a Southern Confederacy; which is but a solemn declaration of these States, that they will not submit to the Northern idea of restricting slavery to its present limits, and confining it to the slave States.

And why not submit to this exclusion from the Territories, the common property of all the States? Because the South believes this Northern policy of restricting slavery to its present limits, would ultimately destroy the institution. And can there be any reasonable doubt as to the policy we should adopt? Should the period ever come when the Southern Confederacy shall have acquired more territory than can be properly settled and cultivated

14

by the then white and black population, then it will be time enough to import African slaves. The gentleman from Dallas [Mr. Morgan], argues, against this Ordinance, that it reflects upon our ancestors, brands the business they followed as a great crime, and indorses the Abolition stigma upon slaveholders. With due respect to the opinions of that gentleman, I hold this to be an unfair argument. It assumes the position that this Ordinance, if passed, makes the Slave Trade an offense which is *mala in se*, unless so amended as to contain an express declaration that the Slave Trade is neither immoral nor unjust. Gentlemen upon this floor declare they will not vote for prohibition without such amendment. It is unusual to state, in any prohibitory law, whether the evil is bad in itself, or made evil by the penalty imposed for the public good. I shall vote for the prohibition, because the African Slave Trade is contrary to the good policy of the State; not for the reason that it is against good morals. I believe the traffic to be sinful; but this is not the sole ground of my opposition to it. I would prohibit it as a great evil to the South.

What room will we have for our white population, when the ports of the country shall have been opened to slaves from Africa? Even now a considerable part of the white population of the country occupy the inferior lands. Shall we drive them to the mountains, or force them to remove to the Northern States, to make room for African slaves not wanted by the country?

It is well known that the Border Slave States, as well as the Northern States, suppose that the opening of the Slave Trade is one of the chief objects of a Southern Confederacy. I am for setting them right on this subject, so far as this State is concerned, and without delay. Not one of the Border States would consent to join the Southern Confederacy, and take the African Slave Trade. We owe it to our fellow-citizens in those States, to ourselves, and to the cause of the whole South, to place the State of Alabama in its true and appropriate position upon this important question.

MR. POTTER said:

Mr. President—The question before us demands that every member of this Convention shall take position, either for the Substitute or the Ordinance reported by the Committee. And it does really appear to me, sir, that the debate which has sprung up here, has taken a very wide range and a strange course. It is quite astonishing to me, sir, that the Slave Trade itself, and the institution of slavery as it now exists amongst us, should be treated of as if they were perfectly identical in point of morality; and more astonishing still, to hear such sentiments as have been uttered upon this floor, in regard to this trade.

Now, sir, it is not perceived how anything that can be said, concerning the morality or immorality of the African slave trade, can be considered pertinent to the question now before us. Yet, as this subject has been introduced here, I am free to say that, while I conscientiously believe that it is our duty to support and perpetuate the institution of slavery as it is, still it is my honest conviction that the Slave Trade, as it was formerly carried on, and as, in all probability, it will be conducted in future, if tolerated, is immoral in its tendency and effects.

This view of the subject does not necessarily involve in guilt those who, by purchase or otherwise, may become the owners of slaves.

This question certainly ought to be settled on principles of policy alone; and the State of Alabama ought to adopt such measures as her present sovereign and independent position demands; and she should assume such ground, on this important question, as will place her in a proper attitude before the world. That this may be done, it appears to me, sir, that a positively Prohibitory Ordinance is preferable to a mere resolution of instruction, which may or may not influence the action of the approaching Southern Convention.

All the arguments offered in support of the Substitute, upon which we are soon to cast a vote, appear to be founded upon the assumption that a Southern Confederacy will very soon be formed. But it should be remembered that such a Republic exists at present only in prospect, and our hopes, in this regard, may or may not be realised. It therefore becomes us to act in our present condition, as true policy dictates to be best. And as the Ordinance will more effectually secure the object sought, I prefer its adoption to that of the Substitute.

WITHDRAWING TROOPS FROM FLORIDA.

Mr. CLEMENS, from the Committee on Military Affairs, made the following report:

The Committee on Military Affairs, to whom was referred a Resolution, requesting the Governor to recall the Alabama Volunteers, now stationed at or near Pensacola, in the State of Florida, have had the same under consideration, and instructed me to report back the same, and recommend its adoption.

SECRET SESSION

Mr. Clemens said:

Mr. President—I have examined, with much care, the proposition which has been by me submitted to the Convention; and I have come to the conclusion that the Alabama Volunteers ought to be withdrawn from Florida at this time. It is understood, from communications made in conversations, by Mr. Malory, late Senator in the Congress of the United States, from Florida, that there has been an agreement with Mr. Toucey, Secretary of the Navy of the United States, that there are to be no hostilities in Pensacola harbor, by the United States forces, until the 4th of March. If this be true, and of that there can be no doubt, there is now no use for our troops in Florida.

They are there without the slightest military preparation, having been ordered off in great haste; and many of them have left their business entangled and their families not provided for.

These considerations, however, might not be of much weight, if the services of these troops were essential to Florida or to the public safety at Pensacola. But there is a day coming, sir, when the services of these troops will be needed—needed, too, in all their vigor; and for that day it is our duty to provide.

They are now quartered in a place where they themselves are satisfied that their time is wasted, and they can do nothing for their country. The life of idleness which they now lead, will disgust them with military service, and they will grow weary of the camp before they have an opportunity to exhibit their valor or to use their arms.

I read from a letter, just received, by one who is well posted on this subject:

Warrington Navy Yard, Florida, } January 26, 1861.

Dear Sir: I received, last night, your obliging favor of the 22nd instant, and I hasten to give you my views of our military position and condition. On the 15th instant we arrived here with upwards of 400 men, which made our force here about 1,000 men. Since then about 400 others have arrived, which makes our present number 1,400. We came under the belief that all things were ready, and that an assault would be made upon Fort Pickens in twenty-four hours after our arrival. We hastily left important business at home, and many left clerkships and unprovided families, with the assurance of an early return. We have been here now twelve days, in utter supineness and indolence, doing nothing, and despairing of our doing anything. The most intense disgust and dissatisfaction pervades the camp.

We have had abundant time to put ourselves in an impregnable position, but we have done almost nothing. Fort McRae, which is the second best position, is in our possession, but utterly neglected. For an entire week it was left unoccupied, and now it is occupied by one company of light infantry. Not a gun is mounted, though 150 are there, and among them three very fine new columbiads. There is also there an abundance of ammunition.

From this letter, Mr. President, and from other sources of reliable information, I am satisfied that these troops are becoming heartily discouraged at Pensacola, and if we persist in keeping them in this situation, we will be spoiling our best soldiers.

Mr. Watts said:

It is understood that the steamer Brooklyn, with two companies for the reinforcement of Fort Pickens, has recently sailed for Pensacola. Has the Chairman of the Committee on the Military [Mr. Clemens], any distinct information as to the terms of the agreement spoken of? I am unwilling to trust implicitly to rumors of agreements. What is this agreement?

Mr. Clemens said:

I know nothing more of the terms of the agreement than what is derived from Senator Mallory's statements, before referred to.

The gentleman [Mr. Watts] is right as to the sailing of the Brooklyn; but we have no certain information as to her destination. Doubtless it is for Pensacola. But we have no means of preventing this reinforcement. The Macedonia is now in the neighborhood of Fort Pickens. She has, doubtless, before this time, reinforced the garrison at Fort Pickens.

I have as little confidence in agreements with Mr. Buchanan as the gentleman from Montgomery has. But we cannot, by keeping the troops in Florida, prevent these contemplated reinforcements. For this service our troops are utterly useless at this time, with such means as are at their command.

Mr. Brooks, the President, [Mr. Webb in the Chair,] moved to amend by inserting after "Governor," the words, "if, in his discretion, the public good should require it." This, it seems to me, Mr. President, will reach the views even of those who seem most earnestly to favor the passage of the Resolution. I do not profess to have military experience, but having confided this matter to the Governor, I think it ought to be subject still to his discretion and better judgment. If this amendment be adopted, the Governor can then be controlled by such circumstances and exigencies as may now surround him, or as may hereafter arise. I was present [with Mr. Morgan,] at the interview between Mr. Mallary and the Governor. I am satisfied, from my understanding of the substance of that interview, that it would be highly improper and unwise, now to withdraw the troops.

[Here, Mr. Brooks stated his understanding of the interview between the Governor and Mr. Mallary.]

In this interview, Mr. Mallary and the Governor discussed the propriety of removing the troops. The conclusion, as I understood, was, that it would be improper now to withdraw them—especially, unless the Governor of Florida should recommend it. Mr. Mallary at first wished the troops withdrawn, but changed his opinion. This change of opinion was the result of a full investigation of the subject.

If this Convention wishes to take upon itself to be the Commander-in-Chief of our Military operations, we will have a good deal to do.

My conclusion is, that we should leave this matter with the Governor, in whose discretion we have already placed it, and in whom we have reason to place the utmost confidence.

Mr. CLEMENS said:

The Convention may not wish to take upon itself to be Commander-in-Chief of our Military operations, but the Convention did take charge of this thing. Our Resolution authorized the Governor to send troops to Florida. This was against my protest; and if we have taken one wrong step, it is no harm to retrace it. I have no objection to invest the Governor with all reasonable discretion. There is no discourtesy meant towards either the Governor of Florida, or to the Governor of Alabama. This Resolution has been postponed until to-day, in deference to the Governor.

As to the suggestion of the gentleman from Mobile, [Mr. Dargan,] that if recalled they ought to be sent back if necessary; this would be improper. We will have no right to send them back

—no right to impose any new restrictions or regulations on them. They went without terms.

MR. BROOKS said:

I withdraw my proposed amendment, and offer another, which I think will reach the whole matter: strike out the word *"required"* and insert the word, "authorized."

MR. WILLIAMSON said:

Mr. President—I have great regard for the opinions and wishes of the Governor. He is wise and prudent. If he thinks these troops ought not to be withdrawn, we ought to stand by him. It is already said that Fort Pickens has been reïnforced. If we withdraw our troops it will be said that we have backed out, and the news will be heralded from one end of the country to the other —despiriting our friends and giving aid and comfort to our enemies.

MR. MORGAN said:

Mr. President—The proposition to withdraw our troops from Pensacola, involves many delicate questions of duty and policy, viewing it in every light. I am constrained to differ from the opinions advanced by the distinguished Chairman of the Committee on Military affairs. Having no knowledge of military science, and no experience to aid, I can only decide for myself the course we should pursue, by accepting one or two propositions involved in the Resolutions as they address themselves to a man of common sense. It has been stated, on high authority, that the Bay of Pensacola is so commanded by the forts and batteries in our possession, that no hostile fleet can enter, although it may be supported by the whole power of Fort Pickens. It is stated, also, that a war vessel can reïnforce Fort Pickens in despite of any batteries we have the means to plant on Santa Rosa Island. If Fort Pickens has not already been reïnforced, it may be assumed as a fact, that it will be reïnforced whenever the United States Government chooses to do so. Certainly, with a full garrison, and with the assistance of a fleet that could sweep every approach by land to Fort Pickens, the reduction of that Fortress may be expected to terminate the war, if war ensues. This will be the base of military operations, to be extended into Alabama, Georgia, and Mississippi, and even as far North as Tennessee, and will be the last position that we can take in the war. Our only hope of defence in that quarter, consists in our ability to prevent the introduction of war ships into Pensacola Bay, and to prevent the landing of a hostile force on the main land in such position as to keep open communications with Fort Pickens. Should such force effect a landing, and secure Barancas and Fort McRea, we would be at every disadvantage, and might expect to be overrun, until the line of the invading force should be so weakened by extension, that we could break it.

If these are correct views of the question, it is a matter of the highest importance that we should hold our position near Pensacola at every hazard, and regardless of expenses. To abandon the Forts on the Bay, or to leave them open to attack, would be to peril everything without any corresponding advantage, or any real necessity. Two reasons have been urged why we should withdraw the troops. The first is, the pacific disposition of the President, and the other is, the irregular manner in which our troops have been raised and organized for this service, tending, as is alledged, to cause them to be dissatisfied, and giving ground for apprehension that they may become demoralized by a life of wasting inactivity. I have as much faith in the pacific intentions of the President as could be inspired by frequent and positive assurances of peaceful intentions on his part, and by several acts, which sooner or later he has sanctioned, tending directly to war. I hope the President is pacific, but faith shudders to plant its feet on uncertain ground. If the President and Cabinet, with their advisers, intend to keep the peace, they will add an agreeable feature to a list of disappointments of a disagreeable character. Still, I hope for peace during the present administration, for no man ought willingly to commence war who cannot possibly conduct it to a conclusion. Mr. Buchanan ought not to bequeath to Mr. Lincoln the opportunity to continue a war, or to conclude a peace upon terms disparaging to his reputation. But war exists at Pensaloca, if the President, or the Congress, chooses to recognize the fact. Our troops, under command of the Governor of Florida, made war on Commodore Armstrong at the Navy Yard, and demanded its surrender to the power of superior force. The United States flag was hauled down, and another flag was hoisted and saluted. True, this was done in reply to a warlike movement on the part of Lieutenant Slemmer, who destroyed what munitions of war he could not remove, and having spiked the guns in Barrancas, retreated to Fort Pickens. But whoever opened the war, it certainly was prosecuted until the Navy Yard was surrrendered to the State of Florida, and it is now held as a conquered post. The President might conceive that it would be lawful and proper to attempt to retake the position, now in possession of our troops, by the display of a superior force—a demand and surrender. And he might signalize the fact by hoisting the United States flag when it floated over Commodore Armstrong, in the place of the flag now floating over the Navy Yard.

If our troops are withdrawn, and if Florida and Mississippi should imitate the example, these posts would at once be occupied by United States troops, and still no blood would be spilled. Once reinstated in that position, we might never expect to regain the possession of these forts and batteries from the U. S. troops without great loss of life. Looking at the matter in this light, I can see nothing but danger in the movement if we now abandon these forts, as we must do if our troops are withdrawn. I agree that the troops there now are exposed to many perils incident to a garrison life, and to the more serious danger of becoming disgusted with the service. I also agree that they are under no legal compulsion to remain there, and I am anxious to see their places supplied by regular soldiers, or volunteers, for a fixed term of service, I doubt not but that many of those now at Pensacola would remain for a term of service, and I feel sure that not a man there would return home if he could know that his services were needed by the State. No duty would be irksome to them, if the State would be benefited. So soon as we can supply their places, they ought to be relieved. We owe it as a duty to these gallant men who suddenly answered the call of the State, and took up the line of march for the service of the State with unquestioning devotion to its cause. But by all means, and at every sacrifice, let us maintain our ground at Pensacola. The impossibility of maintaining our position there ought never to be admitted until we have made every effort to that purpose. If an enemy can disembark troops at Pensacola, accompanied with heavy batteries, Mobile would soon fall into his hands, and Fort Morgan would be cut off from communication with the interior. New Orleans would be an easy prey, and the commerce of the Mississippi would fall into his hands. If there is another point on the Gulf, within striking distance of Mobile or New Orleans, where a fleet could so successfully disembark large masses of troops and heavy guns, I am not aware of it. I take it for granted that if there is such a point, the military skill of the United States officers would have placed it in a strong position of defense. I must believe that the loss of our present defences at Pensacola would expose us to the greatest danger. We will not advance the cause of Peace by a retreat from the Fortifications we have taken, nor by receding from the position we assumed in demanding their surrender. If the policy of the United

States is to make war, it will not be wanting in various pretexts to justify the course. If the policy of that Government is to be peaceful, it will not find occasion of offence towards us, because we considered the conduct of Major Anderson at Fort Sumter, and of Lieutenant Slemmer at Fort Pickens, as a threat of war. I fully justify the course of Gov. Moore in seizing the Forts and Arsenals in Alabama, and would feel very happy to justify the Governor of Florida if he had taken Fort Pickens even at the sacrifice of life. I impute no blame to him that he did not act more promptly, for we well know that Florida was unprovided with soldiers at the critical moment, and that Alabama was still hanging suspended in doubtful discussion on the Ordinance of Secession.

As the proposition, which I have advanced, to raise five hundred men by enlistment to supply the places of the Volunteers now at Pensacola, does not meet the approbation of the Chairman of the Committee on Military Affairs, I will on to-morrow submit another plan, by which the existing Ordinance, in reference to military preparations in the State, can be extended to the protection of the coast defences of the Gulf, and so as to prevent or repel invasion in that quarter.

Mr. JEMISON said:

I am no military man, and for this very reason—for the satisfaction of myself and those who are not military men—it is proper that all military movements of this character should be sustained by arguments addressed to our common sense, so that even he who is not a military man may be convinced to his satisfaction.

I saw no reason for sending these troops to Florida, in the first place. The argument then was, the Governor wishes it. Now, when we propose to withdraw them, it is objected to for the same reason—the Governor objects to it.

The condition of our soldiers who are now in the Forts is disagreeable to them, and unprofitable to us and to the public service. They are powerless to do good and potent to do evil. Disgust, and its consequence, idleness and discontent pervade their ranks. Why retain them where they can accomplish nothing? Shall we sacrifice our young men, the very flower of the country, merely for a little military parade? I apprehend that there is not now, with military men of judgment, any one who thinks of attacking Fort Pickens. There are not enough men in the State of Florida and Alabama both, under the present situation of affairs, to take this Fort.

It is as important to know when to fight as it is to fight.

We began this matter wrong foot foremost. Let us retrace our steps, put ourselves right, so that we may be the better ready to meet the great issue when it comes.

Mr. BROOKS:

Mr. President—I regret very much to differ in opinion with the Chairman of the Military Committee. But this discussion has confirmed me in my original opinion.

I am surprised at the remarks of the gentleman from Tuscaloosa [Mr. Jemison.] I think he does injustice both to the Governor and to the Convention. The troops were not sent to Pensacola at the request of the Governor of Alabama, but at the request of the Governor of Florida, through a telegraphic dispatch. The Convention acted upon its own convictions. The facts were adverted to, and all the surrounding circumstances referred to in an elaborate and animated discussion. And it is the opinion of many who are best acquainted with the condition of things at Fort Pickens, that if our troops had reached Pensacola twenty-four hours sooner, we might have taken the Fort. As it is, our mission was not fruitless—if we did not get all, we got much—large quantities of arms and munitions of war.

Sir, we have placed those troops under the charge of the Governor of Florida. Would he not have a right to complain should we thus unceremoniously withdraw them? And if we do withdraw them, what will be the consequences? The Federal troops will take possession of the places now held by our forces. Is this desirable?

It is objected that there may be blood-shed. But the troops do not make this objection. When soldiers consent to go to the field of battle, they go with the expectation that there will be bloodshed.

I do not adopt the opinion of the gentleman from Tuscaloosa, [Mr. Jemison,] that our troops in the Forts are disgusted and discontented. I have it from one who knows—from one who commands a Company in one of our Forts—that a different state of feeling exists; that the troops are satisfied, and ready for duty.

But, sir, at all events, the Governor of Florida ought to be advised of our wishes to withdraw the troops, in order that he may send his own to occupy the Forts.

If we do withdraw the troops, we will occupy a very awkward position, not only before the people and Governor of Florida, but before the world. There is no good reason for such a course.

It should not be done. Then let the Governor of the State have the discretion to do, in the premises, whatever circumstances may warrant.

Mr. JEMISON said:

I have not mentioned the authority upon which I based my remarks as to the present discontented condition of the troops in the Forts; but I have as good authority as the Captain to which the gentleman from Perry [Mr. Brooks] has reference, and if that gentleman will go with me, I will show him the authority upon which I spoke.

Mr. WATTS said:

Is Alabama a Republic or not? Are we going back into a Union with the Black Republicans? What is the meaning of withdrawing our troops from the Forts? What are we to do? Are we to abandon our positions? How are we to repel any invading force? Are we now to yield, as if without a struggle, to the power of Buchanan, or of Black Republicanism? It seems so to me; for there is no proposition coupled with the one to withdraw, by which the places of these troops are to be supplied. Sir, we need Fort Pickens and we must have it at every hazard. Instead of withdrawing these troops, we ought to send more, and carry on with the utmost rapidity our fortifications. We must do this, or the world will vote us cowards. We have got a small advantage, in the outset, and now it is proposed even to abandon that! We must even withdraw from Fort Morgan, it is said! Shall we give up Mobile, too? If we are to be led back to Black Republicanism and reconstruction, let us know it. I do not wish to be led back blindfolded.

The Forts in Florida are of more importance than the Forts in Alabama. They are equally important to Georgia, Louisiana and Mississippi—much more important even than Fort Sumter. Florida is not in a condition to take her own Forts, by reason of her immense coast. We must help her; and in helping her we help ourselves. We must not act under the supposition that the Southern Congress may do this or that. We do not know yet what the Congress will do.

Mr. CLEMENS said:

Mr. President—I have listened to the gentleman from Montgomery, [Mr. Watts,] with a great deal of pleasure, as I always do;

though it would be difficult to conceive a more complete misapprehension of the subject than he has exhibited. The question is not whether we can take Fort Pickens, nor yet whether we ought to take it. It is much more simple in its character, and requires for its proper understanding, neither military knowledge nor learning of any kind. It is a plain question of justice to men who have manifested a most commendable alacrity to obey the call of the State.

The volunteers now at Pensacola went there under an order from this Convention, explicit and unmistakable in its terms. They were sent there to remain only *during the deliberations of this body upon the Ordinance of Secession.* In point of fact, that time has passed. By no rule of construction can it be held to extend beyond to-morrow when our adjournment shall take place. Many of them abandoned profitable situations at home to obey our orders. Some of them left families without the means of support during a lengthened absence. All of them went at a day's notice, and all of them were unprovided with the most common necessaries for a campaign. Those necessaries have not been supplied by this State, or the State of Florida. Contrary to all military rule, the command was taken from their own officers, and entrusted to a junior in rank. That junior, during a temporary absence, offered to them a still grosser insult, by assigning the command to a Captain. But all this has been submitted to in a spirit of patriotic devotion, to which my military experience furnishes no parallel. They have served out their time. The period for which they agreed to serve has fully expired, and we are gravely deliberating whether we shall compel them to remain contrary to their wishes, and in violation of their agreement.

Sir, we are at the beginning, as I believe, of grave and long continued troubles. We are entering upon a career in which the arm and the heart of every soldier in the State will be needed; and it is an unhappy policy to begin by disgusting and demoralizing the most enthusiastic of that volunteer army, upon which we shall be compelled mainly to rely for the defence of our firesides.

You have no right to keep them without their own consent. They went upon no terms but the provisions of an Ordinance, which has been fully complied with. They may shoulder their muskets to-morrow and return, and there is no power lodged anywhere to try them, and punish them for disobedience. Their officers are without commissions from the State, or any authority but that which has been voluntarily confided to them by the men. The privates have taken no oath, signed no muster roll, and agreed to no stipulation. There is nothing to prevent their return but a sense of public duty.

The gentleman from Montgomery complains that, in offering a resolution to withdraw these men, I have made no provision to supply their places. Sir, it was not necessary. I paid the gentleman the compliment of supposing that he knew what this Convention, of which he is a distinguished member, had been doing. I could not believe that he was ignorant of the fact that the power to do all which is necessary to be done in the premises had been vested in the Governor by the 5th Section of the Ordinance, to provide for the military defence of the State. The power of the Governor to accept the services of *any number* of volunteers for that, or any other service, which, in his judgment, may be necessary for the State, is only limited by the restriction, that they shall be accepted for a term not less than twelve months, unless sooner discharged. If a permanent occupation of Forts Barancas and McRae is contemplated, it would surely be better that their garrisons should be composed of troops having the longest term of service to run. I cannot see the disgrace of substituting the one for the other. Nay, more, sir, I cannot see the disgrace of withdrawing them entirely without any intention of replacing them by others. They confessedly hold the Forts and the Navy Yard by sufferance. It is conceded that they can be compelled to evacuate them in two hours, by the fire of Fort Pickens, aided by a man-of-war. Their occupation of all their positions depends upon the forbearance of their enemies; and it strikes me that it would be more honorable, as well as more prudent to withdraw, while a choice is left them, instead of waiting to be run away in disgrace.

I do not mean to discuss the feasibility of taking Fort Pickens by assault. I have opinions upon that point, which I may have occasion to express at another time. What I mean to assert now is, that it is an absurdity to keep a force in position in front of a fortified place, and in point blank range of its guns, which is powerless to prevent reinforcements, and too weak even to defend itself if attacked. If Fort Pickens is to be assailed we want more men; if it is not, we have too many.

These, sir, are my opinions. They are expressed with entire respect for those who differ from me, and without a particle of feeling. I have a public duty to discharge, which would be poorly performed if I did not say that, to my apprehension, the retention of those troops where they are can serve no good end, and may be productive of serious calamities. Besides, I repeat, that every soldier of that command has a right—an obsolute right, to expect his recall, and will have just ground of complaint if it is not ordered.

To place myself fairly upon the record, it is necessary that I should call for the "yeas and noes," upon laying the amendment upon the table, since the adoption of the amendment is equivalent to a defeat of the resolution.

The Convention refused to pass the Resolution, and the matter of removing the troops was left with the Governor.

CITIZENSHIP.

Mr. Herndon moved to amend as follows: "Insert in section 4th between the words "person" and "vote" the words, "natives of any of the States or Territories of the United States."

Mr. Beck offered as a substitute for Mr. Herndon's amendment to insert after the word "person" in the first line, "who at the date of the Ordinance of Secession was a citizen of the United States of North America." Accepted by Mr. Herndon.

Mr. Dowdell said:

I cannot vote for this amendment. When a man shoulders his gun, and puts his life in jeopardy to defend my country, I will give my consent to no discriminations against him because of the place of his nativity. Already it has been stated as a fact, that the first company which tendered their services to the Governor, ready to march to the place of danger, embraced men of foreign birth, who would be excluded from citizenship by the provisions of this amendment. This case shows the injustice of the law, without the necessity of resorting to any supposed illustration of its impolicy. Sir, we have now separated ourselves from the old Union, and I hope that we shall keep free from the dangerous heresies which not only marred the beautiful theory of a Republican Government, but were fast destroying Republican liberty. Let us commence by discountenancing distinctions among white men at the South. Let there be but two classes of persons here—the white and the black. Let distinction of color only, be distinction of class—keep all white men politically equal —the superior race—let the negro be the subordinate, and our Government will be strong and our liberties secure. I am perfectly willing to throw around citizenship all proper safe-guards

—to elevate and dignify the privilege, but not at the expense of equality between white men. Say to the man who fights your battles—bears the burdens of Government, that you must *never* vote nor be allowed a voice in the laws under which you are to live, nor *ever* enter into competition with your fellows for posts of honor in the civil service of your adopted country, and you put upon him the brand of inferiority. There is no longer equality—the great principle is violated—he is below his neighbor—distinctions commence—classes are authorized by law, the bane of a Democratic Republican Government. There is no proposition clearer to my mind, than this—banish African Slavery from among us and you destroy Democratic liberty. For liberty under the form of a Democratic Government, without African Slavery, is in my opinion an impossibility. The necessity of society demands the discharge of menial duties. Those who shall discharge them, must and will occupy the position of an inferior. Let that inferior class be composed of the African, and the equality of the white race is maintained—otherwise, grades in Society will follow, first social then political, destructive not only of the form but the life of Democracy. White people will be divided into a lower and higher class, liable to, and promotive of constant conflicts, and tending certainly to the disfranchisement and slavery of the menial or inferior class.

Then let us beware, and scrutenize closely any measure which looks to the least difference in political or social position between individuals of the white race. Whilst it is our duty to throw around the privilege of citizenship the proper safe-guards, let us be cautious that we do not plant the seeds of aristocracy which shall hereafter spring up and ripen into a fruitage of death to democratic liberty. Let the true and only test of difference in social or political life among us be—

"Worth makes the man, the want of it the fellow."

Mr. SHORTRIDGE said:

Mr. President—I am somewhat surprised at the reasons assigned by my friend from Mobile, [Mr. Dargan,] in opposition to the 4th Section of the Ordinance now before the Convention. The effect of his argument is to deny the doctrine of expatriation, and to reëstablish the old and exploded dogma of perpetual allegiance, as expounded in the common law.

[Here Mr. Dargan asked and obtained leave to explain.]

Mr. Shortridge resumed:

I must confess that the explanation of the gentleman from Mobile has not tended to enlighten me. He has rather thrown a denser fog around the subject, through the dim obscurity of which I am unable to see my way.

In addition to the arguments of the gentleman from Montgomery, [Mr. Watts,] in support of the fourth Section, it strikes me others may be urged. The question of naturalization or citizenship is a very different one now from that which agitated political circles in 1854, '55 and '56. Then, the South as the weaker portion of the Union, might well look with alarm and distrust on the large tide of emigration which was flowing on the country, and which was diffusing itself over the North and West. Thus, the Abolition vote was increased, and the anti-slavery sentiment stimulated; and even in cases which denied the right of suffrage to the emigrants, they were, nevertheless, rated in the census, and indirectly became instruments to augment the power of the enemies of Southern institutions. Now, however, the scene is changed. We, of Alabama, have cut the cords which bound us to the Union. We have no longer cause to dread the despotism of that majority, whose aim and end has been to stifle justice and liberty, and to trample on the Constitution. Our policy now should be to invite men to live with us who are willing to fight with us. Wherever a white man can be found—it matters little where born—who will enlist under our flag and march to the field to defend our independence and our homes, he should be honored with the rights of citizenship. Some gentlemen have spoken disparagingly of foreigners. Sir, I would as soon trust an Irishman or a Dutchman as a *Yankee*. Nay, sir, I am prepared to make the avowal, that I could repose more confidence in the fidelity and patriotism of these humble men, than in thousands of those natives who lounge in the saloons or strut on the streets of Boston.

There is yet another reason which induces me to look with favor on the 4th Section of this Ordinance. It is this: the Government at Washington, in the event of war, will attempt to seduce to its support, volunteers, by offers of large bounties of lands. This policy is already actually introduced into Congress. We have no resources of a similar kind with which to invite recruits. But we can bestow the high position of citizenship to such as by their valor shall earn it. This is more than an offset; for it carries along with it the most valued privileges, both political and personal, which can be conferred.

I hope the motion to strike out will not prevail.

Mr. Whatley said :

Mr. President—The amendment of the gentleman from Mobile [Mr. Dargan] proposes to strike out the 4th Section of the Ordinance, and thus deny the right of citizenship to those who shall actually enlist in the army of the State, "and be engaged in actual service" in the defence of her rights. Sir, if we are willing that they shall mingle with us in the bloody field of battle, *much more* should we be willing, when the battle is fought and the victory won, that they should mutually share with us the fruits of our common toil. Gentlemen have spoken of "paupers and criminals" becoming citizens of the State, and if a stranger had stepped in and heard this debate, particularly the remarks of the gentleman from Mobile, [Mr. Dargan,] he would have thought the gentleman was making a "Know-Nothing" speech, in his denunciation of foreigners. But, Mr. President, in the language of Holy Writ, "you shall not muzzle the ox that treads out the corn." If they have entered our ranks, and thereby manifested their adherence to our cause, it is but a poor privilege that we should say to them, they may become citizens of the land they have helped to defend.

Gentlemen say that persons may become citizens, who have entered our army and not served exceeding ten days. Well, grant it. If they have entered our army and been *honorably discharged*, that is sufficient. They have showed the *quo animo*. They have made manifest on which side of this *great fight* between the North and the South they are willing to array themselves—in this they show themselves the friends of *equality and justice* in preference to *fanaticism and Black Republican domination*. I would infinitely prefer such a citizen, be he foreigner or pauper, to a Massachusetts Yankee, or even to a Southern-born citizen, whose heart is with the North in this trying issue.

Then, away with the idea of disfranchising those who have fought with us and for us, whether they are foreigners, or "to the manor born." We want men whose souls are with us, and whose hearts are in the right place.

Mr. Watts said:

Mr. President—Before the vote is taken, I beg to make a single suggestion ; and that is, that many members of the volunteer companies, which have just entered the service of the State, are foreigners. Will you, at such a time, adopt this amendment, and thereby declare to these very soldiers, that, although they may go and fight the battles of the country, still, they shall not be citizens ?

Mr. Herndon:

Mr. President—Influenced by the remarks of the gentleman from Montgomery, [Mr. Watts,] just made, I shall vote against my own amendment.

Mr. Smith, of Tuscaloosa, said:

Mr. President—The views I have held upon the laws regulating naturalization have been considered as ultra.

The reasons and arguments surrounding this question under a new Confederacy, in which will probably not be included any except slaveholding States, will be materially changed. The proclivities of a foreigner's mind are always with the majority of the community in which he settles. The popular current controls him. If he goes amongst Free-soilers, he will have free-soil proclivities. If he goes amongst Slaveholders, he will have slaveholding inclinations. We have lived to see the great North-west controlled by foreigners to a very great extent. The few that have settled in the South are true to Southern institutions.

But, without touching the merits of the main question, the subject upon which I am now called to vote being only for the moment, and not to settle the question of citizenship permanently, I am willing to say, that my stringent views, at all events, will now be relaxed, under the suggestions made by the gentleman from Montgomery, [Mr. Watts,] for I think that whoever enters the army of the State, with an honest view of fighting for her honor and independence, ought to be admitted to citizenship. Therefore, I vote against the amendment.

Mr. Webb said:

Mr. President—I do not agree with the gentleman from Tuscaloosa [Mr. Smith.] That a foreigner should be willing to enlist in the service of the State is not a reason sufficient to induce me to change my opinions on the great question of naturalization. I think that the foreigner who enjoys a residence in, and the protection of, the State, and who refuses in time of danger to fight for her, ought to be hung.

This discussion was continued some time, when, upon the vote being taken, Mr. Herndon's amendment was lost.

DEBATE ON THE AFRICAN SLAVE TRADE RESUMED.

Mr. YELVERTON said:

Mr. President—I do not flatter myself that what I am about to say, will receive the sanction of this Convention, or the approbation of this age. We are beset with prejudices and preconceived opinions on all the questions of slavery opinions, which, I apprehend, if closely examined, will be found to have taken this origin from the arguments of our enemies—men and classes, who for years have been industriously employed in the single business of holding up this institution in aspects of exagerated deformity which have made it hideous in the estimation of mankind. Even the friends of this institution, as it exists amongst us, have been more or less imbued with something approaching to prejudice, on that particular branch of the Slave question which I am now about to approach. Most of you here will differ with me now—but I look forward with the fullest confidence to the time—and that no distant day—when I shall be vindicated, and the opinions I now hold and utter, will be the prevailing sentiment of an enlightened nation—the decision of the whole country, recognized and adopted after the maturest deliberation and the best experience.

Sir, I am neither for the opening of the African Slave Trade now, nor for closing it forever. I wish to place the question in a shape to be settled hereafter by our own people—in our own councils, and in our own way.

I here read an Ordinance which shadows forth my views, and which I would propose, if circumstances would allow. [Mr. Y. read as follows:]

SEC. 1. *Be it ordained and declared by the people of the State of Alabama, in Convention Assembled,* That the State of Alabama will, and hereby does, retain exclusive jurisdiction and control for herself of the question of the African Slave Trade; and hereby vests in the Legislative Department of the State, full powers, at all times to legislate for Alabama upon that question, in accordance with the future will, necessity and circumstances of the people of that State.

SEC. 2. *Be it further ordained,* that all laws, organic or otherwise of the United States, or of the State of Alabama in conflict herewith, are, and the same is hereby repealed, so far as the State of Alabama is concerned.

SEC. 3. *Be it further ordained,* that a copy hereof be furnished to the several Governors of the Slaveholding States—and that a copy also be furnished the Southern Congress, soon to assemble in the City of Montgomery, in the State of Alabama.

It is said by some that the world is against us on the Slavery question. My answer to this (tho' it is not conceded) is—that if it be true, then, we ought either to own all the Slaves, or surrender all we have in deference to the unholy prejudice of our acknowledged enemies. As our people are not for this surrender, let every man own as many as he is willing and able to buy—and let the market to which he resorts be open, free and unrestricted, so that the same laws of Trade that regulate the prices of other commodities, may regulate this.

This question of Slavery is the rock upon which the Old Government split: it is the cause of secession. Let us leave it no longer doubtful, nor in a condition to bring our New Government into new troubles. In framing a new Govenment, let us avoid the errors of the old; and we can best do this with success by laying our foundation in *principle* rather than in *policy.*

I am wedded to principle. "Principles are eternal." Let our *policy* of *concession* and *compromise,* ever drifting and ever changing, be forever repudiated by us. In the formation of this New Government everything should be well considered and thoroughly matured. Let us do what we mean, and mean what we do.

Suppose the Border States continue to remain with the United States Government—especially the States of Maryland, Virginia and North Carolina? These three States have been the great Slave markets for the Cotton States. If they stay out of the Southern Confederacy they will be as *foreign* to us as is Africa. We now pay them about as much for one negro as eight would cost us from Africa; and their slaves are no better for labor. Here, then, we discriminate in their favor against ourselves. The discrimination would be hard, even if we remain the same people. Again, would not our people, in the event supposed, feel indignant at being compelled to buy negroes from one *foreign* nation at exorbitant rates, and also be compelled *not to buy* from another foreign market? This would be a very qualified and expensive liberty.

We often hear, in this and other places, the word *Free Trade!* Sir, what is *free trade* without a *free market?* It is an absurdity. This discrimination to which I have referred, amounting to prohibition, is the very annihilation of Free Trade, and renders the term ridiculous.

But it is said that we must pet the old States. I have every respect for them, their interests, and even for their prejudices. I would yield them all courtesies, give them all honor. But the idea, that if we close the door against all other Slave markets, we will thereby bind these old Slave States the more closely to us, and thus influence them to join us in the Southern Confederacy, is, in my estimation, paying these old States but a poor compliment. It would be insinuating that the mere matter of a *slave market* would be sufficient to operate upon their minds and hearts in these great times—times when the minds and hearts of Freemen should only be moved by the spirit of patriotism and the cries of liberty.

But the policy indicated in the Ordinance I would propose, (which no doubt is susceptible of improvements and amendments;) could accomplish everything we desire in a direct way. The State would be vested with power to open a trade or not, as circumstances might warrant. If these old States come into the New Confederacy there would be no clamor for *reopening* a trade with Africa. Meantime, no action would be demanded by the people, and the question would rest. Now look at this question in another attitude: suppose these old States remain out of the New Confederacy and our people *on that account* should desire to purchase slaves elsewhere, and to be protected by law in doing so? Here in your Ordinance is a Constitutional barrier that ordinary legislation cannot break down; and I do not believe that such a barrier should be erected at this time, just as we are inaugurating a new state of things.

We know that slavery exists in Africa, and that the African slaves for labor are equal to United States slaves; that the money required to pay the United States for one will pay Africa for eight. We know that slavery is a social, moral and political blessing. We know that the Bible speaks of Slavery as an institution permitted; and that Jesus Christ, while on earth, found slavery in existence and did not condemn it, but commanded slaves to be obedient to their masters; we know that neither the Bible or the New Testament has any decrees for slavery and Slave trade in one country and against it in another. From these promises the doctrine of States Rights, and the doctrine of free trade in Slaves as property, are deducible.

Your Ordinance, by restricting the privilege of buying slaves in Africa and confining the market to the United States, seeks to prostrate at one fell blow, both these great principles; the principle of State Rights, in which all our public property centres, and the principle of *Free Trade*, which controls the economy, and makes or unmakes the fortunes of the people.

Slavery and Cotton go hand in hand together; they have produced wonderful results. Strike down Slavery, the subordinate, and your haughty "King Cotton," as you proudly call him—that monach who has been the great architect of our fortunes, and who has erected in our midst such a power that we have grown, in our own estimation at least, to be invincible—will dwindle into a petty tyrant, under whose embecile administration our grandeur will subside and our civilization will perish.

I have ever been astonished at the shrewd Yankees for making war upon Slavery, since it is known that slave labor has built them up socially, nationally and commercially. *Now* they begin to see their folly; and as they go *down*—(which process will be rapid,) they will at no distant day rebuke themselves for having placed beyond their reach the power to regain what they have lost.

It has been said that Europe would not recognize our independence on account of slavery. This is a mistake. I have ever believed that the English are a calculating people, content to attend to their own affairs and let others do the same. They, too, are largely interested in the product of slave labor. They have not the weakness to believe that they are responsible for our institutions, any more than we are responsible for their forms of Government. We shall soon have the pleasure to know that the Government of the Confederate States is fully recognized by all the nations of the earth. Soon we will be pointed to as the greatest civilization on earth; we have all the elements to make us so.

We are destined to extend greatly our productions, and to widen the fields of our labor; and with that expansion there will be necessarily an increased demand for slave labor; and I cannot see the economy, statesmanship, wisdom or justice in throwing obstacles in our own way.

By reference to the history of this question it will be seen that in the year 1787, the South was the first to draw the dagger upon herself on the slavery restriction. Doubtless from good motives, but it was a *policy*, the effect of which in my opinion has caused much, if not all the troubles which have followed. Since that time the Northern antagonism to Slavery has been gradually increasing. It was regarded then as a means for its ultimate overthrow. Such great men of that day as Henry, Jefferson and Jay were associated with restriction, and Virginia more decided then for emancipation than New York or Massachusetts. The Hon. T. R. R. Cobb, of Georgia, a member elect to the Southern Congress, in his great book on Slavery, on this question and in this connection says: "So general was the feeling that the Ordinance of 1787, which excluded Slavery from the Northwestern

Territory (out of which the present populous and thriving Northwestern States are formed,) was ratified by the first Congress of the United States, with but *one* dissenting voice, and that from a delegate from New York, the entire Southern vote being cast in its favor."

I allude to this more as a warning than as a reflection upon those concerned.

The Government was then in its infancy; cotton had not been cultivated, and the great value of slave labor not tested; perhaps, too, the influences which a more refined civilization, combined with the great powers of religion, had not shed their holy influences upon, and ameloriated the condition of the Slaves themselves.

But now the argument is not that slavery is an evil, nor that slavery is not profitable, but the fears that fanaticism will be enraged; that slavery may become a burden; that we may have too many; and with some who have as many negroes as they want and are rich by the high price of their property, it is urged that more and cheaper negroes, and a new market might lessen their estates in value, by bringing down the prices of negroes, and making productions too abundant. It is thought that the increase from natural causes will be sufficient for all practical purposes; to that class of owners who are governed by mere dollars and cents, this argument must be plausible.

By far the larger proportion of our people who aid in bearing the burdens, both in war and peace, may take different views. They are as loyal to the Government, and to the institution of slavery as are the largest slave-holders in the Confederate States. They are not as able to purchase—many, not able to purchase at all on account of the prices being too high; they may think that they have at least equal rights to a voice in this matter; and if they do not desire that other cheap slave markets may be opened at this time, yet they would doubtless prefer that the privilege *to have them opened hereafter* would be secured to them.

We have vast amounts of wild lands, which were unavailable, while prices were high, for the poor could not purchase. But statesmen became liberal, and reduced the price of these lands, by which millions have been enabled to secure homes for themselves and families, who, before, were houseless and uncomfortable. Here was a great inducement to the houseless to be industrious and economical in order to enjoy the blessing. I have seen the good effects of this liberality. It is everywhere to be seen in the States where the public lands remained wild. I could now point out hundreds in my section of this State, and within the circle of my acquaintance in Florida, who were, before the graduation law, homeless, and in distress, and who are now comfortable, making plenty; adding to the wealth of the country, educating their children, and enjoying all the blessings of comfort and independence! These people feel a new pride, and take an additional interest in all that concerns the general welfare of the country. This class of citizens could soon save money enough to go into the slave market; and becoming slave-holders, would thus have an actual pecuniary interest in slavery.

I could offer many other reasons why *the question itself* should be left to the people of the States for their own control in future, and upon such terms and regulations as might best suit their condition. Slavery, like great financial affairs, can as well be regulated by time, place and circumstances. No one would think of banking in a community where, from a want of trade, money would not be profitable. Nor will people buy negroes at any price in time when slave-labor will be valueless. Those who calculate upon too much being produced if slavery is increased beyond natural causes seem to overlook the increase of the white population from natural causes also; and the increased demand ahead of us that must come with the necessities of a growing population. They also seem to forget that slavery may be worth something for other purposes than raising cotton. They lose sight of the great moral effect, and seem to hold, that Christianity does not require us to teach the lessons of the Bible, and explain the effects of Christianity upon the poor slave, except when profit follows.

But we are told that the subject may rest very well where it is; that our Convention will refuse to pass the Ordinance which absolutely forbids forever the reopening of the African Slave Trade, and will only pass Resolutions requesting Congress to pass such an Ordinance as would prevent it; and that it is expressed in the Resolutions that this is from public *policy*. Still, I would prefer not giving any advice at all to Congress on this subject. Let us remain silent, unless we pass such an Ordinance as the one I have read. This Southern Congress will doubtless be composed of the wisest and best men in the South—representatives from every section of the cotton States—men who are deeply learned in the wants of the South; of wide experience in practical legislation: to these great spirits of the land, meeting together for the grand purpose of combining their knowledge and intellectual powers to build up a new nation, and to develop the vast resources of this great people, let us leave this vital question. Whatever my own private views may be, I should yield to their better judgment my hearty acquiescence, though I might then be unwilling to surrender my opinion.

It may be, that under a new Constitution to be formed by the Southern Congress this prohibition of the African Slave Trade may find a place in the organic law of the Confederacy. If this should be the case, as a loyal citizen, I shall abide by and support it; still, we may expect that same Constitution to provide a mode by which it may be changed. Whatever mode that may be, whether by two-thirds, or by Conventions of the States, I have the fullest confidence that the day will come when the people will demand a change. I predict, sir, that the time is not far distant which will develope such a state of affairs that the reöpening of the African Slave Trade will be considered as essential to the industrial welfare and prosperity of the cotton States.

If this occasion authorized it, I could suggest a plan for the successful reöpening of this Trade; but the plan would be considered out of place, until the country is ready for the Trade itself. I, therefore, leave this for the future.

I said, in the beginning, that I spoke on this occasion without the hope of being able to produce conviction here. But the importance of the subject demanded of me an expression of opinion. Whether this opinion is wise or unwise, only the future can decide. My reputation with posterity is of small importance when compared to the great interests of this the greatest people on the face of the earth. Whatever is best for them is best for me; so that, if my views are overruled by you, I shall still look for my consolation in the superior wisdom of your decree.

MR. STONE said :

Mr. President—The Resolutions of the gentleman from Lauderdale, [Mr. Jones,] instructing our Delegates to the Southern Convention to insist upon the enactment of such restrictions as will prevent the reöpening of the African Slave Trade, meet my hearty approval. They go sufficiently far to accomplish the object desired, and yet are not liable to the misconstruction which might be placed upon the Ordinance reported by the Committee. I am in no humor, at the present time, to do anything that could even be tortured into a concession to the anti-slavery fanaticism of the North. The Southern States will soon be in council to deliberate upon a Constitution which is to recognize and protect the right of property in slaves, and I am unwilling, at the very beginning of our existence as a pro-slavery Confederacy, to incorporate into the organic law of our State language that would certainly be construed into a condemnation of the principle of slavery. Sir, in a moral point of view, I should feel no more hesitation in the purchase of a slave upon the coast of Congo, or in the kingdom of Dahoney, than I should in the slave markets of Richmond. The morality of slavery is settled by Divine Law, and with that decision all should be satisfied. So far as the African himself is concerned, the Trade that removes him from a land of ignorance and spiritual darkness to a land of civilization and Christianity, is certainly a blessing to him. He is found a wild, lazy cannibal, and is converted into an industrious and useful member of society. It is upon grounds of public policy alone; it is upon the idea that it might be disastrous to Southern interests, that I base my opposition to the reöpening of the African Slave Trade. That Trade would introduce a vast number of additional laborers into our Southern cotton fields, which would increase greatly the production of cotton, and necessarily depreciate the price of the article. The great danger to which the cotton States especially are subjected, is an excessive supply of cotton, to be followed, necessarily, by low prices. If we were to employ in the culture of cotton in Alabama double the number of hands now employed, the effect would be to double the production and to reduce the price of the article one-half. The price depends upon the demand, and this demand will continue the same, whether you import Africans or not. An over-stocked cotton market is always followed by low prices; but when the supply falls short of the demand, the price rises. It is the interest of our cotton planters that the price should be kept high. He produces the article for sale. Other nations are interested in obtaining cotton at the lowest prices. England is now endeavoring, by every means in her power, so to increase the cotton supply as to glut the markets of the world, knowing that she can then buy the article at her own price. This British policy of increasing the supply of cotton would be ruinous to Southern interests; it would make cotton a drug in the market. Instead of being King, it would become a beggar. Sir, we should be careful to do nothing that would depreciate the value of the products of slave labor. We should keep the institution as profitable as possible, for there lies its permanence and safety.

But it is argued, Mr. President, that the reöpening of the African Slave Trade would so reduce the price of negroes as to bring them within the reach of almost every man among us, and that the institution would thus be strengthened by having more persons interested in its preservation. It is true, sir, that low prices might increase somewhat the number of slaveholders, but still, the large planters and capitalists who own most of the rich and productive cotton lands would become much the largest pur chasers. High prices would give much more strength to the institution than low prices, because, as you reduce the value of the slave, you reduce the pecuniary interest which the master has in his slave property. If the value of the slaves in Virginia were now reduced one-half, the slaveholders of that State would listen with much more patience to schemes for general emancipation. It was when negroes were low that emancipation parties were organized both in Virginia and Kentucky. But when the price of this property rose, and when the institution came to represent so vast an amount of the wealth of the State, it became the interest of all to sustain and defend the system. The high price of slaves is the best security against the overthrow of the system. We have, then, too deep a pecuniary interest in this property not to be true to it. The State will then protect it, because it represents so much of the wealth of her citizens. The theories and schemes of fanaticism will fall before the substantial pecuniary interests of the State. The great strength of the inhabitants is in its value—its value to the owner—its value to the State—its value to commerce, to manufactures and to civilization. But if you destroy that value by reducing the price of the products of slave labor, and by reducing the price of the slaves themselves, you thereby destroy the strongest safe-guard that surrounds the institution.

But, Mr. President, the Southern Confederacy has at present no unoccupied territory to which the institution of slavery may be extended. Whether it is to be our policy to acquire territory beyond the seceded States, remains to be seen. If our limits are to be circumscribed, and we are to have no territorial expansion or outlet, then to increase the number of our slave population by importations from Africa would be disastrous. Should the border States refuse to join the Southern Confederacy, the introduction of slaves even from that quarter should be strictly prohibited. Our slaves from natural increase alone double every twenty-five years. From that source, in twenty-five years, we shall have in Alabama near a million of slaves. With such a dense slave population within the limits of our State, if the number was still to be increased by importations from Africa, it would soon require all our best lands to produce a sufficiency for their subsistence. Much of our best soil would become exhausted in furnishing a subsistence for such a population. Slaves would become a charge upon their owner, and soon we would be compelled to emancipate them.

It is true, Mr. President, that the interests of the South may demand territorial expansion, for expansion seems to be the law and destiny and necessity of our institutions. To remain healthful and prosperous within, and to make sure our development and power, it seems essential that we should grow without. Arizona and Mexico, Central America and Cuba, all may yet be embraced within the limits of our Southern Republic. A Gulf Confederacy may be established in the South, which may well enjoy almost a monopoly in the production of cotton, rice, sugar, coffee, tobacco and the tropical fruits. The trade of all tropical America, combined with that of the cotton States, would make our Confederacy the wealthiest, the most progressive and the most influential power on the globe. Should the border States refuse to unite their destiny with ours, then we may be compelled to look for territorial strength and for political power to those rich and beautiful lands that lie upon our South-western frontier. Their genial climate and productive soil; their rich agricultural and mineral resources, render them admirably adapted to the institution of slavery. Under the influence of that institution, these tropical lands would soon add millions to the commercial wealth of our Republic, and their magnificent ports would soon be filled with ships from every nation. Slave labor would there build up for the Southern Confederacy populous and wealthy States, as it has built up for the late Union the States of Georgia, Alabama, Mississippi, Louisiana and Texas. To do this with sufficient rapidity, it is sometimes argued that more slave labor will be required, and that the reopening of the African Slave Trade will become a necessity. But we have as yet added no territory to the seceded States, and it is doubtful what will be our policy as to the extension of our limits.

Mr. YANCEY said:

Mr. President—No subject has been brought before this Convention, apart from the question of Secession, which is at all comparable to this in importance. Without reference to its social and political aspects, it is of immense interest. It touches every point of the circle of our industrial relations. It affects, in some degree, an almost inconceivable value in property in this State—probably one thousand millions of dollars worth in slaves and land alone. A question so vast and profound, must command the most serious consideration; and I should not do justice to myself, Mr President, were I to permit the vote to be taken without defining my position upon it. When a question in the late Union, few public men took more pains to be understood upon it, than myself; yet no public man has ever had so little benefit from his own clearly defined positions. I hope, then, I shall be patiently heard here; for, from this stand-point, speaking as a representative of the people to the people in Convention, and probably for the last time as a public man, I may hope to be understood—and no longer to be misrepresented.

This subject first commanded my serious consideration when it was brought up in the Southern Commercial Convention in 1858. At the previous annual meeting of that body at Knoxville, my name was placed on a Committee, which was to report upon the expediency of reöpening the African Slave Trade to the Convention, which was to meet in this place in May, 1858. I had given no authority for, nor assent to, this appointment, and knew nothing of it, until I saw the fact stated in the newspapers—for I was not a member of that Convention, and, indeed, had never attended any of its sessions. When the Convention met in Montgomery, the Chairman, Mr. Spratt, made a report from that Committee, elaborate in its argument, which recommended the adoption of a resolution declaring it proper to reöpen the African Slave Trade. Such a report, in parliamentary consideration, is taken to be the report of every member of the Committee, unless the dissent of a member is expressed in some form. I had never attended a meeting of the Committee—had never had an opportunity of consulting with it—knew nothing of the report until it was read in the Convention. Not concurring in the conclusion arrived at by the Committee, a necessity was at once imposed upon me, to take position upon the question; and I asked the Convention to allow me, until the next day, the privilege of presenting a minority report. The Convention acceded to my request, and on the next morning, I presented such a report, which I now read:

MINORITY REPORT FROM THE COMMITTEE ON THE AFRICAN SLAVE TRADE

"The undersigned, one of the Committee appointed by the late Commercial Convention to report upon the subject of the African Slave Trade—not having had time to read and digest the report of the Chairman—submits the following as more specifically expressive of his own opinions.

The distinctive feature which characterizes Southern industry is slave labor. Before the formation of this Government this feature was a characteristic of Northern labor, in a limited though practical degree.

This species of labor was recognized by the Federal Constitution, and one of its provisions [Art. 1, Sec. 9, paragraph 1,] expressly provides against the passage of any law prohibiting the foreign Slave Trade, within a given period.

In the year 1807 this trade was declared by Congress to be illegal, and in 1819 an act was passed to send national armed vessels to stop our vessels from engaging in the trade, and in 1820 an act was passed declaring it to be piracy.

The effect of these laws have been to restrict the expansion of this peculiar species of Southern labor, by the usual laws which govern trade in all other species of property, and to keep down the price of Southern lands; while Northern labor, in addition to its own natural increase, has received the stimulus of an average emigration of white labor, in some years reaching as high as half a million persons.

The operation of this law has been a direct governmental discrimination against the South on this vital question affecting its prosperity—its labor. The act is, in the opinion of the undersigned, but a part of that system of discriminating laws, which, affording bounties to Northern industry, have been restrictions upon the industry of our own section, and which have enriched and built up one section, while they have been as shackles upon every effort made by the other to rise to national prosperity.

The spirit of these restricitive laws has passed into and become the leading idea of a powerful and most successful sectional majority, which declares that no more slave States shall be admitted into the Union.

Without expressing any matured opinion, in the views submitted, as to the expediency of reöpening the slave trade, the undersigned believes that the laws prohibiting the foreign Slave Trade are in violation of the spirit of the Constitution, and are unjust and an insult to the South, and, therefore, ought to be repealed; and submits for the consideration of this body the following resolution:

Resolved, That the laws of Congress prohibiting the Foreign Slave Trade ought to be repealed. W. L. YANCEY.

Such, then, is the record of my position in the Convention—showing conclusively three things:

1st. That I had no part in introducing the African Slave Trade issue into the Convention.

2d. That I expressed no "matured opinion" as to the policy of reöpening that trade.

3d. That the only position which I urged the Convention to take was to resolve "that the laws of Congress, prohibiting the Foreign Slave Trade ought to be repealed."

Immediately after the adjournment of the Convention, such a wide-spread misrepresentation of my course on that subject prevailed, that a friend requested me to give a public refutation of them. I did so, in a letter to Mr. Thomas J. Orme, dated May 24th, 1858. I read an extract or so from that letter:

MONTGOMERY, May 24, 1858.

Mr. Thomas J. Orme: SIR—I received your note of the 20th inst., a few moments since. My opinions on matters of public interest are always at the command of my countrymen; and as it is quite uncertain when the official report of the proceedings of the late Convention will appear, I will give you my views in brief on the matters you propound.

1st. I did not introduce the subject of the African Slave Trade into the late Southern Congress.

* * * * * * * * *

When the Convention met at Montgomery, the Chairman of that Committee, Mr. Spratt, made an elaborate report in favor of the reopening of the African Slave Trade. I had never read it, nor knew of its contents, until it was read in the Convention. The presumption is, that all members of a Committee approve of a report, unless they express a dissent. As I was not prepared to give an unqualified approval or dissent to all the arguments and propositions of that elaborate paper, justice to myself required that I should explain my position on that question; and on the next morning I wrote and submitted a brief report of such views on the subject as I had formed an opinion upon, and upon which I was prepared to stand.

2d. It will be seen by reading my report, that I neither recommended or disapproved of the reopening of the African Slave Trade; in which, in reality, I have not matured and fixed opinions, but to which my mind is favorably inclined.

What I did recommend, was simply the repeal of the laws of Congress making the Foreign trade in slaves piracy, on the ground, chiefly, that these laws stood on the Statute book as a direct condemnation by our own Government of the institution of slavery, in its moral and social aspects; and indirectly operated to restrict our political power.

In making this recommendation, my care was not so much for the African Slave Trade, but was to strip the Southern ship of state for battle; to furl and cut away every sail that would impede her movement; to cast loose every rope that would be a drag upon her progress. We have now the moral condemnation of Christendom upon us. We have, since 1807, borne the stigma placed upon us by the laws of our own Government, making foreign trade in slaves a piracy. We have, since 1851, had the stigma of Congressional laws placed upon the internal Slave Trade, also; a law which makes a slave free, if a citizen of any of the Southern States should carry him to the District of Columbia for sale.

* * * * * * * * * *

Repeal the laws of Congress, and the States would each preserve the power to allow or prohibit that trade. I am for repealing those Congressional laws, and for leaving the matter to be regulated by the States themselves. I expressly disclaimed any desire to make an issue upon this matter in the South. I have no such desire. Hence I did not press the matter to a vote.

* * * * * * * * * *

Neither am I for making the issue of disunion now upon the African Slave Trade, or any other question; though individually prepared for the issue, when the South shall deem the time has arrived to resist the accumulated wrongs of half a century of hostile legislation. I expressly disclaimed such intention in the late Convention.

* * * * * * * * * *

Yours, &c., W. L. YANCEY."

The Southern Commercial Convention met again at Vicksburg, Miss., in 1859. I was not a member, but that Convention, from motives doubtless of the kindest personal consideration, appointed me to deliver an oration before "an African Labor Supply Association" at Mobile, in the event of the failure of Mr. Spratt to do so. The first information I had of this was in the columns of a newspaper, and I at once wrote to Prof. J. B. D. DeBow, President of that Convention. I read that letter:

" MONTGOMERY, Ala., May 23d, 1859.

"J. B. D. DeBow, Esq., New Orleans: DEAR SIR—I see by the newspapers that an African Labor Supply Association was formed at Vicksburg, just after the adjournment of the late Southern Convention. In the published proceedings I also notice that Mr. Spratt was selected to deliver an address at the next meeting of the Association, and I was chosen as one of two alternates. The Constitution of the Association. as it appears in the public prints, is indefinite as to the designs of the Association, or, I should rather say, as to the manner in which it will promote the supply of African labor.

"I therefore address you, as the President of the Association, and request of you a full explanation of the aims of the Association. and of the means by which it is to be obtained. Particularly I desire to be informed whether the Association, in the event that the laws of the United States against the importation of Africans as slaves, cannot be repealed or declared unconstitutional, designs to encourage the Slave Trade between this country and Africa, Cuba and Brazil in violation of those laws.

"Yours Respectfully,
" W. L. YANCEY."

To this enquiry I received such a reply, that I deemed it proper publicly to restate my position on this question; and I did so, in a letter to the editors of the Montgomery *Advertiser*, a part of which I will read:

"MONTGOMERY, June 13, 1859.

"*Messrs. Editors*—I enclose for publication the within correspondence, as conflicting views and misapprehensions have been expressed, in regard to the objects of the formation of the African Slave Labor Supply Association.

" I was not present when this Association was formed, and was not consulted either in reference to its aims or to my selection as one of the alternate orators. While I am grateful for this evidence of esteem and confidence, it is but due to the Association and to myself to say, that I am not prepared, at present, to go farther than is justified by the minority report and resolution upon the subject of the African Slave Trade, made by me to the Southern Convention when in session at this place, in May, 1858, and which was, in substance, adopted by the same body, recently in session at Vicksburg, by a large majority. * *

" Whether the African Slave Trade shall be carried on, should not depend on that Government, but upon the will of each slaveholding State. To that tribunal alone should the question be submitted; and by the decision of that tribunal alone should the Southern people abide.

"Yours Respectfully,
" W. L. YANCEY."

But even this was not sufficient to stay the tide of misrepresentation, upon which a class of public journalists and small politicians sought to maintain a popular existence; and hence, the public ear was yet vexed with them—not to keep me out of office—(for I was no candidate, and had not been for twelve years or more)—but to undermine any influence which I might exercise in favor of the spread of enlightened and elevated views of all questions affecting Southern interests—a policy which mere politicians have felt to be destructive to their selfish aims for the last few years.— Hence, a friend in the county of Tallapoosa wrote to me, and called for another expression of my views. I at once replied to him; and I read the closing paragraph from that letter:

"MONTGOMERY, June 16, 1859.
"*James D. Meadows, Esq.*—DEAR SIR :   *   *   *   *
As to rëopening the African Slave Trade, that is a grave question of the highest political and economic import, and should be decided alone by the several States—each for itself, and with reference alone to the industrial interests of each. The time for its decision has not arrived ; and as I have formed no opinion upon its expediency, with that thoughtfulness which its great importance demands, I will not discuss it here.
"Very Respectfully,
"Your fellow-citizen,
"W. L. YANCEY."

This review of my past policy on this subject, must be conclusive to all candid minds, on several points—

First, That while "favorably inclined" to the revival of the African Slave Trade, I have never expressed any "matured opinions" on the subject, nor advocated it.

Second, That the only policy proposed by me, was a repeal of the laws of Congress prohibiting said trade ; not for the purpose of giving license to it, but because they were a Federal condemnation of the institution of slavery.

Third, That its allowance or prohibition was a question which each State should decide for itself.

The key to my course on this question will be found, Mr. President, not in a disposition to encourage trade in African slaves, but in a determination to do all in my power to check the free-soil tendencies of the Federal Government, and to place the South in possession of all her offensive and defensive resources.

Examine for a moment the progress and the position of slavery, and the warfare upon it, previous to the Ordinance of Secession. Previous to the Declaration of Independence the African Slave Trade was in full operation—recognized as legitimate by the whole civilized world—carried on by Kings and Princes, as well as by the more ordinary trader—sanctioned by the laws of nations—protected by the courts, as well as by fleets, and the negro was a slave in all the original British Colonies, as well as in the Spanish and French possessions in the Western Hemisphere. In the new order of things instituted by our ancestors, this institution was left as they found it. Though they struck the shackles from the white man, they sanctioned them upon the limbs of the African race. Recognizing the fact that there were two distinct races of human beings here—and that they had existed distinct—the master and the slave, since God's curse upon the children of Ham, they provided for the perpetuation of that distinction as being right, both politically and morally. The Declaration of Independence brought freedom, with its guaranties of self-government, and of the writ of habeas corpus, and trial by jury to the white race alone. The Articles of Confederation were based upon this order of things; and the Federal Constitution, designed as a "more perfect Union," but perfected and perpetuated the great distinction. It was made by our ancestors, in their own expressive language, "to secure the blessings of liberty to ourselves and our posterity." It was founded on the inseparable and divinely instituted relation of freedom to the white man and slavery to the black man, of a political, civil and moral distinction, between the destinies of the children of Ham and of the descendants of Shem and Japheth. The Constitution is an organic human utterance of the Divine decree—"Cursed be Canaan; a servant of servants shall he be unto his brethren."

It is true, that the germs of Abolitionism were even then to be found in the policy of Virginia and Maryland; but it is equally true that this policy did not prevail. The debates in the Convention were based upon utilitarian, and not on moral views of the question. [I insert here extracts of the debate alluded to in the speech.]

By reference to Madison's papers, the draft of a Constitution will be found as reported by the Committee of Detail. It did not provide for a prohibition or tax on the importation of slaves. On this a debate sprung up. I quote from that debate the views of leading delegates:

Mr. L. Martin, of Maryland, proposed to vary article 7, section 6, so as to allow a prohibition or tax on the importation of slaves.

Mr. Ellsworth, of Connecticut, was for leaving the clause as it stands. Let every State import what it pleases. The morality or wisdom of slavery are considerations belonging to the States themselves.

Mr. Sherman, of Connecticut, was for leaving the clause as it stands.

Col. Mason, of Virginia. He lamented that some of our Eastern brethren had, from a lust of a gain, embarked in this nefarious traffic. He held it essential, in every point of view, that the General Government should have the power to prevent the increase of slavery.

Mr. Ellsworth, of Connecticut. He said, however, that if it was to be considered in a moral light, we ought to go further, and free those already in the country. As slaves also multiply so fast in Virginia and Maryland that it is cheaper to raise than import them, whilst in the sickly rice swamps foreign supplies are necessary, if we go further than is urged, we shall be unjust towards South Carolina and Georgia. Let us not intermeddle.

Mr. King of Massachusetts, thought the subject should be considered in a political light only.

* * * * * * * * * *

He remarked on the exemption of slaves from duty, whilst every other impost was subjected to it, as an inequality that could not fail to strike the commercial sagacity of the Western and Middle States.

Mr. Gouverneur Morris of Pennsylvania, wished the whole subject to be committed, including the clause on imports. These things may find a bargain among the Southern and Northern States.

The matter was committed. The committee made report, in substance, as the section now stands in the Constitution, excepting that the committee reported in favor of the year 1800.

Gen. Pinckney of South Carolina, moved to substitute 1808 for 1800.

Mr. Gorham of Massachusetts, seconded the motion.

Mr. Madison of Virginia. "Seventy years will produce all the mischief that can be apprehended from the liberty to import slaves."

On the motion, which passed on the affirmative, New Hampshire, Connecticut, Massachusetts, and three other States, voted aye. New Jersey, Pennsylvania, Delaware and Virginia, no.

The first part of the report was then agreed to, as amended, as follows. The migration or importation of such persons as the several States, now existing, shall think proper to admit, shall not be prohibited prior to the year 1808. New Hampshire, Massachusetts, Connecticut, Maryland, North Carolina, South Carolina, Georgia, voted aye—7. New Jersey, Pennsylvania, Delaware, Virginia, no,—4.

That debate conclusively shows that the "morality or wisdom of slavery were considerations belonging to the States themselves," and that the Convention was indisposed to "intermeddle," and, when at last it yielded and consented to do so, it was "considered in a political light only," and "formed the subject of a bargain among the Southern and Northern States" touching "imports." That bargain is thus expressed in the Constitution.

"The emigration or importation of such persons, as any of the States now existing shall think proper to admit, shall not be prohibited by the Congress prior to the year 1808, but a tax or duty may be imposed on such importation, not exceeding ten dollars on each person.

Notice the terms—"shall not be prohibited by the Congress prior to the year 1808." What does that mean? Is it an injunction or command on Congress to prohibit after 1808? Clearly not. It is only an injunction on Congress that it shall not prohibit between the date of the formation of the Constitution and the year 1808. Is it a prohibition after the year 1808? Clearly not. It is only a constitutional guaranty up to the year 1808. It does not declare that the trade shall be prohibited after the year 1808, only that it shall not be prohibited before that time. If Congress had seen fit to pass no law upon the subject after the year 1808, who could have complained that Congress had neglected to perform a constitutional duty?

The object of this argument is not to prove that Congress had no power to prohibit that trade after the year 1808, though, in my opinion, it were an easy task to show, by aid of the tenth amendment ["the powers not delegated to the United States by the Constitution nor prohibited by it to the States, are reserved to the States respectively, or to the people,"] that the clause prohibiting Congress from the exercise of power, is clearly not a delegated power; and not being "prohibited by it to the States," is as clearly a power "reserved to the States respectively, or to the people thereof." But my object is to show that the framers of that instrument, so far from considering the foreign trade in slaves an evil, either morally or politically, considered it a political and an industrial blessing; and they acted on the belief that after the year 1808 they would not need it. They argued the need of more slaves, and sanctioned their importation until the year 1808. And even if they assented to its prohibition then, it was not because the trade was a moral or political evil, but because, in their opinion, the industrial wants of the South would then be supplied. They argued the "inequality" of forcing South Carolina and Georgia to buy their slaves from Virginia, when they could be had cheaper from Africa. They based their action on circumscribed views of the necessity for more slave labor. They wisely determined not to cripple the growing prosperity of the South, but to give to it as many slaves as the South, in their opinion, needed. They made no discrimination between slave property and jackasses or silks, so far as "importation" was concerned. They allowed South Carolina, and slave buyers, "to buy where they could buy cheapest," to buy in Africa or Virginia, as they thought proper, upon the principles of free trade.

I turn now, Mr. President, to another branch of this subject. The framers of the Constitution, in the same article which prohibits Congress from interfering with the slave trade prior to

1808, delegated to the Congress the power "to define and punish piracies and felonies committed on the high seas, and offenses against the law of nations." I desire to raise the question: What did they mean—what was the intention of the framers? Surely they knew what were piracies and felonies, and the law of nations? As they were traders in slaves—as they bought African slaves—as they encouraged this foreign trade by making a discrimination in its favor, which they made in favor of no other trade (refusing to permit Congress to prohibit it for twenty years), as they guarded it against even an amendment of the Constitution, surely they never dreamed that the foreign slave trade was either a piracy, a felony, or an offense against the law of nations, or that it would ever be so considered by the Congress. And as assuredly they never gave to the Congress power to declare that to be a piracy which they had so often done, and which they determined should be constitutionally done for twenty years longer. Consider the character of piracy. It is the most offensive form of crime. It involves all other great crimes—murder, rape, robbery, treason. The pirate's hand is against every body, and every one's hand is against him. Could it be within the range of probability that our ancestors designed that Congress, the day after the twenty years of protection to the slave trade had expired, should declare that they had indulged in and protected a trade so offensive, so henious, so abhorrent to the law of man, of nations and of God, so assimilated to murder, rape, robbery and treason, that it might then be declared and punished as piracy? Why, sir, the very pen which wrote that delegated power, doubtless wrote that prohibition of power; and the power, when delegated, was as fixed, immutable and unchangeable when first written, as language and thought could make it. When delegated, its extent and scope were fixed, and could be no greater then than now, can be no greater now than then. The power to declare and punish the foreign slave trade as piracy, was either then delegated, or it was not delegated. If it was then delegated, the Congress could, at the first session, have declared that trade to be piracy. That it could not do that, however, is clear, from the clause guaranteeing the trade against such legislation. The Congress possessed no such power when the Constitution was formed. It was not then delegated. Now, sir, the Tenth Article of Amendments to the Constitution, says that "the powers not delegated to the United States by the Constitution, nor prohibited by it to the States, are reserved to the States respectively, or to the people." If that power was not then delegated, it was "reserved to the States respectively, or to the people." And I now ask, when, and where, and how the States or the people, since then, have parted with that power?

And yet, in 1820, the Congress enacted a law declaring the foreign slave trade to be piracy, and punishing it as such. The spirit that gave birth to it was the spirit of abolition, then in the ascendant, a spirit which, while thus condemning the fountain-head of slavery to be a great and henious wrong, a moral and a political evil—while thus shutting off the increase of slavery from the East, by a violation of the Federal Compact, triumphantly turned to the West, and planting itself on the Western borders of the States, imperiously demanded that its expansion should cease, and that no more Slave States should be admitted into the Union.

Yes, sir, the same Congress that violated the Constitution by classing the African Slave Trade as a Piracy, also violated that instrument by the enactment that no more Slave States should be formed out of the common public domain lying North of the Missouri Compromise Line. Abolition, thus triumphant, wielded a double-edged sword against our institutions. Migration of slavery from the East was pronounced to be piracy—emigration of slavery to the West was forever prohibited. Who dares, at this day, to contend that either measure was right in itself, or was not a blow at slavery itself? Certainly no friend of the institution can be found to do so.

And yet, Mr. President, a delegate in this Convention [Mr. Posey, of Lauderdale] has asked that the foreign slave trade shall be pronounced by this body to be felonious; and another delegate [Mr. Jameison, of Tuscaloosa] has made a motion to strike out of the amendment proposed by the junior delegate from Lauderdale [Mr. Jones], the words "public policy," because, if left in, we declare that this Convention is opposed to reopening the foreign slave trade from "public policy" alone, and not from moral considerations. It seems to me that gentlemen are looking at this question from Mr. Jefferson's stand-point of 1787, and from that of Mr. Rufus King, and the disciples of Wilberforce in 1820, and are not willing to be advised even by the majority of the Federal Convention that wisely considered the question only in the light of industrial interest. Mr. Jefferson, imbued in the wild French theories as to "Liberty and Fraternity," denounced slavery to be a great political evil in the earliest days of the Republic. Religious fanaticism, after causing the ruin of the Western Island colonies of Great Britain, then crept into our country, and in 1820 succeeded in engrafting upon Mr. Jefferson antagonism to slavery, another and more mischievous falsehood, and that was that slavery was also a great moral evil. Under the influence of the conjunction of these two theories, the war upon our institutions commenced. And what has been the result in the South, where the practical working of slavery is known, and where the responsibility rests? A complete change has taken place in public opinion. Thirty years ago, there were few in or out of our churches or public councils who did not believe that slavery was both a moral and political evil. But to-day that opinion is changed, and there are but few who do not believe it to be both morally and politically right. If it were not so, our people would at once take steps to get rid of it.

Such, Mr. President, were some of the leading considerations, which induced me to advocate a repeal of the odious Federal laws on the subject of the foreign trade in slaves, and to leave that question to be decided by each State for itself alone. A repeal of those laws would not have operated to revive and reöpen the trade, as some have said; for some of the States, our own, for instance, have laws forbidding it, and treating their violation as other instances of smuggling were treated. They provided for the confiscation of all slaves introduced from Africa.

Another consideration actuated me in looking favorably upon the policy of reöpening that trade; and that was the then political necessities of the Southern States. They were in a contest for power in the late Union—an attempt to preserve the balance of power in the Senate. That could only be done by keeping pace with the North, in forming new States. But how vain were such efforts, with negroes at an average price of one thousand dollars a-piece. The North, with a large houseless, landless, shiftless population, not knowing where the shelter of to-night or the bread of to-morrow was to be obtained, as soon as Territories were opened for emigration was enabled to pour in her restless and dissatisfied thousands; whereas the South, with a bare supply of valuable labor, hardly enough to till her cleared lands, was in no condition to compete for the possession of those Territories, even under the most friendly aspects of the slavery question. To enable her to do so, it would have been necessary to give her an abundance of slaves—more than enough to till her rice and cotton and corn fields, and to build her railroads; and the only source from which that supply could have been obtained was Africa. This, I say, induced me to be favorably inclined to the foreign Slave Trade, but was still not of sufficient weight to decide me to advocate it.

And well, Mr. President, might one have paused before making such a decision. Think, for a moment, of the position of the South in the industrial world; think, for a moment, of her growth in prosperity, of the stand-point in civilization which she has reached. Compare the South of 1860 with the South of 1787. In 1787, having but about a half-million slaves, and not exporting a bale of cotton—in 1860, having four million slaves, and exporting four and a-half millions bales of cotton. In 1787, our ancestors looked to an increase of slavery with a view to a more extended cultivation of "the sickly rice swamps of South Carolina and Georgia." What would have been their ideas, as to the need of increase of slaves in the South, could they have seen twelve million acres of swamp-land and upland, extending from the Atlantic Ocean to the Rio Grande, whitened with the cotton culture, and constituting the main-spring of the world's commercial and manufacturing industry?

How insignificant was the value of slavery, as viewed by them, to the utility of that institution to the civilized world to-day! The true value of slave labor was a sealed book—never opened to the consideration of mankind till Whitney discovered the cotton-gin, and Arkwright patented the spinning-jenny. By these inventions Agriculture received a new dignity and worth, and Commerce opened new fields for its enterprise. And to the South what sources of prosperity did they reveal! All the world produces bread—but one portion of it produces the cheap universal material with which that world is clothed; and that portion may be said to be chiefly confined to the Gulf States. These States can open cotton land enough to produce ten million bales of cotton, when the wants of the world shall require it. Great as is the prosperity of the North, of England, and of France, and of Germany, that prosperity would wither like a weed pulled up by the roots in mid-summer, were they deprived of their trade in our cotton bales.

The consequence has been, that negroes, once worth but two hundred dollars, are now worth fifteen hundred dollars; lands once worth ten dollars, now sell for from fifty to seventy-five dollars. Within a life, by simple agricultural skill on cotton culture, men have amassed immense fortunes; and within half a century, a culture commenced in a small strip upon the Atlantic seaboard, has opened the forests for a depth of fifteen hundred by a breadth of over five hundred miles—and to-day gives employment to the commerce and manufacturing skill of the entire civilized world.

Well, Mr. President, might one have paused ere he undertook to meddle with the foundations upon which this magnificent and unparalleled prosperity rested. Well might visions of future political aggrandizement have melted away before a reality of prosperity, so grand and so amazing.

But, sir, if such considerations induced a doubt under the old regime, they dispel all doubt under the new. In our anticipated Southern Confederacy, there will be no "irrepresible conflict" amidst its elements. With a homogeneous people, accustomed to slavery, holding it in reverence for its origin and its effects—with similar institutions, similar climate, similar productions, and a compact and valuable territory, there will be no domestic enemy to excite our vigilance, and to call for defensive or offensive measures. With no territories to people, and no balance of power to strive for and to sustain, we shall need no other supply of labor than the ordinary laws of natural increase and emigration of owners with slaves will give us in abundance. This condition of things may never be altered. Our only outlet for expansion must be through Mexico—and I throw it out as a suggestion—that it is, at least, doubtful whether we should wish an expansion in that direction, that would bring with it the recognition of such a mass of ignorant and superstitious and demoralized population, as Mexican States, if annexed, would necessarily bring. Upon one point I have no doubt, and that is, that we should never extend our borders by aggression and conquest. Springing into existence a nation in all its full proportions, by the disruption of the late Union, like Minerva from the cleft head of Jupiter, I would hope that, like that goddess, our young Republic would be distinguished for justice and wisdom, and that every portion of it would indignantly repudiate that spirit of rapacity and iniquitous conquest which Governor Houston has announced, in order to induce the noble State of Texas to pause in her advance towards a union with her sister seceding States in the formation of a Southern Confederacy.

But, Mr. President, I am extending my remarks beyond the limits which I had assigned to myself. I have, however, another suggestion which I wish to make. From what I have said, you will perceive that I am opposed to the African Slave Trade, under the present order of things, from considerations affecting our industrial interests alone. At the proper time I shall move an amendment, proposing that the Southern Confederacy shall prohibit the trade in slaves from any foreign quarter; and I shall do so from two sufficient considerations: First, because we will have as many slaves in our Confederacy as our Territory can profitably support; second, because we should offer inducements to the slave States, which have not yet seceded, to do so.

The argument I have already made, is in a large degree applicable to the first point. In addition, it may be said, that if we do not adopt a policy of exclusion, as wide as I have suggested, and if the other slave Sates should not secede, we shall be flooded with their slaves beyond the natural demand for them, and hence be injured to that extent. If they join their fortunes to ours, then the usual inter-State Slave Trade will be continued, and we shall have an increased territory for their labor, commensurate to the number of slaves added. But if they do not join us, if they choose to adhere to the Union, to retain their alliance to the North in preference to that with us, then it must be clear that they will be compelled to get rid of their slaves by sale or abolition. All of those States—Virginia, Maryland, Delaware, Kentucky, Missouri, North Carolina, and Tennessee, are heavy grain and stock-growing States, and if they get rid of their slaves, could'still prosper to a large degree. If they remain in the late Union, they will be powerless to protect their slaves; and in time, the pressure will be so great on that institution, that they will endeavor, by sale, to get rid of every slave they have as a necessity. The only place where they can sell them, unless my suggestion shall be adopted, will be in the Southern Confederacy. If allowed to do so, then near two millions of slaves will be precipitated upon our market, at any price. Worthless to their owners, who will have to choose between abolition and any price they can get, they will be thrown upon us in quantities far exceeding our necessities, and will hence depreciate the value of those we now own, and throw in our midst more than we can profitably work. Thus we shall have all the evils of the African slave trade thrown upon us. To allow these States this opening, in the circumstances that surround them, will be for us to throw away the greatest power we hold over their action. If, however, we shall simply prohibit the trade in slaves from any quarter outside of the limits of the Southern Confederacy, then will those border States have presented to them this grave issue: shall they join the South and keep their slaves, or sell them, as they choose—or shall they join the North, and lose their slaves by abolition?

That issue will be for each of those States to decide for itself, of course; and I cannot for a moment believe but that, in time, each would decide, from motives of self-interest, as well as from equally weighty considerations in favor of good government, to join the Cotton States, and thus present to the world the South united, prosperous and powerful, for all the purposes of peace or of war.

Mr. Dowdell offered the following amendment as an additional section:

Resolved, That we regard the Institution of Slavery, as it exists in the slave-holding States, South, to be a moral, social, and political blessing; and the people of Alabama, do now, and should hereafter discountenance any and all attempts, either directly or indirectly, by legislation or otherwise, to hinder its growth and expansion.

Mr. DOWDELL said:

Mr. President—By offering this amendment let me not be understood as advocating the policy of reopening the African Slave Trade. The lateness of the hour forbids a full discussion, and I shall only make a few suggestions.

The adoption of the substitute would indicate a distrust on the part of this Convention, of the morality of the Institution. The amendment which I offer, if adopted, will exclude such an idea. It declares a truth most verily believed among us, the assertion of which, at this time, may do much good; it can possibly do no harm. Outside of the slave-holding States an opinion prevails, that we are divided on this subject—that we have advanced no further than mere apologists for an evil entailed upon us—that we would gladly escape, were it possible. That opinion should be corrected.

The world should know that the Southern people are agreed upon the moral question—that we regard this Institution among us a positive good—a blessing both to the white and the black races—that our consciences are clear, and that we, an undivided people, are prepared to maintain that truth. The declaration of it in solemn form, is demanded to meet successfully the errors on the subject, that prevail to an alarming extent in the Christian world. I have confidence in the power of truth. It must at length prevail, whatever be the odds against it now. Opposed to the policy of reopening the African Slave Trade now, yet, I cannot vote for this substitute. I will consent to no policy which binds posterity upon a subject not radically and morally wrong.

We have just dissolved the Union because a distinction was recognized between slave property and other kinds of property hostile to the former. Shall we ourselves, at the outset of our Government, acknowledge the justice of such distinction by unfriendly discrimination, and fix in our fundamental law absolute limits to the growth and diffusion of this persecuted species of property? Does not the substitute offered by the gentleman from Lauderdale make such discrimination?

Examine it closely. What does it propose? Why, that we shall *instruct* our Deputies to insist upon such restrictions as will effectually prevent the rëopening of the African Slave Trade. I enquire with what power do we invest our Deputies? To propose organic laws for ratification; in a word, to make organic laws. Therefore, this substitute, in effect, contemplates the incorporation of restrictions upon this trade in the Constitution. First, then, you discriminate between slave and other property; next you fix this discrimination hostile to slavery, in the organic law, beyond the reach of ordinary legislative discretion. Although not designed, it casts odium on that Institution. Change the kind of property to be effected by the substitute, and who would vote for it? Let us see. Suppose it should read thus, "that our Deputies are instructed to insist upon such restrictions as will effectually prevent the trade in horses," this Convention would say, our people would say not so, let us buy horses where we can buy them cheapest. Let us account for the difference. The world favors the traffic in horses—does not regard it a moral evil—and we should risk nothing therefore, by voting down such restrictions, if attempted; but the outside world regards slavery to be a moral evil, and we must, I suppose, respect the sentiment, at least, show due deference to it by active legislation in behalf of the heresy. Sir, for, one I protest against so suicidal a policy. Let us do nothing from which an inference might be drawn, that we regard either the Institution, or the trade morally wrong. Let us rather assert the truth, that both are morally right—assert it boldly and openly. There is strength and safety in this course. A temporising policy will weaken, if not destroy us.

If we do not regard the African Slave Trade to be morally wrong, I ask gentlemen why do they desire to incorporate a prohibition of it, in the organic law? The Constitution of the United States contains no such prohibition. The argument just made by the gentleman from Montgomery, [Mr. Yancey,] establishes this, beyond all question. No strict constructionist will contend that any such power to prohibit was granted by that instrument. Shall we, then, insist that our new Constitution shall contain a clause condemnatory of our peculiar Institution, which the old Constitution did not? Are we to make it worse instead of better for us? Then adopt this Substitute, or the Ordinance of which it is an amendment, and it will be there, so far as Alabama may have a voice in the Southern Congress. But gentlemen are mistaken when they suppose such a course will conciliate the border slave-holding States, and encourage them likewise to secede. I do not believe it will. They will be governed by other considerations. They will sooner or later unite their fortunes with us. To avoid temporary injury, however, we ought not to refuse to declare a great truth, and one so important to us. The assertion of it may be temporarily detrimental, but to refrain from its assertion involves greater evil. If it be impolitic to reöpen the foreign Slave Trade, let it be prohibited by Congress or the Legislature, but ignore the subject on the organic law, and leave it to legislative discretion. Their action can be readily adapted to the necessities of the times, and should be based upon grounds of expediency altogether. It is doubtless, inexpedient for Alabama, at this time, to insist upon reöpening the trade. It may never be expedient for her to do so. Let it be so, but let her keep the power in her own hands, to be exercised or not, in the discretion of her people. Especially should she not insist on being bound herself, restrict the action of other States and people beyond the wisdom of the fathers, who made the old Constitution. They extended the trade for twenty years, unalterable by amendment of the Constitution, and although Congress, at the expiration of that time, prohibited the same, the power was assumed and clearly unconstitutional.

The result of the usurpation was to strengthen the North, and weaken the South; to destroy the equilibrium of power, and render a separation absolutely necessary to our political freedom and the safety of our Institutions. Are we prepared to engraft the same error upon our new Confederacy; to plant it deep in our organism, by making it a part of our Constitution? I trust that it will not be done. I do not desire to see the causes in operation to reproduce "the irrepressible conflict" in our borders, to avoid evils of which, it became necessary to dissolve the old Government. I do not believe that the Institution of slavery will be put in jeopardy by the prohibition, but sooner or later, it will, I fear, create the necessity for another separation to preserve it. We have escaped, by promptly seceding from the Union, the tyranny of unrestrained majorities. We are now beyond the power of their Legislative action, but we must reflect, that we cannot retire beyond the influence of laws which govern the world.

It is a law that the hungry will hunt for bread; that wherever the wages of labor are remunerative, there labor will go. I ask gentlemen to tell me, what will prevent the white laborers of the North from leaving low wages at home to secure, by immigration to the South, the high wages which must continue to rule here, if the number of slaves be restricted to the natural increase? You may attempt to prohibit immigration by refusing the privileges of citizenship, and imposing other political disabilities, but they will come nevertheless. Bread, to satisfy the cravings of hunger, will be an inducement to immigration, superior to all such prohibitory enactments. Social inequality itself would not deter the hungry from the land of plenty. They will come, and with a large surplus population, settle the middle and healthy latitudes, driving the dearer labor of the slave to the shores of the Gulf, and to the alluvial bottoms of the South-west. But, sir, I never wish to see that day. I hope it may never come, at the South, when safety to the institution of slavery shall require social or political inequality to be established among white people. No, sir; never let it come. Let us now adopt a course to prevent it—a better course—one consistent with Southern ideas and conservative of slave property and all other kinds of property. Let us keep the white race as they are here now, and ought ever to be—free, equal and independent, socially and politically; recognise no subordinates but those whom God has made to be such—the children of Ham—and whose subordination to a superior race secures their happiness, protection and moral elevation.

A simple act of secession, then, will not stay the tide of immigration, and the influx of white laborers from the North will likely introduce the very evils which we have endeavored to avoid. How long it will be before the evil becomes serious, I cannot tell. But, sooner or later, it will be upon us, unless the demand for labor at the South shall be supplied from some other source of a cheaper character, and consistent with our present labor system.

Then, Wisdom dictates, Mr. President, that we should not tie our own hands, nor the hands of those that come after us. If deemed expedient now, let us prohibit the introduction of Africans from abroad, but keep the prohibition out of the fundamental law.

Another reason, let me offer here, why the Legislature or Congress should be left free to act in its discretion upon this most important subject: The border slaveholding States might be induced to remain in the old Union. Should this be so, their people would expect to disconnect themselves from the institution of slavery, as other States have done, by selling their slaves to us at remunerative prices—at all events, without loss. A change of institutions would work a change of sympathies and affections. We must not lose their friendship, certainly not, by a process which shall make us pay for that loss at the rate of a thousand dollars apiece for their slaves. No, sir; let us hold their friendship by keeping them a slaveholding people. Let them keep and cherish their institutions. We can get, if necessary for our people, supplies elsewhere much cheaper.

Besides, sir, another reason might be given why it would be unwise to bind ourselves to any particular policy. A most cruel and inhuman system of Slavery has been countenanced by Great Britain and France under the name of "coolies" and "apprentices." Suppose, either or both of those Countries should, in contempt of the Monroe doctrine, choose to introduce such systems of labor into Mexico or the Central American States, and thereby plant their African apprentices in proximity to our borders, with a *purpose* to limit our expansion, hinder our growth, and eventually supplant and undermine our Slavery institutions, but under the plausible pretext of producing their own cotton, rice and tobacco. Of course, tied down, as we should be by this Constitutional prohibition, we must quietly submit, or engage in a war expensive, perhaps disastrous, to prevent it. Are we dreaming? Are we fast asleep? Will England hesitate to enter, wherein her interests invite? Has she not already expended untold treasures in the East, in the vain effort to supply her factories with Cotton? Will she quietly submit to her losses, and forego an object so cherished and so necessary to her political mercantile and soical independence? Let me tell you, she will not. Eng and will endeavor to make her musquito protectorate the basis of a policy which shall take in the Country from the Rio Grande to the Isthmus.

Give us a surplus of African Slaves, and the advantage of our proximity to that Country, and the still higher advantage of our humane and ennobling system of labor, and we can without force, effectually prevent the introduction of "coolies" and "apprentices," and thus avoid the risk and necessity of collision to secure safety to ourselves and security for our humane system of African Slavery. By a timely and judicious policy, we could settle the neighboring States and Territories with their opposition, and thus carry peacefully and by purchase, our institutions as far South as soil and climate and production would with profit invite Slave labor. To do this we must not tie our hands and cripple our energies, because a fanatical outside world believes African Slavery to be morally wrong, and the African Slave Trade to be infamous. We must dare to do right—leave the Legislative power unrestricted, to be exercised according to the wisdom and necessity of its own times.

Then sir, I hope that however much we may be opposed to the reopening of the African Slave Trade at this time, we shall vote down both the substitute and the Ordinance, which proposes permanent restrictions upon Legislative freedom and discretion— that we shall leave our Legislators free and untrammeled, on this subject, to meet and repel the dangers which threaten us—to embrace the benefits, which must result to us, to the white race, to the African, yea, to all minkind in extending, threatening, and perpetuating Slavery institutions. It secures the equality of the white race, and upon its permanent establishment rests the hope of democratic liberty.

Mr. Potter said:

Mr. President—Sir, this debate has taken a strange course. Gentlemen upon this floor, not content to discuss this measure upon its true merits, have wrung into the debate the morality of this trade. This, I think, sir, is highly improper, for the reason that we are not assembled here to adopt a code of Morals, as was so justly remarked, a few days since, by my friend from Green. But we are here, sir, to consider and do what the true policy of Alabama demands; and this subject should be considered in its political, and not in its moral aspects. When this measure was before us a few days ago, I took occasion to express my convictions as to the morality of this trade as it was once carried on, and as it might be conducted again if tolerated, and I trust my expression then was so qualified as not to be misunderstood. Sir, the amendment proposed, simply strikes out a qualifying clause which states that we are acting upon the "ground of public policy." Now sir, it is clear to my mind that all has been done by this body has been done upon principles of policy. We could have proceeded on no other principles. For had measures been proposed here, to be adopted or rejected upon principles of morality in cnntradistinction to the principles of policy, then certainly we should have had some understanding upon the subject at the out set. As this was not done, the presumption must be, that we have proceeded upon principles of policy alone. In this we have evidently been right. And these principles should still control us in all our deliberations and proceedings. Holding these views, I favor the amendment now proposed and hope it will prevail; for certainly the resolution before us needs no such qualification as this clause proposes.

Mr. Watts proposed a substitute for the Resolution as follows:

Strike out all after the word "Resolved," and insert:

That, in the opinion of this Convention, it is unwise and inexpedient to reopen the African Slave Trade, and the Convention of seceding States should adopt measures to prohibit the importation of slaves into the Southern Republic for sale *from any source.*

Mr. Smith, of Tuscaloosa, said:

Mr. President—There is something in this amendment that demands examination. Let us look at it cautiously. It is fraught with evil and disaster. There is an old saying, that "whom the gods intend to destroy, they first make mad;" and it does seem to me that we are rushing upon our fate with blind fury and heedless inconsideration.

We have made strangers and enemies of three-fourths of our countrymen, and now we propose deliberately to flout the faces of our friends; for, as I view this amendment, it is nothing less than a threat of defiance held out to the border slave States, carrying, in a closed hand, a bribe. This, doubtless, is not the intention of the mover of this amendment, but it is the interpretation that all the world will give the proposition. It simply says to the border States, if you do not come you shall have no slave market here; if you do come, you can have a slave market.

What is the all-important question that we should now keep constantly in view? We have dissolved the Union; declared ourselves independent. The building up of the new State, so far as the organic form of law is concerned, however important, is still secondary to the greater question: Having declared our independence, and set up for ourselves, how are we best to preserve that independence, and to sustain our position? Taking this, then, as the great question, let us stand upon it, and look upon ourselves in the attitude in which this *amendment places us.*

We have already been told, some days ago, in this Convention, by the gentleman from Montgomery, [Mr. Yancey,] that great apprehensions prevailed in the border States—Kentucky, Virginia, North Carolina and Tennessee—that the Gulf States designed to reopen the African Slave Trade; that he had himself received letters from distinguished persons in those States, informing him that but for the fear that the new Confederacy would reopen the African Slave Trade, there would be a much stronger and more general movement in those States in favor of dissolution. If this be a true state of the public mind in those States; if the fear that the new Confederacy would reopen the African Slave Trade, checks the feeling and the movement in those States in favor of dissolution, would not the adoption of this amendment, at this particular time, have a like effect? If, before this Southern Confederacy is formed, Alabama should say to North Carolina and Virginia: "*We will not import slaves from your State*," will it not check the feeling and movement toward secession there?

These old States are the sources of your own blood. If you will not bear a threat patiently, is it sensible to suppose that they will bear it? If a threat arouses you, will not a threat arouse them? If a threat throws you upon your dignity, and stirs the fountains of your scorn and indignation, will it not do the same with the citizens of the old States? They are bone of your bone, flesh of your flesh. They sent out the pioneers to cleave away the wilderness; to drive out the panther and the bear; to risk the tomahawk and scalping knife, and to brave all the horrors, privations and disasters of border life, for the sake of civilization. It is the land of their inheritance, by nature and by blood. But now, "clothed in a little brief authority," you lift your hands against your sires. You have grown rich in lands, in slaves and in money; plenty falls in your laps, and gold rolls at your feet. In the splendor of your prosperity you forget the land of your nativity and the graves of your ancestors. When Joseph grew rich in Egypt, and had gathered abundant stores to feed the famine-struck nations, his father and his brothers were the first in his grateful recollection; and thus he illustrated the beauty of that Divine Decree—" Honor thy father and thy mother, that thy days may be *long in the land which the Lord thy God giveth thee.*"

It is said by the gentleman from Montgomery [Mr. Yancey] that, by prohibiting the introduction of slaves from the border States, we shall offer them inducements to secede and join us. I do not adopt this sentiment. It would be measuring the patriotism of the border States by dollars and cents.

The best way to secure their coöperation and union is to treat them as brothers and as fathers; to claim their countenance and their strong arm as due to us by the indissoluble ties, not only of a common interest, but of common blood.

One of the objections to the reöpening of the African Slave Trade is, that it will operate injuriously on slave property in reducing its value, by placing the native African in the market at a lower price. If we wish the coöperative action of the border States, we should not only give them assurances that the African Slave Trade shall not be opened, but we should so shape our measures here as to relieve them entirely of all apprehensions now entertained by them as to the results of secession upon the permanent, present and future value of their slave property.

Suppose the border States refuse to indorse the wisdom of the policy of secession, and decline to join us; shall we treat them as enemies, then? They may not join us in the political movement, but still they may be our friends. Not favoring our political disunion, but, remaining in the old Union, they would be potent to do us good or evil. Shall we, by thus closing our doors against them, so inspire them with contempt or carelessness as to make them fold their arms and be neutral in the great struggle that we are courting with the North? No, sir. Let us *claim* them as brothers; and they who would scorn your threats, would come flocking in thousands in answer to the more natural appeals for their alliance. They will be the bulwarks over whose battlements the enemy would have to climb before he could reach your borders. Their hearts would be the first to feel the cold steel of the invader.

Sir, I have been pained at the injustice which leads us to lay the foundation of a war without the consent of the very people who will have to do the fighting when the great day of battle comes. That they will do this fighting when the day comes, whether they join us in a political union or not, I have never had a doubt. When the appetite of the North shall crave the blood of the South, that South will present an unbroken front. Political considerations and federative unions will all be postponed for this necessary alliance of defence. If this war is expected— and who does not expect it?—if this war is expected, why, at this early day, seek to mar the harmony of that fraternal sentiment that pervades the entire South?

We who have been in favor of consulting and coöperating with the border slave States, and who have yielded our wishes for the sake of public unanimity, and have come heartily into the support of the State under all emergencies, are now called upon to sit by quietly and see these old States flouted in the face with a threat! This is ungenerous. And are not the border slave States as vitally interested in this momentous movement of dissolution as we are? Nay, sir, are they not, in a practical sense, more so? They lose a hundred slaves to our one. They lie upon the borders of the enemy, with no defensive barriers between. A Kentucky negro that can swim a few hundred yards can obtain his freedom in an hour. If these and other great considerations were not sufficient to move you to pause for a consultation with these old States, may we not hope that at least you will now pause and consider this question well before you declare the citizens of these States to be *foreigners*. They have populated your State; you share their glories; your neighbor, Tennessee, fought your great battles when you were children, and shielded your mothers from the Indian tomahawk! Talladega was made historic by the solemn war tramp of the immortal Jackson, the blood of whose gallant soldiers enriched the soil of Alabama! And now, in one rash hour, you propose to make foreigners of that people, who fed upon acorns while serving you in the day of your direst necessity. Will you cast off such tried friends as these, and go drifting upon the great sea of uncertainty for other allies?

> "The friends thou hast, and their adoption *tried*,
> Grapple *them* to thy soul with hooks of steel;
> But do not dull thy palm with entertainment
> Of each new-hatched, unfledged comrade."

Enthused as we are at this time; lifted up by the spirit of Patriotism; exhilarated by the excitements that surround us, and animated by the contemplation of the novel position we occupy before the world; exultant of our prospects, and confident in the valor of our people, and the universal determination that prevails in the land to sustain our independence to the last extremity, we may yet over-estimate our strength and count without our hosts. And you who expect that the cotton States alone will be able to sustain this contemplated war, without the aid of your neighboring sisters, do over-estimate your strength, and count without your hosts. I know the unbending spirit and the unquailing valor of the people of Alabama; but courage is not the only sinew of war. I know the wealth of our people and the prodigal liberality with which it will flow, when needed, for the public safety; but wealth is not the only sinew of war. It may be that, in some respects, we are not ready for an immediate outbreak of active hostilities. There is no need of rushing into war. We must not be the invaders. Let us husband our resources; arrange our engines and prepare for the conflict; and, in doing this, while we defy our enemies, *let us hold fast to our friends.*

Upon vote taken on Mr. Watts' amendment, it was defeated.

Mr. Jemison moved the previous question in order to cut off all amendments, and the ayes and noes being demanded, the result was, ayes 29, noes 37 ; so the call for the previous question was not sustained.

Mr. Johnson said:

Mr. President—I rise not for the purpose or with the desire to make a speech, but of making an explanation.

I had been inclined to vote for the substitute offered by the gentleman from Lauderdale, although not as strong in its prohibitory provisions as I would like; but, sir, when the additional Resolution offered as an amendment by the gentleman from Chambers, was passed. I was not only astonished, but will most certainly be compelled to vote against the substitute as amended. If I understand the question correctly, we are prohibited from voting on the "Ordinance" reported by the Committee, even though we refuse to pass the substitute, for the Convention, in refusing to sustain the call for the previous question, did, in a parliamentary sense, refuse to entertain the main question or Ordinance; and hence if we vote against the substitute, the inference is natural, that we are opposed to the expression by this Convention, of its disapprobation of, or opposition to, the reöpening of the African Slave Trade.

I am unwilling to place myself upon the record in such way as to admit of that construction, and hence the necessity for this explanation.

The substitute offered by the gentleman from Lauderdale, asserts in the preamble, that we are opposed to the reöpening of the African Slave Trade, "upon the grounds of public policy," and therefore puts to rest the supposition that we are opposed to it upon the grounds of its immorality.

The Resolution proposes to instruct the Deputies elected by this Convention to the Southern Convention to insist upon the enactment by the said Convention of such restrictions as will effectually prevent the reöpening of the African Slave Trade, because we are opposed to it *upon the grounds of public policy.* The additional Resolution which has just been passed by way of amendment, asks that the Southern Convention shall, by Legislation, prevent any detriment to the growth or expansion of the Instituion of slavery; because it is a blessing morally, socially and politically.

In other words, the gentleman from Chambers would have this Convention ask of the Southern Convention the growth and *expansion* of the Institution.

The gentleman says his Resolution contains no such idea; that it simply intends to assert that slavery is a blessing; but when we examine the last, which is the saving and binding clause of his Resolution, we find that it is an invitation for the expansion of slavery, and that too in connection with the subject of the African Slave Trade.

How, sir, would that Convention, when it came to passing a law upon the subject of the African Slave Trade, be best able to carry out the idea of the gentleman? Most assuredly by reopening the African Slave Trade, for that is the cheapest and quickest way of expanding it. Yet we say in the same Resolution, that we are opposed to this traffic upon the grounds of public policy. There seems to my mind to be a contradiction implied at least. To my mind it is clear, that by this Resolution as amended, we intimate very clearly to the Southern Convention or Congress, that the people of Alabama are not only not averse to, but in favor of, the reopening of the Slave Trade with Africa.

To this sentiment, sir, I cannot subscribe, although I will go as far as the gentleman himself, in declaring that slavery is not an evil, either morally, socially or politically.

If the amendment had stopped with that expression, I could have voted for the substitute without violence to my views on this subject; but when it is added to, and qualified as I have intimated, I cannot vote for it.

We *propose*, by this resolution, to express our *qualified* disapprobation of the African Slave Trade, and yet, to my mind, we invite the revival of that traffic.

I regret the necessity which impels me to vote against the Substitute as amended, and I regret still more, the passage of this amendment by the Convention, for I feel assured that there is a large majority of this Convention that would like to record their opposition to the reopening of this traffic.

MR. DOWDELL's amendment had been adopted as a part of the Substitute for the Ordinance, originally reported by the Convention.

MR. WATTS moved to reconsider the vote on the adoption of Mr. Dowdell's Resolution, which motion was carried, and the question being on the adoption of Mr. Dowdell's Resolution, the ayes and nays were demanded, and it was lost—ayes 19, noes 40.

The question was then upon the final adoption of Mr. Jones' Resolution as amended, which is as follows:

WHEREAS, the people of Alabama are opposed, on the grounds of public policy, to the reopening of the African Slave Trade: therefore,

Resolved, That it is the will of the people of Alabama that the Deputies elected by this Convention to the Southern Convention, to meet at the city of Montgomery on the 4th day of February next, to form a Southern Republic, be and they are hereby instructed to insist on the enactment by said Convention of such restrictions as will effectually prevent the reopening of the African Slave Trade.

The Resolution was adopted with only three votes against it.

LAST DAY OF FIRST SESSION.

Mr. KIMBALL offered the following Resolution, [Mr. Webb in the Chair:]

Resolved, That the thanks of this Convention be tendered to the Hon. William M. Brooks, the President, for the able and impartial manner in which he has discharged the duties of his position.

Which Resolution was unanimously adopted.

Mr. WHATLEY moved that a Committee of three be appointed by the Chair to wait on His Excellency the Governor, and inform him that the Convention is ready to adjourn, and inquire of him if he has any further communication to make to this body. Carried,

And the CHAIR [Mr. Webb] appointed Messrs. Whatley, Jemison and Jewett, said Committee.

The Committee, on returning, reported that the Governor had no further communication to make to the Convention.

Mr. WHATLEY called up his motion to adjourn, which being agreed to,

MR. PRESIDENT BROOKS addressed the Convention:

Gentlemen of the Convention—The time of our separation is at hand. Permit me, before we part, to express my gratification at the vote of thanks unanimously tendered me by your honorable body, during my temporary absence from this Hall.

No one could be more sensible than myself of my want of proper qualifications for the high and responsible position of President of this Convention. When partial friends intimated an intention to place me in this position, I endeavored to dissuade them from their purpose. Never having served in any legislative body, and entirely unacquainted with Parliamentary Law, I suggested the names of others more able and experienced, and more worthy than myself of the place; but the choice fell on me. I accepted the office with exceeding diffidence, relying, however, upon your kind assistance and generous forbearance, in which I have not been disappointed. In my official action I have doubtles committed many errors; these you have kindly overlooked. In bearing testimony to my impartiality, I feel that you did me no more than simple justice.

The business for which we were called together was of the most momentous character. No other political body ever assembled in this State to consider and decide upon issues of like magnitude. Submission to Black Republican rule and consequent ruin, degradation and dishonor upon one hand, and the dissolution of the Union by the withdrawal of Alabama on the other, were the fearful alternatives. The issue was not of our seeking: we have been driven to to it by imperious necessity. We have met it resolutely and boldly, and, with a full sense of the responsibility, have chosen the alternative of secession and independence.

The scenes which transpired in this Convention on the 11th day of January, 1861, are indelibly impressed upon our memories. They will live imperishable in history to the last syllable of recorded time. It was the most solemn and impressive occasion of my life. Differences of opinion existed amongst us—honest differences, freely and frankly expressed and duly appreciated. We did not differ as to the question of submission or resistance to Black Republican domination. No, all feeling the necessity, were solemnly pledged to resist; we differed only as to the time and mode of resistance. We unbosomed ourselves to each other in remarks eloquent, heartfelt and patriotic. A deep sense of the solemnity of the occasion and of the great importance and responsibility of the act about to be done, pervaded the entire assembly. Stout hearts and brave ones—hearts which had remained unmoved through the thunder and carnage of battle, now heaved with strong emotions and were melted. Tears flowed freely down the cheeks of men unused to tears. Everywhere in our midst were manifested signs of deep patriotic feelings struggling within our bosoms. At length, by common consent, the vote was taken, and the Ordinance of Secession—that great Act of Deliverance and Liberty—was adopted. Immediately we were united; differences of opinion sunk into utter insignificance before the high purposes of patriotic devotion, and we stood pledged, the one to the other, to sustain this the Sovereign Act of the people of Alabama, with our lives, our fortunes and our sacred honor.

Before and after we assembled, attempts were made to excite in the public mind distrust of our purposes. At one time it was darkly hinted that in the exercise of the unlimited power confided to us, we might betray the people and establish a Monarchy; at another, that we would remain in perpetual session, ruling over the liberties of the people. Time has shown the injustice of these suspicions. We have become the tools of no man's ambition. In the exercise of our extraordinary powers we have faithfully endeavored to promote the good and the safety of the people. In a short time we will cheerfully return our authority to those who gave it, confident that we have not abused our trust.

We are about to return amongst our constituents; let it not be said that we countenance, much less encourage, opposition to the act of Secession. As true men, we will cheerfully labor to remove all dissatisfaction, if any, and urge our people to rally around and sustain the liberties and independence of our beloved State. However we may have differed as to the remedy of secession, *the deed is done.* Alabama is a free, separate and sovereign State: as loyal and united people, we will maintain her independence or perish in the conflict. We are in the midst of perils; Peace, smiling Peace, may, I trust will, be our lot. But this may not be so. Our Northern foes, under the same malign influences which have hitherto marked their conduct, may wage against us an unjust and wicked war. If so, let it come. We will do all that men should do to avoid it, but we will not cower and shrink from the contest; we are prepared to meet whatever fate betides us. As Freemen, we may become Martyrs to Liberty—*we were not born to be slaves.*

Alabama has withdrawn from the Union, moved thereto by a sense of self-preservation; she is now free. Does any one entertain a lingering hope that she will enter that Union again—that she will once more place her fortunes, her destiny, the happiness and liberties of her people within the power and under the control of the Black Republicans of the North? If any man entertains such a hope, he has read the signs of the times to but little purpose; and let me entreat him, as he values the blessings of equality and freedom, to dismiss it at once and forever as an idle and pernicious dream. There is not—there cannot be any peace and security for us in such a reconstructed Union. We have, I confess, many true friends at the North, but too few to render their assistance available. They will, as heretofore, be unable to resist the dark tide of aggression which has threatened to engulf our liberties under and through the agency of a common Government. Looking back at the many grievous wrongs under which we have so long suffered at the hands of our Northern *brethren*, and reflecting upon the threatened perils from which we have escaped by withdrawing from the Union, I cannot but rejoice at our deliverance; and this joy is increased by an abiding conviction that come what may, sink or swim, live or die, survive or perish, Alabama will never again enter its ill-fated portals; no, *never—never—never*. I bid you one and all farewell.

The Convention adjourned until the 4th of March.

HISTORY & DEBATES OF THE CONVENTION.

SECOND SESSION—FOURTH OF MARCH, 1861.

I shall no longer adhere to the plan of dividing this work into particular days; as a continuance of that plan would swell the volume beyond the proportions originally designed for it. I shall keep up a history of the more important events, and make the divisions of the subjects discussed without regard to the day; thus I will be enabled to group the speeches on each subject together.

The Convention re-assembled, on the 4th of March, 1861, in the Hall of the House of Representatives, and resumed the consideration of its unfinished business. The attendance, the first day, was not large; but, on the second, nearly all the delegates appeared. There was no abatement of the interest felt in public affairs; but the great question of Secession having been decided, the deliberations of the Convention were not now of such absorbing interest.

REDUCTION OF THE SIZE OF COUNTIES.

Mr. JOHNSON, of Talladega, brought before the Convention, during the first session, a proposition to reduce the size of the counties. This subject occupied much of the attention of the Convention, and was received with favor; but the ruling objection to it (and the one which caused its final defeat), was, that at this particular time, it would be unwise to introduce for public discussion amongst the people, a question so calculated to excite division and discontent in the counties.

Mr. Johnson said:

Mr. President—I shall content myself, sir, with making a simple statement of facts connected with this question, and leave it with the Convention.

It is, I believe, a universally admitted fact, that our counties are too large; and almost as universally admitted that they should be reduced, if it can be done without inflicting injury upon any locality or interest.

In order to arrive at a just appreciation of the facts connected with, and which should govern our action in relation to, this subject, we must particularise to a limited extent.

We have, Mr. President, in this State, large numbers of citizens who are compelled to travel a distance of thirty, and, in some cases, forty miles to their county site.

Those large populous counties necessarily have a great deal of business on their court calendars, and there is, consequently, great uncertainty as to the time when a particular case will be " reached " and disposed of in these courts.

Our Circuit Courts frequently hold three weeks, and citizens of the county having business in court, either as jurors, witnesses, or parties litigant to suits, living in the remote portions of the county, are greatly inconvenienced, forced to neglect their home interests, and therefore to be heavily taxed.

These and other difficulties attending this subject, tend, to say the least of it, to a denial of justice in the courts, and a direct representation in the Legislature.

The people have evinced more interest in this question, than any other of a secondary nature which has been before this body. We have before us various memorials, numerously signed by respectable and intelligent citizens of the State, asking that some change shall be made in this particular.

The Ordinance reported by the Committee simply proposes to authorize the Legislature to establish new counties, where the necessities of the people require it.

And I assume that the necessities would be urgent before the requisite two-thirds vote, in both Houses of the Legislature, could be obtained.

Mr. President, there seems to be a misapprehension as to the effect of this proposed Amendment to the Constitution.

Gentlemen allude to this Ordinance as though it was a proposition to establish new counties containing five hundred square miles, regardless of the wishes of the people, or the rights which may be jeoparded by it. Such, sir, is not the case. We simply propose to authorize the Legislature, by a two-thirds vote, to establish new counties, to contain *not less* than five hundred square miles, and where it will not reduce the old counties to a less size.

In order, then, to protect, as far as possible, the original county organizations, and interests incident thereto, we propose that the line of no new county shall be established within less than twelve miles of the old county sites; and providing, further, that it shall require a two-thirds vote of the qualified electors of a county to change a county site.

These safeguards are thrown around this proposition, in the belief that they will be ample for the protection of all classes and localities. If, then, there are counties which will not be benefitted by availing themselves of this Amendment to the Constitution, they will certainly not be compelled to do so, and will therefore not be effected injuriously by the passage of this Ordinance.

I will now, Mr. President, notice briefly some of the objections which are urged to this Ordinance.

It is said, sir, that if we pass this Ordinance, we will increase the representation.

It is only necessary to refer gentlemen to the Constitution, as it will read when amended, which asserts that new counties, as to the right of suffrage and representation, shall be considered as a part of the county or counties from which they were taken, until entitled, *by numbers*, to separate representation. This, certainly, meets that objection fully.

Another objection is, that it will endanger the permanency of the present county sites, which we think is groundless, for we have specially provided against this objection, by refusing to allow a new county line to be established within less than twelve miles of the old county sites, and by requiring a two-thirds vote of the electors of a county to change a county site.

Thus, sir, we have certainly endeavored to protect those local interests and vested rights. In short, Mr. President, we have endeavored to present this proposition in such shape as to enable those citizens whose interests will be promoted by the change, to avail themselves of it, while those who do not desire any change, in this respect, will not be affected by it.

Now, sir, may I not appeal to gentlemen of this body, to lay aside any local prejudice, and in that spirit of courtesy and magnanimity which has so far characterized them upon this question, meet this proposition in such way as to benefit a large class of our citizens, while they reflect no injury upon any class.

I beg of gentlemen, as a matter of right, as well as magnanimity, to pass this Ordinance, and thereby enable those citizens of our State who are so deeply interested in this matter, to present their claims to the Legislature; and if they are of such a character as to challenge the support of two thirds of that Body, in the name of common justice let them have it.

Our State, sir, has fewer counties, in proportion to the extent of her territory, than any other State on this Continent.

These counties were established, and this injudicious Constitutional restriction was imposed upon the Legislature, at a time when our State was sparsely populated, and the people illy able to incur the expense that would have been made necessary by laying off the State into small counties.

That day, sir, has long since passed. Every portion of our State now teems with the happy results of an intelligent and prosperous population.

The business which necessarily springs up in every county, has so vastly increased as to render it absolutely necessary that every important office in those large, populous counties, shall be filled by a double set of officers.

I have said more, sir, than I intended, knowing, as I do, that nothing I could say would affect the action of any member on this floor. Yet, from a sense of duty to myself and my constituents, and from an earnest desire that this act of sheer justice should be consummated, I have deemed it an indispensable duty to trespass upon the time of the Convention far enough to make this statement of facts, and, as far as possible, to disabuse the minds of those who have misapprehended the intentions of the friends of this measure, and the provisions of the Ordinance.

Mr. President, I have done, and shall content myself with an expression of this Body voting yeas and nays.

Mr. McLanahan said:

Mr. President—My objections to the Majority Report on County Boundaries are sufficiently set forth in the Minority Report, but inasmuch as I made the Minority Report, it will not be deemed improper for me to explain these objections. It is certainly true, and by me admitted, that this Convention is clothed with extraordinary powers; but we were assembled only in view of the act of secession, and acts incident thereto. The Government has been dismembered, and for this Convention now to enter upon the work of remodeling the counties, will be taking upon itself a responsibility, which has not been desired or expected, and it is but right that the people should be consulted before such an important change in the fundamental law of the State shall be made. The public mind is already greatly agitated, and needs quiet rather than further agitation.

Most of our counties have been formed for more than forty years, the county-sites are permanently located, and any change in the boundaries of the counties may tend to disturb and remove the same, which would be an interference with vested rights, and for that reason should not be adopted.

Our Constitution already limits the number of Representatives to the lower branch of the General Assembly to one hundred, and to the Senate to one-third that number; the proposed change will greatly increase the number of counties, and the result will be to leave the small and weak counties without separate representation; and from necessity they will be compelled to vote with their larger and stronger neighbors.

The proposed change will but lessen the probabilities of the counties securing the services of able and efficient officers, for as you lessen the number of population in the county organization, you lessen the opportunity for the people to select wise and efficient county officers in every department.

It is certainly desirable that every county should have separate representation, but it will be impossible so to reörganize the counties, as to give to each a separate Representative, unless the Constitution is so amended as to increase the present number, and this should be avoided, for our Legislature is now quite numerous enough; in the State of Georgia, they have over three hundred Representatives, and this in consequence of their great number of counties; their Legislative body is not only expensive to the State, but is unwieldly and tardy in its action.

The formation of new counties in the State will lead to a great deal of excitement and speculation in the location of the new county-sites.

I know, Mr. President, that some of the counties in the late Creek Territory are large, containing much over nine hundred square miles, the present Constitutional limits; some of them containing, I believe, from eleven to twelve hundred square miles; and there are some few localities in which I think a new county might and should be formed; but I prefer that gentlemen make their independent applications, and that each application rest on

18

its own merits. The gentleman from Henry, it will be remembered, has introduced an Ordinance to make two counties out of the county of Henry; this, I think, is a meritorious proposition, and I expect to support it, and will support any isolated proposition which is made, to rest on its own merits, provided territory and population will justify it; but my objection to the Majority Report is, that it unsettles every county in the State, and there are at least nine-tenths of the people, and especially in the old counties, who do not desire any change. For these reasons, I have offered the Minority as a substitute for the Majority Report, and hope the same will be adopted by the Convention.

MR. RALLS said :

Mr. President—I do not propose to detain the Convention with any lengthly remarks, but simply to make a few suggestions, and answer some objections that have been urged against the passage of this Ordinance.

There is one thing, sir, that certainly has not escaped the attention of this body. It is this: Some measure, disapproved of by some of the members, is put upon its passage, and then, forsooth, these members meet us with the very *convenient* argument: Oh! the people did not send us here to make such and such changes in the Constitution. But when these members are in favor of any particular measure, although it may involve some radical change in the Constitution, and although there has been no expression of the popular will, yet all their conscientious scruples are held in abeyance, and they can, and do heartily support said measures. Now, Mr. President, it does appear to me that the proposition embraced in the Ordinance under consideration is exceedingly reasonable. It is not to inaugurate any new principle of government, or to *force* upon the people any change, which will be offensive to them. But it is simply to confer upon the Legislature the power to establish new counties, under certain wholesome restrictions. And now, Mr. President, those who oppose this Ordinance, put themselves in this position: They say to the people—although you live at a very inconvenient distance from your county-site—although the discharge of your public duties may be attended with a great tax upon your time and purse, and protracted absence from your families—and although in order to attend your courts, you may have to cross large rivers, that at some stages of the water cannot be crossed but with great difficulty and danger, and although all these facts may be made to appear to the satisfaction of even two-thirds of both branches of the Legislature, and they as an act of simple justice might be disposed to grant you relief, yet we will deny them the power to do so, and you shall still suffer all the inconveniences of your position. Now, let us look at the safeguards thrown around this Ordinance, and see if there is any probability of any unnecessary increase in the number of counties in the State. No new county shall be established but by a vote of two-thirds of both branches of the Legislature, and shall not contain less than five hundred square miles. Now is it at all likely that two-thirds of that honorable body, after a full review of the whole ground, would establish a new county, unless it was manifest that the wants of the people immediately interested required it? I think not. And then the protection of the county-sites already established; no county-line shall run nearer than twelve miles to these places; and no county-site shall be changed without a vote of two-thirds of the legal voters of the county in which said town is situated. This is certainly ample protection to vested rights.

Again, we are told that the expenses of the State Government will be greatly increased, and as a proof of this, that there would be a decided increase in the number of Judges. By no means, sir. There would be no increase of litigation, because of the increase of counties. The population and business of the State would in every particular remain the same. Those large and populous counties, that now hold court two weeks, would loose a part of their Territory and business, so as to hold Court only one week; and a Judicial circuit could contain a greater number of counties, but yet, be served by the Judge in the same time, because of holding Court only one week in each and every county, instead of two weeks, as in many cases is now done. And there is one instance at least in which there would be a saving of expense to the State; and that is in the milage of witnesses in State cases. But, Mr. President, even if there should be some increase in the expenses of the State, I hope that gentlemen will not be so ungenerous as to deny to their fellow-citizens, like privileges with themselves. I hope the Ordinance will be adopted.

Mr. POTTER said:

Mr. President—Were it not for the deep and abiding interest which I feel in this subject, I would not trouble the Convention with any remarks at this time.

But, sir, this measure is now before us, and it is highly important that we dispose of it properly. The argument, that we were not convened for this purpose, (so frequently urged by those who wish to defeat measures here) cannot be legitimately used now;

for we have actually undertaken to revise and correct our State Constitution. This cannot be denied. And certainly a favorable opportunity is now presented for making this amendment, which has been so long desired, and which is so much needed.

There is, sir, a marked difference, in one respect, between the proposed change, and some others which have been adopted; for in other cases barriers have been placed in the way of future legislation, though such legislation may be necessary for the good of the State; but in this case we simply desire to remove a barrier out of the way, so that hereafter such legislation may be had as the wants and interests of the people require. Assembled as we are, for the purposes which called us together, it is plainly our duty to do all we can to promote the welfare of every portion of our State, and to meet the just expectations of those who ask us to provide a remedy for existing evils.

Now, Mr. President, it is well known that in many parts of this State, the people are laboring under serious disadvantages, because of present constitutional provisions, in regard to the size of counties, and they are now, and have been for years, greatly dissatisfied, and we have abundant reason to believe that this dissatisfaction will continue to increase, until relief is obtained by some such change as is now proposed. And it is therefore important that we embrace this opportunity to do justice to such citizens, by making a change which has been so long, and so earnestly desired.

Arguments have been used by gentlemen of this Convention, to defeat this measure, which appear to me, sir, to be utterly futile. It is said that the formation of new counties, will leave the old ones too small; but, sir, this cannot take place under the restrictions which are thrown around this amendment, for while it proposes to change the minimum size of a county, from nine hundred to five hundred square miles, no old county can be reduced below this size.

The objection that the number of Representatives in the Legislature will be increased, is also without foundation, for it is provided that no new county shall be entitled to separate representation until it is entitled by numbers, thus sufficiently guarding this point. But, be it remembered, that the time will come when, either the number of Representatives will be increased, or the ratio changed. It is urged that the expenses of the State will be increased. How this can be, sir, I confess I am totally unable to see, for surely the establishment of new counties will not necessarily augment the business of our Courts. And when we consider the amount of mileage saved, on the part of those who attend court, we find a considerable reduction of expenses in small counties, to say nothing of other savings.

Besides, sir, when we estimate the advantages secured to the citizens of counties of convenient size, in the way of traveling, returning home at night, saving tavern bills, and attention to domestic affairs, during Court terms, and on other occasions, it will be seen that it adds greatly to their convenience, and interest to have such counties. And I take this occasion to say, that those who are so situated as to need new counties in this State, who earnestly desire to have them, and who are now urging their claims upon us, will not, nay, cannot be satisfied to remain in their present condition.

The fears that many seem to indulge, in regard to the permanency of present county sites need have no existence, for if two-thirds of the voters of any county have to decide the question of change, their decision ought certainly to be satisfactory, and with this provision in the amendment now proposed, no Court-house properly situated, can be in any danger of removal.

For these, and other reasons which might be urged, I respectfully insist that this measure be favorably considered, and indulge the hope that the amendment will be adopted.

Mr. Morgan said:

This subject has been discussed in some of its political aspects, by several gentlemen, who addressed the Convention, on a similar proposition introduced by a select Committee, of which the gentleman from Talladega, [Mr. Johnson] is Chairman. If the Convention is still in doubt about the necessity of a change in the existing constitutional area of nine hundred square miles to the county, it must be the result of an apprehension, that the disturbance of this area would be followed by a train of evils, or difficulties not provided against in the propositions heretofore submitted to the Convention. In the amendment which I have offered, I have attempted to meet all the difficulties as yet suggested, and some that have occurred to my mind. Another embarrassment has been called up by the remarks of the gentleman from Calhoun, [Mr. Whatley,] which is outside of the special matter involved in the amendment, but deserves to be carefully noticed. The gentleman suggests, that such amendments to the Constitution are not within the just powers of this Convention; because they are not expressed in the Act of the Legislature, which he is pleased to denominate the Commission under which we act.

The Act of the Legislature has nothing to do with our powers, further than to provide, in a legal way, for the election and assembling of the Convention. In these respects, even, it is not indispensable to the authority of any act we proposed, that there should have been an act of the Legislature calling a Convention, for in the absence of such an act, (there being no restriction in our Constitution, confining the people to a particular mode of procedure,) they could assemble, by their delegates in Convention, and exercise the "political power inherent in the people," and maintain their " indefensible right to alter, reform, or abolish their power of government, in such *manner* as they may think expedient."

The only effect of the Act of the Legislature is to preserve the legality of the action of the Convention, and it does not assume to define or limit our powers when legally assembled.

The people can come together in the exercise of their "inherent power," and disregard the loyalty of their action, but this would be a revolution. If they assemble in pursuance of the will of the State as expressed in the Act of the Legislature, (which is the ordinary expression of its sovereignty) there is no revolution, because the people give their consent by a law, to the assemblage of the Convention, and thus all the powers and departments of the government harmonize in their action, and the movement is set on foot *by the State* and not *against the State Government by the people*.

It would require a very strong case of necessity to justify the people in assembling themselves without the express sanction of the law, for the purpose of changing their form of government, and I rejoice that no such attempt has ever been made in our State. I prefer that the Constitution should contain a provision which shall hereafter place this matter on clear and safe grounds. It is better to have such a provision made in the Constitution than to have to be supplied by Acts of the Legislature.

Being legally assembled here, and moving on in harmony with all the powers and departments of the State, when we have recognized in all our acts, and by whom, in turn, we have been recognized and obeyed, we are not engaged in a revolution against the State, but we, who, alone even represent the State in this particular, do engage the State in a revolution, if you please, by dissolving its connection with another and different Government of which the State was a part.

This great act performed, the question arises, do our powers cease at this point?

The act of dissolution was performed in the exercise of the highest sovereignty.

If we derived our authority from the Legislature to do this act, then it is the General Assembly that is sovereign, and not the people. The converse of the proposition is true. The Legislature is a department of the State, a mere repository of certain powers, ascribed to it by the people in the Constitution. It expresses the voice of the State, in one form only, and is confined by the Constitution to one certain set of powers and duties. Our power is directly from the people, and we here speak the supreme voice of the people—the true political power in the State. We are the people assembled by their Delegates in Convention.

If the Legislature could confine the power of the Delegates of the people in Convention, it could also restrict, or abolish the power of the people to assemble here; or it could, in disregard of the "bill of rights," destroy the power of the people to elect Delegates, or to demand the rights secured to them, as individuals, in the Constitution. We are above the Legislature and the Constitution, and are only confined to the great purposes of securing and protecting the rights, honor and interests of the people, according to the form of Government under which we have lived, and which the people desire to preserve.

If we improve the Constitution by amendments, we better the State, and protect the interests of the people. If our amendments do not change the form of Government or disorganize its great divisions of powers, we work no revolution in the State. We could not depart from the established republican form of Government and preserve the political or moral consistency of our action; but while we keep within these bounds, we may adjust and improve the machinery of Government as we think best, because these things all contribute, in the end, to the wise and safe exercise of the power of the people in the great purpose of all republics, the security of self-government on a basis established in a written Constitution.

We have found it necessary to amend the Constitution in many instances, in order to give effect to the Ordinance of Secession. In our original Constitution there were such recognitions of the United States as were utterly incompatible with the Ordinance of Secession. These recognitions were not necessary to the instrument in any respect, and we have contributed much towards placing the State upon its well recognized and high position as a Sovereign power by striking out these points of the Constitution and supplying their places with other words. In doing this, did we transcend our powers? If not, it is because these changes were needful to protect the interests or honor of the people, and not because they are included in the "commission" contained in the act of the Legislature. The "commission" did not instruct us to secede from the Union, and our secession has found its warrant in the "commission," because we decided that act necessary to protect the honor and interests of the people. If we find that another act, less assimilating to revolution, is needful to be done in order to protect the interests of the people, shall we hesitate to perform it because it is not expressly mentioned in the "commission?" Let us not hesitate on matters of so little weight, to do what is best to be done for the good of the State.

The existing area of the counties in this State was prescribed at a time when a large part of what is now the most populous region of the State was a wilderness, inhabited almost entirely by Indians. It was the commencement, and then necessary to have very large counties. Indeed the white population was so sparse that for a number of years they were not able to build safe jails or respectable Court Houses. It has become a very different matter now. In some of these counties the population has so increased that, while there are only fifty-two counties in the State, and one hundred Representatives in the House, some of those counties have three and others four Representatives from merely agricultural districts, where they have no large towns.

The reason of the rule has ceased, and the rule becomes a burthen to the people. I deprecate small counties, and I learn that Georgia has reaped a bitter experience in the reduction of the size of the counties. But an excessively large county is even worse than one too small. The expense to individuals living remote from the Court House, the loss of time in travel, the increased expenses attending the administration of Justice, in witness fees, and by other means; the consequent denial of Justice in many cases, the wrangles about the removal of Court Houses, the political differences that divide counties on such questions, the influence of localties on the general legislation of the State, all admonish us that a change to a reasonable area is desirable.

The amendment which I had the honor to propose seems to me, to settle all these troublesome matters. It provides for an area of not less than six hundred square miles to each county. Some of our counties do not much exceed that area now. It requires a two-thirds vote to change a county boundary, on the part of the Legislature and of the people concerned. It provides against separate representation of a new county until its population shall entitle it to such representation on a ratio adopted to supply only one hundred members from the entire State. The embarrassments being all removed, the naked question is: shall the convenience of the people be subserved when no person or place can possibly be interfered with by our own action? I leave this question to the Convention, and trust that the response to it will be favorable to the change.

This question was discussed in all its various points, at different times, but the Ordinance was finally defeated.

ON THE LEGITIMATE POWERS OF THE CONVENTION.

The proposition to prohibit future Legislatures from contracting public debts, without, at the same time, providing the means of liquidation, being under consideration,

MR. BUFORD,* of Barbour, said:

Mr President—The chief difficulty that I find in voting for this measure, supported as it is by so many distinguished gentlemen, and with so much zeal and ability, has been entirely overlooked in the argument.
Are we indeed the whole people? with unlimited jurisdiction over every possible subject of legislation? with rightful power to subvert the foundations of society, and shape the Organic Law and Policy of the State at pleasure?

Mr. MORGAN, of Dallas:

Every Ordinance we pass reads: " We, the people of the State of Alabama."

MR. BUFORD:

Yes! While acting within the purview of our commission, we stand in the stead of the people, and may well say, " We, the people." But when I look around, and find in this chamber, not our million of inhabitants, but only one hundred individuals, I ask, are these hundred " the people of Alabama," or only their agents? Manifestly only the latter. Now, whence came our agency? Did we appoint ourselves, and confer our own powers? I confess, Mr. President, we seem to talk and act as if such were the case. Then, if we are not the whole people, but only their agents, it is evident we have no power which they have not conferred.

---

* Hon. Jeff. Buford, who had been elected, from the county of Barbour, to fill the vacancy created by the resignation of Hon. Alpheus Baker, was introduced by Hon. John Cochran, and took his seat in the Convention on the 13th of March.

Concede that, in order to the most liberal construction of our jurisdiction, we may look to the history of the times, the attending circumstances, and the motives which influenced the grant. Still, when we turn to the Joint-Resolutions of the General Assembly, under which the Governor convened this body, and consider them, whether in themselves or in the light of their historical circumstances, we are left in no doubt, either as to the terms of our commission, the motives which induced it, or the end it was intended to accomplish. By words, either of recital, or of direct cession, all are put down in plain, unambiguous language. These Resolutions constitute our sole letter of attorney.

Now, sir, what are the evils and dangers recited in this our commission; and from which we are empowered to deliver the imperiled State? Do we find there (as this proposition, and the arguments urged in its support would lead us to infer,) any complaint of grievous taxation, resulting from debts contracted by improvident and faithless representatives, in the ordinary course of legislation? any authority to heal that disease? to deliver from that danger? That portion of "the people" by whom I was sent, thought the object was to save them, not from their own representatives, in the ordinary functions of legislation, but to deliver them from the power of faithless allies, who were usurping their liberty of internal self-control, and seeking to degrade all the Southern States to the level of their servile population. This, sir, is what my constituents imagined, and what I, too, imagined, was the scope and limit of my authority.

Are we right? Let us condescend, for a moment, to consider and analyze the power-of-attorney under which we all must needs admit we are acting. Yes! "power-of-attorney." And we may not disdain the homely term; for our grant is no wild gush of unlimited generous confidence, but a cautious, technical thing of paper and ink; in which, after carefully reciting the probability that a sectional party, by success in the then pending Presidential election, would possess themselves of the machinery of the Federal Government, and wield it to our destruction, authorizes (in the event of that success,) the assembling a Convention of *delegates* of the people, with specific instructions "To consider, determine, and do whatever they may deem necessary to our protection."

Protection against what evils and dangers, Mr. President? Common sense replies, "Only against the evils and dangers then in contemplation." None other is referred to. No other was urging. No other was thought of, or in any degree prompted the call of this Convention. And there is no need to invoke the lawyers' rule of construction, that the expression of one object is the exclusion of another.

Gentlemen lay stress upon the generalities in our Bill of Rights, and the first principles therein recognized.

They remind us that "Political power is inherent in the people;" and that they have the "inalienable right to alter, reform or abolish, their form of Government, in such manner as they may think expedient."

Now, suppose we admit (and this is more than the other side contends for,) that the people may, without being called by the Legislature, lawfully assemble, *en masse*, and do whatever they will; does it therefore follow that if, after so assembling, and finding it impracticable to deliberate and act in such multitudes, they conclude that they are satisfied with their Government as it is, save as to certain evils which they specify, and the reformation of which they confide to certain individuals, whom they nominate as their delegates or agents in that behalf. And suppose "the people" then disperse, but the delegates remain? Now, "all power is inherent in the people," but does it follow that therefore these delegates may exercise all power?

The question is too absurd to be seriously entertained. And if such delegates moved an inch beyond their specific instructions, the Judicial Tribunals would be bound to hold their action for naught.

Now, in what does the case we have supposed differ from the one at issue, where, there being no prior assembling *en masse*, the mouth-piece of the body politic has, in the first instance, specified the dangers to be guarded against, and called, not a Convention of the people, *en masse*, but a Convention of their delegates, to provide against these specified dangers? The Legislature has acted in the stead of the people; the people have accepted their action, and have sent their delegates. For what purpose? Of course, only for the purpose indicated in the call; no other could have been contemplated. To say, then, that a Convention of delegates, called for specific purposes, is "above the Legislature and above the Constitution," if thereby it is meant to affirm they are untrammeled by the objects of the call—is to say they are above the people.

But gentlemen who claim omnipotence for a Convention assembled for special objects, tell us, in a reassuring sort of way, that these delegates, though they are, in fact, "the people," yet "they cannot depart from the established form of Government, and must preserve the political and moral consistency of their action."

Now, if such Convention be the people, then, under the Bill of Rights, they may "alter their form of Government, in such manner as they may think expedient:" *i. e.* they may change any given form to any other form of Government.

It is but too palpable that this careless use of the words "the people," and "We," as applicable to the people, *en masse*, or their delegates indiscriminately, is not only a misapplication of terms, but a dangerous confusion of ideas.

It is no answer, but a mere sophistry, to say that the Legislature cannot restrict the "political power inherent in the people." For if (as is our case), instead of the people themselves assembling, and directly delegating power to their agents, they accept the legislative call, then they accept it with all its restrictions; and there would seem as much oversight of good faith, as of reasonable inference, in any other conclusion.

Will gentlemen, impatient of logical difficulties in the case, venture to claim that the representative is not bound by the will of his constituents? Why, sir, the admission that he "cannot depart from the established form of Government, but must preserve the moral and political consistency of his action," is a bar to any such assumption, and concedes that delegates are not the people, nor above them, but only subordinate agents, and subject to trammels which "the people" may disregard, "as they may think expedient."

Yes, sir! I concede to my friend from Dallas, that while *bona fide* acting within the fair scope of our delegated power, either in the direct act of seceding from the hostile Government, against which the legislative Resolutions (adopted by "the people," as their deed-of-attorney,) authorize us to protect the Commonwealth, or while doing anything incident to such secession, and necessary to make it safe or effectual, then we, in fact, stand in the very stead of "the people of Alabama," and may well say, "We, the people." But when we trample their commission under foot, and usurp authority not conferred, we become a mere lawless mob—we deno alize, and sap our legitimate authority, and bring reproach even upon the measures we have rightfully adopted

I ask, Mr. President, how can the Captain, who habitually disregards the orders of his superiors, control his own subordinates? And how can the Colonel influence his Captains when he himself usurps authority, and sets the example of disobedience?

No, sir! Man is more an intellectual and moral, than physical being; and human control belongs rather to moral than physical force. Yes, Mr. President; rightful influence is a connected chain, reaching from the throne of the Almighty to the footstool of humanity, where crouches the humblest slave. And at whatever point a link is broken, all below is insubordination, confusion and anarchy. Can we ignore the inexorable laws of logic; can we ignore principle, truth, and God, and still expect to maintain our moral power? I warn gentlemen, when we usurp jurisdiction not confided to us, we destroy our prestige and influence with our constituents; and giving just cause for disregarding our authority, in one particular, we invite suspicion of illegality, and provoke opposition to all our measures.

Sir, the friends of Secession will have burdens enough to carry, and possibly sins enough to answer for, without turning to the right or the left from the straight and narrow path of our limited duties.

This measure proposes a radical change in a long-settled policy of the State, involving momentous interests, well calculated to arouse fierce passions, and array factions in a blind antagonism, that may overshadow and put in jeopardy the great principles and interests specially and solely confided to our charge. Why should earnest, single-minded secessionists, needlessly array the friends of internal improvement, of banking, and of the credit system in general, against their cause? Are they unconscious that thousands, with potent influence at the polls, appreciate no principle but the palpable dollar, and find nor music nor joy in rights and liberties unattended with present ring of metal?

Gentlemen confidently say, there is no Reconstruction party in Alabama, and that there will be none. Disregard of possible danger may prove a fatal security; and I beseech the true friends of our movement to beware lest, in heedlessly rushing forward, we stumble, fail, and find a stronger enemy upon us. And especially, sir, why meddle with this exciting, and therefore dangerous topic, when our action, being beyond our commission, would necessarily be nugatory? For it needs no argument to prove that the agent cannot bind the principal wherein he has exceeded the powers specified in his commission.

I cannot see how this measure is either within the express grant of power to us, or in any way incidental to the same.

It is by no means certain even that it will popularize our great measure of secession with the people. Those who like it will think we have only done our duty; while those who disapprove, will regard it as an usurpation, and a wrong, for which the whole movement will be held to answer. Benefactions are soon forgotten, while injuries are neither forgotten nor forgiven.

I understood my distinguished colleague to intimate that "We, being sent here to protect property, and this measure being eminently conservative of property, it is therefore within the scope and object of our powers."

Now, Mr. President, I submit that while our commission is of much higher import and dignity, it is, in one respect, by no means so broad. We are sent to protect, not so much property, as white supremacy, and the great political right of internal self-control— but only against one specified and single danger alone, *i. e.* the danger of Abolition rule. Now, if A commission B to guard his sheep-fold against the wolves, it is true that sheep are property; but it does not therefore follow that B may lawfully imprison A to prevent his frequenting the tavern or gambling-house, although both these practices may be very destructive to A's property.

And beside, Mr. President, suppose we had rightful cognizance in this matter of legislative creation of debts, still what of its practical utility, in view of the facility of always providing some specious means for their liquidation? This would tempt to frequent evasions of the Constitution in this respect, and, by thus demoralizing the public mind, tend gradually to subvert the whole instrument. It seems eminently impolitic to introduce into the Fundamental Law provisions of such easy evasion. The New York Constitution, in order to prevent bank suspensions, directs all suspended banks to be turned over to the Receiver; and yet even the Judiciary, a few years ago, when public expediency demanded suspension, evaded this provision by construing it as applicable only to banks without assets of value equal to their indebtedness.

I choose, however, to place my refusal to take cognizance of this question on the single ground of want of legitimate power over it.

But while a restraint, practically commensurate with the object here intended, I would regard as an eminently conservative feature of the Organic Law, I cannot shut my eyes to the fact that, as civilization progresses, credit, and the power, to some extent, to anticipate future means, seem to become more and more necessary, to enable both individuals and nations to keep even pace in the march of human progress. Nor can I see how one generation can foreknow all the wants and exigencies of another. This proposition, it is true, excepts occasions of actual war and threatened invasion. But suppose whole cities, within our borders, should be destroyed by fire; or suppose long famine, or some other unforeseen calamity, should happen, when the public treasury was empty, must the houseless and hungry therefore perish rather than draw upon reasonable hopes of the future? Famine has been frequent in the history of many nations; and I remember when the miseries of a terrible conflagration, in Charleston, were materially mitigated by South Carolina lending her credit to enable the citizens to rebuild their homes. The banking facilities of New Orleans, which, to an incalculable extent, have appreciated the crops of Louisiana, have been chiefly built up on State credit, loaned to the banks. And Louis Napoleon, the greatest statesman of the age, originated the "*Credit Mobilier,*" an institution in Paris, whose special office it is to facilitate and advance useful enterprises, by lending its interest-bearing bonds, which are negotiated for money—in short, by a loan of its credit.

Indeed, in countries where heavy mercantile transactions are most cheaply and successfully conducted, an abundance of sound interest-bearing securities are deemed indispensable. And, as civilization advances, in the same ratio we find multiplied the labor-saving and interest-saving devices of credits, counters, interest-bearing stocks, and representatives of money.

That these things, like all human inventions, are attended with evil, there can be no doubt. And their abuse may even endanger the simplicity of a pure Republic. But in an age of credit, it may, perhaps, admit of question whether individuals or nations can keep pace with the general progress without, at least, a rational and temperate use of similar facilities to those enjoyed by rival cotemporaries.

But, sir, whatever may be true or false in regard to these speculations, in the absence of any overwhelming, or even urgent, necessity, and seeing that we are not "the people," but only their agents, I cannot consent to our assuming powers which, by failing to confer, they have reserved to themselves.

Mr. YELVERTON said:

Mr. President—I have no disposition to prolong this discussion, and but for its vast importance, should not add a single remark; but I feel called upon to offer a few reasons which influence me to vote for the substitute offered by the gentleman from Barbour, [Mr. Cochran.] I approach it with feelings of delicacy after listening to the able and distinguished gentlemen who have addressed the Convention on the subject. My responsibility to my constituents for my action upon this, as well as all other questions, induces me more particularly to examine and understand what I do.

An organic principle is sought to be changed by the amendment. It is urged that it will forever protect the faith and credit of the State; that it will hold a complete check upon, and prevent improper legislation; that it will not interfere with existing obligations; that it will prevent corporations from the organization of such power and influence as might without restraint enable them to control the elections of members to the Legislature.

and to control the Legislature itself. It seems to me. Mr. President, to have the merit of settling these things firmly and unmistakably, and of providing effectually against involving the State in debts to be thereafter met with taxation. It has a very high and strong claim upon me as a Representative, upon the ground that it meets and sustains the well-ascertained will of our people *against State aid*, or against the loan of the State's credit or means to Railroad or other corporations.

I assume that the people of the State have, through the ballot-box, and after the most thorough discussion, decided against all manner of legislation *looking to State aid in any form;* and whatever may have been our individual opinions before such appeal and judgment, it is now our duty to treat it as a settled question.

The substitute, Mr. President, provides directly that the Legislature shall not create a debt against the State without providing at the same time the means to pay it—debt or appropriation in case of war excepted. I have noticed with care the objections presented by the several gentlemen who have opposed its adoption. The objections are various, and chiefly as to policy. The gentleman from Barbour, [Mr. Buford,] who has just addressed the Convention at great length, and with his accustomed ability, presents the question of jurisdiction, by denying the Convention power to act; other gentlemen have also alluded to this point. Now, sir, have we this power, or is this Convention a mere unlawful assemblage, or a body whose powers are limited to a particular act or class of acts? Gentlemen assert, by way of illustration, that we were assembled by virtue of Joint Resolutions of the State Legislature providing for a Convention. Let us examine this by reference to the Joint Resolutions themselves. You will see that the Joint Resolutions were passed with great unanimity, providing for the call of a State Convention upon the election of certain sectional candidates for the Presidency and Vice-Presidency. The election passed off, and the contingency contemplated (or feared) by these Resolutions happened—Lincoln and Hamlin were elected. Now, gentlemen, mark, if you please, the *question of power* as we proceed. You argue that the call was *pacific*, to prepare for secession. The Resolutions say, "to consider what is best to be done."

If the gentlemen will allow it, I think I can easily demonstrate that the power behind the throne was greater than the throne itself. I concede that the Legislature had power to do what it did. I honor that noble body of true men for their act. They evidently knew that the Resolutions they passed were not conclusive upon the people, and only looked to any assemblage of the people in Convention, because the people had a right to disregard the call; they had a right to vote for and elect Delegates committed against holding a Convention—against "considering what was best to be done," and more especially as many of them did elect Delegates committed against secession. Suppose then, sir, for further illustration, that a majority of this Convention had decided against secession, would not the reasoning of the gentlemen, applied to that view, prove that we had assembled to declare and ordain *against secession?* But this, you see, would be disastrous to *the policy* of the gentleman from Barbour, [Mr. Buford,] and might prove too much, or, at least, something which neither that gentleman or myself desired; for we both ardently desired secession. I put to the gentlemen, as States-Rights men, the question, whether the people parted with their power to alter or change their form of Government, either in their Convention, providing for Union with the United States, or in their ratification of the admission of the State into that Union? By reference to either of these decrees of the people of Alabama, it will be seen, in language strong, plain and clear, that this great right was reserved; and that all other rights, powers and privileges, which were not delegated to the General Government, were retained in the State, *in the people*; thus the supremacy, majesty and power of control of the State by itself, for itself, has always existed, and was never more potent than now.

Mr. President, the gentleman from Barbour [Mr. Buford] is an able constitutional lawyer of long experience, and of profound learning, and is equally distinguished for his great devotion to Southern and States' Rights, and has for many years contributed largely to the advancement of these great principles; and I must confess, sir, that I was much surprised to hear that distinguished gentleman utter the words which left an impression that he was in doubt as to the power of this Convention on this subject; and to place that doubt upon the ground that the Convention had not been called for the purpose of changing our Constitution in any other respect than such as was demanded to render complete the withdrawal of the State from the United States. Other gentlemen have also alluded to this question of power; and here I propose to show that this question of power has been well considered and ably reported upon by the Judiciary Committee of this Convention, of which the honorable gentleman from Montgomery [Mr. Watts] is Chairman, and whose Report was unanimously sustained.

The subject which called forth that Report was the Ordinance introduced by the gentleman from Mobile, [Mr. Humphries,] proposing the repeal of an Act of the late session of the Legislature, called the "Stay Law;" and while the Committee were unanimous in their opinion as to the power of the Convention to legislate upon this and other subjects, yet they were also (properly, as I think, and as the Convention decided,) of opinion that it would not be treating the Legislature with proper respect. Here the power is ascertained and promulgated, and here, too, is a line drawn between power and policy.

Sir, this Convention has power to control the Legislative, Executive and Judicial Departments of the State; it has all power, or it has none.

I have opposed every proposition to refer to the people any action of this Convention—my reason for such refusal has been the same on all occasions: The people are here; this Convention is the people; here is the sovereignty, the power and will of the State; but still, I am willing only to do whatever is necessary to be done. Gentlemen argue that the Constitution does not need the amendment proposed, because the policy sought to be changed has so long existed. The same argument may be applied to every other change which has been or may be made. It is also objected, because a Convention can be called to revise the Constitution. I grant the call could be made; but as the State is here in Convention, I prefer to save the expense and time of another Convention. Gentlemen say that it might be right as an Act of the Legislature, but not as an Ordinance of a Convention.

The question for the Convention to determine is simply, whether the measure is right, and if so, whether the right may not be better secured by a clause in the Constitution, than by an Act of the Legislature? I wish to aid all I can in making the Constitution as perfect as it can be made. It is a fact well known that many attempts have been made to call a Convention; that many defects have been pointed out and complained of by the people. Why this? Because, sir, the Constitution, though suited to the condition of the State in its infancy, is unsuited to its gigantic manhood. At the last regular session of the Legislature, when the Resolutions of which we have been speaking were passed, a Bill was also passed, calling a Convention of the people to revise the Constitution; and my recollection is that our very able and worthy Chief Executive [Gov. Moore] assigned as one of his reasons for withholding his approval of the Convention Bill was, that the Legislature had provided—*by these Resolutions* "to consider what is best to be done"—for the assembling of a Convention. The prediction of His Excellency was prophetic; his motive a good one, which was to save the State the expense of two Conventions, when one would answer all the purposes. This act, like all the acts of that great and good man. [Gov. Moore,] commend him to the lasting gratitude of the State.

Mr. President, as a member of the Committee on Public Lands, I have on my desk a Minority Report, that I have drawn up to present to this Convention against the Majority Report of its Chairman, [the Hon. O. S. Jewett.] That Report is in favor of making large donations or gifts of the public lands to several Railroad Companies and corporations thereinmentioned. I take the view that *this is State aid*, and that as, the State has decided against that policy so conclusively, we owe it to the people to settle the question in solemn form. I hope I may be excused for alluding to this subject, because I fear that I will not, for want of time, be able to get the ear and action of the Convention upon my Report, and the Ordinance submitted with it. This Ordinance contemplates the setting apart the lands and the net proceeds of the sales thereof, to the payment of the debt now existing, and hereafter to be created on the State by reason of its secession; it also provides that no appropriations out of that fund shall ever be made for any other purpose than paying the debts of the State, while any debt exists against the State.

If, Mr. President, the Substitute in question be adopted, and no donation or appropriation is made by the Convention, a check at least will be held upon the Legislature. I am for this, and hope to see it adopted, as I believe it will in future accomplish great good. But, sir, if the time allows, I shall urge upon the Convention to concur in my Minority Report, and to adopt the Ordinance, I submit with it, as that Ordinance will put it out of the power of the Legislature to make donation or appropriation, and provide for its being paid *or given out of this land fund;* and on these questions I beg to be pardoned if I suggest to the Convention the propriety of bestowing more attention. It is, I think, certain that the State will in future have to pay for these lands; but if not, and they should become our property, by the Act of Secession, then certainly there can be no objection to apply them to the payment of the expenses which follow the Act; and this vast amount of land will be found to be a large item. The Convention has already settled a great Constitutional principle bearing a close relation to the subjects under consideration : I mean the amendment adopted, which prohibits taxation to raise funds to aid the building of Railroads, &c. If the land fund goes to pay the debts of the State, then every tax-payer in the State is equally interested, because to that extent he will be freed from taxation;

but, sir, if the lands are given away to corporations, these selected corporations only will be benefitted; and if it should happen that the State should have the lands to pay for—after the lands are given away, who then doubts the payment? It would have to come by taxation. Who also, I ask, would doubt the general dissatisfaction of the people? They would have proper cause for indignation. Let us carefully guard against any and every cause for producing dissatisfaction among our people, who have so long and so nobly proved themselves loyal to the State.

Mr. President, when it is settled that the State will not aid companies in building Railroads, a healthy state of things will be developed. It is a fact of which we may justly boast, that our State has great wealth as well as intellectual power; great pride too, in our onward march to prosperity; then the immense capital of the State, which is now inactive will be brought into requisition; then there will be but one question, that one will be, *what Road will pay?* Such will be built, and such only ought to be built.

[Mr. Yelverton thanked the Convention for the attention he had received; and remarked that he would then *settle off with* some of his distinguished friends in the Convention; which he did in a most humorous manner, dealing good hits, right and left, including himself in his jests. This part of the gentleman's speech was especially amusing; but we will not attempt to report it, as it would be impossible to preserve the manner, which is usually the soul of wit.]

ON THE POWER OF TAXATION.

Section 32 of the Constitution being under consideration, Mr. DARGAN moved to strike out "private or quasi-public," in the last line of said Section, and insert, in place thereof, "other than Municipal corporations."

MR. JEMISON made an inquiry of the mover of the Amendment to explain his object.

MR. DARGAN said:

I will explain: my object is to carry out the precise idea of the Committee, but to express it in language that cannot be misunderstood, either by the people or the courts. I am not satisfied with the word, "*quasi*" or *quasi-public*. The words I propose, *other than municipal*, conveys the idea better and more unmistakably. I had supposed really, that the Amendment had been accepted.

THE PRESIDENT:

The Chair would remark to the gentleman from Mobile, [Mr. Dargan,] that it was not in the power of the Committee to accept the amendment.

Mr. WATTS said:

Mr. President—Would it be in order to move to strike out the whole of the section during the pendancy of the amendment? If so, I would like to test the sense of the Convention on a direct vote upon the section.

THE PRESIDENT :

The Chair thinks not: the merits of the question could not be reached in that way, without the violation of one of the rules of the Convention.

MR. WATTS said:

Mr. President—The object of the section is obvious. It will be recollected that our Legislature has, on various occasions, passed acts authorizing city corporations to tax their citizens for Railroad purposes. Mobile was authorized to levy a tax in aid of the Mississippi and Ohio Railroad. The tax-payers, to the extent of their tax, become stockholders, and thereby interested in the success of the Road. The enterprise has been eminently successful, and is now approaching its conclusion. No other Act of the Legislature could have done so much towards the perfecting of that Road ; for, from a small town, under the influences of this great Road, Mobile has grown to be the largest city on the Gulf. Selma was authorized to do the same. That city has also shared greatly in the benefits of this system. The grand object of these Legislative acts was, to advance Railroads, and to open and push forward a great system of Internal Improvements. The system has worked admirably; and it may indeed be said, that the great Ohio and Mississippi Road never would have been completed, but for this very act of the Legislature, giving to the city the right to levy a tax on property-holders for the advancement of the Road.

If this system has worked well, why change it now? The adoption of this motion will prevent a like consummation in other Roads, already in progress; it will indeed be a death-blow to Internal Improvements in Alabama. Such a course can but have the most disastrous effects upon the Railroads in Alabama. How are Internal Improvements to go on? How, if you throw around your Legislature such iron bands as these? Sir, you should change the name of this Ordinance, and give it the more appropriate title: an Ordinance *to destroy all works* of Internal Improvement in the State of Alabama.

It is objected, that you must not tax a man without his consent. Sir, if a man is unwilling to share his fortune, in this way, in the promotion of the general good, when he must necessarily participate in the benefits of a growing fortune, he ought to be forced to pay his proportion. No man ought to be allowed to stand by idly, with his hands in his pocket, and wait for his more energetic neighbors to bring value upon *his* property by their industry, risk and enterprize.

Sir, let us leave this matter to an untrammeled and enlightened Legislature—a Legislature whose acts, on this subject, have already been pronounced constitutional by our Supreme Court. If the Legislature, having been heretofore, and so long entrusted with this power, has done no harm, why refuse longer to leave the power in hands which have been so prudent in the use of it? Why thus seek to tie them up forever, by this fundamental restriction?

Sir, there is another and paramount reason why this clause should not be adopted by this Convention at this time. This Convention was assembled for a specific purpose, and with no regard whatever to making the constitutional alteration here attempted. It was assembled in anticipation of great national emergencies arising out of our difficulties with the North, and to discuss the necessity, and mature the plan of a separation from the Union. It was for the accomplishment of the *one* great act of Secession for which it was assembled. That act has been done. And the right we have to interfere with the Constitution is confined to such changes as the independent position we have assumed make necessary in the perfect accomplishment of this grand object. The Constitution must be so changed as to meet and harmonize the new Government; but it was never intended that we should go to work radically, to reform and amend our State Constitution. This was never thought of by the people when they elected the Delegates to this Convention. And, in my opinion, we ought only to amend the Constitution wherein it is absolutely necessary to meet the contingencies of the separation.

Mr. GIBBONS said:

He was glad that the gentleman from Montgomery [Mr. Watts] had so fully stated his reasons for the opposition he made to the proposed Amendment. It was one of the gravest questions that had been submitted to this Convention during its existence, and, in importance, was second only to the Ordinance of Secession itself.

Here, Mr. President, let me refer to certain principles now settled for the interpretation of Constitutions, and on which the proposed Amendment is based:

1st. It is well settled, that in the interpretation of the United States Constitution, no powers could be given to it by construction. It possessed simply such powers as were clearly granted, and all others were excluded. But, secondly, in the interpretation of State Constitutions, the State Legislature possesses all power not *directly prohibited*. Hence, it became necessary, if we would restrain a State Legislature in its action, we must do so by express prohibitions in the Constitution itself, as the Legislature would possess all power not prohibited by the Constitution.

Now, if these principles are correctly stated, I ask any gentleman to take up the Constitution of Alabama, and see where he finds any protection to private property? Where is the prohibition in our Constitution which forbids the Legislature to say that the house or the horse of A. shall become the property of B. ? Where is the prohibition to the Legislature from taking money out of the pocket of one man and putting it into that of another? The Legislature surely has that power, unless it is somewhere prohibited. The only clause in our Constitution that tends to protect private property is, that "*private property shall not be taken for public use, without just compensation.*" Well, sir, at first glance, it would seem that the *major* proposition would necessarily contain the *minor*, and that if they could not take private property for public use, without compensation, much less could they take private property for private use, without compensation. But this does not seem to have been the construction of the Courts. On the contrary, they seem to have considered that they were only authorized to consider those things prohibited which were expressly prohibited, and nothing was so, by construction; and accordingly, the Supreme Court of this State have gone the full length, and have decided that a tax which is confessedly levied for the benefit of a private corporation is constitutional, by virtue of the unrestrained taxing power reposing in the Legislature.

Now, sir, let us look for one moment at the proposition under discussion, and what it is in itself. It reads as follows, to-wit: "Taxes shall not be levied for the benefit of individuals or corporations other than municipial corporations, without the consent of the tax payer." Why, sir, one would suppose that the proposition would commend itself at once, not merely to the good sense, but to the conscience of every member of the Convention. The argument in its favor commences in the Decalogue and reads: "*Thou shalt not steal;*" and again, "*Thou shalt not covet thy neighbor's goods.*" Gentlemen are violently opposed to the proposition as it stands, but, sir, now let us see what the converse of the proposition is, and necessarily the doctrine for which gentlemen contend: "Taxes, then, shall be levied for the benefit of individuals and private corporations;" and this power now existing in the Legislature, they propose to leave there unrestrained, and are shocked that the Committee have proposed to limit the power for the protection of private property. Why, the proposition as above stated, is one that must shock the moral sense of every right thinking man! That my property, which I have acquired and call mine, can, by a simple fiat of the Legislature, be taken from me and vested in another man, is a proposition that shocks the moral sense. It is in vain to say that the Legislature will never exercise this power, tor they have, in effect, done it, and the Supreme Court have declared the act constitutional. Gentlemen propose to do by legislative enactment what they would scorn to do as individuals; what, as individuals, they would not dare do, because in so doing they would be amenable to the Penal laws of the country. Gentlemen may shelter themselves behind an act of the Legislature in the exercise of the power under discussion, but they must recollect that, in morals, it is not the less *robbery*, notwithstanding they may shelter themselves behind a legislative enactment. It is proposed by gentlemen to leave in the Legislature a power, and to justify the exercise of that power in a mode that would not receive the sanction of any despot or tyrant on the face of the earth. I know of no potentate or power on the face of the earth, however despotic or tyranical, that has ever presumed to take money from the pocket of A. to put it into the pocket of B. Dynasties and despots there are, and have been, who have levied taxes upon their citizens for purposes of public enterprizes, such as Railroads and other public works, but then the improvements for which the taxes were expended remained the property of the Government, and were in turn employed for the benefit of the tax-payer, and the franchise put at low rates with a view to his convenience and benefit. But the power contended for by gentlemen is simply to enrich A. at the expense of B., and this by legislative enactment.

Gentlemen talk largely of the necessity of retaining this power for the purpose, as they say, of building up Railroads and other internal improvements. Yes, sir, gentlemen are so thoroughly run mad upon the subject of Railroads, and Railroad companies, that they become utterly oblivious of the morality of the means they employ to bring them into existence. Well, sir, Railroads are now the order of the day. The public mind seems to have become enthused upon that subject to the exclusion of all other subjects in which the public have an equal interest. The resources of the country, say they, must be developed. The bowels of the earth must not only be speedily dug out, but must be carried off. That is all very well, Mr. President, and I have not one word to say against it. In those matters, however, I would always act as I would in other matters of private enterprize. If I wanted a Road and others wanted it also, I would unite my capital or credit with theirs and build it. But I certainly would not steal the means of carrying it out. Now, sir, suppose we leave the taxing power of the Legislature in the same condition as we found it on assembling here; a power, in fact, unlimited, whether for the benefit of the public or for the benefit of individuals, or private corporations: who can tell how long the public sentiment will run in favor of Railroads? Suppose it should take a religious turn and it should be deemed important that churches should be built in every township in the State, would not the enthusiasts upon this subject have the same right to call upon the Legislature to tax the people to build churches and to build up religious societies, as those have who worship the god of this world? Who will rise up here and say that the wealth of a State is, in importance, superior to its morals? Have not moral and religious corporations the same right to have taxes levied for their benefit as Railroad corporations? What guaranty have we that the exercise of this power will be confined to Railroad corporations? Does not the principle contended for by gentlemen apply as well to churches, hotels, turnpike roads, bridges, ferries, and even theatres? The public have an interest in all these, and each of them have the same right to call upon the Legislature to levy taxes in their behalf as Railroads. All the difference between them this day is, that the popular sentiment to-day has a decided tendency to Railroads over and above all other things; but this is no evidence that ten years hence it will be so. The moment that popular enthusiasm takes a different channel and runs in a different direction, then that subject becomes the one of paramount importance, and the Legislature is invoked to build it up, and no matter at whose expense.

Now, if private property is worth anything; if it is commendable to be industrious and economical, and thereby to become thrifty and wealthy, then it becomes important to protect property as well from the inroads which the Legislature may make upon it as against those which individuals may make. It should, in fact, be sacred. The citizen owes to the commonwealth in which he lives full allegiance, and this includes his aid in support and in defence of that commonwealth. Taxes, therefore, may well be levied upon him for this support and this defence. This power is not denied, nor is it sought to interfere with it in any manner whatever. But I deny most emphatically that the Legislature ought to have the power either to take my money and give it to my neighbor, or to take it and give it to a private corporation, that seeks to run a Railroad by my dwelling, or to make any other improvement that, in its nature, is a private enterprize.

Mr. JEMISON said:

If this proposition is adopted, it will put it out of the power of certain cities which have already created Bonds, and have them now outstanding, to comply with their obligations.

Mr. COCHRAN said:

The difficulty suggested by the gentleman from Tuscaloosa, [Mr. Jemison,] can be obviated by the *proviso* which I will offer, if the gentleman will yield me the floor for that purpose. I would not be willing that the Committee's proposition should be adopted without such an explanatory amendment. It was not the design of the Committee to interfere with existing obligations. [Mr. Cochran read his amendment, providing that the proposed change should not, in any way, apply to existing liabilities.]

Mr. JEMISON said:

If the Section, as amended by the Committee, should be adopted, this proviso would be necessary, and would relieve the proposition from the objections I suggested. The city of Tuscaloosa has contracted a debt, by authority of an act of the Legislature, for the purpose of aiding in the construction of a Railroad, and, although I did not vote for the tax, I am in favor of meeting the Bonds in good faith. But, even with the *proviso* of the gentleman from Barbour, [Mr. Cochran,] I am still opposed to this amendment of the Constitution. I would prefer to leave our citizens free to be taxed if they choose; and I am not willing to admit that a man must never be taxed without his consent. Men are often unwilling to be taxed; and to say you shall not tax a man without his consent, is equivalent to saying you will not tax him at all. The money you get from a man by his consent, would be more properly called a contribution than a tax.

MR. DARGAN said:

I will explain my motive for voting for this amendment. What is the meaning of the word "Tax?" It is money levied for public use, by the State, and for which the tax-payer expects no return, except the protection of the State. It is a burden which the tax-payer owes to the State for his protection. This meaning is perverted when the power is used for any other purpose: more particularly is it perverted when the money is caused to be paid for the purpose of procuring certificates of stock. When raised for such purposes, there is an implied contract—it is a bargain between the parties—therefore it is a perversion of the power to levy a tax. Thus you can force money from a tax-payer, for the benefit of private individuals, against his will. It is a violation of the Constitution thus to raise money by taxes. The Constitution says: "the property of no man shall be taken for public use without just compensation." Money is property. I am willing to advance the public interest by my purse, but not by the perversion of a great principle.

This amendment will not arrest the progress of public improvement, as insisted on by the gentleman from Montgomery, [Mr. Watts.] He proposes to force an unwilling tax-payer—you will coerce me to become a stock-holder, though I am unwilling to subscribe for the stock, upon the ground that I am a tax-payer. Yet I answer you, this is not a legitimate tax. It is not tax, but an invasion of my right of property—it is a *violent seizure*. The old policy is fraught with danger and injustice. The large property-holder is at the mercy of the small property-holder; and in such communities as Montgomery and Mobile, those who have little or no property, are largely in the majority, and can force the large property-holders to do as they please, if you give them a chance to do it at the ballot box.

The Railroad system of Alabama will prosper as rapidly under this proposed amendment, as under the old system—and even with more harmony, and on a just principle.

If you assume the right to tax your citizens to build Railroads, why may you not do it upon the same principle, for the purpose of building a line of Steamers? You may as well charter a Stock Company to build and run a line of steamboats from Montgomery to New Orleans, and raise the money by taxing the property-holders of Montgomery, upon the specious grounds that the steamers will improve the commerce of the town, and thereby enhance the value of the property of the tax-payer.

Sir, this is an important question; we are framing an Organic Law for a new State—let it be so framed in language and meaning that it cannot be misinterpreted—so that under the Law, the property of all men may be equally secure.

Mr. Watts said:

The gentleman from Mobile, [Mr. Dargan,] and the gentleman from Monroe, [Mr. Gibbons,] have not presented this question in its real aspect. They have represented me as advocating a new policy.

Mr. Dargan:

The gentleman misstates me. I wish to change a policy which has heretofore been pursued, and which the gentleman, [Mr. Watts,] wishes still to adhere to.

Mr. Watts said:

Alabama is forty-two years old, having been formed into a State in 1819, and this amendment proposes a change—an interpolation into the Constitution of something unknown—something unheard of; and it is my motive to prevent this interpolation. Has any harm been heretofore done by the authority of any act of the Legislature on this subject? Is the policy, the practice and the happy experience of forty years to be cast away? Before this is done, will you not require those gentlemen who advocate this change to show some good reason for it? If, in forty years experience, no damage can be found to have grown out of the old policy, why should we abandon it? The gentleman from Monroe, [Mr. Gibbons,] seems really to be afraid to sleep, lest the Legislature during his slumbers, may invade his rights of property. Surely, he cannot have spent many quiet nights during his residence in Alabama; for the policy which inspires him with such apprehensions has always prevailed in the State.

It need not be disguised, Mr. President, that this proposition springs from the wishes of a few dissatisfied individuals. This old policy of taxation for the benefit of Railroads, having operated injuriously in some respects, to the private interests of certain individuals, all the weight of their legislative influence is brought to bear against it here. We should not legislate for such persons, but for the general good.

In regard to the tax by the city of Mobile for the Great Mississippi and Ohio Railroad, which has conferred such vast benefits upon that city, I understand that, at the time of taking the vote, there were only *seven* votes recorded against it! I am amazed that this dissatisfaction should come from Mobile.

It is urged that you should not tax a man without his consent. Sir, there are classes that should be taxed without their consent; there are men who refuse to aid in all improvements, because the investment does not pay satifactory dividends. They prefer to loan their money at two and three per cent. a month, and thus grind the very citizens who build up the country. Shylock refuses to aid in building a Road which will enhance the value of his own property—but he loans his money at usury to the citizen, who, not only returns him his unholy per cent., but who adds increased value to his property. This is his double thrift. Such a man ought to be taxed, and forced to pay, if unwilling to pay. His soul does not rise above a picayune; his vision is limited by the end of his nose; he is almost unfit to be an inhabitant of a thriving city. Such men are not the class for which we ought to legislate. In casting about for the beneficiaries of legislation, they ought to be regarded most, whose lofty feelings and enlarged views extend, not only to the advancement of their private interests, but to the growth and development of the country—to the building up of cities—to the spread of civilization, and to the general prosperity.

Mr. Dargan said:

I have said before, that a Tax, in its proper sense, is a sum of money required by the Government of its subjects, to enable the Government to perform its proper functions, and for which the subject receives no other return than that of protection. It must, therefore, be levied for the Government, and not for a private corporation, or for the use of a private person.

Hence, all taxes levied for the benefit of Railroad Companies, (unless it be with the express consent of the tax-payer,) are improper and unjust, and is a departure from one of the great objects of Government—the protection of private property. But if the tax-payer consents to the tax, and thereby receives stock to the extent of the tax he pays, this is not strictly a tax, but is in the nature of a contract, by which the tax-payer becomes a stockholder in the Company; or, if he should consent to the tax without receiving anything in return, still, the consent expressly given, justifies the levy of the money, not as a tax in its proper sense, but as a sum of money contracted to be paid on a legal consideration.

If it were true, Mr. President, that the progress and completion of Railroads required a departure from the great principle— *the protection of private property*—I should hold on to the principle at the expense of *Railroads*. But the amendment, in my judgment, will not impede in the slightest degree the building of Railroads, or the making of any other public improvement. It only prohibits the making of such Roads or public improvements upon improper principles, or rather in a legal, not in an illegal manner.

I think that all communities will aid willingly by consenting to a tax, when the work is of such a character as promises public benefit and commercial advantages. True, there may be *some few* who may object, but the number will be *few;* and it seems to be the object of the opponents of this amendment to reach those few; and to effect that object, they would sacrifice one of the most valuable principles of Government, and to initiate the doctrine, that private property may be taken without the consent of the owner, and without confiscation, if a majority be of opinion it will be a public benefit.

I would not, Mr. President, violate this great principle for such a purpose. It will be a poor compensation for the destruction of such a principle that we extract from a few *misers*, as they have been called, a small sum of money by way of *tax*; and I cannot think how a wise statesman would, for such a purpose, impair a principle so vital to the peace and happiness of society.

But, Mr. President, the opponents of this amendment do not seem to understand it in another view. They say it will prevent all cities and municipal corporations from undertaking any public work, or the erection of any Railroad. In this they are mistaken. If a municipal corporation be authorized by its charter or by an Act of the Legislature, to subscribe as a stockholder to a Railroad, the amount subscribed will be a debt that the city will owe, and must pay it in the same manner that they are bound to pay any other debt. But then the stock will be property belonging to the city, and the dividends, if any ever be realized, will relieve the tax-payer *pro tanto*.

The amendment does not prohibit the Legislature from enabling a city or incorporated town from becoming a stockholder; therefore, the Legislature may give such authority; and if the Committee who reported the amendment intended by it so to restrain the Legislature, they have failed to accomplish the object they had in view. But I do not understand that it was so intended by the Committee. The great object, as I am informed, the Committee had in view in proposing this amendment to our Constitution, was to place beyond cavil or doubt the great principle that private property, "whether money, land or personal property other than money," should be held *sacred*, and beyond the power even of the Legislature, unless taken for taxes in its proper and legitimate sense.

Mr. GIBBONS said:

Mr. President—As the gentleman from Montgomery has alluded to personal matters affecting myself, I crave the indulgence of the Convention for a few moments more; and that, I promise, shall close my connection with this debate. The gentleman has alluded to the Mobile and Ohio Railroad, as one that was entirely and successfully built by the tax that was levied upon the real estate of the city of Mobile. Permit me, sir, to say that that railroad was not built by that tax. True, the tax contributed to build it, to the extent that it went; but if the Road had depended upon that tax alone for its construction, it would not have been built to this day. The tax levied was one million of dollars, and the first estimate of the Road, by the engineer, was over ten millions. If it had depended upon that tax alone, levied upon Mobile property the Road would never have gone beyond the limits of the State of Alabama. Sir, the Mobile and Ohio Road was built because it was an improvement cherished by all classes of people, and because all were its friends, and none were its enemies; because every one felt disposed, and called upon, to do all in his power for its completion. The tax, in itself partial, and in its nature entirely unequal, being confined to real estate alone, was voted almost universally (only six votes being cast against it). But so deep was the interest felt in the enterprize, that no one complained of injustice, but all directed their efforts to the accomplishment of the work. This was the secret of the building of that Road

The gentleman from Montgomery [Mr. Watts] says I am dissatisfied with the action of the citizens of Mobile, in the matter relating to the great Northern Railroad. The gentleman will permit me to say that he is mistaken. I am not dissatisfied with anything that the citizens of Mobile have done, as a body. The dissatisfaction of myself, and those that acted with me, did not arise from anything that the citizens of Mobile had done, but it arose from what other parties had done, unauthorized, by the citizens of Mobile.

The gentleman from Montgomery [Mr. Watts] calls upon us to

trust still the Legislature, and triumphantly asks, "Has the Legislature done any harm?" Mr. President, I do not know whether or not the Legislature of Alabama have done any harm; but I do know, that by virtue of their power to levy taxes, they have imposed upon the city of Mobile the duty of contributing, to the great Northern Railroad, some twenty-three hundred thousand dollars, without their consent; and I know, further, that the Supreme Court of Alabama has pronounced this law, levying such tax, constitutional. Whether it is harm or not, depends very much, I presume, upon the medium through which we view it. To me it is harm; to the gentleman, and to the stockholders in the Company, I doubt not it is no harm whatever. A large mass of property-holders, with myself, thought it harm, and tried to get relief by application to the Courts of the country. But the Courts replied to us thus: "We must administer the law as we find it; we cannot make laws to meet particular cases. Inasmuch as this taxing-power is unrestrained by the Legislature, we are not authorized to pronounce the law unconstitutional, however unjust it may be in itself." This, sir, is our answer; and it is the answer I, for one, expected to receive, if the case ever was made to turn upon the Constitutional question. I have been satisfied for years, that under the current of the decisions of the Courts of the country, there was no protection whatever in our Constitution for private property. This defect is what we now propose to remedy, by this Amendment. I certainly would be prepared to trust the Legislature still, if I had not seen and *felt* that that body had entered upon a career of legislation that will inevitably lead to the most unmitigated tyranny. Amendments, similar to the one proposed, have been called for and adopted by almost all of the Northern States. We cannot claim for our Legislature greater purity than theirs; and yet they have been forced to protect private property, by clauses directly in the nature of prohibitions, upon their Legislatures.

The gentleman from Montgomery [Mr. Watts] does not pretend to deny a single principle that we state, but simply because, as he says, I and the gentleman from Mobile have been injuriously affected by a particular case, therefore the principles that we avow, and the arguments by which we support this Amendment, must be entirely disregarded. Mr. President, particular cases, affecting me or any one else, have nothing to do with the question under discussion, except as they may serve for illustration. As illustration, I am not afraid of them, and commend them to the examination of every member of this Convention.

The gentleman from Montgomery seems particularly anxious

to become the guardian of the Misers and Shylocks. as he terms them, of the State; and he wants this power left with the Legislature, in order that he may make *them shell out.*

The gentleman forgets that the Misers and the Shylocks of this country hold their property and their money by the very title and right by which the gentleman from Montgomery asserts the principle of devoting his to Railroads. They hold and re'a'n their property by the same principle precisely that the profligate spends his. Now, if the gentleman is justified in taking, by force, the key of the chest of the Miser or the Shylock, unlock the same, and take their money, by the same right he may take the property of the spendthrift, and devote it to Railroads. Each is an interference with that perfect dominion over property which each citizen possesses by the laws of nature and society, and which cannot be interfered with but at the risk of society itself. The very reason that the gentleman gives for interfering with the property of the Miser and the Shylock, to divert it to Railroads, would apply to every species of public improvement, and amongst all those improvements, if taxes could be levied for all. Neither the gentleman, nor any one else, would be envious of the Misers or the Shylocks in their midst, for there would be none within their reach. Those that such legislation did not ruin and reduce to poverty, would flee beyond the jurisdiction of these laws. But, sir, we are told that this Amendment ought not to be adopted, because it is not properly within the scope of the powers of the Convention. That this Convention came here to pass the Ordinance of Secession, and such Acts as are incidental to it, and nothing else. Mr. President, I know not where gentlemen get their ideas of the duties of this Convention. They certainly do not get them from the Act of the Legislature calling the Convention; and I shall never yield my assent to that narrow view of my duties in this Convention, until I see some authority for it. My ideas are that it is our duty to pass all Ordinances, and make all Amendments to the Constitution that ought to be made, and thereby save the expense of another Convention.

Those are my views of my duty here; and with those views I must vote for this Amendment to the Constitution, to protect private property.

But the gentleman says, we have lived under the Constitution over forty years, and trusted the Legislature all that time—and why not trust it still? Mr. President, that argument, if it proves anything, proves too much. If it is of any force whatever, it goes to the extent of doing away with every Constitutional provision. The gentleman may be prepared for such a move as that, but I am not, and I trust the Convention is not. Well, sir, if it is important to have anything secured by Constitutional guarantys, it surely must be acknowledged that private property is next in importance to personal rights; and while the latter are well secured, there is not, yet, the first guaranty for the former.

Mr. Cochran said:

I would not be willing to vote for the Amendment reported by the Committee, without the explanatory proviso which I have offered, intended to meet the objections suggested by the gentleman from Tuscaloosa [Mr. Jemison]. This proviso having been adopted, I will endeavor to call the attention of the Convention to the real question presented by the report of the Committee. And I must say, that so wide and excursive has been the range of debate, that, had I not been on the Committee, and thereby well advised of the object of the proposition, I should myself be somewhat bewildered in the pursuit of the real question now at issue.

If the subject is worthy of the discussion had upon it to day, it is certainly worth the time of the Convention to listen to an explanation, which will show the extent of the proposition, as intended by the Committee.

It was not the intention of the Committee to interfere with the Legislature, in its power to levy legitimate taxes. It leaves the Legislature entirely unrestricted on that subject. The leading object of this proposition is, to protect private property. It will be seen then, at once, that many matters have been referred to in this debate, which are not at all natural or applicable to the subject. Shylock has been denounced, and the large-hearted man lauded. Neither of them has anything to do with the subject. The proposition asserts the principle that you shall not take money out of one man's pocket, without his consent, to advance the interests of a corporation.

Is there anything terrible in this? Is there any startling innovation here, filled with coming disasters to the State, or to the rights or interests of the people? The Legislature, heretofore, has had and has exercised unlimited power to levy, and to authorize the levying of Taxes. We propose, simply, to restrict that power, but to leave the Legislature free and unrestrained in the exercise of its legitimate duties on this subject

We wish to preserve untouched the dominion of man over the property he has acquired. This is a settled and time-honored principle—an Anglo-Saxon right—which must not be left to the discretion or the supposed justice of any Legislative Tribunal.

What is the great inducement of man to accumulate property? What, but that he may use it as he pleases, and dispose of it according to his will? The miser is as much entitled to the protection of the law, as your large-hearted man. We may indulge a private contempt for the Shylocks, and a corresponding admiration for the large-hearted men of the land, but the law must make no distinction. The law must be general; else, indeed,

"There *is no force* in the decrees of Venice.'

But we are told that Shylock must be forced to disgorge! Sir, where is the end of such doctrine as that? The same principle that destroys Shylock's rights, destroys the rights of your *large-hearted* man. If you cramp Shylock, you cramp the large-hearted man also. The one holds his wealth by virtue of the great principle of personal dominion over personal property; the other gives his money liberally—bountifully—by virtue of *his* dominion over *his* property.

But we are told that it is not one of the legitimate duties of this Convention to act at all on this question; that we were convened for another and specific purpose; that that purpose has no connection whatever with this question. Sir, the leading object of this Convention is, to *protect property*. It was the great *property* question which led to our assembling. We had trusted a Government with the important duty of protecting our property in which it had signally failed—and we took into our hands the *dominion over our own property*. Instead of protecting our property, that Government sought to destroy it. We seceded—to assert the great principle that we will use our own property as we please. It was the duty of the Federal Government to secure me in the free enjoyment of life, liberty, and property. When it ceased to do that, it absolved me from my allegiance.

We have heard much of the inclinations of men to make two and three per cent. per month on their money—and that these are the men who are unwilling to subscribe to railroads, because that sort of stock will not contribute to gorge the appetite of Usury; and that these men ought to be circumvented by the ingenious devices of the Legislature, and reached in the way of taxes upon their property. Sir, no more destructive principle could be asserted. It is of the same class as the one already referred to—of forcing Shylock to disgorge. Its very foundation is in *force*; and force is not law—but the vital principle, the lever, of destruction. *Force* is not the companion, but the great antagonist of the law.

Mr. Humphries said:

I regret very much, Mr. President, to have to come in contact with my two distinguished colleagues [Messrs. Dargan and Bragg] on this subject. But if I were to remain silent, under the circumstances, I should be remiss in my duty; especially as the interests of Mobile have been frequently referred to in this discussion. The citizens of Mobile would be greatly dissatisfied if this measure were adopted, and I am free to express my astonishment that any citizen of Mobile should favor such a proposition, in the face of the great benefits that have resulted to that city from the very policy which it is now sought to destroy.

Mr. Humphries spoke at some length on the Mobile and Ohio Road, referring to the aid which it had received from the corporation of the city of Mobile, and the great benefits that the Road had brought the city and the country; spoke of the class of persons that had opposed it, and referred to several instances wherein individuals who had opposed the Road had been made rich by it in the increased value of their property.

Mr. Gibbons:

I am not opposed to the Road, but I object to the manner of raising the money to build it—taking money from the community and giving nothing in return.

Mr. Humphries:

Our experience shows that there have been returns—the most substantial returns in the increase of trade; the large advances in city property; the growth of the city, and the wide-spreading prosperity of her citizens.

If the citizens of Mobile had a vote on the same proposition by which this Road was originally aided by their city, it would be carried, three to one, now.

I am not so much surprised at the position of Judge Dargan. He is opposed to Railroads; always has been; they make too much noise; they disturb him and frighten his children.

Whether this policy of city corporations granting aid to Railroads will be for the general benefit of the State, I will not speak—am not prepared to speak; but I am willing that the rest of the State should have, at least, the chances of trying it. It would look like ingratitude for the city of Mobile, after having reaped benefits from the policy, now to deny it to the other portions of the State. I am not willing to say that the State at large, or any city in the State, shall be deprived of the benefits of a policy which, having been tested by Mobile, has proved to have been of great advantage.

MR. MORGAN:

I arise to do what I have never done before—to give the reasons for my vote. Dallas County is as much interested in Railroads as any county in the State. I am myself a stockholder, and so far am identified with all that pertains to Railroad enterprise and Railroad success. A large portion of my constituents are deeply interested in the defeat of this measure, and yet, I shall vote for it. This is a delicate position; but I am making a fundamental law for an infant State; and having discovered a false principle, I feel it my duty to remove it. What is that principle? That you may raise money by taxation without the consent of the tax-payer, upon the presumption that the enterprise upon which the money is to be used will enhance the value of the property taxed. This principle ought to be taken out of the Constitution. The Legislature needs to be restrained. I am in favor of this restriction and of some others. The Legislature has no right to pass a law taxing a citizen, except for the legitimate purpose of supporting the Government. I would, then, restrict the Legislature; and I would so guard the Treasury that no extraordinary debt should be contracted for the State by its legislative agents, except for the emergencies of an insurrection or rebellion.

The Section is now so worded that no technical issue can grow out of it, and no bond or obligation heretofore entered into can be affected by it. It presents a naked principle of Government, undisguised and needing no explanation, proclaiming the doctrine that the people shall not be taxed, except for the legitimate support of the State.

I feel the delicacy of my position, and regret that I am compelled to vote against what I suppose to be the present wishes of my constituents; but in this I am acting for the future prosperity of a people whose fundamental laws ought to be matured without regard to sectional or local inclinations.

MR. WHATLEY said:

Mr. President—I was on the Committee that reported this Amendment. I do not think it ought to be adopted. I agree with the gentleman from Montgomery [Mr. Watts] in his unanswerable argument touching the jurisdiction of this Convention. We are not here for the purpose of revising the Constitution. We were called for the one specific purpose of dissolving the Union, and of adapting the Constitution and Laws to the exigencies and emergencies of the radical change which Secession necessarily makes in our situation. This done, our powers cease. The question of Taxation is remote from that of Secession—is not by any means connected with it, and is not in any way affected by it. The subject of Taxation, as much, if not more, than any other question, belongs to the Legislature; it is always of present and immediate interest between the people and the Representative; it is a matter of annual consideration and regulation ; a subject upon which the constituent is expected to be consulted every year. Let us leave it where it belongs.

But the policy proposed is, in my mind, objectionable. It is a stroke at Internal Improvements in this State; and this is the time for Alabama to make vigorous efforts in the way of Internal Improvements. On this question we are confessedly behind the age. Our sister, Georgia, is far in advance of us ; and this is owing to her rapid and onward career in Internal Improvements. We have made a beginning; we have many roads in progress. We begin to feel the spirit of the age, and our progress is onward. Do not let us now, at this juncture, adopt a policy which will crush Internal Improvements—and such will be the inevitable result of the adoption of this measure.

Georgia, the Empire State of the South, owes her present enviable position to the mode by which she, in part, built her roads. She did not hesitate to tax her people ; their money was used freely, by millions, for the general prosperity. She is now reaping her reward.

I admire the candid remarks of the gentleman from Mobile [Mr. Humphries]. He admits the great benefits resulting to the citizens of South Alabama from the former prevalence of the policy which you now seek to destroy; and expresses himself as unwilling, now, after having reaped these benefits, to deny the same to other portions of the State. This is liberal and just. Give us in North Alabama the same chance you have had in South Alabama.

And this is the time when we shall need all aid and all encouragement. Alabama must now depend upon herself; she must look to herself alone ; and she need not shrink from the contemplation if she has a fair chance. Our hills, mountains and valleys groan with mineral wealth, coal and iron in abundance. All we want is facilities for manufacturing, and roads to market.

But the gentlemen are mistaken in the law to which they have referred.

The positions taken by the gentlemen from Monroe and Mobile, that there is no protection to private property under the law, as construed by the courts, is certainly without foundation. The gentleman from Monroe says, the Legislature might say that my house shall be yours, and that my horse shall be another man's. The gentlemen have not properly read the existing law. In the case of Dorman vs. the State, 34 Alabama, the Court say that private property shall not be taken, except by *due course of law;* and the Court says, due course of law is equivalent to a judicial trial, and not a legislative enactment. The same principle is recognized in the case of Sadler vs. Langhorn, 34 Ala. Then, sir, the Legislature cannot transfer my property to another person, by *a simple legislative enactment,* but only by a jury trial, or, at most, by a trial at common law.

DEBATE ON THE PUBLIC LANDS.

Upon a motion made by Mr. Jewett, to reconsider the vote by which the Public Lands in the State were fixed at a price dependent upon the length of time they had been in market,

Mr. JEWETT said:

I have been absent for a short time from the Convention, and during that absence, a very important matter has been under consideration.

Your attention has been occupied with a discussion of the price at which the Public Lands of the State shall be offered to purchasers, at private sale. This is, in fact, the most important question arising under this Ordinance; for unless you establish a proper basis for the disposal of these Lands, they will become a plague, instead of a benefit to the State. Too low a price will throw large bodies of the Lands into the hands of capitalists and speculators, who will purchase and hold them from market until their increased value will cause them to be again offered for sale, at greatly enhanced prices; and too high a price fixed upon them, will effectually prevent any sales by the State—whereas its true policy undoubtedly is, to dispose of the entire body of vacant lands at an early day.

The interest of the State will not be subserved by its continuing to occupy the position of proprietor of lands that can only become valuable by actual cultivation and improvement. Its true object should be to invite immigration, and dispose of the fee simple to all such lands as will meet with demand from actual occupants and cultivators. So soon as the tide of immigration sets towards any portion of the State, its lands immediately come into market, it matters not how long previously thereto they may have been offered for sale without finding purchasers.

I find that a vote has already been taken, in which a price has been fixed, dependent upon the length of the time the lands have been, or may be in market, and subject to private entry under the Laws of the United States, and of this State.

It is my design, to show the Convention that the result of this course will be unfortunate, not to say disastrous to the State. Large bodies of Public Lands lie in the Southern and Middle portions of the State, and I understand, also in the mountainous parts of North Alabama, that have been in market a long time. These lands are not valueless; they have not been sought for because they were remote from navigable streams and Railroad conveniences; they are valuable for the timber upon them—for the mines of coal, iron, and other minerals they contain, and for the deposite of massable limestone, and other valuable building materials to be found upon them. These lands, I say, only require to be brought into notice by the construction of Railroads in their neighborhoods, and they are daily increasing in importance, from the Internal Improvement policy, which appears to have become a fixed idea at last in our State.

In my own section of the State, there are large tracts of vacant land, well timbered, but otherwise of small value, that will be certain to become saleable when penetrated by Railroad. These lands will, before long, be in demand, and will very readily sell, in the neighborhood of Railroads, for the largest price fixed upon our Public Lands, in this Ordinance. But these have, many of them, been offered for sale since 1819, and at the price which this Section as amended fixes, will be offered for sale at twenty-five cents per acre. The inevitable result of which, will be to cause large entries of such lands by capitalists—their withdrawal from market for many years, and a consequent injury to those portions of the State in which they lie. It will always be ascertained before the location of the route of any Railroad, where they are to run, with sufficient certainty to enable speculators to enter the most valuable sections of land contiguous to its line, and any one conversant with such matters, must readily perceive how the low price fixed upon these lands, will operate upon the interests of the

State. For these reasons, Mr. Chairman, I move to reconsider the vote by which the price of the Public Lands has been fixed, at double the graduated price established in Section twenty-nine of this Ordinance.

On his proposition to cede the Public Lands in Alabama to the Confederate States,

MR. CLARKE, of Marengo, said:

I shall vote for the substitute just read, because I believe justice to our sisters of the Confederate States, and the interest of the people of Alabama, require its adoption. The Ordinance offered, concedes the title of Alabama to the Public Lands within her limits. She acquired that title when she resumed all of her rights of sovereignty; but that the States forming the United States have equitable rights in this property, she has already admitted by expressing her willingness to account for the same, on a settlement with the United States, if any such is ever made.

It cannot be doubted, that prior to the secession of Alabama, every State in the Union had the same interest that she had to the Public Lands within her borders. These lands had been ceded to the United States Government in trust for the States. If this be so, has this interest been forfeited? We say to the United States: if you will settle fairly with us, we will account to you for your share of this property. Why do we make this proposition? Because we feel that it is just and honest, that we should do so; as each of the States forming the United States, had as much interest in those lands as we had, and if we refuse to pay for such interest, it is because they withhold from us our interest in property which is equal to theirs. We act on the same principle that a party at law does, in setting up his set-off.

But, sir, that principle will not apply to our associates in secession. They withhold no right we had to any property within their borders, as far as I am advised; if so, we do not complain of it. Then, sir, why should we deprive them of their rights in this property? Suppose Georgia and South Carolina, or either of them, were to say to Alabama: we had the same right to your Public Lands before you seceded, that you had, and we demand our share—we are willing to account to you for your interest in any property within our borders. Could Alabama refuse it, unless she was willing to commence her political life anew, by refusing to her sisters what she was willing to concede to a hostile stranger?

But, sir, the States forming the Confederate States, have not only the right to an equal participation in this property, growing out of their former title, but our title is to be perfected by them; either through the influence of the Confederate States as a nation, or by the power of her armies on the field of battle. Then, sir, if the equitable rights of our sisters are equal to ours in this property, and they have perfected our title thereto, common justice requires that it should be the common property of all. But leaving out the moral obligation which we should rigidly observe, the interest of our people requires that we shall turn over this property to the Confederate States. If the United States and the Confederate States, have a peaceful adjustment of the matters now in controversy between them, each will have to account for the property they possess, in which both are jointly interested. If the Confederate States have the possession of the Public Lands, the whole matter can be settled without embarrassment. There will be no danger of this property being wasted in grants to schemes of Internal Improvement, as our Constitution wisely prohibits such appropriations. If on the other hand, Alabama appropriates it to her own use, we shall see our Legislatures beset by Railroad Companies, and other corporations and societies, clamoring for grants and donations, and in a short time all of the lands of any value will be squandered away. Experience teaches us that my prediction will be fulfilled. Then, sir, if in a treaty between the Confederate States and the United States, we are required to account for these lands, we must resort to taxation to redeem our pledge and discharge our duty. If we are never called on to settle with the United States for the value of these lands, I venture the prediction, that we shall be, some day hence, by Georgia or South Carolina, if the lands are worth anything; and we shall be compelled, for reasons I have before stated, to recognize their rights, and respond to such call; and then our people will be taxed to replace that which has been recklessly wasted.

If the lands are worth nothing, then our State should not be burdened with their management and disposition; they ought to be a fund for the common benefit of all the Confederate States.

I believe the passage of this Ordinance will relieve our Federal Government of embarrassment, and the people of our State from heavy burdens; and will remove a cause which may be a source of discord and contention between the States of our Confederacy and the State of Alabama.

[Mr. Morgan replied to Mr. Clarke, after which Mr. Clarke proceeded:]

I have but little to say in reply to the gentleman from Dallas, as he has not attempted to controvert the soundness of the reasons advanced in support of the substitute.

The gentleman says, Texas is unwilling to surrender her lands —which I think probable, as none of the Confederate States, excepting herself, can pretend that they ever had any interest in a foot of her soil. When Texas was annexed to the United States, she retained all of her lands, and in any settlement hereafter to be had with the United States, I apprehend it will not be contended that she will have to account for property in which the other States, or the United States Government, never pretended to have any interest.

The gentleman next cites Florida, whether on reliable authority or not, I am not advised. If, however, it be true that Florida eschews the rights of her sisters in her lands, it does not prove that she is acting justly, or that they will not some time hence demand a settlement and accountability of their interest; and we cannot be justified by her unjust and unwise course. It is the duty of the seceded States to cultivate the most kindly relations, and it would be the part of wisdom to set Florida a good example, with the hope that she may repair her error.

The gentleman says, the Confederate States have no interest in our lands, and whilst it would be generous in us to give away our property, honesty does not require it; and in the same breath, says, honesty requires us to account to the United States for the value of the lands, if we ever enter into a settlement with that Government, of the matters in dispute. I must confess I cannot understand on what principle, or by what process of reasoning, he has attained his conclusion.

If honesty requires us to account to the United States for these lands, it is because each State forming the Union was equally interested in this property, which the gentleman is willing to admit. Then, it is conceded that the seceding States had every right that the States remaining in the Union had, and I cannot see how those separating from us can retain their rights, whilst those acting and uniting their destinies with us, lose theirs. It may be safer to gratify our avarice at the expense of friends who would submit rather than expose us—a degree of forbearance we might not receive from our *Northern brethren.*

The Ordinance to dispose of the Public Lands being under consideration,

Mr. Jewett said:

I have been surprised to hear two or three members of the Convention propose to turn over to the action of the Legislature, which will not be in session for nearly a year to come, all matters embraced in the Ordinance, reported by the Committe on Public Lands; and still, more surprised to hear assigned, as a reason for such course, that we are not sufficiently informed upon the subject to act with prudence and safety at the present time.

It certainly argues a want of information upon the questions involved, and particularly shows an ignorance, on their part, of the scope and design of the Ordinance now under consideration. But I am at a loss to discern how they can charge this body with such want of knowledge as is requisite to dispose of the Public Lands which have now become the property of the State; and am very far from being convinced that the Legislature is a more competent body than our Convention, to do all that is necessary in the premises.

To show you how injudicious it will be to refuse to consider the Ordinance reported, and adopt, in lieu thereof, the crude propositions of gentlemen, I need but call your attention to the manner in which one of them proposes to meet such difficulties as are apparent upon a single glance at his plan. He merely proposes that we shall reenact the laws of the United States formerly in favor in this State, in regard to the disposal of the public lands. And when it is suggested that the condition of affairs is materially altered by such changes as have grown out of secession; and that there is no officer in the State upon whom we can devolve the duties of supervising and regulating the many matters constantly occurring in the different Land Offices, he proposes, without a moment's hesitation, to invest the Governor of the State with the same power as was previously vested in the President of the United States in that respect, when it must be known to every man conversant with the laws of the United States, that the President had the most insignificant duties to perform in respect to the Public Lands—his signature to all the patents for land being affixed by a private Secretary, and his power to review and pass upon the decisions of the Commissioner of Public Lands and the Secretary of the Interior being merely appellate. I repeat, that I am surprised to see so grave a question as the disposal of the public domain, embracing several millions of acres of land, attempted to be settled here by the passage of three or four Resolutions, or the adoption of an Ordinance of some half a dozen sections.

The entire question involved in the repeal of the Ordinance of 1819, which ceded the waste and unappropriated lands of the State to the United States Government—and our State's future policy in regard to such lands, has been before the Special Committee appointed at the former meeting of this Convention, to consider these matters, and they have engaged the earnest and careful attention of the Committee. After considering these questions in all their bearings, and the propriety of pursuing a line of policy similar to that which induced the State to cede all its vacant lands to the United States Government, when it entered the old Federal Union, the Committee have come to the unanimous conclusion to recommend a different policy, and to advise the State to retain the Public Lands for its own use, and to dispose of them under its own laws and regulations. They have accordingly reported the Ordinance now under consideration, which establishes a Department of Public Lands, appoints officers to carry into effect the laws and regulations for the sale of the lands, fixes the prices and establishes the mode of selling the lands. It further confers privileges upon actual settlers and the occupants of neighboring farms, and establishes preëmption rights; following, in these respects, the laws of the United States, which obtained previous to our withdrawal from the Union. There are, also, some general provisions for the correction of mistakes by purchasers and land officers, and certain regulations to prevent fraud and favoritism.

These matters, as I have said before, have been carefully prepared, and are entitled now to the attention of this body, commensurate with their importance.

The Ordinance makes no disposal by grant or otherwise of the lands themselves, or the proceeds arising from their sale, to any Railroad, or for any purpose of education or otherwise; and so far as remarks have been made in this debate upon the impolicy of diverting the public lands, or the proceeds of their sale, from revenue purposes, they are wholly foreign to the true issues under consideration.

This Ordinance, as I have previously remarked, merely proposes to supply such laws as are requisite to enable the State to sell its vacant lands, in place of those laws of the United States previously in force, and repealed by the Ordinance of Secession.

To have our Land Offices closed, and all the lands withheld from market until the Legislature can meet and enact laws for their entry and sale, will greatly embarass our citizens, and hinder the settlement of many portions of the State, in which lands are now sought for improvement and cultivation. This Ordinance has been prepared with a view of establishing a system for the disposal of the vacant lands of the State, very similar to that in operation under the United States Government, for a like purpose, and which has been found to operate well, both to the citizen who desired to purchase, and to the Government which occupied the position of proprietor of the land.

There are features in this Ordinance, as reported under the instructions of a majority of the Committee, which do not meet with the approval of every member, and some of which, I am free to say, are objectionable to me; such, for instance, as the establishment of County Land Offices, under the charge of the Judge of Probate, for the sale of the Public Lands. These features, however, if equally objectionable to the majority of the Convention, may be easily corrected, and the Committee expected that, in many respects, the Convention would make alterations and additions to the Ordinance; but it is urged, most earnestly, that no reason exists for rejecting the whole Ordinance, and particularly those parts which are satisfactory to the Convention, because other parts may not meet with like favor.

I suggest, that the whole subject be taken up in a Committee of the Whole; that we entertain all motions for amendment; debate fully all suggested alterations; and I have no doubt we shall be able, without the consumption of much time, to embody in this Ordinance as safe and prudent regulations for the disposal of the lands of the State, as any future Legislature could enact upon the subject.

Mr. WHATLEY said:

Mr. President—The gentleman from Marengo [Mr. Clarke] denies our right to the Public Land within the State. In this I disagree with him. I contend that we have not only the equitable right, but the legal right to these lands. How did these lands originate, and who was originally the owner of the same? These lands were ceded by the State of Georgia, by the Articles of Agreement of 24th April, 1802. What was the object of the cession? One of the objects of the cession was to create a *common fund* for the United States, for the defence of the States. That object has now ceased; we no longer ask the United States for defense or protection; we have taken our defense into our own hands. "The reason ceasing, the law itself ceases." The United States not being required to afford protection, the funds provided for that purpose should not remain vested in the United States.

Mr. President, another and more important object of the cession by Georgia, as stated in the 5th Section of the Articles of Cession in 1802, is to "form a State, to be admitted as such into the Union," on an equal footing with the other States. Now, sir, I contend that as soon as Alabama assembled in Huntsville, in 1819, in her sovereign capacity, she then assumed her sovereignty and right of *eminent domain*. She was then clothed with the legal title to these lands, and fiduciary trust of the United States was discharged. The Government has impliedly admitted our right to these lands, when Alabama was admitted into the Union. The United States required that Alabama "should forever disclaim all right and title to the waste and unappropriated land lying within the territory of Alabama." If the State did not own the lands by virtue of her sovereignty, why did the United States require the State to disclaim and cede all her rights to these lands?

Certainly our right is clear to these lands. We have retired from the partnership on account of the violation of the articles of that partnership. We have a right to hold the assets in our possession until the account is settled. Sir, we do not fear that account—we have much less than our full share.

The Confederate States have not requested us to transfer these lands to them; and have we any assurance that other States intend to transfer their lands?

It is said, if we take these lands we shall have to pay an exorbitant price for them—the price which the Government asks for the same. This is not the law, sir. In no case are we liable for more than the reasonable value of said lands, however much the Government may charge for them. [Ainsworth vs. Patillo, 13 Ala. Reports.] Then, sir, if we have to pay for them, it will only be what they bring in market—what is received by the State.

MR. WATTS said:

Mr. President—I do not propose, at this late day of the Convention, to enter into an extended discussion of this important and complicated subject. I wish simply to make some suggestions in the way of argument, to show that the amendment of the gentleman from Marengo, [Mr. Clarke,] should not be adopted; and to show why the amendment which I shall offer ought to be adopted.

The proposition of the gentleman from Marengo is to cede all the Public Lands within Alabama, to the Confederate States of America. In his reply to the gentleman from Dallas, [Mr. Morgan,] he has said that there is doubt as to Alabama's title to the Public Lands within her borders. If his last statement be true, his proposition ought not to be adopted. His proposition to cede is a full answer to the assertion that Alabama has no title. Alabama certainly cannot, and ought not to convey a title to a thing which she does not own. I have no doubt that the effect of Alabama's Secession, and the establishment of her independence of the United States of America, invest her, according to settled principles of international law, with the title to all the lands within her border. I will not now enter into the argument to show this.

But, sir, we ought not, in my judgment, to cede these lands to the Confederate States. The ownership of these lands, by the Confederate States is in no way essential or important to the success of these States. If we look to the past history of the United States touching this subject, we cannot fail to discover, from various reports made to Congress, that as a source of revenue, the Public Lands have never been of service to the United States. The costs of purchase or other acquisition, have far exceeded, in dollars and cents, the amount ever received from them into the Treasury.

The advantage arising from the public domain has not consisted in money; but in furnishing homesteads for families, increase and stability of population, and in all the progress and wealth which spring from the cultivation of the soil, and in the contentment and happiness, and patriotic impulses which cluster around *fixed habitation* and *permanent homes*. So fully was it shown, in the Congress of the United States, that the Public Lands were worthless as a source of revenue, and that they served but as the fruitful fountain of dishonest combinations and "log-rolling" schemes of corruption, that, as long ago as fifteen years, the great Carolina Senator, with the ken of a prophet, and the wisdom of a sage, proposed, that the whole should be relinquished to the control and ownership of the States in which they were located. We shall be unwise if we remain untaught by the history of the past.

I have an amendment, which I shall offer at the proper time, which declares that these Public Lands belong to Alabama; that they shall be under the control and subject to the disposition of the General Assembly, to be appropriated to three specific purposes, viz: One-fourth to citizens of Alabama, heads of families, destitute of lands; and that the remainder shall be appropriated to the purposes of Education and Internal Improvements.

I will read the amendment, which I propose to offer:

Be it further ordained, That the General Assembly shall appropriate one-fourth of the Public Lands, now unsold, and unappropriated, under rules to be prescribed by the General Assembly, to citizens of this State, heads of families destitute of homesteads; and the remainder to the purposes of Education and Internal Improvements.

Here, Mr. President, are three great purposes to be accomplished: The first looks to the *stability* of our population, and encourages that manly independence which animates the heart of him who has a spot of earth he can call his *own;* that love of country, which has its root at the hearth-stones, and happy homes of the humble, yet independent tiller of the soil. Had I the time, I could show by the light which issues from two thousand years of the world's history, *that the beginning of civilization, in every age and every country, has been coeval with the cultivation of the soil;* that from the seeming curse imposed on man, by the Almighty: " In the sweat of thy face shall thou eat bread!" has grown the greatest temporal blessings ever conferred on our race. And we all know, that in times of war, we look with confidence, for the defence of our liberty and honor, to the soldiers who come from the hills and valleys of the land, with hearts full of the thoughts of home and the holy memories of the *fireside.*

The first object to be acccomplished by my amendment needs but to be named to meet the approval of the Convention.

The second is Education.

This needs from me no lengthened comments on the benefits of education. In a Government whose basis is the *people*, it needs no argument, to show, that the wisdom of its administration, its power, prosperity and progress, depend on the intelligence and virtue of its citizens. We are admonished by the advancing civilization of the age, and by the love we bear to republican institutions to spread broad-cast, the light of knowledge through our land. Our own State Constitution, adopted forty years since, declares that " schools and the means of education shall forever be encouraged in this State." The means heretofore adopted have fallen far short of fulfilling the purposes; and if these puolic lands can thus be appropriated, they will furnish the means of equalizing and making sure and steadfast the benefits intended to be conferred by our past compacts and legislation. The inequalities in the distribution of the funds heretofore devoted to education can then be avoided, and the whole harmonized into a Common School System, through which every child in the State may have education as free as the air he breathes

The third object to be accomplished is Internal Improvements.

I know that it is fashionable with certain gentlemen to decry Internal Improvements. Opposition to such improvements by the old Federal Government, has been so long the watch cry of party, that many people confound them with improvements within each State by its own Legislature. Two things could not be more different than the powers of a State, and those of the Federal Government. The latter has no powers except those delegated in its Constitution; whilst, by the terms of almost every State Constitution, the Legislative power extends to all proper subjects of Legislation, restrained alone by its own, or the Federal Constitution. The geographical situation of Alabama requires as a part of a wise policy some encouragement to a system of Internal Improvements. North and South Alabama are separated by mountain barriers, such as to make us almost two separate and distinct people. This should not be so. Along these mountains and valleys cannot be found the wealth to aid in the construction of such improvements as will make the people of Alabama *one people*. This can only be done by the aid and encouragement which the whole people as represented in the General Assembly, can give to a particular part, for the great good of the whole State. It is now within the power of this Convention, without expense to the people, to do what every Alabaman who loves his State earnestly desires to be done. Our whole people can become a homogeous and united people; the North and the South, the East and the West, identified in interest, in purpose, and in destiny.

The fact that you have, in the Amendments to our Constitution, restricted the power of the General Assembly, makes the more necessary the adoption of the policy I urge. That which has made our Mother Georgia, the Empire State of the South, may double the population, the wealth and power of Alabama. Let us not turn over these Public Lands to our Legislature to become the prolific source of log-rolling squabbles, and party combinations and speculations. But let us now fix the *purposes* to which they shall be appropriated. The purposes to which I propose to devote them, form the pillars of the greatness of every civilized people : *permanent, honest,* and fixed population, *intellectual wealth,* and commercial power, constitute the glory and the grandeur of a Republican State.

THE RATIFICATION OF THE PERMANENT CONSTITUTION.

The Permanent Constitution was submitted to the Convention on the 12th March.

Mr. Jemison offered a Resolution, providing that the Permanent Constitution be submitted for ratification or rejection, to a Convention of the people, to be hereafter elected.

Mr. JEMISON said:

Mr. President—I think this is the plan which we ought now to pursue. The question is a grave one, and surrounded with many difficulties. It must be admitted, that when we were elected to this Convention, it was not contemplated, either by us or by the people, that we should be called upon to ratify a New and Permanent Constitution. It is true, that the language used in the Joint Resolutions of the General Assembly, authorising this Convention, *may* be construed so as to embrace in its meaning this power: and indeed, every conceivable power; but we should look not only to the intention of the Legislature at the time, and to the reasons that induced them to act, but we should look carefully to the present state of the public mind. So far as I am individually concerned, I have no great preference for the plan that I propose, and I am moved to it by the respect that I have for the people, as well as by what I conceive to be my duty to them. I do not wish thus to avoid the responsibility of a direct vote on the ratification here, for I should have no hesitation whatever to vote for the ratification now.

That there is great dissatisfaction prevailing in some sections of the State now, in reference to our acts heretofore, there is no doubt; and we must recollect too, that this dissatisfaction, to some extent, at least, is owing to the fact, that the Ordinance of Secession was not submitted to the people. We should have respect for their scruples and wishes. And I can conceive of no more effectual way of satisfying the people now, than by submitting to them this Constitution for ratification. I would have no fear of the result.

There is no pretext now in the way of this course. We cannot plead the want of time, nor the necessity of hasty or rapid movements. And, in my opinion, unless we have better reasons for immediate ratification here, and at once, a refusal on our part to submit it to the people, or to their newly elected Delegates, will greatly increase the dissatisfaction. So far as I am concerned, I endorse the Constitution fully, and am prepared to vote for its ratification.

MR. BROOKS, the President, [MR. WEBB in the Chair,] said:

There can be no use in the course suggested by the gentleman from Tuscaloosa; no necessity for it—it will be a mere waste of time.

[Mr. Brooks was proceeding with his remarks, when Mr. Morgan asked and obtained leave to offer a substitute.]

MR. WATTS:

There is no earthly use in the amendment offered by the gentleman from Dallas, [Mr. Morgan,] as will be seen by reference to the Preamble to the Constitution. The Constitution provides that only the seceded States can ratify.

MR. MORGAN:

I wish to adapt our language to the plain comprehension of the people, so that there should be no misunderstanding. If we ratify, and the other States do not, we will then have two Constitutions.

MR. WATTS:

How can that be, when the Constitution provides that it must be ratified by five States, before it is binding?

MR. MORGAN:

Explained further his position, and made some general observations in favor of the policy of ratification by this Convention, at once. The people would never ratify by a direct vote. This doctrine of a direct vote of the people on ratification, was absurd and odious. A reference would give rise to many distracting questions. The African Slave Trade question would be brought in; the question of Reconstruction, with all its agitating features, would be brought in; and many other questions of sufficient abstract merit to excite the people and arouse opposition, but of no useful importance. Our fathers never would have ratified the Old Constitution by a direct vote.

Mr. Dargan said:

Mr. President—It ought to be gratifying to us, who are friendly to this Constitution, to hear such unanimous expressions of praise bestowed upon it. It meets with general approbation here—we have heard no objection urged against it. If it is so perfect that the Representatives cordially endorse it, this argues that it will receive the approval of the citizens. Then, why not adopt here, and at once, that which we know will be approved by our constituents? If we have the legal right and power to adopt and ratify it, and this, no one seems seriously to deny, why postpone action? The relations we bear to our constituents authorize us, in matters of great delicacy like this, to take upon ourselves the responsibility of action.

I have thought that war would be inevitable; that our redemption would have to be worked out by war. This may be, or may not be. From present indications, there are some hopes of Peace. But whether we are to have Peace or War, all must admit that our success must greatly depend upon unity of action, and the earnestness with which we push our measures.

It is proposed to have a new set of Delegates to ratify this Constitution. That would be unwise, for new Delegates would be harrassed with new questions and new issues. If you look to the dissatisfaction that is said to prevail, you see it is, to some extent, confined by geographical limits. The adversaries of secession, will seize the occasion of a new election to introduce the destructing elements of reconstruction, and other kindred questions. Such efforts, if earnestly made, would produce the most unhappy state of public feeling; leading, probably, even to war and bloodshed. If we are now of one mind, let us seize the golden opportunity, for we have in our grasp peace, prosperity, and security. Let us ratify this Constitution, and close the subject at once.

Mr. Kimball said:

Mr. President—The refusal to send the Permanent Constitution of this Confederation to the people of the State of Alabama, for their endorsement or rejection, is to my mind unfair and illiberal. Have the people of the State of Alabama no rights as a sovereign community? Now, sir, it is my purpose to vote for the Constitution, and in doing so, I desire that I may be placed in a condition to justify myself, the Constitution, and the action of a majority of this Convention. Will the Convention refuse the consummation of so desirable an object? Is the Convention determined to fetter us hand and foot and send us home, unprepared to defend and justify the action here?

In the hot haste to adopt the Ordinance, on the ground that Alabama should secede before Lincoln's inauguration, does not now exist. Time is now no special consideration; we have full time to confer and deliberate. Send us home prepared to defend your action on the subject of this Constitution, and I am satisfied that we will be enabled to satisfy, and to reconcile the people. This Convention must be apprized, that we are pledged by our people, to refer the action of this Convention to them, for their rejection or endorsement. That the people of the State should be united, is certainly desired by this Convention and the country. In the results of the old Government originated the idea of secession, on the ground that the Government, under the old Constitution, was a failure. This induced the State Convention to adopt the Ordinance of Secession, to create a new Government and a new Constitution, based on the old one. Now, Mr. President, in the formation of a Permanent Government, the term would imply strength and durability. If so; if the old Government so formed, was a failure, where is the additional guarantee that this one is not also a failure? Is this stronger than the older one? This Government claimed the right of separate State secession, and by that process, dissolved the old one; then here is the precedent, and any State of this new Government may, with a less reason, destroy the present at pleasure.

Then, Mr. President, the gentleman from Mobile, [Mr. Dargan,] says, not a member of this Convention has objections to the new Constitution. I do assure the gentleman, that I have; but they are not insuperable; and it is my intention to vote for the Constitution.

Mr. CLARKE, of Laurence, said:

Mr. President—Shall the Constitution of the Confederate States of America be submitted to the people, for their ratification or rejection? In other language, shall the people govern themselves? What a singular interrogatory to be propounded, in a deliberative assembly of the 19th Century! If a similar question had been asked in the bloody days when Robespierre *murdered*, it would have excited little surprise; but, sir, that the delegates of a people, whose freedom is their proudest boast, should even entertain a question of this character, is a political phenomenon—a significant paradox. Sir, are mildew and decay about to fall upon the principles established by the conflicts and consecrated by the blood of the revolution? Is the great fundamental law of all free governments, about to be repealed? Has experience demonstrated that the patriotic people of Alabama are incapable of self-government? Has the mere act of secession wrought such a wonderful change in their capacity? Is it possible that such things shall be "and overcome us like a summer cloud without our special wonder?" The solemn matter for the arbitrament of this Convention, is not what degree of responsibility each delegate is willing to assume. The self-complacent and defiant air with which members flippantly declare that it is our duty to lead, and not to follow the people, is a specious *argumentum ad hominum* addressed to personal vanity, and can only affect those who are afflicted with this most contemptible of human frailties. If considerations of individual responsibility alone were involved, I would dare as much as any other member in the *right* direction. The true question is, how far is this Convention willing to aggress upon the clearly defined rights of the people! Sir, the refusal to refer the Constitution to the people, whom it is to govern, for their ratification or rejection is a bold, unauthorized and dangerous advance in the *wrong* direction, and can only be justified by the reasons which tyrants have always quoted in defence of their usurpations. I am not willing, at least, without the excuse of some overruling necessity, to assume the responsibility of doing *wrong*. We assembled here for the patriotic purpose of protecting, and not of infringing, popular rights. To establish more firmly the great principles of civil liberty, and not to subvert them—to preserve, and not to abolish, the land-marks of our fathers. That this Convention does not possess the unlimited power, asserted by those who are opposed to the reference, is perfectly manifest. Th e p ainest principles of construction, when applied to the warrant of our commission, sufficiently demonstrate the truth of this proposition. "We are convinced," in the language of the resolutions of the General Assembly of the State, passed at the session of 1859–60, "to consider, determine and do whatever in our opinion, the rights, interests and honor of the State requires to be done," on account of the election of a Black Republican President to the Chief Magistracy of the Federal Union. The power hereby conferred creates nothing more than a *general* agency for a *special* purpose. In consonance with the mandate of these resolutions the Convention determined on the 11th day of January, ultimo, that the "rights, interests and honor" of the State required that the Ordinance of Secession should be passed, and acted in harmony with that decision.

Now, sir, it is a correct principle of construction that whenever a power is expressly granted, all others of an auxiliary character which are necessary to make it effective pass by implication. It follows, therefore, as a legitimate consequence, that whatever incidental acts are made necessary by the principal one of secession, this Convention ought to perform. Having withdrawn Alabama from her connection with the old Government, whatever Ordinances are necessary to adjust the State to her new political status should be enacted, and no more. When this much is accomplished, the members of this body ought, modestly, to consider themselves *functious officio*. If they assume to do more, their acts will wholly transcend the letter and spirit of their authority, and only be successfully defended upon the hypothesis of the existence of some such overpowering necessity as would itself justify an actual usurpation of power. No such necessity exists. The powers of the Provisional Government are ample for the protection of the State, its citizens and their property, at least during the short time which would be requisite to enable the people to elect fresh delegates to another Convention. Sir, the latitudinous construction given to our Letter of Attorney, by those who seem so fond of the exercise of a "little brief authority," would be infinitely amusing if it were not so utterly absurd. Whatever they have resolved upon, they find no difficulty in discovering power to authorize. As often as their commission is doubtful or obscure, their construction invariably results in an enlargement of their powers; and when their facile *construction* fails to give the power which they desire to exercise, they take it any how. When they are told of their usurpations, they politely reply, in courtly euphemism, "we are only assuming the responsibility." They forcibly remind one of the three celebrated interpreters of their father's will in the Tale of the Tub: When the most ingenious and artful construction had been resorted to in vain to find a warrant for their desires, they very *wisely* added a codicil of their own invention.

But, sir, I am indisposed to argue a proposition so perfectly plain and simple. Grant, *ex gratia argumenti*, that this Convention does possess the power to ratify the Constitution—are there no reasons of expediency which render it highly impolitic and unsafe to exercise it? The political mind of the State is already much agitated and aggrieved—the times are troublous and revolutionary —in some sections the people are mad and discontented—the Southern Confederacy only inaugurated—the experiment incomplete and the fate of the Government by no means determined. The policy of this Convention should be to appease and not to inflame —to allay and not to foment popular excitement; and, if possible, to extinguish the latent fires that smoulder amid the ruins of the old Government. Not only are the people expecting, but they are earnestly desiring, that the Constitution shall be referred. This is not the peculiar wish of any one party—it is the common demand of all. The people, *submissive to rule*, as this body seems to think, know their rights, and will insist upon their assertion. It is quite easy to incur their displeasure—but to assuage it, "*hoc opus hic labor est.*" The man who, voluntarily and without the shadow of an excuse, not only spurns their will, but violates a great prinple of enlightened government to do so, will be held to a rigid accountability. By all means the Constitution should be submitted to the people for their own examination and study. Let its principles be well canvassed, and its provisions thoroughly understood—then, if the people shall ratify it, the Government will rest upon a solid and durable foundation. Its permanency will be insured. The people, if they ratify it, will love it and submit to it cheerfully, because it will then be the Government of their own selection. But, sir, if you impose it upon them, what assurance have you that it will survive the first wave of popular indignation? Why, sir, if every word of this Constitution smacked of inspiration itself, and had been promulged amid the lightnings and thunders of a modern Sinai, it could not be expected to outlive the rage of a disfranchised people. Let it be understood that the great right of man to govern himself, is in danger; is to be overthrown, and once more the armor of Liberty will glitter upon a thousand sun-lit hills; again the songs of the free and the watchwords of the brave will echo through our valleys, and the masses, rising in the majestic grandeur of a popular upheaval, like the great globe when shaken by the throes of an earthquake, will topple this Constitution from the purple heights of its imperial despotism. The provisions of the Constitution itself, will not be considered. The people will regard its ratification by this Convention as conclusive testimony that their rights have been outraged. The refusal to refer, therefore, involves an experiment hazardous in the extreme and eminently foolish, because it is wholly unnecessary to be made. This Government, sir, like the old, must be founded upon the consent of those who are to live under it. A Government erected upon any other basis cannot, in the nature of things, be otherwise than ephemeral, and of right ought not to be. The history of all such is graphically written in the fate of Iturbide—one day illustrious, the next fallen. A people so long accustomed to the usages of free institutions, will hesitate much before they surrender their inherent right of self-government. If the Constitution is a good one—which I by no means deny—the highest motives of patriotic duty would require its ratification, and there is no doubt that an intelligent people would do it. If, on the contrary, the Constitution is a bad one, no sane man will dare to say that it ought to be ratified. Whether it is good or bad, therefore, the most powerful reasons demand its reference.

There is no necessity for the immediate ratification of the Constitution; and moreover, such telegraphic celerity and indecent haste are wholly inconsistent with the solemn importance of the subject and the grave consequences which are to follow the act. When delegates deliberated calmly, States were slow to ratify permanent Constitutions. The States of Rhode Island and North Carolina were engaged for nearly two years in considering the old Constitution, before their final action upon it. The strength, power and resources of the Provisional Government render haste not only unnecessary, but absolutely inexcusable. If there is no necessity for immediate action, in the absence of all other reasons, courtesy to those who have deputed us hither, and a proper respect for their opinions, imperatively demand that the Constitution shall be submitted to them. Life, liberty and property, are considerations of no ordinary character, and are regarded by the people with the liveliest jealousy and the most watchful attention. The Government designed for the protection of these grave interests ought to be established only after the freest election, the fullest discussion, and the calmest deliberation.

Many other reasons of an equally cogent character connected with the history of this Convention and its proceedings, powerfully persuade us to pursue the most liberal policy, and to submit the Constitution to the people.

The Convention itself was called in a very irregular, if not in an unauthorized manner. The usual course, and the one adopted by other Southern States, of first submitting the question "Convention or no Convention?" was cavalierly ignored, and the Governor peremptorily required to call a Convention without consulting the popular will. The next palpable contempt for public opinion manifested in the unique proceedings of this body, was its flat refusal to refer the Ordinance of Secession to the people. The wiser and more republican policy of other seceding States, was expressly repudiated. Thus, the poor privilege of even expressing their opinion of an act which destroyed a Government sacred in the estimation of many, was superciliously denied. Whether these acts are invasions of the fundamental principles of self-government, it is immaterial to inquire. Whether they are real or imaginary injuries is wholly unimportant—the people entertain their own opinions upon these subjects, and will no doubt express them, and that, too, in a very emphatic manner, whenever an opportune occasion is presented. If, in addition to all of these just grounds of complaint, another insult is to be offered to popular intelligence and sovereign right; if, as the crowning act of aggression, and last scene in the drama of usurpation, the great principle of all *free* government, that the people have the right to frame the system of government under which we live, is to be rudely assailed and recklessly subverted by an inconsiderate, unjustifiable and inexcusable refusal to refer the Constitution to them, what opinions will the people of the State form of this Convention? By what name will history characterize it? How shall posterity regard it? It will be a by-word and reproach wherever the name of Civil Liberty is respected. If this policy is adopted, the arrogant declaration that the Convention is omnipotent, will indeed assume an air of fearful portent. Omnipotent! But whether for good or evil, is a question of momentous interest. Little, alas, did the bright-plumed genius of Civil Liberty, when she winged her flight from the royal oppressions and monkish persecutions of the Old World to build her gorgeous palace on the flowering wilds of the new, dream that she would meet her doom by the assassin's knife, and find a grave in the home of her adoption!

It is no answer to these arguments to affirm that the failure of the Convention to ratify the Constitution will impair the credit of the Confederate States. Brokers, Shylocks and money-mongers are an astute class of speculators, and will need no prompter to inform them *who* ratified the Constitution. No shrewder men can be found, and no one knows better that if the ratification of the Constitution by the Convention is a practical invasion of the well-recognized principles of republican Government, that so far from augmenting, it would materially diminish the credit of the Government. The argument that a reference to the people will result in unfortunate divisions among them, is not entitled to the smallest share of respect. Temporary dissatisfactions among a people are prevented at grave expense, when the great principles of free government are the price. The only other reason assigned for the immediate ratification of the Constitution is, that a second Convention would necessarily entail considerable public expense. Ye gods! Barter the liberties of a people for paltry pelf? Enslave a State to protect its Treasury? Cautiously protect the pecuniary interests of a people, while you coolly deprive them of their rights? An Oligarchy with its heel upon the neck of Liberty speculating about economy! Without intending any disrespect for the gentlemen who offer it, I entertain for this argument no other feeling than that of the profoundest contempt.

Much more might be said, Mr. President, but I forbear. These considerations are sufficient to convince me that it is a high duty which we owe our constituency to refer the Constitution to them for ratification or rejection. Without expressing any opinion concerning the merits of the Constitution, I shall vote against it exclusively upon the ground that I am unwilling to depart from republican usages and the time-honored land-marks of a free people. I am not disposed to decide a question for my constituency which I think it is their clear right to decide for themselves. I am acting in obedience to a great principle. No remonstrance, persuasion or reproach can make me depart from it. With it I am willing to "survive or perish." I came here the representative of a free people, and so help me God, I will return as I came. I hope, sir, the Constitution will be referred.

MR. STONE said:

Mr. President—The reasons assigned by gentlemen in favor of submitting this Constitution for ratification to another Convention, only confirms me in the opinion that it would be unwise to adopt that course. What, sir, would be the condition of things in Alabama, if new elections were now ordered? The remarks of gentlemen show, beyond a doubt, that angry and bitter discussions would result from another contest, in this State, for delegates. The public mind would again become agitated; new divisions would spring up among our people. The most active efforts would be made by ambitious partisans to inspire distrust and dissatisfaction with the political action of our State. Our divisions would be exposed and magnified in the face of our enemies; our friends, both at home and abroad, would despair of ever seeing us a united people; and all this, sir, at a time when union, harmony, brotherly feeling, and concerted action among ourselves, are so much needed to secure the great objects of the Southern movement. Sir, I desire to see no fountain of bitterness now opened up among the people of the State. The old antagonisms that have grown out of discussions of the questions in past contests, instead of being revived among us, should be buried forever. But, Mr. President, we are told that the people should be consulted, with reference to the Constitution which is to be adopted for their Government. Sir, they have been consulted. Everywhere, they have declared their unalterable attachment to the principles of the Constitution of the United States. The Constitution of the Confederate States, which we propose now to ratify, is substantially the same instrument as the Constitution of the late United States, under which we have lived so long. No change in the system has been introduced. Amendments, it is true, have been made; but they are such as our experience has demonstrated to be eminently wise, and such as must meet the cordial approval of every Southern man. Sir, it is no new system of Government that we propose to adopt. We are entering upon no untried experiment. We are organizing a Government upon principles which our people have approved for the last seventy years. Secession arose from no hostility to the Constitution, but from the fact that the Constitution was annulled by a sectional majority. The triumph of a Higher Law party, pledged to the destruction of our Constitutional Rights, forced us to dissolve our political connection with hostile States, and to organize with those who, in good faith, would execute the Constitution. Rather than give up the principles of the Constitution, the Southern States have given up the Union. And yet, sir, we are told that we must call another Convention, to see whether the people approve these principles or not!

It is objected, further, Mr. President, that this Body has no authority to ratify the Constitution, and that we were not elected for such a purpose. If that be true, sir, it is decisive of the question; for we should exercise no authority which has not been delegated to us. But to determine this question of authority, we must refer to the Joint Resolutions or 1860, under which this Convention was called. The Resolutions required the Governor to call a Convention of the people of the State, upon the election of a Black Republican President, to "consider, determine, and do whatever, in the opinion of said Convention, the rights, interests and honor of the State of Alabama require to be done, for their protection." This, sir, is the charter from which we derive our authority, and which clothes us with full power to act. This Convention is not only authorized to ratify the Constitution, if in our opinion "the rights, interests and honor" of the State of Alabama require its ratification, but it is our duty to do so. What is our present condition? With six of our Southern sisters, we have seceded from the United States, and have established a Provisional Government for our protection. Our independence has not yet been recognized. The Government at Washington is in the possession of a Black Republican President, hostile to our "rights and interests;" and the Inaugural Address, just delivered, is a declaration of war against our State. We are notified by the highest authority, that the *force* necessary to hold the public property within the jurisdiction of our State, and to collect the duties on imports, will be used against our people. The Government at Washington, yet strong and thoroughly organized, has its army, its navy, and its treasury. Its credit is well established. It enjoys the most friendly relations with foreign powers. It is now in a hostile attitude to our State, and no one can say how soon a collision of arms may occur. Sir, we have no time for delay; we must prepare; and no preparation will be so certain to bring success and triumph to our cause, as the establishment of a permanent, efficient and well-organized Government. Such a Government would be more powerful in war, and more persuasive to peace. Sir, the necessities of the times require that the Confederate States should adopt, without delay, a real, substantial Government—one armed with all the power to resist any shock to which we may be subjected; a Government complete in all its parts, established upon an immovable basis, and possessed of all the elements of national strength. Such a system will immediately place the Confederate States in the strongest possible position to maintain their nationality against any force that may be brought against them.

Such a Government will also be more certain to obtain the recognition of foreign powers, because its stability will be then placed beyond question, and it will be the surest guaranty to those powers of the fixed and irrevocable determination of our people to maintain their independence at every hazard. It will put to flight, now and forever, all hopes of Reconstruction, and would prove to the world that our separation from the North is "final, complete, and perpetual." But a mere temporary, Provisional system, will neither give us the requisite strength at home, nor position abroad. Sir, it is important that we should secure an early recognition of our independence in Europe, and that we should negotiate with foreign powers the most liberal commercial treaties. With these powers our prosperity and peace are intimately concerned. We are their competitors neither in manufactures or commerce. We produce the great staple which supports their factories and their commerce, and which furnishes employment to their laboring classes. We are the consumers of the articles which they desire to sell. It is their interest to encourage production and consumption in our States, and to extend as much as possible the freedom of trade. Their interest, then, is on the side of peace; and if we would make that interest still more active and powerful in the preservation of peace, we should invite, without delay, the most friendly commercial relations. Let our ministers, then, to whom these negotiations will be entrusted, go abroad endorsed by a Permanent Government. Let them appear at the foreign courts as accredited representatives of a real Nation. Our independence will then be recognized, and we shall take the place to which we are entitled among the nations of the earth.

Again, sir, it may be important for the Confederate States to negotiate, without delay, the loans which may be needed for our defense. Bonds, with the endorsement of a Permanent Government, can be much more readily disposed of to capitalists, and will command much higher rates than the bonds of a mere temporary or Provisional Government. Money is sensitive, and dealers would prefer to invest where there is a solid and substantial basis. The fact that we had established no Permanent Government, would be used to impair our financial credit, and to extort from us the most unreasonable terms. Let us, then, place the financial credit of our Confederacy beyond suspicion; and if unfortunately we should at any time need the "sinews of war," they may be obtained at no sacrifice of our interests.

But a controlling reason which induces me, Mr. President, to favor a prompt ratification of this Constitution, is, that such a course may secure the early coöperation of the Border States. They will then see the kind of Government the Confederate States have established. They will see that our Constitution, in express terms, recognizes the independence and sovereignty of each State—a doctrine which has ever been dear to the people of Virginia and Kentucky—but a doctrine which has been denounced and spurned by the Government over which Abraham Lincoln presides. They will see, further, that the institution of Slavery, in which they have so deep an interest, is recognized, guaranteed and protected, under the provisions of our Constitution; and also that the African Slave Trade, which they apprehend might be reöpened, has been expressly forbidden. The bars and bolts and locks with which the Constitution of the Confederate States has guarded the Treasury, to insure a simple and economical Government, will, it seems to me, command the universal approval of the people of the Border States. Under such circumstances, is it not reasonable that those States, having like interests and institutions, "bone of our bone and flesh of our flesh," will prefer to organize with us, under a Government constructed for the protection of their property, rather than remain united with States hostile in interests and feelings, and under a policy which must certainly result, sooner or later, in the overthrow of their institutions. Sir, it is difficult to believe that the Border States can long hesitate. Let us so act as to deserve their confidence. Let us adopt this Constitution promptly, and send it out to the people of the Border States, so that they may see and know the principles and plan of Government we have finally adopted, and be induced to accept the Government before they become demoralized by further submission to Lincoln's administration.

In every aspect of this question, it seems to me the "rights, interests and honor" of the people of Alabama *do* require the prompt ratification of this Constitution. Sir, it is our duty to ratify it; and if we refuse to perform that duty, we have but half-finished the work we were elected to perform, and disregarded the most solemn trust ever confided to men. Why call upon the people, at a heavy expense, and much delay and agitation, to elect delegates to another Convention, to assemble here, to do precisely what we were authorized and required to do, but what it is proposed we shall leave undone? Sir, I see no substantial reason why we should wait the tardy process of another Convention. It is our duty to act; and we should be ready to meet whatever responsibility attaches to that action. If a restoration of harmony among our people is desirable; if the hostile attitude assumed at Washington, is such as to render it prudent that all the power of the separated States should be immediately consolidated; and if it be important that the Government of the Confederated States should be placed upon a solid basis, and clothed with all the powers and attributes of a Nation; if credit and standing, in the money-markets of the world is a matter of consequence to us in our present condition; if confidence at home, and respect and recognition abroad, are objects worthy of serious effort; if the coöperation of the Border States is sincerely desired—then, sir, we can adopt no course so well calculated to secure these great and paramount objects, as the immediate ratification of this Constitution, which has just been unanimously adopted by the Southern Congress, and which they have sent to us for our ratification and adoption.

Mr. EARNEST said:

Mr. President—But few men occupy the floor less than I do, and none more reluctantly. Like one of old, I am slow of speech, and withal, an exceeding modest man. Perhaps I might say, my diffidence and modesty are excessive. [Laughter.] But I will not occupy the time of the house in apologies, but will say what I have to say and sit down.

If my remarks are to some extent personal, it is the necessity of the case and not an egotistic disposition. I seem to stand here, in political parlance, alone, forming that patriotic party which, for want of a better name, I will call the "Earnest party," [laughter,] lost and cast off by the the Conservative party, and only on trial or probation with the Secessionists. But with a consciousness of rectitude and right on my side, I shall open the doors and receive members into the great Alabama Church, which I soon want to see embrace every man and woman of Alabama, [laughter,] from the North, South, East and West, and from the rural districts of the mountains. I do not propose to discuss the merits of the Constitution, but will simply say that, to me, it is objectionable; yet, the objections which I have to it are of a personal character, and to this generation will make it more acceptable. It conforms in every particular as near the pattern as could be. When it deviates from the pattern, it is improved; and if referred to the people of the seceding States, I have no fears but that it would be approved by three fourths of all. But to refer it to the people would be an innovation—a departure from custom—without a single precedent within my knowledge to sustain the reference. It would be productive, in my opinion, of only evil and no good. It would be putting them to the trouble and expense of an election which they do not want.

The gentleman from Tuscaloosa [Mr. Jemison,] says that he cannot find fault of it, and if submitted to the people, would advocate it. The gentleman from Tallapoosa [Mr. Kimball,] intimates that he will vote for it, and advocate it. Now, if they will in good faith throw their weight into the scale of Alabama, the Lincoln end of the scales will jar the beam with such force, that the last flickering rays of hope will become extinguished, of covering us, and we will soon find the Administration of the fragmental Government, as named by the gentleman from Barbour, [Mr. Cochran,] knocking at our doors for such commercial treaties as will save that Government from anarchy, internal war and starvation. Then, if the idea of reconstruction is one that still prompts them to labor, let me say to them. Present an unbroken front to Mr. Lincoln's reign, and we will soon be able to get such a compromise as we may dictate; one without political disgrace, not proposed to, but dictated by us. None other could I accept. While in the Union, I would have accepted Mr. Crittenden's Resolutions as a Compromise. But I would not dream of reconstruction on them now.

Mr. President, I am digressing from the path that I laid out when I got the floor.

While canvassing my county for a seat in the Convention, things were different from what they are now. I was then in favor of referring the Ordinance to the people for ratification; and if Alabama had been acting alone, that would have been proper and right; and if not so referred, I should have left the Convention and gone home and told my people to strike for liberty; that to delay a day was dangerous. But before the Ordinance could have been submitted, all the Gulf States were out without condition. What then would have been the case? To vote against it was to cut the throat of a father or brother; for how many men in Alabama have not a father or brother in some of the seceding States? I say, then, that the facts and circumstances had entirely changed, and he who voted against secession would have voted to make war on your Southern brethren, in favor of your Oppressor, and for a Government once venerable and great, but which had dwindled into a sectional majority-despotism, leaving not a vestige of our former rights and liberty, while our masters taunt us and laugh at our chains. Now, if this be true—and can any one deny its truth?— would it have been expedient to refer the Ordinance back to the people? Could they have voted a free and untrameled vote? Then, if it would have been useless to refer the Ordinance to the people, with stronger reasons why refer the Constitution of the Confederacy—a thing the people do not want or expect? I voted against the secession of Alabama. But being overpowered and voted out, I promised and pledged myself to go with Alabama, and sustain her in her course. This was not made by the lips only, but was made in good faith, and a promise I have kept with fidelity. When I left here and got home, I met my constituents wherever I could, and in my humble manner presented the facts to the people, not with reservations and inuendos that it was for effect, but that if Alabama fell, I must fall with her; that her fate was mine; that the marriage between us was lawful, and that none should separate me from her fate. These sentiments met with a hearty response from all; and my friends who elected me are to-day ready to scale the walls of Fort Pickens or Fort Sumter, or to make the waves that lave their bases, their winding sheets, and the bay their graves.

Never before have I seen the people of Jefferson so united as they are to-day. It is not for me to say what influence I have exerted in producing this state of feeling. Yet, I may be permitted to say, that I had it in my power by a wish-a-washy course, or by a kind of doubtful, distrusting course, to have widened the breach. Now, let me address a few words to my politicall friends on this floor. Before high Heaven, I believe the only way to avoid war is to show that we are united. It is known that with the late Administration, General Scott, a degenerate son of the South, was the head and front of the coercive policy, and that he had said that if the South was united, they could not be whipped back; but if divided, they would whip back themselves. And from the fact that he directed Mr. Lincoln to box himself up and be shipped by Adams' Express Freight Train, or to keep his wife between him and the people, that his influence is not less with the in-coming than the out-going Administration. Then, let us speak to the Head of the powers "that be," by a unanimity that Scott can understand. Let every man sign the Ordinance and vote for the Constitution, and go home and boldly assume the responsibility; and peace will again perch upon our banner, and our people will call us blessed. No sooner had the fact been announced that more than one-third of the Convention had refused to sign the Ordinance, than it was published in the Abolition papers that when they came down to coerce us, they would get more than one-third of our population to join them in subduing us. They were not here, and did not listen to the eloquent, patriotic speeches of the conservative coöperationists; and if they had been, they would not have published them; or, at least, they would not have made the comments they did on the patriotic letters of the gentleman from Madison, by saying they "were bought up," &c.

In conclusion, allow me to say, without regard to party or past offences, I shall act in harmony with that party who presents the true issue with a firm and determined stand to meet the consequences. And after Peace shall rest as a halo of glory encircling the Confederate States, and the horn of plenty is pouring the blessings of peace, plenty and redemption from Black Republican thraldom in our laps, then I will arraign before the tribunal of justice all precipitative, restless demagogues; and after conviction exercising executive clemency, forgive the past, and only lay them on the shelf, that their places may be filled by conservative men— men who will build up the interests of Alabama—will develope her resources and make her the Eden of the world—even if we shall have to tax a few Shylocks, or Southern men with Northern proclivities.

Mr. Brooks, the President, [Mr. Webb in the Chair,] followed Mr. Earnest, and addressed the Conventon at considerable length. The Reporter regrets that he has been unable to procure a copy of this speech for publication.

Mr. Smith, of Tuscaloosa, said:

The consideration that my opinions, will have but little weight in controlling the vote of this Convention, is no sufficient reason why those opinions should be withheld. The causes which restrained me from uttering my objections to another and more momentous question, no longer prevail; and I feel free to speak upon this subject now with the utmost frankness.

The Constitution ought to be submitted to the people, or to a Convention of Delegates to be elected, with special view to its consideration. I would not insist, that it be put to a direct vote of the people, but would prefer that it be submitted to a new Convention, as proposed by the Resolution of my colleague, [Mr. Jemison.]

I shall insist on this, in respect to the people, in respect to the Convention, and in respect of the Constitution itself, as its friend.

How stands the account between us and the people? Since we know that they will inquire into this, let us make the inquiry ourselves.

This Revolution was begun without the express will of the people. It was inaugurated without consulting the people; this Convention is the creature of the Legislature, which thrust upon the people the performance of the duty of electing the Delegates.

When the necessity of performing this duty came, there was no reasonable time for the examination of causes and effects. The canvass was conducted in the greatest hurly-burly of excitement; and large masses of people voted at the polls in the midst of bewilderment and dismay. The election itself was a necessity which had been created without their advice.

Then, your body is the creature, not of the people, but of the Legislature. What have you done? That you would pass an Ordinance of Secession, was expected. You did pass it, and you refused to submit it to the people; in this, they are offended. You created a new tribunal in the shape of a Congress, and authorized the election of Deputies to that Congress, and refused to give the election of those Deputies to the people; in this, they are offended. And the specious pretext for these assumptions, was the danger of delay—the necessity of prompt and immediate action.

You then have made the Congress; the Congress made the Constitution, and the Constitution is not submitted to you for your ratification. If you ratify it, while you have the perfect privilege of submitting it to the people if you choose, will not the people naturally inquire: in what of all these things have we been consulted?

They find themselves under a new Government! and in amazement, exclaim, who did this? They find themselves in the hands of a new Congress, and exclaim: Who elected this new Congress? Who authorized it?

The answer is, "We are the People!" Sir, that "We are the People," in any except a Representative sense, is absurd. It is the flimsey excuse for usurpations; it has been the characteristic of legislative tyrannies in all ages of the World, from the Areopagus to Cromwell's Parliament.

I do not speak thus to upbraid this Convention for its past action, but in the hope of inducing it to cure, by one single act of magnanimity, all the dissatisfaction that prevails in the public mind, by reason of its usurpations.

The usurpation of power is odious, while the surrender of power is admirable. Men, who otherwise would have perished, live in the annals of time, celebrated for the surrender of power; immortal in humility. Ages are illustrated by such examples.

It may be considered now to be the height of folly, to refer to the wisdom of our fathers, and to the course they adopted in bringing to maturity the old Constitution, since it appears that, at last, they were not as wise as we have supposed; for even their work has proved to have been but the work of men—a great temple to be looked upon with wonder, but to be destroyed in an hour; and the conclusion more suited to the spirit of this age, seems to be: as all things are frail and must perish, therefore we need not waste our time, or employ our thoughts with any thing grand, for grandeur itself will decay. But we, who are willing to look into the past, if not for the solid realities of wisdom, but only for the alluring promises there held up for the stability of Governments, and for the freedom and prosperity of future generations, may yet be gratified and instructed by a brief recital of the history of the formation and ratification of the Constitution of the United States. And though we know that these promises have been illusive, yet we are convinced of one undying truth: that, under that Constitution, in the brief period of three quarters of a century, a nation has arisen, whose magnificence attracts the curious observation of mankind, and challenges the admiration of Sages; whilst its irresistable march to civilization and power strikes the feudal Kingdoms of the Earth with consternation, as the ominous advance of Human Liberty threatens to invade the precints of their consecrated Dynasties.

Let us look into this curious history:

On the 21st of February, 1787, the Congress of the Confederation passed the following Preamble and Resolution:

"WHEREAS, There is a provision in the Articles of Confederation and perpetual Union, for making alterations therein by the assent of a Congress of the United States, and of the Legislatures of the several States; and whereas experience hath evinced that there are defects in the present Confederation, as a means to remedy which several of the States, and particularly the State of New York, by express instructions to their delegates in Congress, have suggested a Convention for the purposes expressed in the following Resolution, and such Convention appearing to be the most probable means of establishing in these States a firm National Government:

"*Resolved*, That, in the opinion of Congress, it is expedient, that, on the second Monday in May next, a Convention of Delegates, who shall have been appointed by the several States, be held at Philadelphia, for the sole and express purpose of revising the Articles of Confederation, and reporting to Congress, and the several Legislatures, such alterations and provisions therein as shall, when agreed to in Congress, and confirmed by the States, render the Federal Constitution adequate to the exigencies of Government, and the preservation of the Union."

Twelve States responded to this call, and on the 17th day of May, 1787, the Delegates met at Philadelphia, and on the 17th of September, of that year, agreed to the present Constitution of the United States; not including the amendments.

Thus it will be seen that, having the articles of Confederation before them, our fathers deliberated four months in maturing the Constitution.

What was the first step taken by this Convention after the formation of the Constitution? On the said 17th of September, 1787, they

"*Resolved*, That the preceding Constitution be laid before the United States in Congress assembled, and that it is the opinion of this Convention that it should *afterwards* be submitted to a Convention of Delegates, chosen in each State by the *people thereof*, under the recommendation of its Legislature, for their assent and *ratification;* and that each Convention, assenting to and ratifying the same, should give notice thereof, to the United States in Congress assembled."

On the 28th day of September, 1787, the Congress passed the following:

"*Resolved, unanimously*, That the said Report, with the Resolutions and letter accompanying the same, be transmitted to the several Legislatures, in order to be submitted to a *Convention of Delegates chosen in each State by the people thereof*, in conformity to the resolves of the Convention made and provided in that case."

In conformity with the provisions of the foregoing Resolutions, the several States ratified by Conventions of the people on the dates as follows:

THE CONVENTION OF ALABAMA.

Delaware,	on the	7th December,	1787.
Pennsylvania,	"	12th December,	1787.
New Jersey,	"	18th December,	1787.
Georgia,	"	2d January,	1788.
Connecticut,	"	9th January,	1788.
Massachusetts,	"	6th February,	1888.
Maryland,	"	28th April,	1788.
South Carolina,	"	23d May,	1788.
New Hampshire,	"	21st June,	1788.
Virginia,	"	26th June,	1788.
New York,	"	26th July,	1788.
North Carolina,	"	21st November,	1789.
Rhode Island,	"	29th May,	1790.

It will be seen, by reference to this table, that Rhode Island deliberated nearly three years; North Carolina deliberated more than two years; Virginia deliberated nine months; South Carolina deliberated eight months; and Georgia deliberated four months!

Who were the men that thus deliberated? We boast of the wisdom of our Fathers. Those were the days of Washington, Jefferson, Madison, Hamilton—men, God-like in attitude and thought, still standing out like collossal statues, illuminating the niches in the shadowy walls of the American Pantheon. They paused over these momentous questions! Are they become dwarfs in our estimation? Verily it would so seem—for *we*, the intellectual giants of *this* day representing the sovereign State of Alabama —*are not willing* to deliberate a *single day* over the instrument that makes a radical change in the Government of the country, involving the destiny of the people! the happiness, the honor, the fortunes, and the lives of millions!

And while the country was pausing and deliberating over the momentous questions involved in the ratification of this Constitution, how were these great men employed? Not in framing quibbles to make usurpations plausible; not in persuading Power to go on and to gather its unholy strength, and to wind its anaconda coil around the newborn liberties of the country. No, sir. In the solitude of their closets they were retired, engaged in the holy duty of penning the immortal argument that was to convince the judgment and answer the just expectations of the people. They did not wish to force their measures upon a generous and confiding constituency; they preferred to respect their scruples, to quiet their apprehension, and to appease the jealousies that are so natural with those who love and would preserve their liberties.

Thus, sir, by a free interchange of opinion between the Sages of the land and the people, the people were made co-workers in the great labor of building the Constitution. They were its architects; they carried the materials on their shoulders, and aided in piling stone upon stone. They had a part in it; therefore they loved and cherished the temple that they themselves had contributed to erect.

This, sir, was the course pursued by the American patriarchs, those immortal prophets of modern times. If we are not grown too wise, let us follow their example.

This new Government has been built up with great rapidity. It seems really the production of magic. Reflection, however, suggests as a reason for this, that the work was performed by our fathers, after long years of tedious toil; and all that we have done is but the chipping the original marble, and the adding an occasional block. Still, it seems the work of magic. The old and received idea has been:

> "A thousand years scarce serves to build a STATE;
> A day—an hour—may cast it in the dust."

It must now be agreed that the first line of this verse is no longer a truth in America; yet the latter is the *fatal* utterance of the experience of this day. But the rapidity with which this new Government has been built, is no evidence of its stability. You remember the story of Aladin and his wonderful lamp. He had but to express a wish to his attending genii, and that wish was performed upon the instant. He desired to have a magnificent palace erected on a favorite hill. When the night came down the hill was naked; in the morning it was adorned with the most gorgeous temple that the sun had ever lighted! Architecture smiled with bewildered delight, and the world was amazed. Aladin was worshipped as a superior being, and the palace remained in its position for years, the pride of the country and the wonder of mankind. But the lamp changed masters, and lo! in an hour the palace disappeared! The power that had created, destroyed it; the hill which it had adorned was left again a naked and desolate heath, and Aladin was persecuted as a magician!

You remember the fancy of a Russian Empress? She was not content with her marble palace; she wanted a change of abode— a variety of magnificence. She ordered a *Palace of Ice* to be built. She had but to command, to be obeyed. Huge blocks of crystal were hewn with exact precision, and in an incredibly short period the palace was erected. Colossal columns of ice studded the glittering porticoes, and the winter sun drew back his eye, dazzled by the gorgeous spectacle. The Empress was delighted. O! that this palace could stand for ever! But alas! the summer came; the frail pile tottered at its base, and dissolved itself in tears, as if weeping over the destruction of so much magnificence. Thus passes away the glories of this earth.

Mr. President, I do not draw these pictures of fancy in the spirit of prediction or of prophecy. I would arrest the shocking calamity of a failure of this Government; and for this very reason I beg the Convention to beware of the insidious growth of self-confidence; it is the poorest evidence of wisdom, and the most unmistakable indication of folly.

Yes, sir, I would arrest the terrible calamity of a failure of this Government; and I would arrest it by building its foundations on the only basis that will be found able to uphold, in a land of liberty, the structure of Government.

This Constitution has no marble base to rest upon. All its materials are perishable; the thought is scarcely less mortal than the paper upon which it is written. Parchment cannot save it from the Great Destroyer; and the leather and the boards within which it is to be confined, will only serve to preserve it the more securely, housing it for the final worm. There is but one way to perpetuate it: Lodge it in the *hearts of the people!* There, and there only, will it find a permanent existence. That is the only foundation upon which the structure of a free Government can rest. Take that base away, and the frail tenement crumbles into atoms. But how is it to find its way to the hearts of the people? How is it to reach that holy lodgement? Let them have a hand in building it. We love the creatures we make. GOD HIMSELF was pleased with his magnificent creation. HE is the type of man. Have you never seen an old architect lingering in the precincts of some palace that he had planned? He loiters around, gazes on its grand proportions, muses upon its pillars, its cornices, its dome; congratulates himself upon his success; regrets when the shades of night shut out the lovely contemplation from his view, and whispers to himself as he retires—" I built it!"

Imagine the great painter, as line by line he draws into existence some beautiful picture. See Raphael, Angelo, Reubens, Guido, leaning with bewildered delight over their own creations, kneeling and kissing the lips that yet had not the tremulousness of vi ality! See the great sculptor, chiseling the divine neck, fashioning the lofty brow, developing the sinewy frame, and dragging Hercules from his home in the solid mountain, to show the modern world this giant of the olden time. The sculptor grows drunk in the contemplation of his own Bacchus, and strong, as he surveys the limbs of his own giant. Even Prometheus so loved the man he made, that he was ready to scale the Heavens in search of a vital spark to animate it.

Thus it has been ever with the human heart—thus it will be ever. Then, if you would lodge this Constitution in the hearts of the people, give them a share in its creation; that when the day shall come that endangers its existence, they may throng around it, as they will, in millions, for its protection, exclaiming, as they rush to its rescue—"We made it—it is ours!" To a people thus inspired, armies and banners, the sword, fire and famine, present no terrors.

I know the people well. I have appealed for position to that tribunal often, and have had my days of success and failure. It is hinted even now, by those whose lives have been spent in the unholy business of nursing their prejudices, that the *people are not capable of self-government*. I deny the assertion. As polluted as their counsels may be made by bad advisers, they are still wise. They are the first to snuff the atmosphere of danger. Their watchfulness is a part of the ever-living jealousy of their rights. They are sagacious to detect and quick to resent the fawning smiles of a hypocrite. They know their true men. It is not amongst the people that political putrefactions gather; it is in the rotten perlieus of Federal Courts, where plotting ministers of State

> "Crook the pregnant hinges of the knee.
> That thrift may follow fawning."

I know, too, the duties of a Representative. There are times and occasions when he should rise above the popular tumult, and aspire to lead and control the misguided multitude. He should scorn the paltry considerations of his own tenure of office, and give himself up to the welfare of the State. He should utter the words of his own sure ostracism, if the country demanded the sacrifice. He who would hesitate to perform this sublime duty, would be unworthy a home in the midst of a free people. And in the examination of the annals which disclose the illustrious names of the brave men who have arisen to perform this great work of rolling back the tide of popular error, I find that they are the very men who had built their homes in the hearts of the people—whose rights and privileges they had protected, and whose follies they could presume to rebuke: the men who have ever acknowledged the supremacy of the people—that multitudinous king, in whom center all the legitimate sources of power. But when a representative is fresh from the people, and knows their well-ascertained will, it is his duty to follow that will.

But let us examine some of the arguments used in favor of the immediate ratification of this Constitution now by the Convention.

It is said that we can the more readily borrow money if the Permanent Constitution should be at once ratified. There is plausibility in this. But it is reported that our loan has already been taken. And whether it be taken or not, there is no doubt of our ability to raise money commensurate with our necessities. The wealth of these States is well known to the world. We will not, I hope, have to depend on foreign loans. When the day of necessity comes, the private fortunes of a people struggling for their rights, and fighting for their homes and firesides, will be freely cast into the public treasury. Between poverty and liberty there can be no debate. In this day, and under the great issues and struggles in prospect, the money is the smallest consideration. Sir, the money must come from the people. If the ranks of your army are to be swelled by the poor, they must be clothed and fed by the rich. I do not despair that all classes will do the duty of men.

But it is said by the gentleman from Pickens [Mr. Stone]—and this argument is not without its plausibility—that the European nations will the more readily recognize us, and the more certainly acknowledge our independence. Let us examine this serious question in all its aspects.

I do not think we ought to have the remotest apprehension on the subject of the speedy recognition of our position as a nation, and the acknowledgement of our independence. The nations of Europe are looking with eager anxiety to the day when they will be permitted to do this. Their lamentations over the fall of the mighty Republic of the West may be sonorous with the expressions of grief; and the smiles with which they welcome us into the fraternity of nations may be moistened by tears; but the swelling bosoms of the friends of Monarchy will heave with giant throes, and the ears of Royalty will be charmed with the dirges of liberty.

Our independence will be speedily acknowledged, and with that acknowledgement will come treaties of alliance! Treaties—the great source of international troubles; treaties, it may be, that surrender, on our part, substances for shadows; treaties, which may be the entering wedges that are to rend in sunder the principles that lie at the foundation of American liberty. I say, *American* liberty—for the word has a broader meaning here than it had in olden climes. It embraces not only all the attributes of Freedom, all the innovations upon Feudal Kingdoms, and all the enfranchising ideas of Representative Government, but, in its grand and majestic sweep, it excludes from American soil the last semblance of European Monarchy. American liberty looks even to the final extinction of all foreign claim to dominion over one foot of American soil. It is a liberty whose body towers aloft from the mountains of the Continent, and whose feet are washed by the two great Oceans of the World.

Sir, in what a strange position do we place ourselves, by calling in foreign allies for our *protection!* Our fathers conquered the Britons in the name of Liberty. We, their degenerate sons, *now* call in those very Britons to *aid us in the protection* of *that* Liberty! Thus, we place this goddess in the tyrannical hands of those from whom our fathers rescued her!

It is a sad day, sir, when an American has to admit that he depends upon *foreign allies* for his *protection.*

Protection! Sir, we proclaimed, in the so-called Monroe doctrine, that on those portions of the North American Continent not already under foreign dominion, no Power outside of America shall place its Governmental foot. Shall we abandon this? Do we not abandon this when we look abroad for an alliance of defense!

We must not depend upon foreign alliances. Our institutions are too essentially different from theirs. They will always demand more than they give. They surrender shadows and demand substances. We have had some experience in these matters with England, as well as with France. The generous sacrifices of the immortal LaFayette, whose impulses were as magnanimous as his services were important, were followed at last by the most exorbitant demands by the French Government. The mission of Jennet cannot be forgotten.

England will never forget her colonies. The gap in her crown, caused by the tearing away of those jewels, has not yet been filled. It is the dream of her political philosophy to see those jewels restored; and English pride, with English ambition, is far-reaching. Her revenge is as deathless as the oath of Hannibal. This never-sleeping desire will run through generations The same spirit of monarchy that crushed the last remains of Cromwellism in England, and pursued the Regicides to the farthest limits of the earth, is still sleepless and vigilant, though biding its time, to restore the jewels of America to the English crown.

On this question, then, of the acknowledgment of our independence by foreign powers, there is nothing to apprehend, except, indeed, the dangers that are to follow an unnatural alliance.

England and France will recognize us with joy; but not with the joy of true friends; it will be the joy of Tyrants that gloat over prospective desolation—the joy of Royalty vaunting over the fall of Constitutional Liberty. Wilberforce, a great collossal prophet, though dead, still looming over the dome of the British Parliament, points with his bony fingers to dismembered America, and exclaims, "Behold the fall of Constitutional Liberty;" and towering above its ruins, " Behold the ' irresistible genius of universal emancipation !' "

Let us beware, then, of foreign friends. England has no feelings in common with us. Her politicians are emancipationists; and it is but a year since Lord Brougham broadly insulted the American Minister in London, on account of American slavery. Nothing but the last necessity should induce a free nation to submit to an alliance for defense with a monarchial one. Monarchy is a political maelstrom, whose vortex is the oblivion of Freedom.

Mr. President, the question of war and peace has been touched in this debate. Whatever we may say or think, on that subject, is, at best, but conjecture. This great question depends much upon the sagacity and patience of our leaders. Precipitation may bring war; caution and prudence may avert it. The bloodiest wars have sprung from the slightest causes. I have never believed that the Northern hostility would reach the point of blood. But be this as it may, it is in war that we shall need the hearty coöperation of the people. They are to bear the toils, fatigues dangers and privations of war. If you get them into war, upon a slight pretext, you must beware of the consequences. And, in view of the probabilities of war, let the people vote for this Constitution. They will then the more readily defend it.

Sir, it is said, on all hands, that there is no fear that the people will ratify. I have no fears; but yet I suspect that there are serious apprehensions felt on this subject by others. There are, gentlemen here who do dread to see this question go to the people. Sir, let them discard these apprehensions. If you will consent for this Constitution to go to the people for their votes, I will be proud of the privilege of taking it in my hand, and visiting the remotest cabin in my county, to proclaim my own approval of it, and to beg the people to accept it.

And do not let me leave anything to be understood or surmised, so far as I am concerned. Whether you consent or not for this Constitution to go to the people for their votes, I will still defend the instrument itself, and even beg the people to forgive you for your usurpations. I will do this simply because I have made up my mind, stubbornly, to do or say nothing to create dissensions, or to divide the people.

PERMANENT CONSTITUTION.

Mr. BULGER said:

Mr. President—As you know, sir, I am in the habit of contenting myself with voting for or against questions pending before this Convention, and relying upon the record thus made, to place me right before the country. But, sir, the Convention, by sustaining the surprising motion of the gentleman from Madison [Mr. Davis], and that, too, after the earnest appeals made to that gentleman, by those with whom he has been acting heretofore, to withdraw his demand for the previous question for a few moments, to allow members to place themselves right on the journals, had been disregarded by him, imposes on me the necessity of submitting a few remarks to the Conventson, that they may be incorporated into the debates of the Convention, and thus place myself right in the history of the country. Sir, unlike the gentleman from Lauderdale, [Mr. Jones] from the time that I witnessed the prudence exercised by the State Conventions, in the appointment of delegates to the Confederate Congress, when they excluded ultra men of all parties, and selected wise, moderate and conservative gentlemen to that responsible position, I entertained high hopes that the action of Congress would be directed by wisdom and prudence and crowned with eminent success. And now, sir, when I listen to the reading of the many wise provisions of the Constitution, I am not disappointed, but gratified, that my hopes have been realized. Unlike the gentleman from Tuscaloosa, [Mr. Jemison,] who contends that this Convention has no right to submit the Ordinance ratifying the Constitution, and insists upon calling another Convention for that purpose;—on the contrary, I believe that we have the right, and that it is our indispensable duty, to submit this question directly to the people, for their ratification or rejection. Where, sir, do we look for the measure of our powers? To our commission, of course. Then, sir, what do we find there? That we are authorized "to consider, determine and do whatever the interest, safety and honor of the State may require to be done." Here we find our commission as expansive as the imagination of man. The only question necessary for us to consider, in determining our authority, is: what does the interest, safety aed honor of Alabama require to be done?—and that it is our duty to do.

I am opposed to the proposition of the gentleman from Tuscaloosa, to assemble another Convention; because such a course is unnecessary, inexpedient and expensive; and the will of the people can be better ascertaind without such expense or inconvenience. And if I could have prevailed on the gentleman from Madison [Mr. Davis] to have withdrawn his demand for the previous question, I would have offered an amendment, which I hold in my hand, which, if adopted, I think would have accomplished that object. [Read! Read! Read!—from different parts of the House.] Sir, I will read the amendment that I desired to offer:

Provided, That said Constitution shall have no binding force upon the citizens of the State, unless this Ordinance be ratified by a majority of the legal voters, voting at an election to be hereafter provided for.

That amendment, if adopted, would have removed the objection raised, as to expense. But the gentleman from Montgomery [Mr. Watts] expresses the opinion, in which the gentleman from Tuscaloosa [Mr. Jemison] concurs, that this Convention has no right to refer this Ordinance to the people, because the Constitution for the Confederate States provides, that when that Constitution is ratified by Conventions of five States, it shall go into effect. I hold, sir, that the Congress possesses no power or right to prescribe the mode by which the States shall ratify the Constitution. But suppose, for sake of the argument, that they have that right. Then, sir, have we not the right to adopt it with such conditions as we think proper? I had thought, as I have heretofore said, that our commission was as expansive as the imagination of man. What are we authorized to do? "Consider, determine and do whatever the interest, safety and honor of the State requires to be done." Then, sir, what bounds are there to our powers here but our discretion? What, even in our opinion would advance the interest, the safety, or the honor, of the State, we should do. Would it not promote the interest of the State to conciliate the people, and reconcile them to the new Government? I think it would. What causes the loudest complaints that we now hear from the people? That we have not paused, in the rapid progress of this Convention, in tearing down the old Government and forming a new one, to consult them. They say, we sent you to the Convention to consider, determine and do whatever the interests, safety and honor of the State required to be done, in consequence of Lincoln's election, supposing that you would permit us to pass judgment upon your action; but to our surprise, you have resolved yourselves into a creative power, and constituted a Congress, and clothed it with power not only to form a Provisional, but both a Provisional and Permanent Government—all of which has been done; and not stopping at the exercise of these extraordinary powers, you have resolved yourselves into a Legislative Body, and continue to exercise the law-making power—thus ignoring the Old Fogie ideas of our Fathers, that all the just powers of Government were derived from the consent of the goverend. Then you have resolved yourselves into a Constitutional Convention, to revise the Constitution of the State, in a manner not known to that instrument; nor content at that, you have again resolved yourselves into a Legislative Body, and passed laws repealable and unrepealable, all regardless of our wishes and without our consent.

Can you, sir, say that those complaints are wholly unfounded? Mr. President, I do not vote against this Ordinance because of objections to the Constitution, but on the contrary, (and what I now say, I desire the distinguished gentleman who proposes to publish sketches of the debates of this body, if he honors me with any notice of what I say, to incorporate in his Reports,) that I think the Congress deserves well of the country, for the wisdom and prudence by which they have been guided in the discharge of this important portion of their duties. And if the amendment which I desired to offer, providing that the Constitution should be submitted to the people directly for their ratification, had been adopted, I would have voted most cheerfully for its ratification, not only here, but at the ballot box at home. But if I stand solitary and alone, I will never vote to fasten upon the people that I have the honor to represent in this Body, a Permanent Government without their consent.

Mr. COMAN said:

Mr. President—I have at no time been troublesome to this Honorable Body. I have had but little, if any, ambition to participate in the various and important discussions which have from time to time sprung up in the progress of business. And I have had still less ambition to place my name conspicuously on the record, by any officious participation in the more unimportant proceedings of the Convention. And, Mr. President, I would now gladly accept any state of facts that would authorize a continued silence on my part.

But, sir, the Constitution proposed for the Confederate States of America has made its advent into this body. It is urged that this Convention shall ratify it at once. I feel it a duty I owe myself, as well as others outside of this body, to say a few words in explanation of the vote I shall give on the subject matter before the Convention, and now pressing to a vote. Since I have occupied a seat on the floor, I have been alone anxious and concerned to do my whole duty to myself, my constituents, and to the State of Alabama.

Up to this hour, Mr. President, I have unwaveringly voted for every proposition submitted to this Convention, to refer this Constitution, for ratification, to the people.

I have done so because I thought it was just and right, and in deference to the great American principle, that all Governments ought to exist alone by the consent of the governed.

In this country, and at this day, a Government created and maintained by the breath of the few. and not by the breath and affections of the many, I take it, is like the house built on the sand; when the floods come, and the rain descends, it will fall, and great will be its fall.

To be durable and worthy of our confidence, it must be built upon a rock, and in Anglo-Saxon America, there is no rock but the people. These views have been, mainly, influential in determining my vote heretofore on the subject of ratification. A very grave and responsible duty lies immediately before me, which is perhaps the most momentous one that has ever devolved upon me in the whole course of my life. How shall I discharge that duty?

The State of Alabama, by the action of this Convention, is this day undeniably out of the Federal Union. She no longer reposes in peace under the vine and fig-tree planted by our fathers.

Where is she?

Out at sea, without chart, rudder or compass.

What pilots are aboard, and how will they compare with such men as Dr. Franklin, Washington, Jefferson and Madison? Posterity must and will answer. History will pass upon them and render up the judgment: there I am content to leave them.

What is called a Provisional Government has been inaugurated. Such a Government is practically unknown to the people and altogether unsuited to their taste. It is only to be endured by the pressing exigencies of our present extraordinary political condition, brought about by the disrupting and revolutionary proclivities of a majority of this body. We are, in my humble judgment, as good as out of doors—shivering in the cold—exposed to many dangers, both seen and unseen. We are in no condition to awe our enemies, or to command the confidence and respect of the world. It is not impossible, that whilst in this unsettled and transitory process, even the liberties of the people may be made to run the gauntlet of the wire-workings, plottings and counter-plotting of unpatriotic and ambitious men—such as may love Cæsar more than Rome. I take it, sir, that we cannot remain in a

Provisional Government any length of time, without incurring the greatest perils to all the interests we hold as most dear and valuable in life.

What shall we do? Prudence and wisdom suggests that we go out without further delay, over this sea of troubles, and inquire if there is no rock of safety; no friendly port where we may find shelter from all impending dangers. We cannot now go back to the old Union, and the old altars of our fathers. Under existing circumstances, that is simply impossible and perhaps undesirable. It is plain to my mind, that it will not do to stay where we are to-day. We must advance, and the next best move, in my humble opinion, we are able to make, is without any fuather delay, or unnecessary circumlocution, to take refuge, at least for the present, in a Southern Confederacy, under the auspices of this Constitution. I therefore, Mr. President, in considering and determining what is best to be done for the honor, safety and interest of Alabama, in this conjuncture of affairs, feel it an imperative duty to vote for the ratification of the Constitution now before the Convention.

MR. SHEFFIELD said:

Mr. President—I ask the indulgence of the Convention for a few moments. Heretofore I have been contented to sit as a silent member; but as some gentlemen seem to think, that members who acted with the Coöperation Party, in opposing the Ordinance of Secession, and who now approve every measure calculated to sustain the action of the State, as having changed their principles; sir, I stand before you to-day, entertaining the same principles that I did on the day I took my seat in this Convention. I came here a Coöperation man—advocating that policy before my people, as the best means of procuring harmony and satisfaction with all the slave States; and the day I received the nomination as a Delegate to this Convention I stated my position clearly before I received the nomination. My position was this: that I believed our State Convention should not act separately; that our Convention should ask a Convention of all the slave States; let them adopt some plan unitedly, and whatever they adopted, I would stand by it. Should any of the States refuse to meet in said Convention, let those act that do meet, and I would sustain their action; and should all the States refuse to meet Alabama, I would not have her recede, but act boldly for herself, and I would stand by her. That I was a Union man upon Constitutional principles, but could be made a disunionist when our Constitutional rights were denied us in the Union. I am one of those who believe in the right of secession or revolution; I was opposed to the Compromise of 1850, and stood almost alone in my county in opposition to it, and advocating the right of secession, whenever the people thought their Constitutional rights could not be obtained in the Union. Mr. President, I entered into the late Presidential canvass with more zeal and energy than I ever did to secure an election for myself, believing that the doctrines of the Douglas Party were the only doctrines that would save the Union of the States, by taking the question of slavery out of Congress, and leaving it in the hands of the people, where it of right belongs. But the majority of the Southern people thought otherwise. Having also advocated before the people that this was a majority Government, and whatever course or policy the State adopted, I felt in duty bound to sustain it—having drawn my first breath upon her soil, she being my mother country, I intended to stand by her; her foes should be my foes—that I would assist her sons in repelling every attempt to invade her soil, either by a domestic or foreign foe; that in the future I intended to vote for every measure brought before the Convention, that was necessary to sustain the State in the position she has taken; that I would not stop to count up the cost, either in money or blood; that I had stated in Montgomery, publicly, on the day the Ordinance of Secession passed, that I knew there was not fifty men in my county who favored the policy adopted by the Convention that day, yet, I knew them to be highminded, honorable, and patriotic, that they would sustain the action of their State, right or wrong, and if necessary, with arms upon the field. On my return home from this place, I canvassed my county, and stated nothing but facts to the people, and I found the result as I stated before the Capitol on the day the Ordinance of Secession passed, almost a unit in favor of myself and colleague signing the Ordinance, and in voting for every measure to sustain that action. My reason for not having signed the Ordinance since my return here, is, that I wanted to see the Constitution; if it had been objectionable, I did not intend to sign it. I have seen the Constitution, and I believe it to be as perfect as it was possible for it to have been; I believe it an improvement on the old Federal Constitution; therefore I am ready at any time to sign the Ordinance of Secession, and in signing it, I do so cheerfully. I am one of those, who believed it to be the duty of the Slave States to demand their Constitutional rights, even at the disruption of the Union. I look upon this secession movement as having been forced upon us by Northern fanatics, after having done all men could do, to save the Union. The history of the country will sustain me in saying that the South has made all the concessions, and has been for years the only Section that cherished a true attachment for the Union, and has been really seeking to perpetuate it. With the South, then, thus driven to the wall, the present struggle, is obviously one of life and death. We could retreat no farther, and to have done so, would have been infinitely more horrible than death itself; it was the duty of the South to settle this question, I do not pretend to say; it was her duty to have acted precipitately, without first exhausting all possible means for an amicable adjustment of the Slavery question with the Northern States It is done, however, and right or wrong, I will sustain her. The question is no longer a debateable one; as long as it was, I fought this secession movement with all the energy I possessed, and would still do so if it would avail any thing; but it would not; it would only be aid and comfort to the Abolitionists, and it would be unmanly and cowardly to desert the State whose laws had protected me in peaceful times, when she needs my assistance. Mr. President, I regret the dissolution of the Union, and to have averted that act, should have been the study of every American. For more than half a century, during which Kingdoms and Empires have fallen, the old Union had stood unshaken; the patriots who framed it have long since descended to the grave. Yet, sir, up to the day that South Carolina broke the link, they stood the proudest monument to their memory—an object of affection and admiration, with every one worthy to bear the American name. In my judgment, its dissolution is a calamity, and upon its preservation, perhaps not only depended our own happiness, but that of countless generations yet to come.

Mr. BAKER, of Russell, said:

Mr. President—The Convention is about to come to a vote on the passage of the Ordinance ratifying the Constitution of the Confederate States. When my vote is recorded for that Ordinance, I shall, in rapid succession, have completed a series of the most important political acts of my life. I voted for the Ordinance of Secession, not because I favored secession *per se*, but because, under the circumstances, I regarded it necessary in order to promote the safety of the South, and to protect her honor. No act of mine in the past had tended to bring about the state of affairs which made it necessary to resort to secession. When from the conduct of others, however, I saw that a dissolution of the old Government was inevitable, and that Separate State Action was the policy by which it was to be accomplished, and that those who adhered to that view were largely in the majority in the Gulf States, I felt it to be my duty to rise above all mere party considerations, and accept, as a last resort, the mode of redress for existing evils prescribed by others.

The action of the Convention which severed Alabama from the old Union is now a thing of the past; the results which must follow it, whether good or evil, will greatly depend, in my judgment, upon the policy we subsequently pursue, and whether or not those of us who voted for it did right or wrong, the events of future years will determine.

I also voted for the measures which had for their object the complete organization of the military force of the State, so that Alabama might be speedily placed in a position to maintain her independence. and to defend by the sword, if necessary, the new relation she sustains to the Northern section of the old Confederacy and to the world.

And now, sir, I come to vote for the crowning Ordinance of the whole—an Ordinance which, if passed by the Convention, will ratify and adopt the Permanent Constitution submitted to us by the Congress for the Government of the Confederate States, and will impart to that instrument force, effect and power, and make it the fundamental law by which this, and perhaps future generations in these States must be governed. I know the Ordinance will be passed by a majority vote. I am entirely satisfied that the Constitution will be ratified by this Convention, but my chief desire is that it may be ratified by a unanimous vote. I am aware that some members prefer to have it referred to another Convention, to be elected by the people, with a view to its ratification or rejection. But that, Mr. President, is not now a practical question. The gentleman from Tuscaloosa [Mr. Jemison] on yesterday submitted an amendment to the Ordinance to that effect, and it was rejected by the Convention. Now, the question is, will the Convention, by its own act, ratify and adopt for the people of Alabama, this Constitution? To the Constitution itself there seems to be no serious objection. All concur in opinion that it is an admirable document, and the only objection to its ratification is that it ought to be submitted to another Convention. With great respect for the opinions of those who entertain this view, I must say, in my judgment it ought not to cost the Ordinance a single vote. Those gentlemen have done all they fairly and legitimately could do to have the Constitution submitted to another Convention. They voted for the amendment proposed by the gentleman from Tuscaloosa, and when that amendment was pending, they urged their views upon the Convention with great force. They have made, each for himself, and caused it to be spread upon the journals, a record on this point, by which not only their constituents, but posterity, can make up a correct verdict. Is not this sufficient? And now, when the main question is presented, disconnected with amendments, may I not with confidence appeal to gentlemen to come as one man and make the vote for the Ordinance unanimous? I can well see how, on yesterday, gentlemen could with propriety urge the adoption of the amendment; but to-day, and since its defeat, I am unable to perceive how they can conscientiously refuse to vote for the adoption of the original Ordinance, especially when it is admitted they find no fault with the provisions of the Constitution.

No question is raised with regard to the power of this Convention to ratify and make of binding force and effect the Constitution, so far as Alabama is concerned. No one disputes our authority, and the exercise of it is a mere question of policy, about which, it seems to me, there should be but one opinion. Individuals as well as nations are more or less the creatures of circumstance, and it is often wise to do, and to do promptly, that which, under a different state of things, our judgment would condemn. By what state of affairs are we at present surrounded? The old Government has been thrown off, and only a provisional one erected. Alabama to-day is sojourning under the roof of a shanty half-way from the old and dilapidated house she has abandoned, to the new and splendid edifice erected for her reception. Shall we tarry longer on the way? Shall we pause in this critical condition to consult our fears, or to consider of reconstruction? Shall we stand still while the cloud of war gathers over our people, and make no haste to carry them under the protection of the best Constitution the world ever saw? Sir, this is not the time nor the occasion for us to pause, or to take counsel of our fears. The occasion calls for action—united, prompt, resolute, determined action. This, and this alone, can shield us from the fury of the impending storm. As for myself, I have embraced this great issue in good faith. I know full well the responsibility, as a member of this body, I have assumed, and, knowing it, I now declare that, "live or die, sink or swim, survive or perish," I am for the new Government, and so help me God, I intend to stand by, sustain and defend it to the end of the chapter.

Sir, let us not be divided. Divisions are dangerous and often ruinous. Unity of sentiment and unity of action inspires confidence, and vastly adds force and effect to a cause in which any people are engaged. Can we not, at this critical moment, comprehend this great truth and act upon it? We are passing through one of the most remarkable revolutions the people of this world ever saw. We are in the very midst of it, and shall we become divided amongst ourselves on a mere question of policy? Shall we falter or retrace our steps? Shall we turn back to the flesh pots of Egypt, and stamp the cause of the South with infamy? No, sir. Rather let us press forward and sustain with our votes this great magna-charta of the rights of white men, based, as it is, upon the great truth that theirs is the superior race; and let us as a unit evince to the world that we are determined to sustain and defend it through evil as well as good report, with our money, our honor and our lives.

MR. JEMISON said:

Mr. President—So far as I am concerned, I entertain no opposition to this Constitution. In all its features, as well as I am enabled to judge, upon a careful examination, it seems to be all that we could desire. Considering its every feature, with some amendments and evident improvements, it is fashioned after the Old Constitution, the one under which we have so long lived, and with the spirit and meaning of which our people have become so well acquainted; with such a Constitution, sir, so framed, retaining all the old guarantees of liberty, and others in addition, which adapts it better to our institutions, preserving and securing a pure Republican Government. With such a Constitution as this, presented to me for my sanction, I can find no reason to oppose it, but every reason to support it.

I hold it to be our high duty, whatever may have been our opinions on other subjects, and however much we may have differed with one another on points of policy, now to support the State under all her emergencies—to sustain her in all difficulties. And it must be a matter of congratulation to every friend to the State, to know that we stand pledged, voluntarily and solemnly, with life, liberty and property, to a man, thus to stand by our State. It cannot be forgotten with what solemnity these pledges were made, even before the passage of the Ordinance of Secession. I appeal to our friends here, that we may not be divided. We cannot separate ourselves from the destiny of our State; we are all in the same vessel, and, sink or swim, survive or perish, we must all share a common fate. I appeal to our friends the more earnestly, and with the more confidence, because this Constitution preserves all the best features of the old one, and, in form and shape, is unquestionably an improvement on its great pattern. I make this appeal to those friends with whom I have acted through all the trying and exciting scenes of this Convention, that they should not now be divided on this question. So far as we and our immediate constituents are concerned, we can safely appeal to the Record, and show that we have done all that men could do, in the honest discharge of our duties, to have this Constitution submitted to the people for their ratification. This is all that a just and generous constituency, such as we have, could require at our hands. Let us, one and all, come up to the support of the Government, such as it is.

I appeal to our friends, as citizens of Alabama, to pause a moment, and reflect in what a position they place themselves by voting now against the ratification. When asked by our constituents why we refused to ratify, our only answer could be—" *The Convention refused to submit it to the people.*" But the answer to that is—" You tried your best, and failed; the question then was, not whether the people should be allowed to vote to ratify, but whether the Constitution was such a one as ought to be ratified?" Then, it seems to me, that every man who is satisfied with the Constitution as it is, should now vote for its ratification by the Convention. It is true, that the Convention has refused to submit this Constitution for ratification to the people, or to a new Convention : but is that a sufficient reason for us to vote against the Ratification of an Instrument whose features we heartily indorse? I think not. For one, I shall feel it my duty to vote for it here, and to advocate it before the people, and thus to sustain my vote.

Suppose the people should be opposed to it? Shall we encourage the popular delusion? Is it not rather our duty—perhaps the highest duty that a representative ever has to perform—to check the popular impulse? Do any of us suppose that it would be better to inaugurate the reign of anarchy—to go home without any Constitution, and leave the country in a state of disorganization, than to have a Constitution fully and completely adopted, whose every feature is perfectly in accordance with our old form of Government, and to the form and shape of which there is no good objection? For one, I shall always be ready to sacrifice myself for the good of my country, and if that sacrifice has to be the result of combatting and beating back popular error, I shall not shrink from the performance of so high a duty.

But there is no danger of this. The people will be satisfied with the Constitution. Even those who opposed secession will prefer a Constitutional Government to an Anarchy. Let us, then, with this certainty before us—of not offending a generous constituency—let us all vote for this Constitution, and present to the world an unbroken front. We can say to our people, as we point to our Record, we obeyed your instructions as far as it was in our power, and when we could not carry out your positive will, we then felt it our duty to protect your interest, and to secure you from the evils of disorganization; therefore we voted for the Ratification.

I would not only be proud to see a unanimous vote in favor of the Ratification, but I would be proud of the privilege of marching up side by side with all of those who have not yet signed the Ordinance of Secession, and sign it. I have not signed it yet, but I intend to do so before this Convention adjourns. This, however, I do not regard as a matter of so overwhelming importance as the ratification of the Constitution; but I hope, and advise, that before we adjourn, we make even *that* unanimous.

Mr. JEMISON'S amendment was

"That the Permanent Constitution be referred to a Convention of the people of the State, the members of which shall be elected by the qualified electors for Members of the General Assembly, at such time and place as this Convention may hereafter prescribe."

Mr. BROOKS, the President [Mr. Webb in the Chair], moved to lay Mr. Jemison's amendment on the table; and the yeas and nays being demanded, the motion was lost.

Mr. DAVIS, of Madison, moved the previous question, and the question was: Shall the main question now be put? The yeas and nays were called, and the motion for the *previous question* was sustained.

Those who voted in the affirmative were—

Mr. President, Messrs. Baily, Barnes, Beck, Blue, Bolling, Bragg, Buford, Catterling, Clarke of Marengo, Clemens, Cochran, Crawford, Creech, Crook, Crumpler, Curtis, Daniel, Dargan, Davis of Covington, Davis of Madison, Davis of Pickens, Dowdell, Earnest, Foster, Gibbons, Gilchrist, Hawkins, Henderson of Macon, Henderson of Pike, Herndon, Howard, Jewett, Love, McLanahan, McPherson, McKinnie, Mitchell, Morgan, Owens, Phillips, Ralls, Rives, Ryan, Shortridge, Silver, Smith of Henry, Starke, Stone, Webb, Whatley, Williamson and Wood.

Those who voted in the negative were—

Messrs. Allen, Baker of Russell, Barclay, Brasher, Bulger, Coffey, Coman, Edwards, Ford, Forrester, Franklin, Gay, Green, Hood, Jemison, Jones of Fayette, Jones of Lauderdale, Johnson, Kimball, McLellan, Posey, Potter, Russell, Sandford, Sheets, Sheffield, Slaughter, Smith of Tuscaloosa, Stedham, Steele, Watkins, Watts, Whitlock, Wilson, Winston and Yelverton.

The question being on the adoption of the Ordinance of Ratification, it was adopted—yeas 87, nays 5.

Those who voted in the affirmatiue were—

The President, Messrs. Allen, Bailey, Baker of Russell, Barclay, Barnes, Beard, Beck, Blue, Bolling, Bragg, Brasher, Buford, Catterling, Clarke of Marengo, Cochran, Coffey, Coman, Crawford, Creech, Crook, Crumpler, Curtis, Daniel, Dargan, Davis of Covington, Davis of Madison, Davis of Pickens, Dowdell, Earnest, Edwards, Ford, Forrester, Foster, Gay, Gibbons, Gilchrist, Greene, Hawkins, Henderson of Macon, Henderson of Pike, Herndon, Hood, Howard, Jemison, Jewett, Jones of Lauderdale, Johnson, Kimball, Leonard, Love, McLanahan, McLellan, McPherson, McKinnie, Mitchell, Morgan, Owens, Phillips, Posey, Potter, Ralls, Rives, Russell, Ryan, Sanford, Sheffield, Shortridge, Silver, Slaughter, Smith of Henry, Smith of Tuscaloosa, Starke, Stedham, Steele, Stone, Taylor, Timberlake, Watkins, Watts, Webb, Whatley, Whitlock, Winston, Williamson, Wood and Yelverton.

Those who voted in the negative were—

Messrs. Bulger, Franklin, Jones of Fayette, Sheets and Wilson.

Mr. Clarke, of Lawrence did not vote, having paired off with Mr. Coleman.

When it was ascertained that only five had voted against the Ratification, there were some earnest speeches made, appealing for a unanimous vote, to those who had voted against the ratification. It was a solemn and impressive scene.

TURNING ARMS OVER TO THE CONFEDRATE STATES.

MR. COCHRAN'S Ordinance to turn over the arms, &c., to the Confederate States, before we had the Constitution submitted to us, being under consideration,

Mr. MORGAN said:

Mr. President—The question now presented to the Convention brings up to our view the relations of this State to the Provisional Government, and the discussion has also brought before us the probable results of the controversy between the Confederate States, and their former associates, in relation to our independence.

I do not attribute to any of those who may oppose this measure, a disposition to reconstruct the old Union, but on the contrary, I claim that their votes and conduct indicate no such purpose.

We were not all elected here, to secure the secession of Alabama from the Union; but we were all elected for the purpose of forming a Southern Confederacy, in the event the State should secede.

So far as I am advised of the condition of public opinion throughout the State, it is not only true that the people desire a Southern Confederacy; but that they demand it; and their greatest fear, as to the results of secession, was that we might not be able to unite with our sister Southern States in a new Government.

If there are still in this State, those who favor a reconstruction of the old Union, they will not persist in their purposes after the people have seen the advantages of our secession.

We have given two unanimous votes in this body. The first was that we would never submit to the election of a Black Republican to the Presidency. The other was given yesterday, when we transferred the jurisdiction over the Forts and Arsenal to the Provisional Government. Two great events, which proved that every pulsation of the political heart was responded to in both extremities of the State. I hope that at an early day we will join in one voice, and proclaim the new Constitution of the Confederate States of America, to the people, as worthy to be the repository of all our rights. I hope that this union of sentiment will be the final solution of all party differences as to the past, and the destruction of all parties in the State, except such as may arise in a generous emulation for the good of the people, and the prosperity of the new Republic.

The proposition now before us, is the same, in principle, as that adopted by the Convention on yesterday It is only applied to a different species of public property. We took this property with the intention of turning it over to the Confederate States, if it should be more needed by them than by ourselves; but we took it as a Sovereign State. The title is with us, and it rests with us to dispose of it. I admit no trust arising out of the capture for the actual benefit of any other Government, but insist that when we turn it over, the accountability is to this State, and rest to the United States. We will account to the United States for it, when they enter upon a general account with us of all unsettled matters, and not before. Our Commissioner did himself justice, and reflected honor on his State, when, after being denied an official audience, in reference to this matter, he notified the President of the United States that hereafter negotiations would be entertained on this subject by Alabama at her Capital, but at no other place.

By turning over the Forts to the Provisional Government of the Confederate States, we have recognized that Government as fully as we could. There is no question open about this matter. Indeed, we recognized it in advance of its formation, by an Ordinance providing for the extension of its juri,diction over us.

Fears were expressed at one time that the Provisional Government would be a despotism. These fears were based on a want of confidence in the love of our people, for the established doctrines of our Republican Institutions. I never, for a moment, felt any dread on this subject. We are fixed and immovable on this point. It would cause more bloodshed to destroy Constitutional liberty, than was ever suffered in efforts to build up Empires. But we are told this measure will be construed into a declaration of war against the Government of the United States. I can perceive no reason for that conclusion, and no force in the argument, that it has not already drawn from other facts. War has been only a question of construction for near three months. The facts, have existed, out of which war has seemed to frown upon the world. If war has not existed, it is only because we have construed that as consistent with peace which was susceptible of the other construction.

Has it been cowardice, that has given us the disposition to deliberate upon this matter? Time will soon prove that it is only our regard for the great interest of the world, and for the history of our race, that has thus far prevented a war. We have been determined to appeal for peace, until the sentiment of honor would impel us to shed the blood of our kindred, who may refuse to allow us to depart in peace.

I think we have now gone far enough. We have made the last overture which I am prepared to sustain. The rejection of the Commissioners of the Confederate States, will be the final blow to all hope of a peaceful settlement of these questions. I do not regard a war, even with the people of the North—lately our brethren—as the worst evil that could attend these times. The demoralization of this generation of people, if it should occur will descend upon their posterity. Odious blotches will be spread over the future history of our race, if we permit ourselves to settle down on dishonorable concessions, rather than make a stand for principle at the expense of suffering and blood.

I have always believed that disunion would bring war upon this generation or the next. I included all its worst horrors, except defeat, when I made a calculation that these were better than submission to wrong. In the end, disunion will bring good; it may be out of evil, but good will result from it. Great good has already resulted from it.

The Churches that have dissevered, and opened the way to our present condition, are stronger in the South, and have done more for morals, education, and christianity than they could have done, had they remained united. It will be so with the State. With a limited sphere of action, and a people united in sentiment and interest, we will be stronger than we could have been under the disadvantages of our enemy within our borders.

We need but one thing to-day to make us at once a great people, and it was that which brought our fathers from beneath the sceptre of King George. We need self-reliance. Should war ensue, we will write some new memorials of our prowess, which will prove to the world again, what we seem to have forgotten, (but other nations will never forget,) that we are capable of all that is required for defence or for aggression.

Southern battle-fields, from Cape Fear to the Rio Grande, have a place in the memory of those who would oppress us.

We have a Southern clime, which in other regions of the earth, has given to the world the brightest examples of valor and enterprize in war. We are not wanting in such examples here.

Give to our people the self-reliance that has reanimated France, under the inspiring genius of Louis Napoleon, and it would only require a chieftain bold and cruel enough to take the lead, to bring this Continent at our feet.

I would not have this condition of public sentiment to supplant our present disposition to do justice, and to discard every resentment that might incline us to a wrong step; but if we are to end this strife by an appeal to arms, I shall confidently expect to see its effects rapidly developed in the display of those characteristics, which will make for us a record in history, amongst the greatest nations of the earth.

With all the prejudice, (for it is nothing else,) prevailing against us, in the minds of distant nations, on account of our laws relating to slavery, they respect us for our firm refusal to be put under the ban of inequality by the people of the North.

All men know that a despotism which attempts to support its pretensions by fraud, is contemptible, and that such despots are cruel when in power, but cowards at heart.

It is impossible for our assailants to conceal the shallow tricks by which they have sought to overreach us. The enlightened world sees through the matter. The bosom of gallant France heaves with contempt at the despicable picture, and England regrets that her posterity can be so base.

How shall we stand in the opinion of mankind, if we allow our Commissioners to be rejected, and sit down with the guns of Sumter and Pickens, (names that crimson at the thought,) frowning defiance at our soldiery? We will be marked as a people who are afraid of a race of artful cowards.

Let us at once place the means of warfare in the hands of our President.

If you will follow him, he will lead us to victory. He has never left a battle-field except in triumph.

His cool courage, his skill in arms, and his unclouded judgment will save us in battle, and consecrate the victory to the good of the people. We may fail for a time, but we shall never be conquered. We may have many bloody battles; but in none of them will our people exhibit a want of patriotism or courage.

The cement of blood will consolidate us as a people, and our minds and our hearts will inspire and control the State.

We must admit the possiblity of war, and its near approach, so that we shall not be self-deceived. Let us insist for peace on proper terms, but spurn it, if it is to be purchased at the expense of justice, and the sacrifice of honor.

DIVORCE.

The Report of the Committee on the Constitution, restricting the granting of Divorces to the single ground of adultery, being under consideration,

MR. HENDERSON, of Macon, said:

Mr. President—I entirely concur with the Committee in the opinion, that the granting of Divorces should be limited to the single ground of incontinence. Marriage being exclusively an Institution of God, it is only subject to the sanctions and directions of His law. No authority less than that which established the Institution, can rightfully dissolve it. The integrity of the Institution rests upon Divine authority, and no human power can disannul, or abrogate it. No part of the law of God is more binding than this; and it were just as absurd for human legislation to attempt to set aside, or nullify the legislation of Heaven upon any other portion of the moral law, as this.

Let us look, Mr. President, at the consequences which have resulted within the last few years, from this departure of State legislation from the ancient landmarks. The facility with which Divorces are granted; the many grounds which legalize them, and the alarming extent to which they have multiplied, are a sad commentary upon the policy of our State in this respect. Upon looking into the Acts of the General Assembly of the State of Alabama for the last twenty years, and collecting the facts upon this subject, I find the following result:

For the years 1840–'41, there were 18 Divorces granted.
"   "   1843   "   " 12   "   "
"   "   1844   "   " 24   "   "
"   "   1845   "   " 32   "   "
"   "   1846   "   " 39   "   "
"   "   1847–'48, "   " 61   "   "
"   "   1849–'50, "   " 67   "   "
"   "   1851–'52, "   " 67   "   "
"   "   1853–'54, "   " 45   "   "
"   "   1855–'56, "   " 106   "   "
"   "   1857–'58, "   " 97   "   "
"   "   1859–'60, "   " 115   "   "

Making in all, (with the exception of the year 1842, which I cannot procure,) the alarming total of 683.

It will hence appear that this evil is increasing with an accelerated velocity. Twenty years ago, eighteen Divorces were granted at a single session of our State Legislature; last year, one hundred and fifteen were granted, showing an increase of more than six hundred per cent. in twenty years! Or if we make the allowance between annual sessions then, and biennial sessions now, the increase is still between three and four hundred per cent. Should not an evil, which is making such rapid strides into the very citadel of society, be promptly arrested, and that sacred Institution, the marriage relation, be restored to its ancient purity? God has thrown around it the most solemn sanctions of His law, and guarded it by the most terrible penalties. He who violates its sacred vows, incurs the most awful penalty which Heaven can inflict; he has his portion "in the lake that burns with fire and brimstone." The Divine Law-giver has thus indicated to us the estimate He placed upon this part of His law. And since the violation of this compact incurs the heaviest penalty, which is in the power of Almightiness to inflict, we may judge of the magnitude of the evil which the guilty party inflicts upon his own soul; upon the victim of his lust, upon the innocent family, upon society, and against God. For let it never be forgotten, that in addition to his own ruin, and all the sad consequences to his family and society, the wretched man has linked another immortal being to his own destiny; to be his accusing spirit in the world of dispair. He has committed *treason* against the most sacred compact which God ever formed for his rational creatures, and has incurred the penalty of treason; total isolation from all human society, and perpetual infamy so long as he lives. Branded with a mark of a Cain, he is consigned to a living death. This, therefore, is the only ground on which the law of God permits a Divorce.

I have said that marriage is a Divine, not a human Institution; and that Divorces for any cause other than the one prescribed by God himself—adultery—are unlawful. The Divine injunction is: "What God hath joined together, let no man put asunder." The interdiction is explicit, universal and solemnly imperative. "Let not *man*," whether as Husband, Judge, Legislator, or what not, "put asunder." It is an Ordinance of God, with which human power may not interfere.

"God never made His work for man to mend." The most sacred interests, as well as the highest happiness of the race, depend upon the maintenance of the integrity of the nuptial relation. Whatever of felicity earth has to bestow, is found in the cultivation of its hallowed virtues. It is the great heart of the entire social and political system. Where it is respected and preserved in its pristine purity, it sends the glow of health through every member of that system; but let it become vitiated or diseased, and the contagion spreads through all the extremities.

As the grounds of Divorce are increased, they become correspondingly numerous. When the National Assembly in France enacted a law permitting Divorces, they became, within three months, as numerous in Paris, as the registered marriages. There were upwards of *twenty thousand* Divorces granted in the empire in eighteen months! "This law," said a distinguished cotemporaneous French author, "will soon ruin the whole nation."

I have no doubt, that one of the most prolific causes of Divorce in this State, is, the practical operations of what is known as the "Woman's Law." As originally enacted, I do not doubt, it was intended to protect her rights. But results have shown, that what was intended for her protection, has proved to be the reverse. It creates, by law, two separate interests in the same family, where God designed there should be but one. In attempting to keep their interests separate and distinct, differences often arise, which the natural selfishness of the parties, and the course of events, intensifies, until final separation is accepted by the parties in preference to perpetual broils. Every lawyer who has had extensive practice, knows the sad truth of this statement. Divorces have more than doubled, in this State, since the passage of this law. It ought never to survive the meeting of another Legislature.

Again: were Divorces limited to the single ground indicated in the report of the Committee, the marriage contract would be framed with more caution. The parties would know that their interests and destiny through life were one; and this would lead them, on the one hand, to practice all those duties of affection and kindness essential to the perpetuity of the relation; and on the other, to exercise that generous forbearance towards each other's faults, which necessity required.

In conclusion, let me add, that as you diminish the grounds of Divorce, you increase the odium of the offense which legalizes it. Let the law embody the correct principle in this case, and public opinion will soon fix upon the guilty party the infamy which his crime so richly merits. The great alternative now is, will this Convention heed the authority of God? or the clamors of the disaffected—or, if you please, the unfortunate? Is it not better to allow this Institution to remain in all its purity, as it came from God, than to compromise it to human convenience? Whenever you relax a principle to fit a special case, you demoralize that principle. Nay, you admit a principle into human jurisprudence which would repeal every proposition of the decalogue which interest or prejudice may demand. You declare that God's law is not binding, when it conflicts with our convenience or supposed interest. In these perilous times, when every man feels a sense of dependence upon the Lord of Hosts, when our entire people are anxious to propitiate his smiles, is it safe for us to inaugurate our State policy, under the new order of things, with so manifest an infraction of His law, which is " holy, just and good ?" I hope, therefore, Mr. President, that the report of the Committee will pass, and that Alabama will place herself beside the only State of the late Union—South Carolina—in which the marriage relation is honored and respected as it came from the hand of God.

LAST DAY OF SECOND SESSION.

Mr. Davis, of Madison, offered a resolution, which was unanimously adopted, expressive of the sense of the Convention, of their high estimation of their Presiding officer, the Hon. Wm. M. Brooks, and returning the thanks of the Convention for the dignified and impartial manner in which he had presided over their deliberations.

Mr. Bulger offered the following resolution, which was unanimously adopted:

Resolved, That A. G. Horn, the Secretary, is entitled to the high regard of the members of the Convention, for the dignified and faithful manner in which he has discharged the arduous duties of his office.

Mr. Webb offered the following resolution, which was unanimously adopted:

Resolved, That the thanks of this Convention are hereby tendered to the Hon. Alex. B. Clitherall, for his faithful and able services, rendered as Assistant Secretary of this Convention.

[Mr. Clitherall had acted in this capacity voluntarily, for the few last days of the Convention, some of the Secretaries being sick.]

Mr. Morgan offered the following resolution:

Resolved, That the Convention tenders its thanks to Frank L. Smith, Assistant Secretary, for his faithful services, rendered at both its sessions.

Some little business was left unfinished, and still pending.

Mr. Brooks, the President, made a farewell speech, heartfelt and touching.

And when the clock struck *Two,* on Tuesday, March 21, 1861, the President announced that the Convention was adjourned, *sine die.*

The reader is referred to the following Appendix for the Reports of our Commissioners to other States. The documents are able, and eminently worthy of preservation.

APPENDIX.

REPORT OF HON. STEPHEN F. HALE, COMMISSIONER TO KENTUCKY, SUBMITTING THE CORRESPONDENCE BETWEEN THE COMMISSIONER FROM ALABAMA AND THE GOVERNOR OF KENTUCKY.

To His Excellency A. B. Moore,
   Governor of the State of Alabama:

 Under the authority of the Commission with which you honored me, I repaired to the city of Frankfort, in the State of Kentucky, on the 26th day of December last. The Legislature of that State was not in session, and no extra session had then been called by the Governor; so that I had no opportunity of conferring with the Legislative department of the Government. I was, however, most cordially received by the Governor, and immediately opened a consultation with His Excellency, Beriah McGoffin, the Governor of the State of Kentucky.

 The nature and result of that consultation is fully disclosed by the official correspondence between us, herewith submitted for your consideration. On the day after my arrival, the Governor issued his Proclamation convening the Legislature in extra session, on the 17th day of January, " to take into consideration the interests of the Commonwealth, as the same may be involved in, or connected with the present distracted condition of our common country."

 Receive assurances of the highest consideration and esteem of
    Your friend and obedient servant,
          S. F. HALE.

To His Excellency B. McGoffin, Governor of the Commonwealth of Kentucky:

I have the honor of placing in your hands herewith, a Commission from the Governor of the State of Alabama, accrediting me as a Commissioner from that State to the sovereign State of Kentucky, to consult in reference to the momentous issues now pending between the Northern and Southern States of this Confederacy. Although each State, as a sovereign political community, must finally determine these grave issues for itself, yet the identity of interest, sympathy, and institutions, prevailing alike in all the slaveholding States, in the opinion of Alabama, renders it proper that there should be a frank and friendly consultation, by each one, with her sister Southern States, touching their common grievances, and the measures necessary to be adopted to protect the interest, honor, and safety of their citizens.

I come, then, in a spirit of fraternity, as the Commissioner on the part of the State of Alabama, to confer with the authorities of this Commonwealth, in reference to the infraction of our Constitutional rights, wrongs done and threatened to be done, as well as the mode and measure of redress proper to be adopted by the sovereign States aggrieved, to preserve their sovereignty, vindicate their rights and protect their citizens. In order to a clear understanding of the appropriate remedy, it may be proper to consider the rights and duties, both of the State and citizen, under the Federal Compact, as well as the wrongs done and threatened.

I therefore submit, for the consideration of your Excellency, the following propositions, which I hope will command your assent and approval:

1. The people are the source of all political power; and the primary object of all good Governments is to protect the citizen in the enjoyment of life, liberty and property; and whenever any form of Government becomes destructive of these ends, it is the inalienable right, and the duty of the people to alter or abolish it.

2. The equality of all the States of this Confederacy, as well as the equality of rights of all the citizens of the respective States under the Federal Constitution, is a fundamental principle in the scheme of the Federal Government. The Union of these States under the Constitution, was formed "to establish justice, insure domestic tranquility, provide for the common defense, promote the general welfare, and secure the blessings of liberty to her citizens and their posterity;" and when it is perverted to the destruction of the equality of the States, or substantially fails to accomplish these ends, it fails to achieve the purposes of its creation, and ought to be dissolved.

3. The Federal Government results from a Compact entered into between separate sovereign and independent States, called the Constitution of the United States, and Amendments thereto, by which these sovereign States delegated certain specific powers to be used by that Government, for the common defense and general welfare of all the States and their citizens; and when these powers are abused, or used for the destruction of the rights of any State or its citizens, each State has an equal right to judge for itself, as well of the violations and infractions of that instrument, as of the mode and measure of redress; and if the interest or safety of her citizens demands it, may resume the powers she had delegated, without let or hindrance from the Federal Government, or any other power on earth.

4. Each State is bound in good faith to observe and keep, on her part, all the stipulations and covenants inserted for the benefit of other States in the Constitutional Compact—the only bond of Union by which the several States are bound together; and when persistently violated by one party to the prejudice of her sister States, ceases to be obligatory on the States so aggrieved, and they may rightfully declare the compact broken, the Union thereby formed dissolved, and stand upon their original rights, as sovereign and independent political communities; and further, that each citizen owes his primary allegiance to the State in which he resides, and hence it is the imperative duty of the State to protect him in the enjoyment of all his Constitutional rights, and see to it that they are not denied or withheld from him with impunity, by any other State or Government.

If the foregoing propositions correctly indicate the objects of this Government, the rights and duties of the citizen, as well as the rights, powers and duties of the State and Federal Government under the Constitution, the next inquiry is, what rights have been denied, what wrongs have been done, or threatened to be done, of which the Southern States, or the people of the Southern States, can complain?

At the time of the adoption of the Federal Constitution, African slavery existed in twelve of the thirteen States. Slaves are recognized both as property, and as a basis of political power, by the Federal Compact, and special provisions are made by that instrument for their protection as property. Under the influences of climate, and other causes, slavery has been banished from the Northern States, the slaves themselves have been sent to the Southern States, and there sold, and their price gone into the pockets of their former owners at the North. And in the meantime, African Slavery has not only become one of the fixed domestic institutions of the Southern States, but forms an important element of their political power, and constitutes the most valuable species of their property—worth, according to recent estimates, not less than four thousand millions of dollars; forming, in fact, the basis upon which rests the prosperity and wealth of most of these States, and supplying the commerce of the world with its richest freights, and furnishing the manufactories of two continents with the raw material, and their operatives with bread. It is upon this gigantic interest, this peculiar institution of the South, that the Northern States and their people have been waging an unrelenting and fanatical war for the last quarter of a century. An institution with which is bound up, not only the wealth and prosperity of the Southern people, but their very existence as a political community. This war has been waged in every way that human ingenuity, urged on by fanaticism, could suggest. They attack us through their literature, in their schools, from the hustings, in their legislative halls, through the public press, and even their courts of justice forget the purity of their judicial ermine, to strike down the rights of the Southern slave-holder, and override every barrier which the Constitution has erected for his protection; and the sacred desk is desecrated to this unholy crusade against our lives, our property, and the Constitutional rights guaranteed to us by the Compact of our Fathers. During all this time the Southern States have freely conceded to the Northern States, and the people of those States, every right secured to them by the Constitution, and an equal interest in the common Territories of the Government; protected the lives and property of their citizens of every kind, when brought within Southern jurisdiction; enforced through their courts, when necessary, every law of Congress passed for the protection of Northern property, and submitted, ever since the foundation of the Government' with scarcely a murmur, to the protection of their shipping, manufacturing and commercial interest, by odious bounties, discriminating tariffs, and unjust navigation-laws, passed by the Federal Government to the prejudice and injury of their own citizens.

The law of Congress for the rendition of fugitive slaves, passed in pursuance of an express provision of the Constitution, remains almost a dead letter upon the Statute Book. A majority of the Northern States, through their legislative enactments, have openly nullified it, and impose heavy fines and penalties upon all persons who aid in enforcing this law; and some of those States declare the Southern slave-holder, who goes within their jurisdiction to assert his legal rights under the Constitution, guilty of a high crime, and affix imprisonment in the penitentiary as the penalty. The

Federal officers who attempt to discharge their duties under the law, as well as the owner of the slave, are set upon by mobs, and are fortunate if they escape without serious injury to life or limb; and the State authorities, instead of aiding in the enforcement of this law, refuse the use of their jails, and by every means which unprincipled fanaticism can devise, give countenance to the mob, and aid the fugitive to escape. Thus, there are annually large amounts of property actually stolen away from the Southern States, harbored and protected in Northern States, and by their citizens. And when a requisition is made for the thief by the Governor of a Southern State upon the Executive of a Northern State, in pursuance of the express conditions of the Federal Constitution, he is insultingly told that the felon has committed no crime—and thus the criminal escapes, the property of the citizen is lost, the sovereignty of the State is insulted—and there is no redress, for the Federal Courts have no jurisdiction to award a mandamus to the Governor of a sovereign State, to compel him to do an official Executive act, and Congress, if disposed, under the Constitution has no power to afford a remedy. These are wrongs under which the Southern people have long suffered, and to which they have patiently submitted, in the hope that a returning sense of justice would prompt the people of the Northern States to discharge their Constitutional obligations, and save our common country. Recent events, however, have not justified their hopes; the more daring and restless fanatics have banded themselves together, have put in practice the terrible lessons taught by the timid, by making an armed incursion upon the sovereign State of Virginia, slaughtering her citizens, for the purpose of exciting a servile insurrection among her slave population, and arming them for the destruction of their own masters. During the past summer, the Abolition incendiary has lit up the prairies of Texas, fired the dwellings of the inhabitants, burnt down whole towns and laid poison for her citizens—thus literally executing the terrible denunciations of fanaticism against the slave-holder—"Alarm to their sleep, fire to their dwellings, and poison to their food."

The same fell spirit, like an unchained demon, has for years swept over the plains of Kansas, leaving death, desolation and ruin in its track. Nor is this the mere ebullition of a few half-crazy fanatics, as is abundantly apparent from the sympathy manifested all over the North, where, in many places, the tragic death of John Brown, the leader of the raid upon Virginia, who died upon the gallows a condemned felon, is celebrated with public honors, and his name canonized as a martyr to liberty ; and many, even of the more conservative papers of the Black Republican school, were accustomed to speak of his murderous attack upon the lives of the unsuspecting citizens of Virginia, in a half-sneering and half-apologetic tone. And what has the Federal Government done in the meantime to protect slave property upon the common Territories of the Union? Whilst a whole squadron of the American Navy is maintained on the coast of Africa, at an enormous expense, to enforce the execution of the laws against the slave trade—and properly, too—and the whole navy is kept afloat to protect the lives and property of American citizens upon the high seas, not a law has been passed by Congress, or an arm raised by the Federal Government, to protect the slave property of citizens from Southern States upon the soil of Kansas—the common Territory and common property of the citizens of all the States—purchased alike by their common treasure, and held by the Federal Government, as declared by the Supreme Court of the United States, as the trustee for all their citizens; but, upon the contrary, a Territorial Government, created by Congress, and supported out of the common treasury, under the influence and control of Emigrant Aid Societies and Abolition emissaries, is permitted to pass laws excluding and destroying all that species of property within her limits—thus ignoring, on the part of the Federal Government, one of the fundamental principles of all good Governments, the duty to protect the property of the citizen, and wholly refusing to maintain the equal rights of the States and the citizens of the States upon their common Territories.

As the last and crowning act of insult and outrage upon the people of the South, the citizens of the Northern States, by overwhelming majorities, on the 6th day of November last, elected Abraham Lincoln and Hannibal Hamlin, President and Vice President of the United States. Whilst it may be admitted that the mere election of any man to the Presidency, is not, *per se*, a sufficient cause for a dissolution of the Union; yet, when the issues upon, and circumstances under which he was elected, are properly appreciated and understood, the question arises whether a due regard to the interest, honor, and safety of their citizens, in view of this and all the other antecedent wrongs and outrages, do not render it the imperative duty of the Southern States to resume the powers they have delegated to the Federal Government, and interpose their sovereignty for the protection of their citizens.

What, then are the circumstances under which, and the issues upon which he was elected? His own declarations, and the current history of the times, but too plainly indicate he was elected by a Northern sectional vote, against the most solemn warnings and protestations of the whole South. He stands forth as the representative of the fanaticism of the North, which, for the last quarter of a century, has been making war upon the South, her property, her civilization, her institutions, and her interests; as the representative of that party which overrides all Constitutional barriers, ignores the obligation of official oaths, and acknowledges allegiance to a higher law than the Constitution, striking down the sovereignty and equality of the States, and resting its claims to popular favor upon the one dogma, the Equality of the Races, white and black.

It was upon this acknowledgement of allegiance to a higher law, that Mr. Seward rested his claims to the Presidency, in a speech made by him in Boston, before the election. He is the exponent, if not the author, of the doctrine of the Irrepressible Conflict between freedom and slavery, and proposes that the opponents of slavery shall arrest its further *expansion, and by Congressional Legislation exclude it from the common Territories of the Federal Government, and place it where the public mind shall rest in the belief that it is in the course of ultimate extinction.*

He claims for free negroes the right of suffrage, and an equal voice in the Government—in a word, all the rights of citizenship, although the Federal Constitution, as construed by the highest judicial tribunal in the world, does not recognize Africans imported into this country as slaves, or their descendants, whether free or slaves, as citizens.

These were the issues presented in the last Presidential canvass, and upon these the American people passed at the ballot-box.

Upon the principles then announced by Mr. Lincoln and his leading friends, we are bound to expect his administration to be conducted. Hence it is, that in high places, among the Republican party, the election of Mr. Lincoln is hailed, not simply as a change of Administration, but as the inauguration of new principles, and a new theory of Government, and even as the downfall of slavery. Therefore it is that the election of Mr. Lincoln cannot be regarded otherwise than a solemn declaration, on the part of a great majority of the Northern people, of hostility to the South, her property and her institutions—nothing less than an open declaration of war—for the triumph of this new theory of Government destroys the property of the South, lays waste her fields, and inaugurates all the horrors of a San Domingo servile insurrection, consigning her citizens to assassinations, and her wives and daughters to pollution and violation, to gratify the lust of half-civilized Africans. Especially is this true in the cotton-growing States, where, in many localities, the slave outnumbers the white population ten to one.

If the policy of the Republicans is carried out, according to the programme indicated by the leaders of the party, and the South submits, degradation and ruin must overwhelm alike all classes of citizens in the Southern States. The slave-holder and non-slave-holder must ultimately share the same fate—all be degraded to a position of equality with free negroes, stand side by side with them at the polls, and fraternize in all the social relations of life; or else there will be an eternal war of races, desolating the land with blood, and utterly wasting and destroying all the resources of the country.

Who can look upon such a picture without a shudder? What Southern man, be he slave-holder or non-slave-holder, can without indignation and horror contemplate the triumph of negro equality, and see his own sons and daughters, in the not distant future, associating with free negroes upon terms of political and social equality, and the white man stripped, by the Heaven-daring hand of fanaticism of that title to superiority over the black race which God himself has bestowed? In the Northern States, where free negroes are so few as to form no appreciable part of the community, in spite of all the legislation for their protection, they still remain a degraded caste, excluded by the ban of society from social association with all but the lowest and most degraded of the white race. But in the South, where in many places the African race largely predominates, and, as a consequence, the two races would be continually pressing together, amalgamation, or the extermination of the one or the other, would be inevitable. Can Southern men submit to such degredation and ruin? God forbid that they should.

But, it is said, there are many Constitutional, conservative men at the North, who sympathize with and battle for us. That is true; but they are utterly powerless, as the late Presidential election unequivocally shows, to breast the tide of fanaticism that threatens to roll over and crush us. With them it is a question of principle, and we award to them all honor for their loyalty to the Constitution of our Fathers. But their defeat is not their ruin. With us it is a question of self-preservation—our lives, our property, the safety of our homes and our hearthstones—all that men hold dear on earth, is involved in the issue. If we triumph, vindicate our rights and maintain out institutions, a bright and joyous future lies before us. We can clothe the world with our staple, give wings to her commerce, and supply with bread the starving operative in other lands, and at the same time preserve an institution that has done more to civilize and Christianize the heathen than all human agencies beside—an institution alike beneficial to both races, ameliorating the moral, physical and intellectual condition of the one, and giving wealth and happiness to the other. If we fail, the light of our civilization goes down in blood, our wives and our little ones will be driven from their homes by the light of our own dwellings. The dark pall of barbarism must soon gather over our sunny land, and the scenes of West India emancipation, with its attendant horrors and crimes (that monument of British fanaticism and folly), be re-enacted in our own land upon a more gigantic scale.

Then, is it not time we should be up and doing, like men who know their rights and dare maintain them? To whom shall the people of the Southern States look for the protection of their rights, interests and honor? We answer, to their own sons and their respective States. To the States, as we have seen, under our system of Government, is due the primary allegiance of the citizen; and the correlative obligation of protection devolves upon the respective States—a duty from which they cannot escape, and which they dare not neglect without a violation of all the bonds of fealty that hold together the citizen and the sovereign.

The Northern States and their citizens have proved recreant to their obligations under the Federal Constitution; they have violated that Compact, and refused to perform their covenants in that behalf.

The Federal Government has failed to protect the rights and property of the citizens of the South, and is about to pass into the hands of a party pledged for the destruction, not only of their rights and their property, but the equality of the States ordained by the Constitution, and the heaven-ordained superiority of the white over the black race. What remains, then, for the Southern States, and the people of these States, if they are loyal to the great principles of civil and religious liberty, sanctified by the sufferings of a seven-year's war, and baptized with the blood of the Revolution? Can they permit the rights of their citizens to be denied and spurned? their property spirited away, their own sovereignty violated, and themselves degraded to the position of mere dependencies, instead of sovereign States? or shall each for itself, judging of the infractions of the Constitutional Compact, as well as the mode and measure of redress, declare that the covenants of that sacred instrument, in their behalf, and for the benefit of their citizens, have been wilfully, deliberately, continuously and persistently broken and violated by the other parties to the compact, and that they and their citizens are therefore absolved from all further obligations to keep and perform the covenants thereof, resume the powers delegated to the Federal Government, and, as sovereign States, form other relations for the protection of their citizens and the discharge of the great ends of Government? The Union of these States was one of fraternity as well as equality; but what fraternity now exists between the citizens of the two sections? Various religious associations, powerful in numbers and influence, have been broken asunder, and the sympathies that bound together the people of the several States, at the time of the formation of the Constitution, has ceased to exist, and feelings of bitterness, and even hostility, have sprung up in its place. How can this be reconciled, and a spirit of fraternity established? Will the people of the North cease to make war upon the institution of Slavery, and award to it the protection guaranteed by the Constitution? The accumulated wrongs of many years, the late action of their members in Congress refusing every measure of justice to the South, as well as the experience of all the past, answers, *No, never!*

Will the South give up the institution of slavery, and consent that her citizens be stripped of their property, her civilization destroyed, the whole land laid waste by fire and sword? It is impossible; she can not, she will not. Then why attempt longer to hold together hostile States under the stipulations of a violated Constitution? It is impossible; disunion is inevitable. Why then wait longer for the consummation of a result that must come? Why waste further time in expostulations and appeals to Northern States and their citizens, only to be met, as we have been for years past, by renewed insults and repeated injuries? Will the South be better prepared to meet the emergency when the North shall be strengthened by the admission of the new territories of Kansas, Nebraska, Washington, Jefferson, Nevada, Idaho, Chippewa, and Arizonia, as non-slaveholding States, as we are warned from high sources will be done within the next four years, under the administration of Mr. Lincoln? Can the true men at the North ever make a more powerful or successful rally for the preservation of our rights and the Constitution, than they did in the last Presidential contest? There is nothing to inspire a hope that they can.

Shall we wait until our enemies shall possess themselves of all the powers of the Government? until Abolition Judges are on the Supreme Court bench, Abolition Collectors at every port, and Abolition Postmasters in every town, secret mail agents traversing the whole land, and a subsidized Press established in our midst to demoralize our people? Will we be stronger then, or better prepared to meet the struggle, if a struggle must come? No, verily! When that time shall come, well may our adversaries laugh at our folly, and deride our impotence. The deliberate judgment of Alabama, as indicated by the Joint Resolutions of her General Assembly, approved February 24, 1860, is, that prudence, patriotism, and loyalty to all the great principles of civil liberty incorporated in our Constitution, and consecrated by the memories of the past, demand that all the Southern States should now resume their delegated powers, maintain the rights, interests and honor of their citizens, and vindicate their own sovereignty. And she most earnestly, but respectfully, invites her sister sovereign State, Kentucky, who so gallantly vindicated the sovereignty of the States in 1798, to the consideration of these grave and vital questions, hoping she may concur with the State of Alabama in the conclusions to which she has been driven by the impending dangers that now surround the Southern States. But if, on mature deliberation, she dissents on any point from the conclusions to which the State of Alabama has arrived, on behalf of that State I most respectfully ask a declaration by this venerable Commonwealth of her conclusions and position on all the issues discussed in this communication; and Alabama most respectfully urges upon the people and authorities of Kentucky the startling truth that *submission or acquiescence on the part of the Southern States, at this perilous hour, will enable Black Republicanism to redeem all its nefarious pledges, and accomplish all its flagitious ends;* and that hesitation or delay in their action will be misconceived and misconstrued by their adversaries, and ascribed, not to that elevated patriotism that would sacrifice all but their honor to save the Union of their Fathers, but to division and dissension among themselves, and their consequent weakness; that prompt, bold and decided action is demanded alike by prudence, patriotism and the safety of their citizens.

Permit me, in conclusion, on behalf of the State of Alabama, to express my high gratification at the cordial manner in which I have been received, as her Commissioner, by the authorities of the State of Kentucky, as well as the profound personal gratification which, as a son of Kentucky, born and reared within her borders, I feel, at the manner in which I, as the Commissioner from the State of my adoption, have been received and treated by the authorities of the State of my birth. Please accept assurances of the high consideration and esteem of

Your obedient servant, etc.,   S. F. HALE,
    Commissioner from the State of Alabama.
Frankfort, December 27, 1860.

EXECUTIVE DEPARTMENT, }
FRANKFORT, KY., December 28, 1860. }

To Hon. S. F. HALE,

Commissioner from the State of Alabama :

Your communication of the 27th inst., addressed to me by authority of the State of Alabama, has been attentively read.

I concur with you in the opinion that the grave political issues yet pending and undetermined, between the slaveholding and non-slave-holding States of the Confederacy, are of a character to render eminently proper and highly important a full and frank conference on the part of the Southern members, identified, as they undoubtedly are, by a common interest, bound together by mutual sympathies, and with the whole social fabric resting on homogeneous institutions. And coming, as you do, in a spirit of fraternity, by virtue of a commission from a sister Southern State, to confer with the authorities of this State in reference to the measures necessary to be adopted, to protect the interests and maintain the honor and safety of the States and their citizens, I extend you a cordial welcome to Kentucky.

You have not exaggerated the grievous wrongs, injuries and indignities to which the slave-holding States and their citizens have long submitted, with a degree of patience and forbearance justly attributable alone to that elevated patriotism and devotion to the Union which would lead them to sacrifice well nigh all, save honor, to recover the Government to its original integrity of administration, and perpetuate the Union upon the basis of equality established by the founders of the Republic. I may even add, that the people of Kentucky, by reason of their geographical position, and nearer proximity to those who seem so madly bent upon the destruction of our Constitutional guarantees, realize yet more fully than our friends farther South, the intolerable wrongs and menacing dangers you have so elaborately recounted. Nor are you, in my opinion, more keenly alive than are the people of this State to the importance of arresting the insane crusade so long waged against our institutions and our society by measures which shall be certainly effective. The rights of African slavery in the United States, and the relations of the Federal Government to it, as an institution in the States and Territories, most assuredly demand, at this time, explicit definition and final recognition by the North. The slaveholding States are now impelled by the very highest law of self-preservation to demand that this settlement should be concluded, upon such a basis as shall not only conserve the institution in localities where it is now recognized, but secure its expansion, under no other restrictions than those which the laws of nature may throw around it. That un necessary conflict between free labor and slave labor, but recently inaugurated by the Republican party, as an element in our political struggles, must end ; and the influence of soil, of climate and local interests, left unaided and unrestricted save by Constitutional limitations, to control the extension of slavery over the public domain. The war upon our social institutions and their guaranteed immunities, waged through the Northern press, religious and secular, and now threatened to be conducted by a dominant political organization, through the agency of State Legislatures and the Federal Government, must be ended. Our safety, our honor, and our self-preservation, alike demand that our interests be placed beyond the reach of further assault.

The people of Kentucky may differ variously touching, the nature and theory of our complex system of Government: but when called upon to pass upon these questions at the polls, I think such an expression would develop no material variance of sentiment touching the wrongs you recite, and the necessity of their prompt adjustment. They fully realize the fatal result of longer forbearance, and appreciate the peril of submission at this juncture. Kentucky would leave no effort untried to preserve the Union of the States upon the basis of the Constitution as we construe it; but Kentucky will never submit to wrong and dishonor, let resistance cost what it may. Unqualified acquiescence in the administration of the Government, upon the Chicago Platform, in view of the movements already inaugurated at the South, and the avowed purposes of the representative men of the Republican party, would, I feel assured, receive no favor in this State; whether her citizens shall, in the last resort, throw themselves upon the right of revolution as the inherent right of a free people never surrendered, or shall assert the doctrine of secession, can be of little practical import. When the time for action comes—and it is now fearfully near at hand—our people will be found rallied as a unit under the flag of resistance to intolerable wrong; and being thus consolidated in feeling and action, I may well forego any discussion of the abstract theories to which one party or another may hold to cover their resistance.

It is true that, as sovereign political communities, the States must determine, each for itself, the grave issues now presented; and it may be that, when driven to the dire extremity of severing their relations with the Federal Government, formal independent separate State action will be proper and necessary. But resting, as do these political communities, upon a common social organization, constituting the sole object of attack and invasion, confronted by a common enemy, encompassed by a common peril—in a word, involved in one common cause—it does seem to me that the mode and manner of defense and redress, should be determined in a full and free conference of all the Southern States, and that their mutual safety requires full coöperation in carrying out the measures there agreed upon. The source whence oppression is now to be apprehended is an organized power, a political Government in operation, to which resistance, though ultimately successful—and I do not for a moment question the issue—might be costly and destructive. We should look these facts in the face, nor close our eyes to what we may reasonably expect to encounter. I have therefore thought that a due regard to the opinions of all the slaveholding States, would require that those measures which concern all alike, and must ultimately involve all, should be agreed upon in common convention, and sustained by united action.

I have before expressed the belief and confidence, and do not now totally yield the hope, that if such a Convention of delegates from the slave-holding States be assembled, and, after calm deliberation, present to the political party now holding the dominance of power in the Northern States, and soon to assume the reins of national power, the firm alternative of ample guarantees to all our rights, and security for future immunity, or resistance, our just demands would be conceded, and the Union be perpetuated stronger than before. Such an issue, so presented to the Congress of the United States, and to the Legislatures and people of the Northern States [and it is practicable, in abundant time before the Government has passed into other hands], would come with a moral force which, if not potent to control the votes of the representative men, might produce a voice from their constituents which would influence them. But if it fail, our cause would emerge, if possible, stronger, fortified by the approbation of the whole conservative sentiment of the country, and supported by a host of Northern friends, who would prove, in the ultimate issue, most valuable allies. After such an effort, every man in the slave-holding States would feel satisfied that all had been done which could be done, to preserve the legacy bequeathed us by the patriots of '76 and the statesmen of '89, and the South would stand in solid, unbroken phalanx, a unit. In the brief time left, it seems to me impracticable to effect this object through the agency of Commissioners sent to the different States. A Convention of authorized delegates is the true mode of bringing about coöperation among the Southern States, and to that movement I would respectfully ask your attention, and through you solicit the coöperation of Alabama. There is yet another subject upon which the very highest considerations appeal for an united Southern expression. On the 4th of March next, the Federal Government, unless contingencies now unlooked for occur, will pass into the control of the Republican party. So far as the policy of the incoming Administration is foreshadowed in the antecedents of the President elect, in the enunciations of its representative men, and the avowals of the press, it will be to ignore the acts of sovereignty thus proclaimed by Southern States, and of coercing the continuance of the Union. Its inevitable result will be civil war, of the most fearful and revolting character. Now, however the people of the South may differ as to the mode and measure of redress, I take it that the fifteen slave-holding States are united in opposition to such a policy, and would stand in solid column to resist the application of force by the Federal authority to coerce the seceding States. But it is of the utmost importance that, before such a policy is attempted to be inaugurated, the voice of the South should be heard in potential, official, and united protest. Possibly the incoming Administration would not be so dead to reason as, after such an expression, to persist in throwing the country into civil war, and we may, therefore, avert the calamity. An attempt "to enforce the laws," by blockading two or three Southern States would be regarded as quite a different affair from a declaration of war against thirteen millions of freemen; and if Mr. Lincoln and his advisers be made to realize that such would be the issue of the "force policy," it will be abandoned. Should we not realize to our enemies that consequence, and avert the disastrous results? But if our enemies be crazed by victory and power, and madly persist in their purpose, the South will be better prepared to resist.

You ask the coöperation of the Southern States in order to redress our wrongs: so do we. You have no hope of a redress in the Union. We yet look hopefully to assurances that a powerful reaction is going on at the North. You seek a remedy in secession from the Union. We wish the united action of the slave States, assembled in Convention within the Union. You would act separately: we unitedly. If Alabama and the other slave States would meet us in Convention, say at Nashville, or elsewhere, as early as the 5th day of February, I do not doubt that we would agree, in forty-eight hours, upon such reasonable guarantees, by way of amendment to the Constitution of the United States, as would command at least the approbation of our numer ous friends in the free States, and by giving them time to make the question with the people there, such a reaction in public opinion might yet take place as to secure us our rights, and save the Government. If the effort failed, the South would be united to a man, the North divided, the horrors of civil war would be averted— if anything can avert the calamity. And if that be not possible, we would be in a better position to meet the dreadful collision. By such action, too, if it failed to preserve the Government, the basis of another Confederacy would have been agreed upon, and the new Government would, in this mode, be launched into operation much more speedily and easily than by the action you propose.

In addition to the foregoing, I have the honor to refer you to my letter of the 16th ult., to the editor of the Yeoman, and to my letter to the Governors of the slave States, dated the 9th December, herewith transmitted to you, which, together with what I have said in this communication, embodies, with all due deference to the opinions of others, in my judgment, the principles, policy, and position which the slave States ought to maintain.

The Legislature of Kentucky will assemble on the 17th of January, when the sentiment of the State will doubtless find official expression. Meantime, if the action of Alabama shall be arrested until the Conference she has sought can be concluded by communication with that department of the Government, I shall be pleased to transmit to the Legislature your views. I regret to have seen, in the recent messages of two or three of our Southern sister States, a recommendation of the passage of laws prohibiting the purchase, by the citizens of those States, of the slaves of the border slaveholding States. Such a course is not only liable to the objection so often urged by us against the Abolitionists of the North, of an endeavor to prohibit the slave trade between the States, but is likewise wanting in that fraternal feeling which should be common to States which are identified in their institutions and interests. It affords me pleasure, however, to add, as an act of justice to your State, that I have seen no indication of such a purpose on the part of Alabama. It would certainly be considered an act of injustice, for the border slaveholding States to prohibit, by their legislation, the purchase of the products of the cotton-growing States, even though it be founded upon the mistaken policy of protection to their own interests.

I cannot close this correspondence without again expressing to you my gratification in receiving you as the honored Commissioner from your proud and chivalrous State, and at your courteous, able, dignified and manly bearing in discharging the solemn and important duties which have been assigned to you.

I have the honor to be, with sentiments of high consideration,
Your friend and obedient servant,
B. MAGOFFIN.

FRANKFORT, KY., Jan. 1, 1861.

To His Excellency B. Magoffin, Governor of the Commonwealth of Kentucky:

Your communication of the 28th ult., in reply to the communication I, as the Commissioner from the State of Alabama, had the honor of submitting for your consideration, on the 27th, has just been placed in my hands, and shall promptly be laid before the Governor of Alabama. Be assured that the communication of your Excellency will receive, from the authorities of the State of Alabama, that full and candid consideration due, as well to the magnitude of the subject discussed, as the high source from which it emanates; and I doubt not, that in the hour of trial, Kentucky and Alabama will be found standing side by side in defense of the rights, interests and honor of their citizens.

In closing our official correspondence, permit me again to express my high appreciation of the cordial welcome extended to me as the Commissioner from Alabama, as well as your many acts of courtesy and kindness to me personally, during my sojourn at your capital.

And accept assurances of the high consideration and esteem of
Your friend and obedient servant,
S. F. HALE.

REPORT OF THE HON. JOHN A. ELMORE, COMMISSIONER TO SOUTH CAROLINA.

MONTGOMERY, January 5, 1861.

His Excellency, A. B. Moore:

Sir: I was honored by your Excellency with the appointment of Commissioner to the State of South Carolina, to confer with her Governor and her Convention, about to assemble on the 17th of December last, on the political condition of the slaveholding States of the Union, in the present crisis. The principal object of my mission was for consultation with that State, through her

Governor and Convention, by a full and free intercharge of opinion, as to the best course to be pursued, in view of the dangers impending over the Southern States, to avert those dangers, and to unite those States in a common union in defence of their rights.

I left this place on the 13th December last, and arrived in Columbia, the place of meeting of the South Carolina Convention, and where the Legislature was still in session, on the 14th, about 5 o'clock, P. M. The lateness of the hour of my arrival, prevented my calling upon the Governor on that evening. My arrival had been expected, and immediately on reaching my hotel I was called on by numerous persons, members of the Legislature and others, who were filled with the deepest anxiety to ascertain the feeling of this State, and who were greatly cheered by the intelligence I felt authorized to communicate.

On the morning of the 15th, I waited on the Governor, [Wm. H. Gist,] at his house, and presented my credentials. I was warmly received by him, who entered into a full and frank communication on the objects of my mission. The state of public sentiment in South Carolina and other slaveholding States, with the Governors of several of which he had been in correspondence, and also in the preparation which South Carolina had made, and was making to maintain her sovereignty and independence, if on her secession from the Union, the Federal Government should attempt to coerce her back into the Union by force.

From the moment of my arrival, I was in constant communication with members of the Legislature, and other distinguished men in that State, and with most of the Delegates to the Convention as they arrived, and sought a full consultation and interchange of opinion on the matters with which I was charged. On the 15th December, the Hon. Mr. Hooker, the Commissioner from the State of Mississippi to South Carolina, arrived in Columbia, charged with the same objects of consultation as myself, with whom I freely conferred on the nature of our mission.

The result of all the information thus obtained, confirmed the opinion entertained by me before I left this place, and in which I was pleased to find that your Excellency concurred. That opinion was, that the only course to unite the Southern States in any plan of coöperation, which could promise safety, was for South Carolina to take the lead, and secede at once from the Federal Union without delay or hesitation; and that any other plan would prevent *coöperation for submission* and *not for resistance.* That the only effective plan of resistance by *coöperation* must ensue after one State had seceded and presented the issue, when the plain question must be presented to the other Southern States, whether they would stand by the seceding State engaged in a common cause, or abandon her to the fate of coercion by the arms of the Government of the United States.

In this opinion, Mr. Hooker also concurred, and on all proper occasions I expressed it not only as my own, but as the opinion of your Excellency.

The Convention was organized on the 17th of December, and on that night Mr. Hooker and myself were invited by it to address that body, which we did. In my speech, I announced to the Convention the character in which I appeared before it, and the objects for which I had been sent, and in substance told the Convention what I had previously said to the members individually, announcing as my opinion, as supported by that of your Excellency, that Alabama, through her Convention, would unquestionably follow the great example set by South Carolina, and that there would be a large majority in our Convention in favor of the secession of our State.

Mr. Hooker expressed the same opinion, and gave the Convention assurances of a large majority in Mississippi in favor of her secession.

On the day of its organization, the Convention adopted a Resolution, that the State of South Carolina forthwith secede from the Federal Union, which passed unanimously, and appointed a Committee to draft and prepare an Ordinance of Secession, and then adjourned to Charleston, to meet the next day at 4, P. M. I regret that I cannot furnish your Excellency with a copy of this Resolution; but on application to the Clerk of the Convention in Charleston for a copy, I was informed by him that owing to the haste in which the Convention had removed from Columbia, some of the papers were mislaid, and this among them, and none of the proceedings of the first day had been or could be at the time printed.

I left Columbia on the 18th at 2, P. M., and reached Charleston about 10, P. M.

No measures of importance were adopted by the Convention until the 20th of December, when the Ordinance of Secession was reported by the Committee, and adopted unanimously, as follows:

AN ORDINANCE

To dissolve the Union between the State of South Carolina and other States united with her under the compact entitled "The Constitution of the United States of America."

We, the People of the State of South Carolina, in Convention assembled do declare and ordain, and it is hereby declared and ordained,

That the Ordinance adopted by us in Convention, on the twenty-third day of May, in the year of our Lord one thousand seven hundred and eighty-eight, whereby the Constitution of the United States of America was ratified, and also all Acts, and parts of Acts, of the General Assembly of this State, ratifying amendments of the said Constitution, are hereby repealed; and that the Union now subsisting between South Carolina and other States, under the name of "The United States of America," is hereby dissolved.

And on its passage the following Resolution was adopted:

Resolved, That the Ordinance be engrossed, under the direction of the Attorney General and the Solicitors, upon parchment, and signed by the President and members of the Convention at the Institute Hall, in the alphabetical order of Election Districts, and be deposited in the archieves of the State.

At 7, P. M., on the same day the Ordinance engrossed on parchment, with the great seal of the State attached, was signed by the President and every member of the Convention.

Many questions were submitted to the Convention, on which no definite action has been taken that I am aware of.

I have authentic information that the Convention passed the following Ordinances and Resolutions:

1—One, to alter the Constitution of the State of South Carolina in respect to the oath of office

2—One, the appointment of Commissioners to Washington.

3—One, to make provisional arrangements for the continuance of Commercial facilities in South Carolina.

4—One, vesting in the General Assembly of the State, the powers lately vested in the Congress of the United States.

5—One, vesting in such Courts as the General Assembly should direct the Judicial powers heretofore delegated to the Government of the United States.

6—One, to define and punish treason against the State.

7—One, in relation to citizenship in the State.

Copies of all which are hereto attached for the information of your Excellency.

There were other important Ordinances submitted to the Convention, but I had no means of ascertaining whether they were adopted in the precise form in which they were offered, but I am satisfied they were passed either in that form, or with some modification. These I attach to the Reports of Committees and addresses, herewith submitted.

I was in the City of Charleston, when, on the night of the 26th of December, Fort Moultrie was evacuated, and Fort Sumter occupied by the Federal troops, under the command of Major Anderson. The greatest indignation was aroused by this violation of the understanding between the authorities of the State, and the Government of the United States From the most reliable sources, I was informed that the State and Federal authorities had mutually given a pledge, that the State should make no attack nor hostile demonstration against the fortresses in the possession of the Government of the United States in the Harbor of Charleston, and that no reinforcements were to be sent to those fortresses by the Federal Government, nor the position of the troops in those fortresses changed, until the question of their occupation or surrender had been attempted to be settled by negotiation between the State and Federal authorities. While the Executive of the United States pretends to disavow the act of Major Anderson in this change of position of the troops, he sanctions the act by permitting this officer to remain in his new position. Casuists will find it difficult to distinguish between the previous order, and subsequent sanction in a question of good faith.

On the morning of the 21st of December, as soon as the removal of the Federal troops from the one fort to the other, was known in the city, the Governor sent a dispatch to Major Anderson asking an explanation of his conduct, which being unsatisfactory, the troops of the State were ordered at once to occupy Fort Moultrie and Castle Pinckney, which was done on the same day, and these fortresses are still in the possession of the State, and will be defended to the last extremity.

From the observations made by men in South Carolina, I am satisfied that the people of that State are prepared to undergo the utmost horrors that war can bring upon a people—to have their lands ravaged and their homes made desolate, before they will submit to subjugation by the Federal Government, or the forces of the Abolition States.

I left Charleston on the 29th of December, on my return home. I was induced to this step from the fact that all the deliberations of the Convention on questions of importance were had in secret, and my presence in South Carolina could be of no further service, as I would obtain no further information than that afforded by the public prints.

I cannot close this communication without mentioning the cordial and complimentary manner in which I was received by the authorities of South Carolina. The privilege of a seat on the floor of the Senate and House of Representatives, and of the Convention, was given to me, and the hospitalities of the State tendered by Resolution of both Houses of the Legislature. In reply to this last courtesy, while acknowledging it in proper terms in the name of the State of Alabama, I felt constrained to decline it, but availed myself of the privileges of the seats tendered by the several bodies, except when the Convention was in secret session.

I reached this place on the 30th ult., at night, and have availed myself of the occasion to make known to your Excellency how I have discharged the duties of my appointment.

With the highest considerations of respect,

I am your Excellency's
Obedient servant,
J. A. ELMORE.

REPORT OF HON. JOHN GILL SHORTER, COMMISSIONER TO GEORGIA.

MILLEDGEVILLE, GA., January 3d, 1861.

His Excellency Governor Joseph E. Brown,
Governor of the State of Georgia—

Sir: I beg leave to hand you herewith a Commission from His Excellency Andrew B. Moore, Governor of the Sovereign State of Alabama, and attested by the great seal of the State, under date of December 21st, 1860, by which I have the honor to be constituted and appointed a Commissioner to the Sovereign State of Georgia, with authority to consult and advise with your Excellency, as to what is best to be done to protect the rights, interests and honor of the slaveholding States.

No duty more agreeable to my feelings could have been laid upon me, at this trying hour in the history of our country, than that of a Delegate from Alabama, the beloved State of my adoption, to Georgia, the beloved and honored State of my nativity.

The unnatural warfare which, in violation of the Federal Compact, and for a long series of years, has been unceasingly waged by the anti-slavery States upon the institutions, rights and domestic tranquility of the slave-holding States, has finally culminated in the election of an open and avowed enemy to our section of the Union; and the great and powerful party, who have produced this result, calmly awaits the fourth day of March next, when, under the forms of the Constitution and the Laws, they will usurp the machinery of the Federal Government, and madly attempt to rule, if not to subjugate and ruin, the South.

In anticipation of such a contingency, and in advance of any of her sister States, the General Assembly of Alabama, on the 24th day of February, 1860, solemnly declared, that "to permit a seizure of the Federal Government by those whose unmistakable aim is to pervert its whole machinery to the destruction of a portion of its members, would be an act of suicidal folly and madness almost without a parallel in history; and that the General Assembly of Alabama, representing a people loyally devoted to the Union of the Constitution, but scorning the Union which fanaticism would erect upon its ruins, deem it their solemn duty to provide in advance the means by which they may escape such peril and dishonor, and devise new securities for perpetuating the blessings of liberty to themselves and their posterity."

In stern pursuance of this purpose, the General Assembly adopted, among others, the following Resolution:

"That upon the happening of the contingency contemplated in the foregoing preamble, namely, the election of a President advocating the principles and action of the party in the Northern States calling itself the Republican Party, it shall be the duty of the Governor, and he is required forthwith, to issue his proclamation, calling upon the qualified voters of this State to assemble on a Monday, not more than forty days after the date of said proclamation, at the usual places of voting in their respective counties, and elect Delegates to a Convention of the State, to consider, determine and do whatever, in the opinion of said Convention, the rights, interests and honor of the State of Alabama require to be done for their protection."

And the same General Assembly, on the 25th day of February, 1860, in response to Resolutions received from the State of South Carolina, inviting a Conference of the Southern States, adopted these additional Resolutions:

1. "*Resolved*, That the State of Alabama, fully concurring with the State of South Carolina, in affirming the right of any State to secede from the Confederacy whenever, in her own judgment, such a step is demanded by the honor, interests and safety of her people, is not unmindful of the fact that the assaults upon the institution of slavery, and upon the rights and equality of the Southern States, unceasingly continued with increasing violence,

and in new and more alarming forms, may constrain her to a reluctant but early exercise of that invaluable right.

2. "*Be it further Resolved*, That in the absence of any preparation for a systematic coöperation of the Southern States in resisting the aggressions of her enemies, *Alabama, acting for herself,* has solemnly declared, that under no circumstances will she submit to the foul domination of a sectional Northern party, has provided for the call of a Convention in the event of the triumph of such a faction in the approaching Presidential election, and to maintain the position thus deliberately assumed, has appropriated the sum of $200,000 for the military contingencies which such a course may involve.

3. "*Be it further Resolved*, That the State of Alabama, having endeavored to prepare for the exigencies of the future, has not deemed it necessary to propose a meeting of Deputies from the slaveholding States, but anxiously desiring their coöperation in a struggle which perils all they hold most dear, hereby pledges herself to a cordial participation in any and every effort which, in her judgment, will protect the common safety, advance the common interest and serve the common cause."

In obedience to the instructions of the General Assembly, and in accordance with his own loyal heart and manly purpose, His Excellency Andrew B. Moore, Governor of Alabama, ordered an election of Delegates by the people, on the 24th day of December last. These Delegates, one hundred in number, will assemble in Convention at Montgomery on Monday next, the 7th instant, and there and then will speak the sovereign voice of Alabama.

There may be found an honest difference of opinion and judgment as to the time and mode of secession from the Federal Union, whether the State shall move at once, for herself and by herself, or await the action and coöperation of Georgia and adjoining sister States, who have with her a common interest, but that the Convention will fully maintain the high and patriotic resolves of the General Assembly, and thus proudly vindicate the rights and honor of Alabama, I do not for a moment entertain the shadow of a doubt.

Events now transpiring, must, at an early day, unite all loyal sons of the South in the defence of the South. We should make haste to be ready for the conflict which is well nigh upon us. "Delay is dangerous—hesitation, weakness—opposition, treason." We honor the gallant State of South Carolina, which accidental and fortuitous circumstances have placed in front of the battle; and Alabama will stand by and make common cause with her, and every other State which shall assert her independence of an abolitionized Government.

THE CONVENTION OF ALABAMA. 397

Alabama sends greetings to her mother—glorious old Georgia, the Empire State of the South—one of the immortal thirteen which suffered, and endured, and triumphed in the Revolution of 1776; and Alabama invokes her counsel and advice, her encouragement and coöperation. Having similar institutions, kindred sympathies, and honor alike imperilled, will not Georgia unite with Alabama and sister States in throwing off the insolent despotism of the North, and in the establishment of a Southern Confederacy, a government of homogeneous people, which shall endure through all coming time the proudest and grandest monument on the face of the earth?

I shall proceed hence to the capital of Alabama, to report the result of my interview with your Excellency to the Governor of Alabama, in time for him to lay the same before the Convention on Monday next; and I shall feel grateful for the honor of being made the medium of bearing any communication which your Excellency may be pleased to make.

With high consideration, I am
    Your Excellency's
      Obedient servant,
        JNO. GILL SHORTER.

        EXECUTIVE DEPARTMENT, }
      MILLEDGEVILLE, January 5th, 1861. }

Hon. John Gill Shorter, Commissioner
   of the State of Alabama:

Dear Sir: On my return from Savannah this day, I find your communication accompanying your Commission from His Excellency the Governor of Alabama, which you did me the honor to send by express, but which was not received till after I had the pleasure of a private interview with you.

The gallant and noble stand taken by your State in the passage of the Resolutions recited in your communication, for the protection of the rights and the vindication of the honor of the State of Alabama and the other Southern States, excited the just admiration of all her Southern sisters. Alabama, in common with the other pro-slavery States, had long endured the injustice and insults of the Black Republican party of the North. That party is now triumphant, and is about to seize the reins of the Federal Government. To this the States of the South can never submit, without degradation and ultimate ruin.

While Georgia may be said to be the Mother of Alabama, she is proud of the noble conduct of her daughter; and will not claim to lead, but will be content to follow in the path of glory in which her offspring leads. We feel well assured that your State will not be intimidated, nor driven from her high position.

While many of our most patriotic and intelligent citizens in both States have doubted the propriety of immediate secession. I feel quite confident that recent developments have dispelled those doubts from the minds of most men, who have, till within the last few days, honestly entertained them.

Longer continuance in a Union with those who use the Government only as an engine of oppression and injustice, cannot, it seems to me, be desired by any party in the Southern States.

Conciliation and harmony among ourselves, are of the most vital importance. Let us, if we have differed in the past, meet each other with just forbearance; and the path of duty will, I trust, be plain to all.

The Federal Government denies the right of a sovereign State to secede from the Union, while it refuses to make any concessions or to give any guarantees which will secure our rights in future. If we yield this right, we become the subjects, and the pro-slavery States the provinces, of a great centralized Empire, consolidated and maintained by military force.

The sovereign State of South Carolina has resumed the powers delegated by her to the Federal Government, on account of the violation of the Compact by the other contracting parties. Her right to declare herself independent is denied, and military coercion is boldly threatened. Shall we yield the right of secession, and see her whipped back into the Union? Never.

Since she seceded, her course has been moderate and dignified. She did not occupy the most impregnable Fort in her harbor, which she could have seized without the loss of a single man, because she had pledged her faith not to do so, in consideration that the Government at Washington would make no change in the military *status* of the Forts, but would permit all to remain as it was at the time she seceded. She kept her faith. What was the conduct of the Federal Government? Its agent who commanded Fort Moultrie violated the pledge given by his Government. The Government disavows his conduct, but refuses to keep its faith by remanding him to his original position. The result will probably be, the loss of much of the best blood in South Carolina, before the Fort can be taken. In my opinion, other Southern States should not be deceived by trusting to such a Government in future.

In view of the threats of coercion which are made by Northern Senators and Representatives, and the probabilities that the like policy now meets the sanction of a majority of the Cabinet, the South can look in future only to her own strength, the justice of her cause, and the protection of the Almighty Ruler of the Universe, for her safety and independence. Prompted by these considerations, I have seized and occupied Fort Pulaski, the stronghold in this State, with a sufficient number of troops and other ample provision to secure it against successful assault. Till the Convention of this State has acted, and decided the question of Georgia's future dependence or independence, I shall hold the Fort at all hazards, and by force, if necessary.

I am glad to learn, by a telegram just received from His Excellency the Governor of your State, that he has taken the same precautions for the protection of the people of Alabama, against the assaults of our common enemy; and I sincerely trust the Executive of each and every Southern State in the Union will at once adopt the same policy; and let us all coöperate in a common defense.

So far as the returns have been received at this office, they indicate beyond a doubt that the people of Georgia have determined, by an overwhelming majority, to secede from the Union so soon as our Convention meets and has time to consummate this important step, which can alone preserve the honor, the rights and the dignity of this State in the future.

I trust that Alabama will not hesitate, but will act promptly and independently, relying, as I know she may, upon the cordial coöperation of Georgia in every hour of trial. The people of the pro-slavery States have common institutions, common interests, common sympathies and a common destiny. Let each State, as soon as its Convention meets, secede promptly from the Union; and let all then unite upon a common platform, coöperate together, and "form a more perfect Union." Our cause is just, and I doubt not, should we be attacked, that the God of battles will protect the right, and drive far from us the scattered hosts of an invading foe.

I regret the necessity which compels me to prepare this response in so short a period. I have no time to revise it. You will please say to His Excellency Governor Moore, that it will afford me much pleasure to receive intelligence at the earliest moment, after the Convention has placed Alabama in the high position which Georgia, by a vote of her people, has determined to occupy so soon as her Convention has time to assemble and deliberate. I am, very truly, your obedient servant,

JOSEPH E. BROWN.

REPORT OF HON. J. L. M. CURRY, COMMISSIONER TO MARYLAND.

MONTGOMERY, ALA.,
8th January, 1861.

Sir—Acting under the authority of the Commission received from you, I visited Annapolis to confer, in person, with the Governor of Maryland. He was absent, and I submitted the enclosed letter, with the request that it be laid before the Legislature when it should be convened.

The Governor, prior to my visit, had declined, on the application of the Commissioner from Mississippi, and numerous requests, more or less formerly presented, from citizens of Maryland, to convene the Legislature to consider the present condition of political affairs. From conversation with prominent citizens, and from other sources, I am firmly of the opinion that Maryland will not long hesitate to make common cause with her sister States which have resolutely and wisely determined not to submit to Abolition domination.

I have the honor to be, with high respect,
Your obedient servant,
J. L. M. CURRY.

HIS EXCELLENCY A. B. MOORE, Montgomery, Ala.

ANNAPOLIS, MD., Dec. 28th, 1860.

Sir--The Governor of the sovereign State of Alabama has appointed me a Commissioner to the sovereign State of Maryland, "to consult and advise" with the Governor and Legislature thereof, "as to what is best to be done to protect the rights, interests and honor of the slaveholding States," menaced and endangered by recent political events.

Having watched with painful anxiety the growth, power and encroachments of anti-slaveryism, and anticipating for the party, held together by this sentiment of hostility to the rights and institutions of the Southern people, a probable success (too fatally realized) in the recent Presidential election, the General Assembly of Alabama, on the 24th of February, 1860, adopted Joint Resolutions, providing, on the happening of such a contingency, for a Convention of the State, "to consider, determine and do whatever the rights, interests and honor of Alabama require to be done for their protection." In accordance with this authority, the Governor has called a Convention to meet on the 7th day of January, 1861, and on the 24th instant Delegates were elected to that body.

Not content with this simple but significant act of convoking the sovereignty of the people, the State affirmed her reserved and undelegated right of secession from the Confederacy, and intimated that continued and unceasingly violent assaults upon her rights and equality, might "corstrain her to a reluctant but early exercise of that invaluable right." Recognizing the common interests and destiny of all the States holding property in the labor of Africans, and "anxiously desiring their coöperation in a struggle which perils all they hold most dear," Alabama pledged herself to a "cordial participation in any and every effort which, in her judgment, will protect the common safety, advance the common interest and serve the common cause."

To secure concert and effective coöperation between Maryland and Alabama is, in a great degree, the object of my mission. Under our federative system, each State being necessarily the sole judge of the extent of powers delegated to the General Agent, and controlling the allegiance of her citizens, must decide for herself, in case of wrong, upon the mode and measure of redress. Within the Union the States have absolutely prohibited themselves from entering into treaties, alliances and confederations, and have made the assent of Congress a condition precedent to their entering into agreements or compacts with other States. This constitutional inhibition has been construed to include "every agreement, written or verbal, formal or informal, positive or implied, by the mutual understanding of the parties." Without endorsing this sweeping judicial *dictum*, it will be conceded that if the grievance or apprehension of danger be so great as to render necessary or advisable a withdrawal from the Confederacy, there can be between the States, similarly imperilled, prior to separation, only an informal understanding for prospective concert and federation. To enter into a binding "agreement or compact" would violate the Constitution, and the South should be careful not to part with her distinguishing glory of having never, under the most aggravating provocations, departed from the strictest requirements of the Federal Covenant, nor suggested any proposition infringing upon the essential equality of the co-States. It is, nevertheless, the highest dictate of wisdom and patriotism to secure, so far as can be constitutionally done, "a mutual league, united thoughts and counsels," between those whose hopes and hazards are alike joined in the enterprise of accomplishing deliverance from Abolition domination.

To your Excellency, or so intelligent a body as the Legislature of Maryland, it would be superfluous to enter into an elaborate statement of the policy and purposes of the party which, by the recent election, will soon have the control of the General Government. The bare fact that the party is sectional and hostile to the South, is a full justification for the precautionary steps taken by Alabama to provide for the escape of her citizens from the peril and dishonor of submission to its rule. Superadded to this sectional hostility the fanaticism of a sentiment, which has become a controlling political force, giving ascendancy in every Northern State, and the avowed purpose, as disclosed in party creeds, declarations of editors, and utterances of Representative men, of securing the diminution of slavery in the States, and placing it in the course of ultimate extinction, and the South would merit the punishment of the simple, if she passed on and provided no security against the imminent danger.

When Mr. Lincoln is inaugurated, it will not be simply a change of Administration—the installation of a new President—but a reversal of the former practice and policy of the Government so thorough as to amount to a revolution. Cover over its offensiveness with the most artful disguises and the fact stands out in its terrible reality, that the Government, within the amplitude of its jurisdiction, real or assumed, becomes *foreign* to the South, and is not to recognize the right of the Southern citizen to property in the labor of African slaves. Heretofore, Congress, the Executive, and the Judiciary, have considered themselves, in their proper spheres, as under a constitutional obligation to recognize and protect as property whatever the States ascertained and determined to be such. Now the opinion of nearly every Republican is, that the slave of a citizen of Maryland, in possession of and in company with his master, on a vessel sailing from Baltimore to Mobile, is as free as his master, entitled to the same rights, privileges and immunities, as soon as a vessel has reached a marine league beyond the shores of a State, and is outside the jurisdiction of State laws. The same is held if a slave be carried on the territory or other property belonging to the United States, and it is denied by all Republicans that Congress, or a Territorial Legislature, or any individuals, can give legal existence to slavery in any Territory of the United States. Thus, under the new Government, property which existed in every one of the States, save one, when the Government was formed, and is recognized and protected in the Constitution, is to be proscribed and outlawed. It requires no argument to show, that States whose property is thus condemned, are reduced to inferiority and inequality.

Such being the principles and purposes of the new Government and its supporters, every Southern State is deeply interested in the protection of the honor and equality of her citizens. Recent events occurring at the Federal Capitol and in the North must demonstrate to the most incredulous and hopeful that there is no intention on the part of the Republicans to make concessions to our just and reasonable demands, or furnish any securities against their wrong doing. If their purposes were right and harmless, how easy to give satisfactory assurances and guaranties! If no intention to harm exists, it can be neither unmanly nor unwise to put it out of their power to commit harm. The minority section must have some other protection than the discretion or sense of justice of the majority; for the Constitution, as interpreted, with a denial of the right of secession or State-interposition, affords no security or means of redress against a hostile and fanatical majority. The action of the two Committees, in the Senate and House of Congress, shows an unalterable purpose on the part of the Republicans to reap the fruits of their recent victory, and to abate not a jot or tittle of their Abolition principles. They refuse to recognize our rights of property in slaves, to make a division of the territory, to deprive themselves of their assumed constitutional power to abolish slavery in the Territories or District of Columbia, to increase the efficiency of the fugitive slave law, or make provision for the compensation of the owners of runaway or stolen slaves, or place in the hands of the South any protection against the rapacity of an unscrupulous majority.

If our present undoubted constitutional rights were reäffirmed in, if possible, more explicit language, it is questionable whether they would meet with more successful execution. Anti-slavery fanaticism would probably soon render them nugatory. The sentiment of the sinfulness of slavery seems to be imbedded in the Northern conscience. An infidel theory has corrupted the Northern heart. A French orator said, the people of England once changed their religion by Act of Parliament. Whether true or not, it is not probable that settled convictions at the North, intensely adverse to slavery, can be changed by Congressional resolutions or constitutional amendments.

Under Republican rule, the revolution will not be confined to slavery and its adjuncts. The features of our political system, which constitute its chief excellence and distinguish it from absolute Governments, are to be altered. The radical idea of this Confederacy is the equality of the sovereign States, and their voluntary assent to the Constitutional Compact. This, from recent indications, is to be changed, so that to a great extent, power is to be centralized at Washington; Congress is to be the final judge of its powers; States are to be deprived of a reciprocity and equality of rights; and a common Government, kept in being by force, will discriminate offensively and injuriously against the property of a particular geographical section.

With Alabama, after patient endurance for years, and earnest expostulation with the Northern States, the reluctant conviction has become fixed, that there is no safety for her in a hostile Union, governed by an interested sectional majority. As a sovereign State, vitally interested in the preservation and security of African slavery, she will exercise the right of withdrawing from the Compact of Union. Most earnestly does she desire the coöperation of sister Southern States in a new Confederacy, based on the same principles as the present. Having no ulterior or unavowed purposes to accomplish, seeking peace and friendship with all people, determined that her slave population, not to be increased by importations from Africa, shall not be localized and become redundant by excess of growth beyond liberty of expansion, she most cordially invites the concurrent action of all States with common sympathies and common interests. Under an Abolition Government the slaveholding States will be placed under a common ban of proscription, and an institution, interwoven in the very frame work of their social and political being, must perish gradually or speedily, with the Government in active hostility to it. Instead of the culture and development of the boundless capacities and productive resources of their social system, it is to be assaulted, humbled, dwarfed, degraded and finally crushed out.

To some of the States delaying action for new securities, the question of submission to a dominant Abolition majority is presented in a different form from what it was a few weeks ago. One State has seceded; others will soon follow. Without discussing the propriety of such action, the remaining States must act on the facts as they exist, whether of their own creation or approval or not. To unite with the seceding States is to be their peers as confederates and have an identity of interests, protection of property, and superior advantages in the contest for the markets, a monopoly of which has been enjoyed by the North. To refuse union with the seceding States is to accept inferiority, to be deprived of an outlet for surplus slaves, and to remain in a hostile Government in a hopeless minority and remediless dependence.

It gives me pleasure to be the medium of communicating with you and through you to the Legislature of Maryland, when it shall be convened. I trust that between Maryland and Alabama, and other States having a homogeneous population, kindred interests and an inviting future of agricultural, mining, mechanical, manufacturing, commercial and political success—a Union, strong as the tie of affection, and lasting as the love of liberty, will soon be formed, which shall stand as a model of a free, representative, constitutional, voluntary Republic.

I have the honor to be, with much respect,
Your obedient servant,
J. L. M. CURRY.

Hon. Thos. H. Hicks, Annapolis, Md.

REPORT OF THE HON. WILLIAM COOPER, COMMISSIONER TO MISSOURI.

Montgomery, Ala.,
January 7, 1861.

To His Excellency A. B. Moore, Governor of Alabama:

Sir—In pursuance of the requirements of the commission to me directed, by the Governor of the State of Alabama, on the 18th of December, 1860, I did forthwith repair to Jefferson City, in the State of Missouri, for the purpose of performing the duties required of me, as Commissioner from the State of Alabama to the State of Missouri; and my communication was immediately had with the then acting Governor of that State [Robert M. Stewart]. I submitted to him my communication, a copy of which is herewith laid before your Excellency, together with the reply of Governor Stewart. The Missouri Legislature was not in session, and would not convene until the last day of December, 1860. Many of the members, however, of both Houses, had assembled at the seat of Government, and it being obvious that I could not await the organization of that Body, with any hope of such prompt action, on its part, as to enable me to be present, and return here in time for the Alabama Convention, an informal meeting of the members of the Senate and House of Representatives was had, in the Senate Chamber, after due publication, and an opportunity was afforded me of being heard, by the members and the people, in the Hall of the House of Representatives, on the 29th of December past; and, after which, action was had by the members who convened in the Senate Chamber, and adopted a preamble and resolutions, which were handed to me, and which I herewith submit to your Excellency.

I will add that, so far as I could learn (and there was a free expression of opinion, from the members and the people of the State of Missouri), that State was in favor of coöperation with the slave-States, and, in the event of a dissolution, Missouri will confederate with the South, and not with the North. Missouri feels and realizes her critical situation, being a border State, bounded North, East and West by free-soil territory, and bounded by a slave-State on the South, sparsely populated. She will move with slow and cautious steps. The present Governor of Missouri, Hon. C. F. Jackson, is decidedly in favor of calling a State Convention, to act in the present political crisis of the country, and his views are fully foreshadowed by his letter of the — December past, as well as in his Message. His letter to Gen. Shields is also here referred to.

Respectfully,

W. COOPER.

LETTER OF GOV. JACKSON.

MY DEAR SHIELDS—I observed in the last *Expositor* a call for a meeting, to take place in Lexington, on the 10th of this month, to consider the course the Southern people should pursue under the menaces and threats of Black Republicanism. From the free and outspoken terms in which this call is made, and the unqualified language used in setting forth the objects of the meeting, those of us at a distance cannot but infer that the good people of "old Lafayette" are determined to assert the rights which belong to them under the Constitution, and set themselves right before the world.

I rejoice to see that the men of all parties have freely signed this call, and I trust in God they will have the metal and the nerve about them, when they shall assemble together, to look all impending danger squarely in the face, and firmly but respectfully declare to the world where they will be found in the fearful crisis which now overhangs our common country. The time has come, in my judgment, when a settlement of all the questions in controversy must be had. That settlement, to be of any value, must be FULL, COMPLETE, and FINAL, and expressed in such terms that no one can doubt the exact meaning of the settlement. In the call for your meeting, you have declared your purpose to demand an "unconditional repeal" of all the personal-liberty laws which have been passed by the free States. This is a step, I think, well taken, and leads in the right direction. But does it go far enough?

Does it reach the heart of the disease? Nothing short of the most positive and binding obligations would I accept in the proposed settlement. Suppose those offending States should agree to repeal their odious enactments, and should actually do it, may they not reënact them the year following? They have already violated one bargain, under the pretence of construing it differently from us. In making the next agreement, let it be made so plain that the wayfaring man, though in a gallop, cannot mistake its meaning. You know the Constitution has not the word slave or slavery in it. Our fathers, who made it, were, in reference to this subject, possessed of a little mock-modesty, or, perhaps, more properly speaking, they were a little too mealy-mouthed to speak out "in meeting," fully what they thought and meant. Now, everybody knows exactly what they meant; yet the Abolitionists and Black Republicans are beginning to deny its true intent and meaning. You know this is so—every man knows it. Should we, then, accept anything less than an amendment to the Constitution, setting forth, in the plainest terms, the exact agreement entered into? I do not know that we should ask this by way of "amendment," but rather as an EXPLANATION of the true meaning of the Constitution. We should also require a proper penalty of every State that failed to comply, in good faith, with the Constitution and laws upon this subject. Each State that permits its citizens, in the way of armed mobs, or otherwise, to obstruct the faithful execution of the Fugitive Slave Law, should be held responsible to the owner of the slave for all damages and costs in the case. It has occurred to my mind that we should demand this, or something like it. I will not differ with friends in the matter of detail, or mere form of the thing; so I get the substance I should feel satisfied.

Some of the Union-savers, and some of our more timorous friends, are insisting that we must wait yet a while longer, until Lincoln shall commit some "overt act." They tell us his election is no good cause for secession. I agree that the mere *form* or *manner* of Lincoln's election does not furnish good and sufficient grounds for secession; but when we consider that Lincoln is the representative-man of the Black Republican party—that he was taken up by the Chicago Convention, and afterwards elected by his party, solely because he was the author of the declaration, that "this Government cannot endure permanently half slave and half free." I ask if his election, under these circumstances, is not committing the "overt act?" Can we regard it as anything less than a declaration of war, upon the whole slave property of all the Southern States? Is it not a moral dissolution of the Union

—a virtual disruption of the Government? For myself, I cannot but regard the election of Lincoln as having brought to a focus all the threats and agitations of the last thirty years; as severing the political ties which have held together the people of the Northern and Southern States; as alienating their affections, and placing them, to a great extent, in the position of two opposing armies, standing in hostile array to each other. But, my dear sir, do not understand me as undertaking to dictate what should be done. I simply took up my pen, on reading your call for a meeting, to say to you that you have my hearty approval and warmest sympathies in this movement. We shall hold a meeting in Saline, on the 14th, and would be glad to have you with us if it would not put you to too much trouble. This is all I intend to say in the outset; but as I have a little space I will add a word more. I think the people of each Southern State should hold Conventions at once, and these conventions should appoint delegates to a general Convention of all the Southern States, where they could all agree on what ought to be demanded, and that all might act in concert in carrying out the measures and policy agreed upon. Had I been acting Governor of the State, I should have called the Legislature together before now, in order that they might consider the question of calling a Convention, and at the same time, if thought proper, to dispatch a Commissioner to South-Carolina, Georgia, etc., etc., asking them, as friends, nfit to go out of the Union, by any hasty step, but remain with us and meet us in Csnvention, and, if go we must, let us all go out together. Let us exhaust all the means in our power to maintain our rights in the Union, let us preserve the Government, if possibly in our power; but if, after having tried all the remedies within our grasp, if these should fail—as I fear they will—then, I say, let us dissolve the connection, and maintain the rights which belong to us, AT ALL HAZARDS, AND TO THE LAST EXTREMITY.

In my arguments upon this subject I have thought it a waste of words and time to discuss the abstract right of secession. To us it does not matter whether it be a Constitutional remedy or not. What right has the Black Republican or his allies to read us lectures on Constitutional rights, after having violated, with impunity, the plainest provisions of the Constitution for more than thirty years? I pray that our friends may not be betrayed into any rash acts or measures. Let there be no threats, no bravado, no gasconading; but firmly and determinedly let us take our position, in the right, and stand by it to the last.

C. F. JACKSON.

JEFFERSON CITY, MISSOURI,
December 26, 1860.

To His Excellency R. M. Stewart, Governor, &c:

Sir: At a late session of the Legislature of the State of Alabama, and on the 24th day of February, 1860, the Senate and House of Representatives of the State of Alabama, in General Assembly convened, adopted the following Preamble and Resolution, viz:

"WHEREAS, anti-slavery agitation, persistently continued in the non-slaveholding States of this Union for more than a third of a century, marked at every stage of its progress by contempt for the obligations of law and the sanctity of compacts, evincing a deadly hostility to the rights and Institutions of the Southern people, and a settled purpose to effect their overthrow, even by the subversion of the Constitution, and at the hazard of bloodshed; and whereas, a sectional party, calling itself Republican, committed alike by its own acts and antecedents, and the public avowals, and secret machinations of its leaders to the execution of those atrocious desings, has acquired the ascendant in every Northern State, and hopes by success in the approaching Presidential election, to seize the Government itself; and, whereas, to permit such a seizure by those whose unmistakable aim, is to pervert its whole machinery to the destruction of a portion of its members, would be an act of suicidal folly and madness, almost without a parallel in history; and, whereas, the General Assembly of Alabama, representing a people loyally devoted to the Union of the Constitution, but scorning the Union which fanaticism would erect upon its ruins, deem it their solemn duty to provide in advance, the means by which they may escape such peril and dishonor, and desire new securities for perpetuating the blessings of liberty to themselves and their posterity. Therefore,

Be it Resolved, By the Senate and House of Representatives of the State of Alabama, in General Assembly convened, That upon the happening of the contingency contemplated in the foregoing preamble, namely: the election of a President advocating the principles and actions of the party in the Northern States, calling itself the Republican party, it shall be the duty of the Governor, and he is hereby required forthwith to issue his proclamation, calling upon the qualified voters of this State to assemble on a Monday not more than forty days after the date of said proclamation, and at the general places of voting, in their respective counties, to elect Delegates to a State Convention of the State, to consider, determine, and do whatever in the opinion of said

Convention, the rights, interests and honor of the State of Alabama requires to be done for their protection.

And on the 25th day of February, 1860, another Resolution was adopted and passed by said body, as follows, (viz:)

"*Be it Resolved*, That in the absence of any preparation for a systematic Coöperation of the Southern States in resisting the aggressions of their enemies, Alabama, acting for herself, has solemnly declared, that under no circumstances will she submit to the foul domination of a Sectional Northern party; has provided for the care of a Convention, in the want of the triumph of such a faction in the approaching Presidential election, and to maintain her position thus deliberately assumed, has appropriated," &c.

Under the foregoing Resolutions, and the influence of subsequent political events, his Excellency Andrew B. Moore, Governor of the State of Alabama, deeming it proper to consult with the slaveholding States of the Union, as to what is best to be done to promote their and our interests and honor, in the crisis which the action of the Black Republicans has forced upon the country, and believing that the Conventions of South Carolina and Florida, as well as the Legislatures of some of the other States would have assembled and acted before the meeting of the Convention of Alabama, and thus the opportunity of conferring with them would be measurably lost, determined to appoint Commissioners to each of the slaveholding States, in time to enable them to report the result of the Convention to him before the meeting of the Alabama Convention, (which will assemble at the city of Montgomery, on the 7th of January, 1861,) that the same might be laid before that body.

The election of members to the Alabama Convention was holden on the 24th December, 1860.

This course was pursued by Governor Moore, because the Southern States could not, without violating the Constitution of the United States, make any agreement, form any alliance, nor enter into any compact for their mutual protection, before separate State secession; and because all that can be done, will be to consult generally as to what would be best; and afterwards to secede separately as emergencies might demand, and thereafter coöperate in the formation of such Confederacy as might tend to the general welfare.

Under this state of facts the undersigned was, by Andrew B. Moore, Governor of the State of Alabama, on the 18th of December, 1860, commissioned to the State of Missouri to consult and advise with his Excellency the Governor of Missouri, and with the Legislature, and all other public functionaries of said State, touching the premises as to what shall be deemed best to be done to protect the rights, interests, and honor of the slaveholding States; and all of which is respectfully submitted to elicit the counsel and opinion of the State of Missouri, as to what is best to be done by the slaveholding States, in the present political crisis, and all of which I respectfully submit to elicit the consultation and advice of the State of Missouri in the premises.

Respectfully,
WM. COOPER,
Commissioner from Alabama.

GOVERNOR STEWART TO GOVERNOR MOORE.

EXECUTIVE DEPARTMENT, }
CITY OF JEFFERSON, Dec. 30th, 1860. }

His Excellency A. B. Moore,
Governor of Alabama,
Montgomery, Alabama.

Sir: I acknowledge with pleasure the receipt of your favor of the 18th inst., accrediting and introducing to me Mr. William Cooper as a Commissioner from Alabama to Missouri, to confer with proper authorities in this State, respecting all matters connected with the present political and governmental crisis in the United States.

I am truly gratified, and the people of Missouri will be pleased to learn, that you have taken a course which looks to a friendly conference of all the slave-holding States. Be assured, sir, that in Missouri we have a lively appreciation of the practical injuries suffered from the interference and depradations of Northern fanatics.

Owing to the peculiarity of our geographical position, being bounded by nearly a thousand miles of free Territory, our State probably suffers more from the loss and abduction of slaves than any of her sisters; and our people are determined to seek redress for their wrongs and full security and indemnity for their rights. At the same time they are, so far as I am advised, equally opposed to separate or immediate action upon a subject of so grave importance.

The people of Missouri will still seek for the acknowledgment and indication of their rights within the Union, rather than "fly from present evils to those we know not of;" and when the terms of a fair adjustment are refused, will be prepared to join with the slaveholding States in united measures for the redress of our common grievances.

For a further exposition of my views on this subject, I beg to refer you to my forthcoming annual message to the General Assembly of Missouri; which you will doubtless receive before the meeting of your State Convention on the 7th proximo, as also that of my successor of whose opinions I am not specially advised. In the meantime, be assured, that every courtesy, which the representatives of a great and generous people know how to bestow, will be cordially extended to the worthy and gentlemanly Commissoner, who comes here honored with the confidence of Alabama.

Yours, respectfully,
R. M. STEWART.

At an adjourned meeting of the members of the Legislature of Missouri, held at the Capitol on Saturday, December 29th, 1860, prior to the meeting of the General Assembly, after the address of the Hon. William Cooper, Commissioner from the State of Alabama, Dr. John Hyer, Senator from Dent, was elected Chairman, and R. C. Cloud, Esq., of Pemescot, was elected Secretary.

Hon. M. M. Parsons, Senator from Cole, offered the following:

"*Resolved*, That we have heard with deep interest the address of the Hon. William Cooper, Commissioner appointed from the State of Alabama, to consult with us in regard to what course the slaveholding States should take under the present crisis, and that we will, during the coming session, express our opinions, officially, upon the questions now distracting the Union, and will furnish his Excellency, the Governor of Alabama, with a copy of such resolutions on the subject as the General Assembly may adopt." which was unanimously adopted.

Hon. Thomas W. Freeman, Representative from Polk, offered the following:

"*Resolved*, That the Secretary of this meeting be directed to transmit a copy of the Resolutions adopted by this meeting to his Excellency, the Governor of Alabama, by Hon. William Cooper, Commissioner from that State."

Which was unanimously adopted, and thereupon the meeting adjourned.

R. C. CLOUD,
Secretary.

REPORT OF THE HON. JOHN A. WINSTON, COMMISSIONER TO LOUISIANA.

January 2, 1861.

Sir: In obedience to your instructions, I repaired to the seat of Government of the State of Louisiana, to confer with the Governor of that State, and with the legislative department, on the grave and important state of our political relations with the Federal Government, and the duty of the slaveholding States in the matter of their rights and honor, so menacingly involved in matters connected with the institution of African slavery.

Owing to the fact that the Legislature was in session only three days, and other unavoidable causes, I did not arrive at Baton Rouge until after the Legislature had adjourned. But I met many members of the Legislative Corps, and communicated with them, and with His Excellency, Gov. T. O. Moore, on the purposes of my Embassy, and have the pleasure to report that the legislative mind appeared fully alive to the importance and the absolute necessity of the action of the Southern States, in resistance of that settled purpose of aggression on our Constitutional and inherent natural rights, by the majority of the people of the non-slave-holding States of the Federal Union; which purpose and intention has culminated in the election of a man to the Presidency of the United States, whose opinions, and constructions of Constitutional duty, are wholly incompatible with our safety in a longer union with them.

In evidence of such a conclusion, the Legislature of Louisiana have provided for a Convention of the people, to consider and take action on the matter; the election of delegates to which takes place on the 7th instant, and the Convention assembles on the 23d instant.

I was rejoiced to find the Governor fully up to the conclusion, that the time had come when the enjoyment of peace and our rights as co-equals in this Confederacy, were no longer to be expected or hoped for; and that the solemn duty now devolved upon us, of separating from all political connection with the States so disregarding their Constitutional obligations, and of forming such a Government as a high sense of our rights, honor, and future peace and safety shall indicate. And that, although the sense of the necessity of such a course, may not yet be so nearly general and unanimous in Louisiana as in some other States, he was of the opinion that the conclusion was hourly gaining ground, that there was no hope of justice or safety to us, except in a separation, and that the State of Louisiana would not hesitate to coöperate with those Southern States who might prove equal to the emergency of decided action.

The State of Louisiana, from the fact that the Mississippi River flows through its extent, and debouches through her borders, and that the great commercial depôt of that river and its tributaries is the city of New Orleans, occupies a position somewhat more complicated than any other of the Southern States, and may present some cause of delay in the consummation and execution of the purpose of a separation from the North-Western States, and the adoption of a new political status.

In consideration of these facts, more time may be required for reflection than might otherwise appear necessary; and as the Convention does not assemble for some weeks, that may prevent action on the question until some time in February. As a point of policy it might be advisable for the State of Alabama to announce her intention, as a foregone conclusion—a fixed fact—that on a day appointed, our relations as a member of the political association known as the United States, had ceased; and that Alabama, acting as a sovereign for herself, in the Act of Separation, was prepared to form such political relations, with States having a community of interest and sympathies, as to them may seem just and proper.

I feel assured, that by such a course of respectful delay on our part, other States would more promptly respond to whatever action Alabama may take, and that there is little or no doubt but that Louisiana will coöperate with the States taking action, and so add dignity and importance to the movement—which is so essential to secure the respect and recognition of foreign nations, and the support of hesitating States.

Should it be considered advisable by your Excellency, to communicate further with the authorities of the State of Louisiana, after her Convention shall have assembled, I will be in Mobile, and can receive readily, by mail, or telegraph, any instructions you may deem it advisable to make; and I will, without delay, endeavor to discharge them. Trusting that the time has come, when not only Alabama, but the entire South, will prove prepared to vindicate her honor by a fearless assertion of her rights, and her determination to enjoy them.

Most respectfully, your obedient servant, etc..
JOHN A. WINSTON.

To His Excellency A. B. Moore.

REPORT OF THE HON. L. P. WALKER, COMMISSIONER TO TENNESSEE.

MONTGOMERY, *January* 16, 1861.

To His Excellency A. B. Moore:

Sir : By authority of your Excellency's commission, I proceeded to Nashville, Tennessee, where, on the 9th inst., I addressed, by invitation, both branches of the Legislature of that State. I beg to report, as the result of my mission, that there is, in my opinion, no doubt that Tennessee will unite with the Gulf States in forming a Southern Confederacy. The right or wrong of secession is not the question submitted for their determination.— *That* may very well be pre-termitted in that State. The Union is dissolved without their action, and the practical question for them to decide is, shall they go with the North or with the South? And in deciding this question the result is obvious. There is a geographical necessity that Tennessee shall unite with the South. Her trade, like the waters of her beautiful rivers, flows southward, and being homogeneous in opinion, in character, and in civilization, her natural sympathies are stimulated by her commercial necessities, and make her drift quietly and surely into the union of the Southern States. I consider this result as absolutely certain.

I cannot close this communication without acknowledging, in behalf of my State, the marked and cordial courtesy with which I was received by all parties in Tennessee.

With sentiments of high consideration and regard,

I am, very truly,
Your friend,
L. P. WALKER.

REPORT OF THE HON. E. C. BULLOCH, COMMISSIONER TO FLORIDA.

MONTGOMERY, ALA., January 15, 1861.

To His Excellency Andrew B. Moore, Governor of Alabama:

Sir—Under the authority of the Commission conferred by your Excellency, and in discharge of the duties imposed by it, I reached Tallahassee on the 3d day of January, at which place and time the Convention of the State of Florida assembled. That Body, without having effected a permanent organization, after a very brief session adjourned until Saturday, the 5th instant, the intervening Friday having been observed as a day of fasting and prayer. On Saturday, His Excellency Gov. Perry, to whom my credentials had been previously presented, communicated the fact of my presence, as Commissioner from Alabama, to the Convention. On Monday, the 7th inst., I was, together with the Commissioner from South Carolina, Hon. L. W. Spratt, formally introduced to the Convention, by a Committee appointed for the purpose, and had the honor to set forth, in an address before that Body, the views entertained by the State of Alabama, as since indicated by the action of her Convention, as to the best mode of protecting the rights, interests and honor of the slave-holding States, urging the promptest action, as, under the circumstances, the truest wisdom, and as furnishing the best hope of a peaceful solution of our difficulties. The friendly voice of Alabama, however feebly uttered, was heard with the most respectful attention, and the opinions expressed seemed to meet the hearty countenance of a large proportion of the Convention.

On the evening of Monday, a resolution, affirming the right and necessity of speedy secession, which had been introduced on Saturday, was adopted by a vote of Sixty-Two to Five; and a Committee was appointed to prepare the Ordinance of Secession, which was reported on Wednesday, the 9th inst. Several amendments, intended to delay any action until after the secession of Georgia and Alabama should be first accomplished, or until the Ordinance of Secession should be ratified by a vote of the people of Florida, were proposed, but they were all lost by decisive votes. On Thursday, the 10th inst., several gentlemen of the minority, who had warmly supported these amendments, and attached very great importance to them, avowed their purpose, notwithstanding their failure, to record their votes in favor of the Ordinance of Secession—thus nobly sacrificing their personal views upon the altar of their country. And at Twenty Minutes past Twelve o'clock, on that day, I had the extreme gratification to witness its passage, by a vote of Sixty-two to Seven—every member of the Convention having been present. I have appended to this Report a copy of the Ordinance, as adopted.

It is due to the minority to state, that no voice in the Convention was raised in favor of submission to Black Republican rule, and that their whole aim seemed to be to make the secession of Florida follow, instead of preceding, that of Alabama and Georgia. If there was a man in Florida, who, with these two States.

out of the Union, desired her to remain in it, his opinions certainly found no organ in the Convention.

The main facts herein stated, in respect to the action of the State of Florida, were immediately communicated to your Excellency, by telegraph, in order that they might at once be made known to the Convention.

It only remains to add, that the warmth and cordiality with which I was greeted by the Governor, the Convention of Florida, and the people whom they represented, as the Commissioner of Alabama, afforded the most gratifying proof that the strong ties of a common cause, a common danger and a common destiny, were deeply felt and appreciated, and the best reasons for hoping that the two States, divided by but a single day in their exodus from a Union of "irrepressible conflict," will soon be closely joined in that new Union of brotherly love, in which a homogeneous people, taking their destiny into their own hands, shall exhibit to the world the noblest phase of Free Government, and the highest development of true civilization.

With great respect, I have the honor to be
Your Excellency's obedient servant,
E. C. BULLOCH.

ORDINANCE OF SECESSION.

We, the people of the State of Florida, in Convention assembled, do solemnly declare, publish and declare:

That the State of Florida hereby withdraws herself from the Confederacy of States existing under the name of the United States of America, and from the existing Government of the said States; and that all political connection between her and the Government of said States ought to be, and the same is hereby totally annulled, and said Union of States dissolved; and the State of Florida is hereby declared a Sovereign and Independent Nation; and that all Ordinances heretofore adopted, in so far as they create or recognize said Union, are rescinded; and all laws, or parts of laws in force in this State, in so far as they recognized or assented to said Union, be and they are hereby repealed.

REPORT OF THE HON. E. W. PETTUS, COMMISSIONER TO MISSISSIPPI.

MONTGOMERY, January 21, 1861.

His Excellency A. B. Moore:

Sir: The rapidity with which information is now communicated from place to place, and the almost hourly occurrence of most important events, render the recitals of this communication a mere repetition of facts already familiar to the public mind: and though the events herein recited, concern the recent dissolution of a great Government, they have already lost much of their absorbing interest because of the rapid succession of other great political changes of a more recent date.

The Convention of the people of the State of Mississippi assembled at the city of Jackson on the seventh day of the present month; and the Hon. William S. Berry, of Columbus, was elected President. Then, after other officers were chosen, the Convention proceeded to the consideration of the great question which they had been empowered to decide.

The object of my mission was made known to his Excellency J. J. Pettus, the Governor of that State, in a formal note, and was by him communicated to the Convention. And, as Commissioner from this State, I was invited to, and accepted a seat in the Convention; and during my stay at the Capitol of Mississippi, I witnessed the proceedings of the Convention, in its secret as well as its public sessions.

The Convention was composed of ninety-nine delegates, including many of the most distinguished men of the State, and its deliberations were conducted with the order, dignity and solemnity fitting the deliberations of a sovereign people changing their form of Government.

There was a large majority of delegates who favored the immediate dissolution of the political connection between that State and the Government of the United States, and a respectable minority was opposed to the separate action of the State; but no delegate favored the continuance of the Union longer than was necessary to obtain the sanction of the Southern States. The debates arising from these differences of opinion among the delegates, were conducted with great courtesy and forbearance. On the one side, the majority did not resort to the parliamentary rules sometimes used to stifle debate; and on the other, the minority opposed no factious opposition to the will of the majority. No bitter personalities marred the harmony of that body, assembled not to honor or to punish individuals, but to direct the destiny of the State, and to save its people from wrongs and dishonor.

On Wednesday, the ninth day of this month, a Committee, appointed for that purpose, reported an Ordinance declaring the State of Mississippi to be separated from the other States of the Union, and also giving the consent of the people of that State to the formation of a Confederacy, on the basis of the present Constitution, with such States as had then, or might thereafter, secede from the then Federal Union.

Various amendments were proposed and rejected; and about 5 o'clock in the evening, the Ordinance was passed by a vote of eighty-four to fourteen. During the call of the roll, several of the delegates made remarks, explaining their votes, and though some of these remarks were most eloquent and patriotic, and were listened to by a large concourse of spectators, there was no symptom of applause, or other disorder, to disturb the solemnity of the scene. When the President announced the passage of the Ordinance, prayer was offered in the most fervent and impressive manner to the great Ruler of Nations, for the peace, protection and prosperity of the new Republic. It was a scene of moral grandeur—the doing of a brave deed by a gallant people, trusting in God.

On the day after the passage of the Ordinance, I was formally invited to address the Convention; but, as the purpose of my mission had been accomplished, and having no authority from the Convention of Alabama, to make any proposition concerning the formation of a new Government, and not even knowing what would be the action of our State, I thought it best that I should not address the Convention, and, therefore, declined the invitation.

The Ordinance of Secession was enrolled on parchment, and it was signed, on the 15th instant, by every delegate except two, who were absent from the Convention. The people of Mississippi are no longer divided. They are of one mind, ready to spend their fortunes and their lives to make good that which their delegates have ordained. As the minority of the delegates made no factious opposition, so the minority of the people are not inclined to make a seditious resistance to the sovereignty of the State. Those who were opposed to changing the form of Government are now, with a patriotism worthy of all honor, determined to conquer or die in defence of the rights and sovereignty of their State.

I left Jackson on the 18th inst., after having informed the Governor and the Convention of my intention to do so.

I have the honor to be, with great respect, your ob't serv't,
                                        EDMUND W. PETTUS.

CAHABA, Dec. 12, 1860.

His Excellency Andrew B. Moore:

SIR: Without waiting to make a formal report of my mission to the State of Mississippi, I write now to give your Excellency such information as I have in reference to the condition of that State.

In my last communication I informed you particularly as to the acts of the called session of the Legislature of Mississippi, and that the Legislature had adjourned before I reached Jackson.

I presented my credentials to Governor Pettus, and was received and treated by him with all the consideration and respect due to the position in which your Excellency had placed me. I also met in Jackson the Judges of the High Court of Errors and Appeals, the Presidential Electors, and other distinguished citizens of that State, all of whom declared that there was a moral certainty, that a large majority of the Delegates to be elected to their State Convention would be in favor of the immediate secession of that State from the Federal Union; and a Confederacy with such of the Southern States as may withdraw from the Union. The Governor of the State, and all others with whom I conversed in Jackson, approved of a consultation with all of the Southern States *in the mode provided by their Legislature*, that is, by means of Commissioners; and they desired their State to coöperate, but only with such of the slaveholding States as would secede from the Union without delay. They look with special anxiety to the action of Alabama, owing to the local position of our State, and the fact that a very large part of their trade is carried on through our seaport. Mississippi has no seaport which is accessable at this time, and, consequently, is not so well able to carry on a separate Government as Alabama. But with the coöperation of Alabama or Louisiana, I am satisfied that Mississippi is prepared for immediate secession.

There are certain facts, apart from the opinions of distinguished citizens of that State, which strongly tend to show that it is the purpose of the State to secede:

The Governor, the three Judges of the High Court, the two Senators and all their Representatives in Congress, the Auditor, Treasurer, Attorney-General and all the members of the State Legislature, (except three,) are in favor of secession, and declare their sentiments without reserve. Such a body of men so united, and including in their body a very large portion of the talent of the State, with the advantages of their official positions, must have great influence in directing the action of the State. And it is not unreasonable to suppose that public sentiment in the State has had some influence on men in the high places.

In the late Presidential election, the party favoring the election of Mr. Breckinridge declared, in Mississippi, through their orators, that if Lincoln was elected, the State ought to secede from the Union. The candidates nominated by that party for Electors, received 40,797 votes; the candidates of the Constitutional Union party received 25,040 votes; and the candidates who preferred Judge Douglas, obtained 3,283 votes. There are sixty counties in the State, and in forty-seven counties, the candidates of the party which nominated Mr. Breckinridge received a full majority of the votes. It is true, that old party lines are destroyed; but it is also true, that nearly all of those who voted for Mr. Breckinridge, and a large number of those who acted with the Constitutional Union party, and some of the friends of Judge Douglas, are now in favor of the secession of their State from the Union. These facts, as I believe, show what will be the action of the State.

Under the Resolution passed by the Legislature, the Governor of Mississippi has appointed J. W. Matthews, of Marshall County, who was formerly the Governor of the State, as Commissioner to Alabama. He is a man distinguished for his practical wisdom, and highly honored by the people of his State. The Commissioner to this State will remain in Montgomery until after the 7th day of January, to consult with your Excellency and the Convention to assemble on that day.

Governor Pettus will send Commissioners to all the Southern States. The Judges of the High Court, the Attorney-General, and Mr. Thompson, the present Secretary of the Interior, are among the Commissioners appointed. Mr. Thompson is to go to North Carolina, if he will accept the position; and Mr. Hooker is to go to South Carolina, with instructions to advise the authorities of that State to secede from the Union without waiting for the action of other States.

The Legislature of the State of Mississippi, last winter, appropriated one hundred and fifty thousand dollars to arm the State. Of that sum the Governor has used about forty thousand dollars. The Treasury of the State is now empty, and, under the laws, there will be no available means until the first of April next, at which time the Tax Collectors are required to pay in their collections. It is estimated that the revenue for the present year will amount to six hundred thousand dollars. This condition of the Treasury being known, the planters of that State have offered the Governor as much money as he thought necessary to provide for the defence of the State; and Gov. Pettus has accepted the loan, but only to the extent of the money appropriated.

Under the instructions received from your Excellency, and in strict accordance with what I believed to be true, I labored to satisfy the Governor of Mississippi and others, that Alabama would dissolve all political connection with the Federal Government, so soon as she could do so according to the forms of law; and that this State would not consent to be represented in a Convention or Congress of the Southern States until she had become a separate Government; and that it would be the policy of this State to form a Confederacy, at the earliest practicable period, with such of the Southern States as had seceded at that time. And I believe that Governor Pettus will advise his State to pursue the same policy. He informed me that he would use every possible effort to secure the coöperation of all the Southern States, provided the final action of his State is not to be delayed.

I was requested by Governor Pettus to call the attention of your Excellency to the present condition of Fort Morgan, and to ask you to consider whether it is not necessary and proper to provide against the possibility of that fortification being again garrisoned by the Federal Government? Fort Morgan is, at this time, as I was informed in Mobile, well supplied with heavy guns, but without men or ammunition, and, though somewhat out of repair, is a strong fortification. Governor Pettus considered that it would not be improper for him to make this suggestion, as his State is interested in whatever relates to the Gulf trade, but more especially as Fort Morgan commands in part the coast of Mississippi.

My necessary expenses in going to and returning from Jackson, amounted to $45\frac{50}{100}$ dollars. Please direct me how to dispose of the sum of $\$150\frac{50}{100}$, now in my hands, of the sum furnished by you.

I have not been able to wait on your Excellency in person, on account of the sickness of one of my children. If your Excellency thinks my personal appearance would be of any service, I will wait upon you at any time and place you may direct.

There are, perhaps, statements in this communication which should not be made publicly known; but it is entirely for you to judge of that matter. If, however, my report to you is to be communicated to the Convention, as a whole, I will ask permission to make it out in a more formal manner.

I have the honor to be, most respectfully,

Your ob't serv't,
EDM'D W. PETTUS.

REPORT OF THE HON. JAS. M. CALHOUN, COMMISSIONER TO TEXAS.

MONTGOMERY, January 19, 1861.

To His Excellency Gov. A. B. Moore:

DEAR SIR—As soon as possible after receiving your Commission to me, to confer with the authorities of Texas, I visited Austin, the seat of Government.

I did not find either the Legislature or Convention in session, and the Governor was absent. For his return I waited, and with him I had a short conference, being kindly and hospitably received by him and the citizens of Texas generally.

The Governor being the only public authority with whom I could confer, I addressed to him a short communication, in writing, which I now inclose, and from him received, to-day, by mail, a reply, for which I could not wait for a personal delivery; this I also inclose.

The citizens of Texas seemed everywhere to be alive to the grave issues which were forced upon them for consideration. I do not deem it proper to give the impression which was made on my mind as to their future action, from what I saw and heard in my hurried trip from Galveston to Austin and back. This, however, is the less important, as her Legislature meets on the 21st instant, and a Convention, called by her citizens themselves, meets on the 28th instant; and from these we shall soon have an authoritative expression of views and course of action.

However unsatisfactory the meagre results of my mission may be, I trust your Excellency will think that I done all I could do, under the circumstances, and in the short time allowed me.

With sincere respect, I remain yours, etc.,

J. M. CALHOUN.

———

AUSTIN, January 5, 1861.

To His Excellency Gov. Sam Houston:

DEAR SIR—I come as the accredited Commissioner of the State of Alabama, to consult and advise with yourself and the members of the State Legislature and of the Convention of Texas, as to what is best to be done to protect the rights, the interests, and the honor of the slave-holding States.

Neither the Legislature of Texas, or any Convention being *now* in session, and my speedy return to Alabama being required, my conference must be of necessity confined to yourself, with a request that my communication to you may be communicated to the Legislature of Texas, when it shall assemble, as I am pleased to learn it will at no very distant day.

In the performance of this my duty, under all the surrounding circumstances, I have only simply to say, that Alabama, through her Legislature, being the first to move in the direction which may probably result in the severance of all connection with the Federal Government, as the only means of saving her citizens from the utter ruin and degradation which must follow from the administration of that Government, by a sectional, hostile majority, desires to assure her sister slave-holding States, that she feels that her interests are the same with theirs, and that a common destiny must be the same to all. That therefore, whatever may be the course which she may deem it proper to take, to meet the dangers by which she, as well as they, are surrounded, she will do so with an earnest desire that there may be, in the present and in the future, an unbroken bond of brotherhood and union between herself and Texas, and every other slave-holding State; that she will not act with rashness or thoughtlessness, but with mature and deliberate consideration; that she will, by all means, endeavor to avoid the doing of any act which may shake the confidence or alienate the friendly feelings of her sister slave-holding States; that whatever may be the determination of her people, to be assembled in their sovereign character, in Convention, on the 8th instant, they will still cover themselves and posterity under the folds of the old Constitution of the United States, in its purity and truth.

It is perhaps my duty to give to your Excellency my individual opinion, that the action of the Convention to assemble on the 7th instant, will be to withdraw the State from the present Union, and to take her position as a sovereign and independent State, seeking and desiring a near and perfect Union with all the other States of the South, as speedily as possible. This will, however, have been decided, one way or the other, and be made known to the Legislature of your State by the time it shall assemble.

Hoping and trusting that there may be no discord between the States of the South—that unanimity, confidence, wisdom, prudence and firmness may mark the course of all, and that a kind Providence may rule over and guide and protect us in our day of gloom and danger,

I remain, very respectfully, your obedient servant,

J. M. CALHOUN,
Commissioner from Alabama.

EXECUTIVE DEPARTMENT,
AUSTIN, TEXAS, Jan. 7, 1861.

To Hon. J. M. Calhoun, Commissioner from Alabama:

DEAR SIR—Your communication of the 5th inst., informing me of the objects of your mission, on the part of the State of Alabama, is before me.

As a citizen of a sister State, bearing an appointment as Commissioner to Texas, from her Chief Executive, I welcome you here, and trust that whatever ideas you may adopt in reference to the political opinions of the people of Texas, you may bear back with you the evidences of their kindness, hospitality and friendship.

Having convened the Legislature of the State, with a view to its providing a mode by which the will of the people of Texas may be declared, touching their relations with the Federal Government and the States, I cannot authoritatively speak as to the course they will pursue. A fair and legitimate expression of their will, through the ballot-box, is yet to be made known. There fore, were the Legislature in session, or were a legally authorized Convention in session, until the action taken is ratified by the people, at the ballot-box, none can speak for Texas. Her people have ever been jealous of their rights, and have been careful how they parted with the attributes of their sovereignty. They will reserve to themselves the right to finally pass upon the act involving so closely their liberties, fortunes, peace and happiness; and when, through the free exercise of that sacred privilege, which has ever, until now, been deemed the best security for the liberties of the people, and the surest means of remedying encroachments upon their rights, they have declared their will, then, and then only, can any speak for Texas. Until then, nothing but individual opinions can be expressed; and mine are entitled to no more weight than a long acquaintance with the people, and a continued intercourse and communication with them would justify.

That there is a difference of opinion existing in Texas, in relation to the course necessary to pursue at this period, none can deny. Citizens, alike distinguished for their worth and public services, hold opposite views; and while all are united in the determination to maintain our Constitutional rights, they differ as to the mode of accomplishing the same. In this I do not include that reckless and selfish class, who, moved by personal ambition, or a desire for office or spoil, desire a change of Government, in the hope that aggrandizement will attend them. I believe, however, that a large majority of the people, recognizing the obligations they owe to the Border States—who have so long stood as barriers against the assaults of Abolitionism, desire to concert such measures as will not only conduce to their safety, but the benefit of the entire South. As Executive of the State, I have deemed it my duty to present to the other Southern States a proposition for a consultation having that object in view. Alabama has not yet responded to the same, and although the tenor of your letter indicates that she will pursue a different course, I trust that when the great interests at stake are duly considered by her people, they will determine to join with Texas and a majority of the Southern States, in an honest and determined effort to obtain redress, for the grievances which the North has put upon us, ere they take the fatal step, which, in my opinion, ultimately involves civil war and the ruin of our institutions, if not of liberty itself.

If Alabama has been the first to move in the direction which may possibly result in the severance of all connection with the Federal Government, it is a matter of pride to me that Texas has, in the time of peril, been the first to move in that direction calculated to secure Southern unity and coöperation. Texas is the only one of the States which possessed, ere her connection with the Union, full and complete sovereignty. Though she brought an empire into the Union, and added vastly to the area of slavery, she arrogates to herself no especial privileges, nor has she yet consulted her own safety or interest, save in common with that of the entire South. Knowing the obligations which she took upon herself when she came into the Union, she has thus far shown no desire to relieve herself of those obligations, until it is manifest that the compact made with her will not be observed. Having made an effort, in concert with her sister slaveholding States, to secure the observance of that compact, and failed in that effort, it would then be her pride to sink all considerations, prompted by her own ambition, and share a common fate with them; but if, on the contrary, they, consulting their own interests and their own inclinations, neither seeking her counsel or coöperation, act separately and alone, and abandon a Union and a Government of which she yet forms a part, Texas will then be compelled to leave a policy whereby she has unselfishly sought the good of the whole South, and will pursue that course which her pride and her ancient character marks out before her.

Were I permitted to trust alone to the tenor of the first part of your communication, and had you given me no assurance of the fact that, although Alabama "desires to assure her sister slaveholding States, that she feels that her interests are the same with theirs, and that a common destiny must be the same to all, and that she will, through her Convention, which assembles to-day, the 7th inst., withdraw from the present Union, and take her position as a sovereign State," I could give you more assurances of my co-öperation, as Executive of Texas, with Alabama in the present emergency. Should Alabama, without waiting for the action of Texas, withdraw from the Union, and Texas, by the force of circumstances, be compelled, at a future period, to provide for her own safety, the course of Alabama, South Carolina, and such other States as may follow their lead, will but strengthen the conviction, already strong among our people, that their interest will lead them to avoid entangling alliances, and to enter once again upon a national career. No claim would then exist upon Texas, for her coöperation has not been deemed important, at a time when it was essential to her safety; and her statesmen will deem that she violates no duty to the South in imperiling once again her Lone Star banner, and maintaining her position among the independent nations of the earth. If the Union be dissolved, and the gloomy forebodings of patriots be realized, in the ruin and civil war to follow, Texas can "tread the wine-press" alone, in the day of her misfortune, even as her freemen trod it in the past; and if she fails in the effort to maintain liberty and her institutions upon her own soil, she will feel that posterity will justify her, and lay no blame at her door. Texas, unlike Alabama, has a frontier subject to hostile incursions. Even with the whole power of the United States to defend her, it is impossible to prevent frequent outrages upon her citizens. The numerous tribes of Indians, now controlled by the United States, and restrained by treaty stipulations and the presence of the army, would, by the dissolution of the Union, be turned loose to provide for themselves, and judging from the past. it is not unreasonable to suppose they will direct their savage vengeance against Texas. The bandits of Mexico have, within the past year, given an evidence of their willingness to make inroads upon us, could they do so with impunity. These are some of the consequences of disunion which we of the border cannot shut out from our sight. If Texas has been compelled to resort to her own means of defense, when connected with the present Union, it is not to be supposed that she could rely for protection on an alliance with the Gulf States alone; and having grown self-reliant amid adversity, and continued so as a member of the Union, it will be but natural that her people, feeling that they must look to themselves, while sympathizing equally with those States whose institutions are similar to their own, will prefer a separate nationality, to even an equal position in a Confederacy which may be broken and destroyed, at any moment, by the caprice or dissatisfaction of one of its members. Texas has views of expansion not common to many of her sister States. Although an Empire within herself, she feels that there is an empire beyond, essential to her security. She will not be content to have the path of her destiny clogged. The same spirit of enterprise which founded a Republic here, will carry her institutions Southward and Westward. Having, when but a handful of freemen, withstood the power of that nation, and wrung from it her independence, she has no fear of Abolition power while in the Union; and should it be the resolve of her people to stand by the Constitution, and maintain, in the Union, those rights guaranteed to them, she will even be proof against the "utter ruin and ignominy" depicted in your communication. A people determined to maintain their rights, can neither be ruined or degraded; and if Texas takes upon herself the holy task of sustaining the Constitution, even in the midst of its enemies, history will accord her equal praise with those who sought only their own safety, and left the temple of liberty in their possession.

Were I left to believe that Alabama is disposed to second the efforts made to secure the coöperation of the South in demanding redress for our grievances, or that her course would in the least depend upon that of Texas, I would suggest such views as sincere and earnest reflection have induced. But as you express the opinion that Alabama will, through her Convention, without waiting to know the sentiments of the people of Texas, act for herself, there can be no reason why I should press them upon your attention, or is it a matter of importance whether they reflect the popular sentiment of the State, or not; they would be alike unavailing. Nor will I enter into a discussion as to how far the idea of the adoption of the Constitution of the United States will be acceptable to the people of the States forming a Southern Confederacy. That Constitution was a compromise of conflicting interests. It was framed so as to protect the slave-holding States against the encroachments of the non-slave-holding. The statesmen of the South secured a representation for three-fifths of our slave property. Whether this, and other provisions of that instrument will be deemed applicable to States which have no conflicting interests, so far as slavery is concerned, is not for me to say; but I cannot refrain from expressing the opinion, that if the proud and gallant people of Alabama are willing to "still cover themselves and their posterity under the folds of the old Constitution of the United States, in its purity and truth," the rights of Texas will be secure in the present Union, so long as that Constitution is preserved and controls the administration of the Government; and although the administration of the Government by a sectional, hostile majority," will be distasteful to the feelings of Texas, if she can, by fair and Constitutional means, induce that majority to yield obedience to the Constitution, and administer the Government in accordance with it, the triumph will be hers, and we will escape the miseries of civil war, and secure to us, and to our posterity, all the blessings of Liberty, which, by the power of Union, made us the greatest nation on earth.

Recognizing, as I do, the fact that the sectional tendencies of the Black Republican party call for determined Constitutional resistance, at the hands of the United South, I also feel that the million and a-half of noble-hearted, conservative men, who have stood by the South, even to this hour, deserve some sympathy and support. Although we have lost the day, we have to recollect that our conservative Northern friends cast over a quarter of a million more votes against the Black Republicans than we of the entire South. I cannot declare myself ready to desert them, as well as our Southern brethren of the border (and such, I believe, will be the sentiment of Texas), until at least one firm attempt has been made to preserve our Constitutional rights within the Union.

In conclusion, allow me to say, that whatever may be the future of the people of Alabama, my hopes and ardent prayers for prosperity will attend them. When I remember their progress, and the evidences they have had of the blessings of free government, I join you in the belief that they "will not act with rashness, or thoughtlessness, but with mature and deliberate consideration." Forty-seven years ago, to prevent the massacre of her citizens, it was upon her soil that I gave the first proofs of my manhood in devotion to the Union. The flag that I followed then was the same stars and stripes which the sons of Alabama have aided to plant on many a victorious field. Since then Alabama has risen from an almost wilderness region, under the fostering care of the Federal Government, and the power embraced in Union, to a great, wealthy and prosperous people, and obtained a position, which, without Union with the other States, she could not have achieved for ages, if ever.

Receive for yourself and the people of Alabama, whose accredited Commissioner you are, the assurances of my esteem and consideration.

I have the honor to be your most obed't serv't,

SAM HOUSTON.

REPORT OF HON. R. H. SMITH, AND HON. ISHAM W. GARROTT, COMMISSIONERS TO NORTH CAROLINA.

To His Excellency Andrew B. Moore, Governor of the State of Alabama:

SIR—We have the honor to report to your Excellency that, under the Commission with which you honored us, we proceeded to Raleigh, North Carolina, and placed our Commission in the hands of His Excellency the Governor of that State, who promptly communicated it to the General Assembly, then in session. We were cordially welcomed to the State, and made its guests. The Governor heartily sympathises with the cause in which we are engaged, and the remedy proposed. The two houses of the General Assembly, through their Committee, tendered us the welcome of the State, and invited us to address them, in the Hall of the House of Representatives, on the subject of our mission, at such time as might meet our wishes. On the twentieth day of this month, the time designated by us, in response to the invitation of the Committee, we met the Senate and the House, and read to them the paper, of which we herewith furnish you a copy. We believe the tone and sentiment of the paper met with approbation. On the night of that day, we each, by invitation, delivered oral addresses to a large assembly, convened in the Hall of the House of Representatives, in which we set forth, at some length, the grievances of the South, and justified our resistance. We also attempted to show that the cause was that of North Carolina as much as it was that of Alabama.

Our Commission being to the Governor and the *members* of the Assembly, we, of course, could neither invite nor expect a response from the Legislature as a Representative Body; but we formed a general acquaintance with the members, and embraced every suitable opportunity of representing to them the views and purposes of our people, and urged the propriety and importance of action by North Carolina, in conformity with that proposed and being taken by Alabama. We found a large number of the members, probably a majority, heartily corresponding with our views, and earnestly devoting themselves to the furtherance and establishment of them. We, however, found party lines closely drawn on the old issues, and that this condition of things interposed a great impediment to harmony of feeling in respect to the present movement. It was understood that the people of the State were holding primary meetings in the several counties, and that the sentiment reflected by them indicated opinions in advance of the Legislature.

The question of calling a Convention was pending before the General Assembly, and it was believed would certainly command a majority, and probably a two-thirds vote, which, by many, was supposed necessary, under the provisions of their Constitution. In the view of this being regarded as a doubtful question, and of the approach of the Christmas holidays, and of the fact that the question was supposed to have received a great impetus among the people since the election of members, and even since the General Assembly convened, action upon the proposition to call a Convention was deferred until after the recess, which the General Assembly has now taken. We found the indications of approval and sympathy with us so strong, as to leave us in no doubt but North Carolina will make the cause of the South her cause, and to convince us that the period is near at hand when she will be acting in full fellowship with us. We, however, found her slower than Alabama for action, and some regret existing that no preliminary joint-consultation and action had been proposed by her sister Southern States.

We also found a strong apprehension that we of the cotton States would endeavor to reopen the African slave trade, to which the people of North Carolina seem unalterably opposed. You will observe the assurances we have given them on this point, in our address, and we need not say that the sentiments we have expressed for our people, meet our undivided approval.

Your Excellency will also observe the assurances we gave them that the movement in Alabama was not one of resistance to law and order, but on the contrary, had for its object the preservation of both, and the protection of our present Constitutional rights.

We found a few leading members of the General Assembly thinking of a middle Confederacy, which idea had, we believe, its origin in the apprehensions above alluded to; but in our opinion the project has little foothold in North Carolina; and we entertain no doubt but she will unite with us in resistance, and in the formation of a new Government, especially if we show, as we trust we shall, that our action is to be characterized by the maintainance of a well-regulated Constitutional Government.

The courtesies and gratulations extended to us, impressed us with the conviction that North Carolina received our mission in the true spirit of fraternal kindness, and we hope it tended to aid the cause, not only by quickening the sympathies of the people towards us, but by relieving them of the fears which we have said were prevailing in respect to our purposes.

We have the honor to be your Excellency's obd't serv'ts,

I. W. GARROTT,
ROB'T H. SMITH.

December 29, 1860.

To His Excellency the Governor, and to the Honorable the members of the General Assembly of the State of North Carolina:

The General Assembly of the State of Alabama, on the 11th day of January, A. D. 1860, by joint resolutions, made it the duty of His Excellency the Governor of Alabama, upon the election of a President of the United States advocating the principles and action of the party in the Northern States calling itself the Republican party, to issue his writs of election for delegates to a Convention of the State, "to consider, determine and do whatever, in the opinion of said Convention, the rights, interests and honor of the State of Alabama require to be done for their protection."

In consequence of the results of the late Presidential election, the Governor of Alabama has issued the writs of election required. The election is to be held on the twenty-fourth day of this month, and the Convention is to assemble on the seventh day of January next.

North Carolina and Alabama have been true and loyal to the Constitution and to the Union. There is no plighted faith which each has not kept. They have stood together in fidelity to the Government, and to each of the States composing the Confederacy. They are bound together by a common duty, a common interest, a common danger and a common honor. North-Carolina has largely contributed to the population of our State, and her sons have brought along with them those principles of integrity, honor, obedience to law, and love of well-regulated liberty, for which she is known and admired, and which have imparted so much of worth and prosperity to the States in which her children have settled. It is therefore fit, that now, in this their hour of trial, North-Carolina and Alabama should consult and advise together; and his Excellency the Governor of Alabama, has charged us with a commission to this our native State, "to consult and advise with his Excellency the Governor, and with the members of this Legislature, as to what is best to be done to protect the rights, interests and honor of the slave-holding States, and to report the result of such consultation." We feel complimented in accepting the invitation of this General Assembly, to appear before them in discharge of the duties imposed upon us.

We believe that the exhibitions of public opinion in Alabama are so marked and distinct, as to justify us in declaring that her approaching Convention will withdraw her from the Federal Union. A result so sad, and so pregnant with consequences to herself and to her sister States, requires that she should have grave and conclusive reasons for the step. Light and transient causes will not justify it; much less should restlessness, passion or ambition influence her action. Her obligations to the other States, to the cause of Free Government, and to the civilized world forbid it. Her hopes of reconstructing, with the other States of the South, a well-regulated Government, which shall "establish justice, insure domestic tranquility, provide for the common defense, promote the general welfare, and secure the blessings of liberty to ourselves and our posterity," alike forbid it.

Our people consider that the Constitution of the United States is the charter of our national rights and duties, by which our fathers bound us to the Union, and under which, in its integrity, our people would be content to live, and would envy none the prosperity it brings; but they think that the past and present conduct, and apparently settled rule of action of the non-slave-holding States, are vialative of its plain letter and spirit—and the people of Alabama, we believe, will no longer be bound by its obligations while deprived of its benefits.

They think the history of the country shows, that some of the non-slave-holding States have, throughout our political existence, proven themselves sectional, and hostile to the rights and interest of the common country. Some of them have opposed every war in which we have been involved, from that of 1812, with Great Britain, to the war with Mexico; have opposed the acquisition of the rich territories we have obtained—even that which gave us the Mississippi river and the vast plains watered by it; and yet these States, with the other non-slave-holding States, have adopted and are acting on the settled policy that we of the South shall be excluded from the Territories, obtained by the common exertions and treasures of the nation; and that to maintain this sectional policy, the Constitution of the United States, as expounded by the grave, well and earnestly considered decision of the Supreme Court of the United States, is to be set at naught, and the Court itself, which made the decision, is to be reformed, not only for general partizan purposes, but for the particular purpose of obtaining a reversal of that decision. A party which announces, as a cardinal article of its creed, the degradation of the highest Court in the world, does, in the opinion of the people of Alabama, offer no rule of Government consistent with well-regulated, Constitutional freedom. Beyond this, is the fact that the plain letter of the Constitution, providing for the rendition of fugitive slaves, has not only been annulled by the non-slave-holding States, but several of them have, by their so-called "personal-liberty bills," made it a highly penal offense for a master to attempt the enforcement of the Fugitive-Slave Law of Congress. So it has come to this, that degrading punishment is the consequence of a citizen of the South going into these States, with the Constitution of the United States in his hand, asking simply for the performance of the guarantees therein provided. Nor are those non-slave-holding States that have not passed such bills, behind their coöperators in practically annulling the clause of the Constitution referred to—for it is well known that in most, if not all of the non-slave-holding States, the rights of the master of the slave are defied and set at naught, and that public opinion, aided by mobs, has as effectually overthrown the Constitution and the Law, as though neither had any existence. Were this state of things the result of some sudden gleam of passion, the people of Alabama might hope that a returning sense of justice would bring obedience to duty; but, unhappily, the past and present prove that such a hope is illusory. The violations of their obligations to us, have been so long continued, and so oft repeated, that the principle has incorporated itself into their education and religion, until the doctrine of the law of conscience has been set up over the supreme law of the land, and hatred to the South and her institutions has usurped the teachings of the Bible. The spirit of sectional animosity has so "grown with their growth and strengthened with their strength," that their matured, cultivated, and trusted statesmen have proclaimed, that the conflict between the sections is "irrepressible," and their people have, in the late Presidential election, responded affirmatively to the announcement.

The election of a President of the United States, of any opinion, however heretical, and however much calculated to disturb the public mind, would, of itself, we think, be considered by our people as of secondary importance; but the recent Presidential election is the inauguration of a system of Government as opposed to the Constitution as it is to our rights and safety. It ushers in, as a settled policy, not only the exclusion of the people of the South from the common Territories of the country, but proposes to impair the value of slave property in the States by unfriendly legislation; to prevent the further spread of slavery by surrounding us with free States; to refuse admission into the Union of another slave State, and by these means to render the institution itself dangerous to us, and to compel us, as slaves increase, to abandon it, or be doomed to a servile war. The establishment alone of the policy of the Republican party, that no more slave States are to be admitted into the Union, and that slavery is to be forever prohibited in the Territories (the common property of the United States), must, of itself, at no distant day, result in the utter ruin and degradation of most, if not all of the Gulf States. Alabama has at least eight slaves to every square mile of her tillable soil. This population outstrips any race on the globe in the rapidity of its increase; and if the slaves now in Alabama are to be restricted within her present limits, doubling as they do once in less than thirty years, the children are now born who will be compelled to flee from the land of their birth, and from the slaves their parents have toiled to acquire as an inheritance for them, or to submit to the degradation of being reduced to an equality with them, and all its attendant horrors. Our people and institutions must be secured the right of expansion, and they can never submit to a denial of that which is essential to their very existence.

The non-slave-holding States, while declaring that we shall not expand, and that thereby we shall be crushed by our slave population, are charging upon us a design to reöpen the African slave trade, and seize upon two or three ineffectual attempts, by Northern vessels, to import Africans into Southern ports, as an evidence of the fact. The charge is a slander upon our people, and a reflection upon their intelligence. There may be, here and there, found an advocate for the measure, as there may in every community be found individual advocates of any heresy; but our people, with almost entire unanimity, would reject the proposition as offensive to their sense of propriety and averse to their interests. They feel no desire to depreciate the value of their own property, nor to demoralize their slaves by throwing among them savages and cannibals. They will look, as heretofore, to the redundant slave population of the more Northern of their associated sister States of the South for such additions to their negroes as their wants may require.

The state of opinion and of conduct in the non-slave-holding States, finds no justification or apology, in any general or special direction of Federal Legislation to their injury. On the contrary, such legislation has been greatly to their advantage and prosperity. The benefits that have been conferred upon them in the shape of tariff laws, navigation laws, fishing bounties, land laws, and internal improvement laws, have been important aids to their material prosperity—a prosperity which is, in fact, to a great extent, the result of burdens upon the agricultural interests of the South.

The apologists of the present state of public mind at the North, sometimes maintain that it finds palliation, at least, in the repeal of the Act of 1820, known as the Missouri Compromise—which, in other words, is a complaint that the North can no longer keep in force a law which the Supreme Court of the United States have declared to be unconstitutional. But the well-remembered history of recent events teaches us, that it was the South which, a few years since, endeavored, in a spirit of concession, to extend the line of thirty-six degrees thirty minutes to the Pacific Ocean, and the North who refused the offer.

The sectional strife has now been conducted with increasing rancor for more than twenty years, until every question of Government furnishes a theme for its discussion. The Halls of Congress have ceased to be places for statesmen, and have degenerated into arenas for strife. Our people have grown tired of the controversy, and can see no good in prolonging the quarrel, and no way to end it in the Union. Submission would but invite new and greater aggressions, until Alabama would become a despised and degraded province. Our people see little hope for the adjustment, within the Union, of questions upon which the public mind of the sections has been driven so wide apart, and discern, in the present temper and conduct of the non-slave-holding States, no spirit of atonement for their wrongs, which could offer peace to the country. Indeed, when the plain letter of the law has been so long and persistently violated, they would not rely upon any adjustment short of farther Constitutional guaranties.

Alabama hopes that, among other evils which public affairs have brought, and are bringing upon her, there may not be added that of a divided South. She sets up no rule of action for her sister States, but hopes to obtain their consultation, advice and assistance; and she repeats, through us, her Commissioners, the expression of her fervid desire that North-Carolina may be with her in counsel and in action, and with her in attempting to uphold the principles of liberty which are engrafted into the Constitution of the United States, and in the hearts of her people, and that the States of the South may be enabled to snatch that Constitution, and those principles, from the desecrating touch of fanatical " higher law." I. W. GARROTT,
ROB'T H. SMITH.

REPORT OF THE HON. DAVID CLOPTON, COMMISSIONER TO DELAWARE.

WASHINGTON, D. C., January 8, 1860.

SIR:—In discharge of the duties imposed by your appointment of Commissioner from the State of Alabama to the State of Dela-

THE CONVENTION OF ALABAMA.   437

ware, I prepared and delivered, in person, to his Excellency,
William Burton, a communication in writing, which I requested
should also be submitted to the Legislature, then in session, and a
copy of which I herewith transmit to you. The health of my
family prevented me from spending as much time with the Governor
and Legislature, as it was my wish and intention to have done.
No reply to my communication has been received. I was assured
that the State of Alabama had the sympathy of many of the citizens
of Delaware in this trying emergency; although the members of
the Legislature, not having been elected in view of the present
crisis, would not, probably, give expression, by a majority vote, to
this sympathy. From the best information which I received, I
have no hesitation in assuring your Excellency, that whilst the
people of Delaware are averse to a dissolution of the Union, and
favor a Convention of the Southern States—perhaps, of all the
States—to adjust and compromise, if possible, existing difficulties,
yet, in the event of dissolution, however accomplished, a large
majority of the people of Delaware will defend the South. An
effort will be made to procure the call of a Convention by the
Legislature, which it is hoped will be successful; and then the
people of Delaware can decide their own course according to their
own conceptions of the requirements of honor, safety and right.

It gives me pleasure to report to your Excellency, my cordial
reception by the officers of the Executive Department of the State
of Delaware, and my very agreeable intercourse with them and
many of the Members of the Legislature.

I have the honor to remain
Very truly yours,
DAVID CLOPTON.
His Excellency A. B. MOORE, Montgomery, Ala.

HON. DAVID CLOPTON TO THE GOVERNOR OF DELAWARE.

DOVER, Delaware, January 1st, 1861.

SIR :—I have the honor to transmit to you the accompanying papers, including a commission from the Governor of the State of Alabama, appointing the undersigned commissioner to the sovereign
State of Delaware, "to advise and consult with his Excellency Governor William Burton, and the members of the Legislature or State
Convention, as the case may be, of said State, as to what is best to
be done to protect the rights, interests and honor of the slaveholding States." With a due appreciation of the delicacy and respon-

sibility of the trust confided, and from an earnest desire to discharge its duties in the manner most conducive to the harmony and co-operation so eminently proper in present emergencies, I address your Excellency this communication, and request that it be submitted to your Legislature.

The necessity of such consultation, and of the appointment of a commissioner for the purpose expressed, implies that these rights, interests and honor are endangered. The causes which have produced, upon the part of the people and Governor of the State of Alabama, this not merely apprehension, but conviction of danger, are indicated in the accompanying commission.

In the succession of party triumphs and defeats which have marked the political history of the country, the power and patronage of the Executive Department of the Federal Government will, on the 4th March next, pass, for the first time, under the control of a purely sectional party, which has succeeded by a purely sectional vote. The principles and purposes of this party, as defined in its platforms and by its leaders and presses, are too well understood to render it necessary for me to recall them in detail, to the notice of your Excellency. The fact that it is a sectional party includes the additional fact that its aim will be, by all the means of legislation and of the administration of the Government, to promote and foster the interests and internal prosperity of one section, and to debase the institutions, weaken the power, and impair the interests of the other section. Its animus, its single bond of union, is hostility to the institution of slavery, as it exists in the Southern States. Its members, numbering nearly two millions of voters, as evidenced by the late presidential election, have been collected from all the other various political organizations; and, although disagreeing totally upon other important political principles, have, nevertheless, ignored all these, and been moulded into a compact mass of enmity to this particular institution, upon which depend the domestic, social, and political interests of fifteen States of the Union; and which institution was recognized, respected, guarded and protected by the convention which framed the Constitution, and by the people of the States by whom it was ordained and established.

The slaveholding States, notwithstanding the vastness of their interests at stake, will be either unrepresented in the Cabinet councils of the incoming Administration, or represented by men who sympathize with this party in its purpose. The same policy will be pursued by the Executive department which the President elect recommended in a public address, when, after having declared the ends to be accomplished, he said: "To do these things, we must employ instrumentalities; we must hold conventions; we must adopt platforms, if we conform to the ordinary custom; we must nominate candidates, and we must carry elections. In all these things I think we ought to keep in view our real purpose, and in none do anything that stands adverse to our purpose." Those men who direct the sentiment, purpose, and action of this party, have notified the people of the slaveholding States that the past policy of the Federal Government is now to be wholly changed; that those principles which have secured our present respect abroad and our past internal prosperity are to be superseded by others which are adverse to the true theory, nature, and designs of the Federal Government.

Mr. Lincoln has left us in no doubt as to his policy. In the address before alluded to, which he delivered at Cincinnati in September, 1859, he emphatically declared: "I think we want, and must have, a national policy in regard to the institution of slavery, that acknowledges and deals with that institution as being wrong. Whoever desires the prevention of the spread of slavery, and the nationalization of that institution, yields all when he yields to any policy that either recognizes slavery as being right or as being an indifferent thing. Nothing will make you successful but setting up a policy which shall treat the thing as being wrong. When I say this, I do not mean to say that this General Government is charged with the duty of redressing or preventing all the wrongs in the world; but I do think that it is charged with preventing and redressing all wrongs which are wrongs to itself. This Government is expressly charged with the duty of providing for the general welfare. We believe that the spreading and perpetuity of the institution of slavery impairs the general welfare. We believe, nay, we know, that that is the only thing that has ever threatened the perpetuity of the Union itself. The only thing which has ever menaced the destruction of the government under which we live, is this very thing. To repress this thing is, we think, providing for the general welfare." He may suppose that the people of the slaveholding States will be satisfied with the assurance that he does not intend to interfere with slavery in the States; but, in thus supposing, he supposes further, that they have not the manhood and honor to assert and maintain, or do not possess the intelligence to understand, their rights in the Territories, or wherever else the jurisdiction of the Government extends; and that they are willing to surrender all the outposts, and leave the citadel unguarded, liable to, first, covert, then open attacks. Notwithstanding this assurance, common sense and experience, our knowledge of human nature and all history teach that, believing slavery to be a moral and political evil, a wrong to the Government, and that these States cannot exist half free and half slave, Mr. Lincoln will exert all his powers, influence, and patronage "to place it where the public mind shall rest in the belief that it is in the course of ultimate extinction."

From these principles and this avowed policy the following propositions may be correctly deduced:

The success of "republicanism" ignores the sovereignty and disregards the rights of the States, by disallowing the concurrent majorities established by the Constitution and perverting the powers of the Federal Government to the redressing of what it may consider to be a wrong in the social, domestic, or local institutions and regulations of any of the States; and by converting that which was intended to be a Federal Republic into a consolidated, centralized power—a despotism of numbers.

Its success destroys the equality of the States, by a denial of common and equal rights in the common Territories; by the effectual exclusion of any representative voice, on behalf of the slaveholding States, in the management of a co-ordinate department of the Government, and by the declared intent to administer that department in a manner hostile to their peace, safety and prosperity.

Its success subverts and defeats the ends of the Constitution. Instead of forming a more perfect Union, it has dissolved the Union, by compelling the secession of one of its members and the anticipated secession of others; instead of establishing justice, it denies justice to fifteen of the States, by refusing to admit any more slave States into the Union, and by the enactment of laws to prevent the rendition of fugitive slaves; it endangers, instead of insuring, domestic tranquility, by the possession of the channels through which to circulate insurrectionary documents and disseminate insurrectionary sentiments among a hitherto contented servile population; it neglects, instead of providing for, the common defence, by permitting, within the limits of some of the States, the organization of plans for the armed invasion of others, and by refusing to surrender the criminals when fugitives from justice; it disregards and impairs, instead of promoting, the general welfare, by compassing the destruction of an inestimable amount of property with all its direful consequences; it will rob us of, instead of securing to ourselves and our posterity, the blessings of liberty, by the extinction of a great domestic and social institution, by the overthrow of self-government, and the establishment of an equality of races in our midst.

Its success overthrows the fundamental principles of the Revolution, by denying the freedom of property. This freedom of property is the corner-stone of social happiness. As has been said, "the rights to life, liberty, and property, are so intimately blended together that neither can be lost in a state of society without all; or, at least, neither can be impaired without wounding the others." To maintain the value of property and realize its fullest advantages, there must be guaranteed permanency, security, and protection. "Republicanism" proposes to place the right to property in slaves under the ban of a consolidated, centralized General Government, and threatens to employ all its powers and resources to the consummation of the single purpose of destroying this single species property. When this shall be done, the right to "life, liberty, and the pursuit of happiness" must be involved in common ruin, for the admission of sovereignty in a government admits the universal claim of governmental sovereignty to despotic power over all these, whether it is, in form, a monarchy, a democracy, or a republic.

From these considerations, your Excellency must concur in the opinion, expressed by the Governor of the State of Alabama, that "the success of said party, and the power which it now has, and will soon acquire, greatly endanger the peace, interests, security and honor of the slaveholding States, and make it necessary that prompt and efficient measures should be adopted to avoid the evils which must result from a republican administration of the Federal Government." You can not be surprised that, in the opinion of the opinion of the people of Alabama, the time has arrived when imperious necessity and self-preservation require them to exercise their right to abolish the present Government and institute a new one, "laying its foundation in such principles and organizing its powers in such form as to them shall seem most likely to effect their safety and happiness.

I am impressed with a sense of this necessity, and contemplating the possible success of this party, the General Assembly of Alabama, at the session of 1859–'60, adopted joint resolutions by which it was made the duty of the Governor, upon the election of its candidates for the Presidency and Vice Presidency, to call a Convention of the people, "to consider, determine, and do whatever, in the opinion of said convention, the rights, interests, and honor of the State of Alabama require to be done for their protection." The Governor, by authority of said joint resolutions, and with the full concurrence of his own opinion, did, on the 6th day of this month, issue a proclamation, calling said Convention to assemble on the 7th day of January next. Commissioned to advise and consult with your Excellency, it would be improper to declare, at this time, and in this communication, what, in my opinion, will be the action of that Convention.

I will simply suggest that the hope of obtaining new and sufficient guarantees, by way of constitutional amendments or otherwise, has abandoned the hearts of all, even the most moderate Southern men. The expressions of republican presses, and the representative men in and out of Congress, the futile efforts of the Senate and House Committees, and the persistent silence of Mr. Lincoln, have extinguished the last ray of such hope. But, even if new guarantees could be obtained, they can bring no sense of security to the Southern mind; they would prove a temporary and delusive truce—a broken reed to pierce hereafter. The slaveholding States have never complained of the insufficiency of the Constitution, or of the want of additional and further guarantees. They have asked no more than the faithful observance of those which are contained in the present Constitution. New guarantees will be utterly valueless without an entire revolution in the public temper, prejudices, opinions, sentiments, and education of the people of the non-slaveholding States. Laws passed in compliance with such new guarantees for the security and protection of property in slaves will avail nothing where their execution depends upon the Republican appointees of a Republican President.

Speaking from what I am assured is the determination of the people of the State of Alabama, and from what I know to be the opinion of her Governor, they do not propose to violate any section or clause of the Constitution in this movement. Whilst Alabama continues a member of the Union the people and chief Executive intend, as it is their proud boast to have ever done, to regard and observe that instrument as a sacred compact. Hence the State of Alabama, being in the Union and prohibited by the 3rd clause of the 10th section of the 1st article of the Constitution, does not propose co-operation in the sense of entering into any agreement or compact with another State or States to abolish the Federal Government, or to secede from the Union. After the State has seceded by separate State action, this prohibition of the Constitution no longer restrains or operates upon the sovereign right "to contract alliances, and do all the other acts and things which independent States may of right do." This sufficiently answers the objection, so constantly urged, that several of the cotton States are determined to precipitate the act of secession, and disregard the situation and interests of their sister slaveholding States by refusing to meet them in convention. The people of Alabama recognize the right of the people of each other State to decide upon any infraction of their rights by the Federal Government, and to determine the mode and measure of redress.

The people of Alabama, however, also understand, and will observe, the comity which should exist between sovereign States, and especially between the slaveholding States. They fully appreciate the position and condition of the border slaveholding States, and are willing and ready to engage with them in a defence of common rights and safety. Identity of interest is a bond of sympathy. Similar dangers suggest the propriety of similar and simultaneous action, as far as practicable. The withdrawal of all the slaveholding States, and the organization of a Southern Confederacy, would possess a moral, political, and physical power which no government would dare to oppose. Yet the people of Alabama will not assume or pretend to dictate to the intelligent, brave, and patriotic people of the State of Delaware what course their safety, interests, and honor require them to adopt, believing that they are competent and have the right to decide by and for themselves. They ask only to advise and consult together.

To secure such consultation, in order to be informed of the views and opinions of the citizens of other States, and to show a due respect for these views and opinions, at the same time avoiding any semblance of a violation of the Constitution, the Governor of Alabama has appointed a commissioner to each of the slaveholding States. It will be my pleasure to advise and consult with your Excellency and the membess of the Legislature, so far as may be agreeable and practicable, and to communicate the views and purposes of your Excellency, and the sentiments and desires of the people of Delaware, to the Governor of the State of Alabama by the time of the meeting of the State Convention.

I have the honor to be, very respectfully, sir,

DAVID CLOPTON.

REPORT OF HON. DAVID HUBBARD, COMMISSIONER TO ARKANSAS.

KINLOCH, Alabama, }
3d January, 1860. }

Governor Andrew B. Moore:

MY DEAR SIR—

On receipt of your letter and appointment as Commissioner from Alabama to Arkansas, I repaired at once to Little Rock, and presented my credentials to the two Houses, and also your letter to Gov. Rector, by all of whom I was politely received. The Governor of Arkansas was every way disposed to further our views, and so were many leading and influential members of each House of the Legislature, but neither are yet ready for action, because they fear the people have not yet made up their minds to go out. The counties bordering on the Indian Nations, Creeks, Cherokees, Choctaws and Chicasaws, would hesitate greatly to vote for secession, and leave those Tribes still under the influence of the Government at Washington, from which they receive such large stipends and annuities. These Indians are at a spot very important, in my opinion, in this great sectional controversy, and must be assured that the South will do *as well* as the North, before they could be induced to change their alliances and dependence. I have much on this subject to say when I get to Montgomery, which cannot well be written.

The two Houses passed Resolutions inviting me to meet them in the Representative Hall, and consult together as to what had best be done in this matter. When I appeared, men were anxious to know what the seceding States intended to do in certain contingencies. My appointment gave me no authority to speak as to what any State would do, but I spoke freely of what, in my opinion, we ought to do. I took the ground, that no State which had seceded would ever go back, without full power being given to protect themselves by vote against anti-slavery projects and schemes of every kind. I took the position, that *the Northern people were honest*, and did fear the Divine displeasure, both in this world and the world to come, by reason of what they considered the *national sin* of slavery; and that all who agreed with me in a belief of their sincerity, must see that we *could not* remain quietly in the same Government with them.

Secondly, if they were dishonest hypocrites, and only lied to impose on others and make them hate us, and used anti-slavery arguments as mere pretexts for the purpose of uniting Northern sentiment against us, with a view to obtain political power and sectional dominion, in that event we *ought not* to live with them. I desired any Unionist present to controvert either of these positions, which seemed to cover the whole ground. No one attempted either, and I said but little more.

I am satisfied, from free conversations with members of all parties, and with Gov. Rector, that Arkansas, when compelled to choose, will side with the Southern States, but at present a majority would vote the Union ticket. Public sentiment is but being formed, but must take that direction.

I have the honor to be truly, &c.,
DAVID HUBBARD.

ADDRESS TO THE PEOPLE OF ALABAMA.

The undersigned, delegates to the Convention of the people of the State of Alabama, feel it their duty to themselves, to their constituents, and to the people of the State at large, to make public the reasons that actuate them in withholding their signatures from the Ordinance of Secession by which the people of Alabama resumed, on the 11th day of January, 1861, the powers previously delegated to and exercised by the Federal Government. This duty is the more imperative, as designing persons have misrepresented, and will continue to misconstrue, their refusal to participate in a mere form of attestation, into opposition and hostility to a solemn act of the State. This act is binding on all citizens alike, and none are more ready than the undersigned, to yield a cheerful obedience to the will of their State, to which they owe their first and paramount allegiance, and none will be more faithful in upholding and sustaining at any price, and at any sacrifice, her interest and her honor, in the attitude she has assumed by this act. If, therefore, the enemies of the State derive comfort from the refusal of the undersigned to sign the Ordinance, the fault will lie with those who misrepresent their motives or impugn their patriotism and loyalty to their State.

The Ordinance derives no additional validity from the signatures of the individual delegates composing the Convention. The affixing these signatures is a mere form of attestation, and might be, and most likely would be, regarded as a voluntary abandonment and retraction of those principles and views of public policy, advocated by the undersigned before the people, and which caused them to oppose the passage of the Ordinance of Secession, [in its present form.] While the undersigned cannot consent to have even the appearance of modifying or relinquishing these views and principles, they do sincerely disclaim all intention to perpetuate the bitterness and animosities of former party divisions, or to encourage new divisions between those who favored and those who opposed separate State action, and they solemnly pledge themselves to a faithful and zealous support of the State in all the consequences that may result from the Ordinance of Secession.

These principles and views of public policy, to which they stood pledged to their constituents, and which have governed their action in Convention, are so well known as to require only a brief enumeration.

First. The great fundamental principle that all representative bodies, exercising a high and responsible public trust, should submit their acts for the approval or condemnation of those by whom the trust was confided; especially when in the discharge of such trust, is involved a radical change in the existing Government, affecting alike the highest and the lowest in the land, and upon which depends the welfare and happiness of not only this generation, but that of the remotest posterity, demanded that the Ordinance of Secession should have been submitted to the people of the State for their ratification or rejection at the ballot box. This principle is the foundation of the whole theory of popular government, and is the only safeguard to the abuses of trust and the usurpations of power.

Secondly. Not only comity, but the interest of all concerned, and of none more than Alabama, dictated the policy of respect fully consulting with all the States whose identity of interest makes their ultimate destiny inseparable from ours, and who are affected almost as much as ourselves by any action on our part, of devising with them, or at least such of them as would join us in a plan of harmonious and simultaneous action, thus presenting in all our dealings with the Federal Government, foreign nations or hostile States, a united strength, a moral power and a national dignity, which no single State could hope to present; of establishing a new Confederacy of all the States engaged in a common cause, before finally severing all connection with the Federal Government, and thus avoiding to the individual States the burdens and dangers of an independent and separate national existence, placing the formation of a new Confederacy beyond the risks and hazards to which it would be subjected by the conflicting interests and views of disunited States, each acting for itself, without concert one with another, and leaving no interregnum during which men's minds could be unsettled, and all material interests jeoparded by the uncertainties of the future. These views of policy the undersigned are convinced are the only ones consonant with prudence and a wise discretion, and the only ones that can lead to a peaceful and successful termination of present difficulties. It is not yet too late to apply them, at least in part, to the management of public affairs, and as we see with pleasure the cheering indications of their being more generally recognised and adopted than during the first effervesence of popular excitement, at the accumulated wrongs and insults of hostile and sectional factions, culminating in the election of a sectional President.

It will not be necessary to add, in conclusion, that in refusing to sign the Ordinance of Secession, the undersigned are actuated by no desire to avoid the responsibilities that now attach, or may hereafter attach, to the act by which the State withdrew from the Federal Union. Not only will they share these responsibilities alike with those who sign the Ordinance, but if it should appear that the public interest or expediency requires the affixing of their signatures, they will unhesitatingly and cheerfully do so—their object being in the present statement solely to defend and maintain the principles and line of policy, the advocacy and support of which was entrusted to them by their constituents, and which they believed to be of vital importance to the future peace and welfare of the State.

With this brief exposition of our acts, and the reasons therefor, we are willing to be judged by a candid public; the truth and sincerity of our declarations and motives, time alone can decide; and upon the correctness and wisdom of those principles and views of public policy, by which we have been governed, "other men and other times" will render a correct verdict.

R. JEMISON, JR.,
WM. O. WINSTON,
JOHN GREENE, SR., }Com.
S. P. TIMBERLAKE,
M. J. BULGER,
A. KIMBAL,
WILLIAM H. EDWARDS,
R. R. WOOD,
GEORGE FORRESTER,
HENRY M. GAY,
WINSTAN STIDHAM,
ARTHUR C. BEARD,
JAMES L. SHEFFIELD,
J. N. FRANKLIN,
JONATHAN FORD,
ROBERT GUTTERY,
W. R. SMITH,

NICK DAVIS,
THOS. J. McCLELLAN,
JOHN POTTER,
S. C. POSEY,
E. P. JONES,
B. W. WILSON,
LANG C. ALLEN,
JOHN A. STEELE,
J. P. COMAN,
HENRY C. SANFORD,
JOHN J. BRASHER,
W. A. WOOD,
JOHN R. COFFEY,
TIMOTHY J. RUSSELL,
H. C. JONES,
WM. L. WHITLOCK.

WITHDRAWAL OF ALABAMA SENATORS.

MR. DARGAN, from the Committee on Foreign Relations, made the following report:

Your Committee, to whom was referred certain resolutions adopted by many of the Southern Senators and members of the

House of Representatives of the Congress of the United States, have had the same under consideration:

They believe that the Ordinance of Secession adopted by the Convention of the people of Alabama, severs *completely* all connections between the State of Alabama and the Government of the United States. That the State of Alabama is no longer entitled to, and ought not to, be *represented* in the Congress of the United States; therefore, that they have instructed me to report the following Resolution:

Resolved, That our Senators and members of Congress of the Government of the United States, at Washington, be informed, that the State of Alabama can *no longer be represented* in the Congress of the United States, as *one* of said United States.

Adopted—*no dissenting voice.*

WITHDRAWAL OF ALABAMA SENATORS.

Mr. CLAY, of Alabama:

I rise to announce, for my colleague and myself, that the people of Alabama have adopted an Ordinance of separation, and that they are all in favor of withdrawing from this Union. I wish it to be understood that this is the act of the people of Alabama, in taking this momentous step. It is nearly forty-two years since Alabama came into this Union. She entered it amid violence and excitement, caused by the hostility of the North against the institutions of slavery at the South. It is this same spirit of hostility at the North which has effected the secession of Mississippi, South Carolina, Georgia, Florida and Alabama. It has denied us Christian communion, because it could not endure what it styles the leprosy of slavery. It refuses us permission to pass through the North with our property, in violation of the Constitution and the laws of Congress designed to protect that property. It has refused us any share in the lands acquired mainly by our diplomacy, our blood, and our treasure. It has robbed us of our property and refused restoration. It has refused to deliver up criminals against our laws who fled to the North with our property, or with blood upon their hands, and it threatened us with punishment, and murdered Southern men who attempted to recover their property. It invaded the borders of Southern States, burned the dwellings and murdered the families. Habitual violators of the rights of humanity, they have exhaust-

ed all that human ingenuity can devise, and all that diabolical malice can invent, to heap indignity upon us, and make us a byword, a hissing and a scorn throughout the civilized world. Yet, we bore all this for many years, and might have borne it many years longer, under the oft-repeated assurance and fondly cherished hope that these things were not the action and feeling of a majority, but a minority party. But the failure of these promises and our hopes have conclusively proved to us that there is no hope. The platform of the Republican party we regard as a declaration of war against the lives and the institutions of the Southern people. It not only reproaches us as unchristian and heathenish, and imputes to us a sin and crime, but adds words insulting and hostile to our domestic tranquility. In its declaration that our negroes are entitled to liberty and equality with white men, it is in spirit, if not in fact, a strong incitement to insurrection, arson, murder and other crimes. And to aggravate the insult, the same platform denies us equality with Northern white men, or free negroes, and brands us as an inferior race. To cap the climax of insult to our feelings, and this menace to our rights, this party nominated for the Presidency a man who not only endorsed the platform and promised to enforce its principles, but disregards the judgments of your courts, the obligations of your Constitution, and the requirements of his oath, by approving any bill to prohibit slavery in the Territories of the United States. A large majority of the Northern people have declared their approval of the platform and candidates of that party in the late election. It is the solemn verdict of the people of the North, that the slaveholding communities of the South are to be outlawed and branded with ignominy and consigned to execration and ultimate destruction. Sir, are we looked upon as more or less than men? Is it expected that we will or can exercise that god-like virtue that beareth all things, believeth all things, hopeth all things, endureth all things, which tells us to love our enemies, and bless them that curse us? Are we expected to be denied the sensibilities, the sentiments, the passions, the reason, the instincts of men? Have not we pride and honor? Have we no sense of shame, no reverence for our ancestors, and care for our posterity? Have we no love of home, of family, of friends? Must we confess our baseness, discredit the fame of our sires, dishonor ourselves and degrade our posterity, abandon our homes, flee our country—all, all for the sake of the Union? Must we agree to live under the ban of our own government? Must we acquiesce in the inauguration of a President chosen by onfederate and hostile States, whose political faith constrains him co deny us our constitutional rights?
t

Must we consent to live under a government which we believe will henceforth be administered by those who not only deny us justice and equality, but brand us as inferiors; whose avowed principles and policy must destroy our domestic tranquility and imperil the lives of our wives and children, and ultimately destroy our States? Must we live by choice or compulsion under the rule of those who present us the alternative of an irrepressible conflict in defence of our altars and firesides, or the manumission of our slaves, and their admission to social equality? No, sir, never! never! The freemen of Alabama have proclaimed to the world that they will not, and have proven their sincerity by seceding from the Union, and braving all the dangers of a separate and independent nation among the powers of the earth. As a true and loyal citizen of that State, approving of her action, acknowledging entire allegiance, and feeling that I am absolved by her from all my obligations to support the Constitution of the United States, I withdraw from this body, intending to return to the bosom of my mother, and share her fate and maintain her fortunes.

Mr. FITZPATRICK, of Alabama:

My colleague has announced our withdrawal from the Senate. I have only to say that I concur in it, and endorse fully all that he has said.

LETTER FROM SENATOR CLAY, WITH CERTAIN RESOLUTIONS.

WASHINGTON CITY, January 7, 1861.

His Excellency A. B. MOORE:

MY DEAR SIR:—At a caucus of Senators from the States of Georgia, Florida, Alabama, Mississippi, Arkansas, Louisiana and Texas, in which all were present but Mr. Toombs and Mr. Sebastian, the enclosed resolutions were adopted; the first and second with but one dissentient, and the third with but four. Members of the House of Representatives from those States were not present, because there was not time to summon them, and in fact, many of them had left this city.

There was a common understanding, that the Senators of each State should communicate the resolutions and action of the caucus to the Governor of their State, to be used as might be deemed best, on consultation with members of the Convention or Legislature, that might be assembled.

I wish to invoke attention to the 3rd resolution, and to make such explanation as is necessary to prevent any misconstruction of the motive of those who voted for it.

It will at once, occur to your mind, that there is a plain incongruity between the first and third resolutions; that after a State has seceded from the present Federal Union, its Senators and Representatives have no right to seats in this Congress. Such must be the conclusion of all who maintain the right of secession. This was admitted by the caucus, not excepting (I believe) one of those who voted for the third resolution.

But the Black Republicans deny the right of secession; insist that the late Senators and Representatives from South Carolina are still members of the respective Houses to which they were elected, and the names of those Representatives (by order of Speaker Pennington,) and of those Senators (without order or objection) are still called, as if present. They are, therefore, estopped from objecting to the votes of Senators and Representatives from other States that may secede before the 4th of March next, if any retain their seats after the secession of their State.

There is a manifest purpose of the Black Republicans in both Houses of Congress, to use the power they may have, when the Senators and Representatives of the Cotton States leave here, to enact every species of legislation which hate of the South and lust of power and plunder may suggest. Bills extending the districts for the collection of revenue, so as to authorize collections on board of war vessels in view of Southern ports—increasing the Tariff and making it discriminate more against the South—increasing the Army and Navy—calling for Volunteers and offering them bounties in land and money—employing the militia—authorizing loans and issuing Treasury notes—indeed, every bill will be passed which they can pass, and may deem necessary to strengthen the arm of Government, and to enable Mr. Lincoln to enforce payment of revenue at Southern ports or to blockade them, or to commence war upon the South, as soon as he is installed in office. Such legislation might, probably, be defeated, if the delegates from the Cotton States, about to secede, remained in their seats till the 4th March; and a new Congress could not be convened before September next, by which time we might be fully prepared for war and strengthened by the alliance of all the slaveholding States.

On the other hand, it may be well asked whether it will comport with the dignity and honor of Alabama, after she has seceded from the Union, to authorize her Senators and Representatives to hold their seats in this Congress? Or can she with credit, pass an Ordinance of Secession and yet direct them to retain their seats?

I submit the resolutions, to be sent to the Convention for their consideration, if you deem it proper or expedient.

I owe it to myself to say, that I do not wish to remain here, and if I consulted my own feelings, interests or opinions, I would not stay a day after the secession of my State.

I am, most respectfully,
Your friend and serv't,
C. C. CLAY, JR.

Resolved, That in our opinion, each of the Southern States should, as soon as may be, secede from the Union.

Resolved, That provision should be made for a Convention to organize a Confederacy of the seceding States, the Convention to meet not later than the 15th of February, at the city of Montgomery, in the State of Alabama.

Resolved, That in view of the hostile legislation that is threatened against the seceding States, and which may be consummated before the 4th of March, we ask instructions, whether the delegations are to remain in Congress until that date, for the purpose of defeating such legislation.

Resolved, That a Committee be and are hereby appointed, consisting of Messrs. Davis, Slidell and Mallory, to carry out the objects of this meeting.

REPORT OF THE COMMISSIONER FROM ALABAMA TO WASHINGTON.

MONTGOMERY, ALA., Feb. 18, 1861.

To HIS EXCELLENCY A. B. MOORE,
Governor of the State of Alabama:

SIR:—On the 25th of January, 1861, I had the honor to receive from your Excellency, the appointment of Commissioner from the State of Alabama to the Government of the United States at Washington City, "to negotiate with the said Government in reference to the Forts, Arsenals and Custom Houses within this State, and the public debt of the United States; also as to the future relations of the State of Alabama, now a sovereign, independent State, with the Government of the United States."

On receiving my commission, I forthwith repaired to the city of Washington to enter upon the duties of the trust which had been confided to me. The day after my arrival, I applied, through the Hon. C. C. Clay, Jr., for an audience with the President of the United States to present my credentials and enter upon the proposed negotiation. I herewith submit to your Excellency a copy of the entire correspondence between Mr. Clay and the President, and Mr. Clay and myself, relating to the mission. By it your Excellency will perceive that the President refused to recognize me in the only character in which I was authorized to represent the State. This, of course, ended my duties as commissioner.

Trusting my action, as shown by the correspondence, may meet with the approval of your Excellency, I have the honor to be, with the highest consideration,
Your Excellency's most ob't serv't.
THOS. J. JUDGE, Coms'r, &c.

MR. CLAY TO THE PRESIDENT.

BROWN'S HOTEL,
WASHINGTON CITY, Feb. 1, 1861.

HIS EXCELLENCY, JAMES BUCHANAN,
President of the U. S. of America:

SIR :—I have the honor to inform you that the Hon. Thos. J. Judge, of Alabama—duly commissioned to negotiate with the government of the U. S., in reference to the Forts, Arsenal and Custom Houses in that State, and the debt of the U. S., is in this city and desires to present his credentials, and enter upon the proposed negotiation.

Will you be pleased to inform me, when it will suit your convenience, to give him an audience, and oblige,
With high consideration,
Your Ex. most obedient servant,
C. C. CLAY, JR.

THE PRESIDENT TO MR. CLAY.

WASHINGTON, Feb. 2, 1861.

DEAR SIR :—In answer to your note of yesterday, I shall be happy to receive the Hon. Thomas J. Judge, as a distinguished citizen of Alabama, either at 12 or 3 o'clock on Monday, as may best suit his convenience.

You are doubtless, aware, from my several messages, that in my judgment, I have no power to recognize him in the character ascribed to him by your letter.

Yours very respectfully,
JAMES BUCHANAN.
Hon. CLEMENT C. CLAY, &c. &c. &c.

MR. CLAY TO MR. JUDGE.

BROWN'S HOTEL,
WASHINGTON CITY, Feb. 2, 1861.

HON. T. J. JUDGE:

DEAR SIR:—I send you a copy of my note in your behalf, as Commissioner, &c., to the President of the United States, and his reply—which has reached me since 7 o'clock, P. M. Please read and advise me of your wishes and purpose, in the premises, by Monday next.

I will defer my departure for a few days longer if I can serve you by remaining. I am respectfully and truly yours, &c.

C. C. CLAY, JR.

WASHINGTON CITY, Feb. 4, 1861

HON. C. C. CLAY, JR.:

I acknowledge the receipt of your note of the 2nd inst., enclosing the correspondence between yourself and his Excellency James Buchanan, President of the United States, relating to my mission as Commissioner for the State of Alabama.

The President declines to give me an audience in the only character in which I sought it, as Commissioner for the State of Alabama, and thereby refuses to receive any proposals from that State, for a settlement relating to the public debt of the United States, contracted whilst Alabama was a member of that Confederacy, and relating to the property in the possession of Alabama, which belonged to the United States of America before the withdrawal of Alabama from that Union.

From this course of the President, it is to be presumed that he has abandoned all claim, or resolved not to make any in his official character, to that property in behalf of his Government; or, that repelling every offer of amicable adjustment, he desires that it shall be retaken by the sword.

But no matter what motive has prompted his unexpected treatment of me, I should be wanting in proper reverence for my State, and proper appreciation of my present relations to her, to sue for peaceful negotiations, since the right of Alabama to send me, and my right to speak for her, have been denied. And if negotiation is to settle our difficulties, touching these Forts and Arsenals, it must be proposed by the President, to the Governor at her Capitol—whither I shall go and report the result of my mission.

Whilst I regret this action of the President, it is gratifying to know that the State of Alabama, by her prompt efforts to do that justice in the premises which has been thwarted by him, will stand justified before the world.

That State having now been placed right upon the record—and under the circumstances, nothing more remaining for me to accomplish as her Commissioner—my mission ceases with this letter.

Permit me to return you my thanks for the valuable aid you have rendered, in endeavoring to advance the objects of my mission, and believe me to be,

Very truly your friend and ob't serv't,

THOMAS J. JUDGE.

MR. CLAY TO THE PRESIDENT.

BROWN'S HOTEL,
WASHINGTON, Feb. 5, 1861.

Hon. James Buchanan,
President of the United States of America:

SIR—I submitted my note and your reply touching the mission of the Hon. T. J. Judge, to him for his consideration, and send you herewith a copy of his response. You will see that he declines to address you on the subject matters of his mission, because he regards your note to me as closing the door against him, as the representative of Alabama, and repelling any offers she may have to make at the very threshold.

I am sure that you desire peace with all the world, and especially with those States which have seceded from the Union. You profess to claim, or holds Forts and Arsenals in those States, only as property of the United States, that you are bound to take care of. It is therefore, matter of surprise and regret, that you not only refuse to trust the people of those States with such property in their own limits and intended for their benefit, but pursue a course tending to destroy that property and to break the peace between your Government and those States. If, recognizing the right of secession, you had received Mr. Judge as Commissioner from a foreign State, and had sent his proposals to the Senate with your approval or objection; or, denying that right you had submitted his proposals to Congress, as those of a Commissioner from a State of the Union ; possibly the independence of the State might have been acknowledged, and a treaty with it formed, or denying its independence, Congress might have agreed to the sale and retrocession of the disputed places. At all events, it would have relieved you of the responsibility you have assumed, of not only refusing to entertain a peaceful proposition from a seceding State, but of preventing Congress from receiving it. I see nothing in the Constitution forbidding the course I suggest, either on your part or that of Congress. It would not have compromised your duty or the rights of the United States.

Certainly the lands for Forts Morgan and Gaines, and for Mount Vernon Arsenal, were ceded to the United States for the erection of such " needful buildings" for the defense and protection of the people of Alabama. For what other purpose should the Government of the United States hold them? But it is too late, if not improper, to pursue the argument.

Alabama has vindicated her integrity to the world. She sends her Commissioner here to purchase the property which her people prefer to hold in their own defence. It is now useless to your Government, except to injure them or their allies or friends. Knowing these facts, they were right to seize it, and are magnanimous to offer to pay to your Government the amount it cost. They cannot misunderstand your course in refusing to receive their Commissioner; that you deny their right to take their destiny in their own hands, or to defend themselves against the Government of the United States, or to resist its authority, and that you mean to control their action by military force.

Their Governor advised you, as soon as possible after the seizure of the forts and arsenals, "that it was done by his orders to make the secession of Alabama peaceful, and to prevent your reinforcing those places, and shedding the blood and sacrificing the lives of her people in endeavoring to maintain the authority of your Government over them." Subsequent events have proven his wisdom and forecast. Your transfer of troops from Northern and Western ports to this city, and to all Southern forts where you apprehend that the people might take them for their defence, to secure peaceful secession, shows your inclination to keep them for their coercion and to prevent peaceful secession. The frowning artillery and armed men brought to the unaccustomed view of the people of Maryland and Virginia, of Charleston and Pensacola, are just causes of offence to those who esteem themselves free citizens—not subjects, masters or servants of Government.

The free people of Alabama will not consent that places of power granted by them to Government for their defence against insurrection and invasion, shall be used in aid of their invasion and subjugation. They regard the uses now made of Forts Pickens, Sumter, McHenry, and others in Southern States, as a gross abuse of the people and trust—a plain ursurpation of ungranted power. And, be assured, that the men of the South will not long endure this constant menance of the power of your Government, or suffer it to stand sentinel over their door-ways, with presented arms, ready to challenge themselves or their friends, or to dispute their ingress or egress. The instincts of mere brute nature, no less than the noblest sentiments of humanity—self-preservation, patriotism, honor and pride of independence—conspire against such deliberate insult and persistent menace of injury. If not surrended for the defence of the people against your standing army, they must and will take them at every hazard and any sacrifice.

Those States that have seceded will never unite with the Northern States under a common government. The idea is preposterous—the ground is hopeless. There has been constant and increasing strife between them for more than a quarter of a century. They differ so widely in principles and sentiments, in morals, in manners, religion and politics, as well as social institutions and habits, that the world knows they are different and uncongenial types of civilization.

They have long seen and felt it, and cannot have a motive for living together that is not purely selfish and mercenary. I trust and believe they will hereafter form separate and distinct governments, in which they cannot love each other less, or harm each other more, than under a common government. The people of Alabama believe their rights will be better respected by the New England and other Northern States, when out of this Union, than they have been in it. The common prevalence in the South of this opinion will forever prevent the rebuilding of the old Union.

With your knowledge of the history of the United States, and the unhomogeneous characters of the Northern and Southern peoples, you must agree with me that man will never witness the rëconstruction of the Union. Then, why hold forts and keep troops in the seceded States, if not to disturb us? Why not take the purchase money offered for them? Left to yourselves, I think you would withdraw your garrisons and sell us the forts;

for you pray for peace and protest against coercion. Take care that your councils do not compromise your honor and your character by evincing uses of those strongholds at variance with your prayers and protests.

A superannuated soldier, whose vanity and ignorance have never failed to provoke contempt whenever he essays to play the statesman, is not competent to advise you. Neither is a mere jurist and scholar, who has lived a recluse, and knows less of living and feeling men than of dead languages and abstract sciences. Trust your own judgment and feelings, and I think you will correct the errors they have committed by transferring your troops from Southern States—where they can only excite suspicions and heart-burnings, and make enemies of those who should be friends—to the western frontier, where war is being carried on against citizens of the United States.

Hoping that good may come out of seeming evil, and that we may not be precipitated into war by your preparations to prevent it, and wishing you the peace and tranquility in your retirement that follows good deeds,

I have the honor to be,
Respectfully and truly,
Your friend and ob't servant,
C. C. CLAY, Jr.

RESOLUTIONS OF THE LEGISLATURE OF NEW YORK.

To His Excellency Andrew B. Moore, Governor of the State of Alabama, Montgomery:

STATE OF NEW YORK, EXECUTIVE DEPARTMENT, }
ALBANY, January 11, 1861. }

Sir—In obedience to the request of the Legislature of this State, I transmit herewith a copy of the concurrent resolutions of that Body, adopted this day, tendering the aid of the State to the President of the United States, to enable him to enforce the laws and uphold the authority of the Federal Government.

I have the honor to be your Excellency's Obd't Serv't,
EDWIN D. MORGAN.

THE CONVENTION OF ALABAMA. 459

Concurrent Resolutions, tendering aid to the President of the United States, in support of the Constitution and the Union:

STATE OF NEW YORK, IN ASSEMBLY, }
January 11, 1861.   }

WHEREAS, Treason, as defined by the Constitution of the United States, exists in one or more of the States of this Confederacy, and

WHEREAS, The insurgent State of South Carolina, after seizing the Post-Office, Custom-House, moneys and fortifications of the Federal Government, has, by firing into a vessel, ordered by the the Government to convey troops and provisions to Fort Sumter, virtually declared war; and whereas, the forts and property of the United States Government, in Georgia, Alabama and Louisiana, have been unlawfully seized, with hostile intentions; and whereas, further, Senators in Congress avow and maintain their treasonable acts; therefore,

Resolved, (If the Senate concur,) That the Legislature of New York, profoundly impressed with the value of the Union, and determined to preserve it unimpaired, hail with joy the recent firm, dignified and patriotic Special Message of the President of the United States, and that we tender to him, through the Chief Magistrate of our own State, whatever aid, in men and money, he may require, to enable him to enforce the laws and uphold the avthority of the Federal Government. And that in defense of " the more perfect Union," which has conferred prosperity and happiness upon the American people, renewing the pledge given and redeemed by our Fathers, we are ready to devote " our fortunes, our lives, and our sacred honor," in upholding the Union and the Constitution.

Resolved, (If the Senate concur,) That the Union-loving Representatives and citizens of Delaware, Maryland, Virginia, North Carolina, Kentucky, Missouri and Tennessee, who labor with devoted courage and patriotism to withhold their States from the vortex of secession, are entitled to the gratitude and admiration of the whole people.

Resolved, (If the Senate concur,) That the Governor be respectfully requested to forward, forthwith, copies of the foregoing resolutions to the President of the Nation, and the Governors of all the States of the Union.

The preceding preamble and resolutions were duly passed.
By order   H. A. RISLEY, CLERK.

IN SENATE, January 11, 1861: The preceding preamble and resolutions were duly passed.
By order   JAMES TERWILLIGER, CLERK.

RESIGNATION OF MEMBERS OF CONGRESS.

The President announced that he had received communications from the Hon. Thomas Fearn and the Hon. David P. Lewis, Deputies to the Confederate Congress, from the State of Alabama, tendering their resignation.

Mr. DARGAN offered the following resolution:

Resolved, That in accepting the resignation of Mr. Thomas Fearn, and Mr. David P. Lewis, two of our Delegates to the Congress of the Confederate States of America, this Convention would express its entire and full approval of the course they have pursued in said Congress, so far as the same has been made public, and tender to them our thanks for the good results, owing, in part, to their labors.

Mr. BEARD said:

Mr. President—I feel constrained, from a sense of duty, to make a few remarks upon the resolution now under discussion. No man in this State better deserves the compliment which that resolution contains, than does Thomas Fearn; and perhaps no individual in this State knows as well, or better, the part he has played in this great Revolution than I do. I have been honored with his confidence; intimate personal and political relations have existed between us for more than twenty years. We have belonged to the same political party; we were both opposed to the policy of separate State secession; but after the passage of the Ordinance, I wrote him a letter, in which I requested him to advise me as to my future course. In reply, he urged me to sustain the State in the position she had taken, assigning, as a reason, that we owed our first and paramount allegiance to our State, and that as Alabama was now the only Union left to us, it was our duty to aid in maintaining it. No man in the State of Alabama could have brought more aid to the Southern Confederacy, more power to allay the excitement, to overcome the preëxisting prejudices in the minds of the people of North Alabama, than he did. Acting upon his suggestions, as well as from a sense of duty, when I returned among my constituents I told them there was no other course or policy for us to pursue but to acquiesce in the action of the Convention; that violently and ardently as I had been opposed to the passage of the Ordinance, I now considcred it a settled question, that it was no longer debateable. It was the Organic Law of the land, and we, as good and patriotic citizens, were bound to sustain it. I say now, that the Constitution which we adopted yesterday for the Confederate States of America, is, to my mind, a satisfactory evidence that Thomas Fearn has played a conspicuous and influential part in its preparation and adoption. Many of the provisions of that conservative instrument were suggested in his letter to me. I might add, that the sentiments contained in that letter induced his nomination by me, and his election by the Convention.

I hope, therefore, that the resolution offered by the gentleman from Mobile [Judge Dargan] will receive the unanimous vote of this Convention.

Mr. DARGAN's resolution was adopted.

ELECTION OF DEPUTIES.

HON. NICH. DAVIS, of Madison, was elected to fill the vacancy created by the resignation of Mr. Fearn; and Hon. HENRY C. JONES, of Lauderdale, was elected to fill the vacancy created by the resignation of Mr. Lewis.

ENDORSEMENT OF THE ACTION OF THE PRESIDENT AND VICE-PRESIDENT OF THE CONFEDERATE STATES.

On Tuesday, March 12, MR. COCHRAN offered the following resolution, which was unanimously adopted:

Resolved, That the election of Jefferson Davis, President, and Alexander H. Stephens, as Vice-President of the Provisional Government of the Confederate States of America, meets with the approval of this Convention, and the same is hereby fully ratified by the people of Alabama.

VISIT TO THE PRESIDENT.

On the 7th day of March, MR. CROOK introduced the following resolution, which was adopted:

Resolved, That the President of this Convention be requested to inform the President of the Confederate States, that it is the desire of this Convention to call on him in a body, at such time as he may designate.

On the next day, the President of the Convention announced that, in pursuance of the resolution of yesterday, he had called upon the President of the Confederate States, who expressed his gratification, and would willingly receive a call from the Convention, in a body, at such time and place as might suit the Convention.

Mr. MITCHELL* moved that a Committee of three be appointed to make the necessary arrangements for the reception of the President; which was adopted—and Messrs. Mitchell, Beard, and Clarke of Marengo were appointed the Committee.

On Saturday, the 9th, Mr. Mitchell, from the Select Committee of three, reported that arrangements had been made, in accordance with instructions given to the Committee, to carry out the desire of the Convention to call upon the President of the Confederate States, in a body. President Davis would be pleased to see the members of the Convention, on Monday night, at 9 o'clock. The Delegates to the Convention will meet at the Exchange Hotel reading-room, at $8\frac{1}{2}$ o'clock. They will be called to order by Mr. President Brooks, and will proceed in a body to the reception parlor of President Davis, when the Presiding Officer of the Convention will introduce each member to the President of the Confederate States.

Mr. Mitchell also reported that the Committee would, at another time, communicate to the Convention the time and place when Vice-President Stephens would be visited by the members in a body.

---

*Hon. C. B. Mitchell, who had been elected from the county of Montgomery, to fill the vacancy created by the resignation of the Hon. Wm. L. Yancey, was introduced by Mr. Watts, his colleague, and took his seat in the Convention, on the 7th of March.

On the night indicated, the members called, in a body, and were introduced by their President. Most of the Cabinet were present, and several of the members of the Confederate Congress.

This visit to the President was one of the most agreeable incidents of the Convention. To the address of Mr. Brooks, President Davis made a short and appropriate response, conceived in the most patriotic spirit, and expressed in fervent and vigorous language.

The President's mode of speech is graceful, earnest and persuasive. With a deep, sonorous voice, is blended a happy, emphatic gesticulation, and a positiveness of manner, so that the hearer is at once struck with the speaker's sincerity.

But few of us had ever seen or heard him before, and all were delighted, as well with the glowing ardor of his sentiments as the determined tone of his resolution.

It would seem that the formalities of such an introduction would be heavy, clumsy and awkward. The contemplation of an hundred men, arrayed in a sort of military phalanx, marching up in couples to be introduced, one by one, to the President, was indeed enough to provoke a smile from the mischievous and the courtly; but this beautiful speech broke the rude shackles of formality, and the cordial attentions of the President to his guests, dispelled the last feeling of the restraint, and imparted to each person, as if by some magnetic influence, the gracefulness and ease which distinguished his own dignified demeanor. For an hour the Chamber of Reception was the scene of the liveliest animation; and the conversation, turning mainly upon the topic of Southern Independence, and the novel position of the young Republic, was characterized by the free expression of those exultant opinions, which, though not clamorous, are at once the best indications of a deliberate determination, and the surest forerunners of success.

It was very beautiful for a patriot to note and meditate upon this assembly, composed of men so lately of antagonistic opinions as to policy, now all binding their hearts and minds to the one common end—the Independence of the Republic; and entering, uninvited, into a common league, not of words, but of intentions irrevocable, to devote all their energies to the perpetuation of their Institutions, and to the preservation of their ancient Liberties.

There were many ladies present upon this occasion, distinguished not more by beauty and grace than by the lively interest they exhibited in the stirring events of the times, and their eager readiness to aid in pushing on the Revolution to success.

This Reception was closed around a convivial and festive table, spread in true Republican style, with plenty to eat and drink, but with no mark of courtly splendor.

The Vice-President, Mr. Stephens, made his appearance, was toasted from the hearts of the guests, and responded in an appropriate speech, which was eloquent in its earnest simplicity.

www.ingramcontent.com/pod-product-compliance
Lightning Source LLC
Chambersburg PA
CBHW051858300426
44117CB00006B/449